CUSTODIANS
OF THE
SACRED MOUNTAINS

CUSTODIANS
OF THE
SACRED MOUNTAINS

*Culture and Society
in the Highlands of Bali*

Thomas A. Reuter

University of Hawai'i Press
Honolulu

02 03 04 05 06 07 6 5 4 3 2 1

Library of Congress Cataloging-in-Publication Data

Reuter, Thomas Anton.
Custodians of the sacred mountains : culture and society in the highlands of Bali /
Thomas A. Reuter.
p. cm.
Includes bibliographical references and index.
ISBN 0–8248–2450–4 (cloth : alk. paper)
1. Bali Island (Indonesia)—Social life and customs. 2. Mountain people—
Indonesia—Bali (Island) 3. Ethnology—Indonesia—Bali (Island) I. Title.
DS647.B2 R47 2002
306'.09598'6—dc21   2001053065

University of Hawai'i Press books are printed on acid-free
paper and meet the guidelines for permanence and durability
of the Council on Library Resources.

Designed by Cindy E. K. C. Chun
Printed by The Maple-Vail Book Manufacturing Group

To all the fellow travelers on the path of life
whose gifts of love and wisdom
have made my journey worthwhile.

Contents

Black-and-white insert follows page 196

List of Illustrations

Acknowledgments

This project would not have been accomplished without the kind support of persons and institutions too numerous to mention. My gratitude extends to them all, even though I will name only a few.

I thank the Australian Research Council for funding this research, and the Australian National University and the University of Melbourne for their institutional support. I am grateful for receiving permission from the Indonesian government to conduct research in Bali and for the courteous assistance of provincial and local government officials. I am indebted also to Ketut Arsana and Universitas Udayana for acting as my academic sponsors. For their practical support in the field, I am particularly indebted to the Kepala Desa of Batukaang and Sukawana, along with I Gede Astrajaya, Ni Komang Suciati, I Wayan Suparta, I Gusti Agung Alit, and, especially, I Nyoman Sabaraka.

Among many friends and informants in the highlands, I especially wish to thank Jero Bayan Kiteg, Jero Bau Jumun, Jero Bau Tongkok, Jero Bau Gesing Almarhum, Jero Bayan Sari, Jero Mangku Pegeg, Jero Mangku Sari, Jero Mangku Gede Cidra Almarhum, Jero Balian Sayang, Jero Made Kaler, Jero Kara, and other elders in mountain villages.

For their valuable comments and encouragement I thank J. Fox, H. Geertz, P. Worsley, D. Schaareman, D. Stuart-Fox, G. MacRae, D. Santikarma, and I Gede Pitana. For having kindled my initial interest in anthropology, I am forever grateful to K. P. Koepping and E. D. Lewis.

Finally, and most of all, I am deeply grateful to Marina and Merlyn for sharing with me the joys and tribulations of life in the highlands of Bali.

Publication of this work was assisted by a publications grant by The University of Melbourne.

INTRODUCTION

This book offers a journey into the world of the Bali Aga, or Mountain Balinese. It tells of a people whose culture for centuries has been shrouded in the shadow of the more celebrated lowland kingdoms of southern Bali. In this interlocal ethnographic account of the elaborate alliance systems of the Bali Aga, highland Balinese culture and society is explored for the first time in all its regional complexity. I hope in this book to convey a deeper appreciation of the Bali Aga people and their place in the fabric of Balinese identities and to contribute to a radical reassessment of prevailing assumptions about the political history, society, and culture of this island. The story of the Bali Aga people further raises important issues about the process and politics of cross-cultural representation in the social sciences and in the world at large.

Bali is renowned as a magical window on Indonesia's classical history, when Hindu empires still dominated what is now the world's most populous Muslim nation. In anthropology, Bali has become a test case for new methods of research and theoretical approaches, and to a wider public the island is familiar as a major international tourist destination. Although tiny compared to some of its neighbors, the island of Bali stands out like a beacon of singular significance from the vastness of the Indonesian archipelago (Map 1).

Balinese culture has been subject to ethnographic scrutiny and reflection like few other cultures in the world. Well-known anthropologists of every generation have contributed to a deeper understanding of Balinese society and thus of human societies in general. From the culture and personality studies of Margaret Mead and Gregory Bateson to the hermeneutics of Clifford Geertz, shifting currents in Balinese studies have provided an excellent indication of shifting currents in anthropological theory. With the case study of Bali at the focus of Western attention for so long, one could be excused for assuming

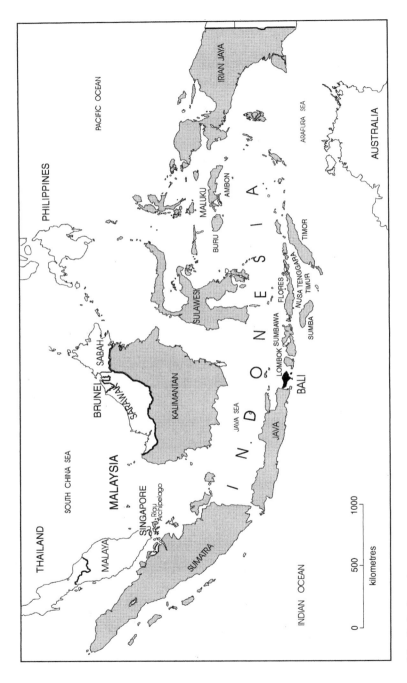

Map 1. Indonesia

that further ethnographic research is unlikely to produce major surprises or new discoveries.

There is one fundamental reason why such an assumption would be incorrect. Tall and brightly lit beacons of culture tend to cast particularly long and impenetrable shadows. As it captured ever more attention from outside observers, the courtly society of southern Bali became synonymous with Bali as a whole. At the same time, the world of highland Balinese culture became almost invisible, like a distant planet concealed by the brightness of its star. In popular and ethnographic representations alike, Bali's mountainous center marks the margins of understanding.

"Representation" is fundamental to the enterprise of writing ethnography and also highly problematic for the epistemology of social science. A recent debate in anthropology has focused on the question of whether ethnographers as particular "subjects" are capable of producing reliable, let alone objective, portrayals of cultural others. Many critics have suggested that ethnographic representations written by positioned researchers are subject to bias and not to be trusted. In response to the fact that the Bali Aga are indeed misrepresented or ignored in most of the academic literature on Bali and in recognition of this general crisis of representation in anthropology and other branches of cross-cultural studies, I have made representation a central theme in this book.

My conjecture is that cross-cultural representation is a necessary and legitimate enterprise after all, under certain conditions. In support of this argument, I have taken a significant departure from the rather gloomy perspective on representational knowledge systems that has become a characteristic of postcolonial and postmodernist approaches by challenging some of the basic assumptions informing the current debate and crisis of representation in the social sciences. Most important, I argue that resource competition is not the defining force in social or cross-cultural encounters among human subjects and, hence, that the subjectivity of individual representers is neither a foundation nor an insurmountable obstacle to the accomplishment of genuine cross-cultural understanding.

The problem of representation became the focus of a perpetual debate in the social sciences as Western scholars engaged in the study of other cultures began to acknowledge that their academic disciplines had originated in a period of European history marked by rapid colonial expansion and that the knowledge generated within these disciplines had served as a motor to the mechanics of Western domination from the beginning. In the course of my research in the highlands of Bali, however, it became obvious to me that a tendency to misrepresent others is not just an issue in cross-cultural encounters with less powerful others. On closer inspection, subjective bias in the construction of personal and cultural identities proved to be a fundamental human conundrum, even for people representing the world from the margins of global and local systems of domination—people like the Bali Aga—and even in their interactions with one another. In this book, the Bali Aga are the focus of analysis as subjective agents of representation, and it is from the perspective of a critical analysis of their representational culture that subjectivity—the central problem of representation—will be approached.

A portrayal of culture and society among the Mountain Balinese, this book is first and foremost an ethnographic representation. The central aim of this ethnography is to explore a complex web of asymmetric status relationships among highland communities arising in the course of their joint participation in complex regional systems of ritual interaction and alliance. The analysis will show how status claims are constructed on the basis of seniority in this society or, more precisely, by distinguishing among different degrees of temporal proximity to a shared and sacred origin. Bali Aga society, unlike a hierarchical system, is founded on a time-based and process-oriented notion of precedence.

I treat status as the fruit of a particular form of representational labor. Theories of status, in turn, provide a fresh perspective from which to address issues left unresolved by conventional theories of representation. My assumption in taking this approach was that the basic communicative processes in social games of mutual representation are more easily revealed by examining cases where the stakes are predominantly symbolic rather than material resources and by employing a status economy rather than a political economy model of analysis.

I hypothesize that the symbolic economies of the Bali Aga and other status-oriented societies rest on a fundamental paradox. An ongoing competition for (and asymmetrical distribution of) symbolic resources is made possible and is simultaneously constrained by an intrinsic need to cooperate. This paradox is particularly salient where the social agents or groups participating in a culturally regulated "game" of mutual representation are primarily concerned with symbolic resources, assuming that social status is achieved by securing the voluntary approval of others. It is reasonable to make this assumption at least for situations where the agents concerned encounter one another under a condition of relative material parity. For much of its recent history, these conditions have applied to highland Balinese society and its economy of ritual status, making it an ideal site for a study of representation processes as they may unfold in the absence of any systematic form of political or economic domination.

The Bali Aga people, however, are no strangers to issues of power. While power differences may not be a major factor in shaping the mutual representations they have constructed of one another, they have also participated and competed—with a distinct disadvantage—on the larger stage of a Balinese politics of identity, as active agents but often also as silent and powerless objects of representation. A further set of questions about representation is thus raised in this study at a level of ethnohistorical inquiry: How have the Bali Aga been represented by more powerful others, and how have they represented themselves to the outside world? Or, put in more general terms: How does representation function under a condition of material disparity?

I argue that the Bali Aga, in their responses to outsiders' portrayals of their culture, have displayed an active and cooperative engagement with, and a vested interest in supporting, the very discourses that allocate to them the status of a politically marginal group. This response suggests that the introduction of material disparities to a game of representation does not necessarily or even typically dispense with a need for cooperation and mutual understanding.

Moving closer to issues of representation at home, I then ask how Dutch colonial intervention in Bali and the accumulation of anthropological knowledge about Balinese society altered the position of the Bali Aga. Whereas a more conventional postcolonial study might stress the impact of Western power-knowledge systems, I argue that the dominant political other for the highland Balinese in the first place has not been a Western colonial power but a changing political and economic elite within Balinese society. From the perspective of the indigenous Bali Aga, the traditional seat of power has been the central palaces of the island's southern kingdoms, and its face a changing aristocracy or modern elite whose sources of power have been located on the outside in one way or another throughout the course of Balinese history. Western images of the Bali Aga were formed on the basis of an increasingly cooperative relationship between Bali's ruling classes and the outside world, established in the wake of initially violent confrontations. This political and economic cooperation was and is underwritten by a process of cultural brokerage and a mutual appropriation of the other's knowledge and power.

These preliminary observations suggest that, along with iron chains of domination, subtle threads of cooperation seem to extend between people of lower and higher status, between marginal and dominant sectors of a society, and between globally powerful and peripheral societies as they engage in a process of mutual representation. They also raise an important general question about representation. Is intersubjectivity rather than subjectivity the primary force in shaping one's experience with others? And if so, does this experience give rise to a human interest in communicative cooperation that may enable us to develop a representational knowledge of others based on free intersubjective exchange rather than subjective bias?

This book takes up the project of studying popular representation in Balinese society, but it is also a project of (ethnographic) representation in its own right. The first project is an exploration of the grounds for the legitimacy of the second. Through an empirical investigation of processes of representation in highland Bali, I endeavor to provide a better understanding of the practical challenges a popular representation system faces and must overcome if it is to prevent the rise of any lasting and pervasive patterns of discrimination and material domination in the society concerned. By tracing continuities in this social dynamics of representation further, across interpersonal, intrasocietal, interethnic, and cross-cultural contexts, I aim to illustrate that some of the same challenges must be met in order to free ethnographic representations from the charge of subjective bias. In short, I hope to illustrate that a system of knowledge, on the condition that it is based on voluntary and free intersubjectivity, can act as a positive constraint on political domination, no matter whether the knowledge concerned is the product of a popular or an ethnographic representation.

From the Mountains of Bali
to the Valleys of Social Theory

In providing an alternative ethnographic portrayal of Balinese society, from the perspective of its indigenous mountain population, this study draws on experiences gained during seven visits over a time span of twenty years, including a major period of eighteen consecutive months of local and regional fieldwork in 1993–1994.[1] The results of this ethnographic research may help to fill an embarrassing gap in the ethnography of Bali by exploring the still mysterious world of its interior highland region.

This is not to suggest that the Bali Aga have escaped attention altogether. Earlier research has provided valuable insights into the local organization and traditions of a few Bali Aga villages (*desa*). The present study, however, pays tribute to a more complex world of mythical connections and ritual interactions in which those and more than one hundred other Bali Aga communities partake. This wider social world is maintained through a vast network of regional, intervillage alliance systems spanning the entire central highland region of Bali and incorporating communities along the island's northern and eastern coasts as well. These important and ancient regional alliance networks are locally known as *banua*, or 'ritual domains'.[2]

The study of Bali Aga alliance networks illustrates the importance of narrative origin histories and ritualized social interactions for systems of status distribution in Bali and related Austronesian societies. In brief, ritual domains in highland Bali are united by the shared orientation of participating villages toward a sacred time and place of origin. Origin sites are identified in elaborate mythohistorical narratives and marked by ancient regional temples. The status system of an alliance network is ritually displayed during annual festivals held at such regional temples in commemoration of the ancestral deities and founders of the domain concerned. The focal concept and value of "origin" inspires the Bali Aga to conceive of contemporary society as a differentiated whole arising from a common source in the past and expanding in a historical sequence of migrations and village foundations. Villages within a domain thus represent way stations on the path of the ancestors, and the ritual status of a particular village is determined by precedence or relative proximity to the sacred origin of this mythical journey. "Precedence" is an analytical concept for describing a mode of status differentiation crucial to all aspects of social organization in the highlands. First conceived by a group of anthropologists based at the Australian National University and conducting research in eastern Indonesia, the concept of precedence and the social systems it describes fundamentally differ from a concept of hierarchy and a hierarchical mode of status distribution, which are conspicuous in anthropological literature on the Indian caste system.

While relevant to general theories of ritual, status, hierarchy, and social organization, this study most immediately contributes to the comparative ethnology of Austronesian-speaking peoples. This group of historically and culturally related societies is dispersed over a vast region—from Madagascar in the far west, across insular Southeast Asia, and eastward across the Pacific as far as New Zealand and Hawai'i. When contemplated from the perspective of its indigenous mountain people and their culture, the island of Bali no longer stands out from the Indonesian archipelago as a local anomaly on account of a strong element of Indian or Hindu influence in its courtly culture and religion. As much as it may hold surprises in relation to the literature on southern Balinese culture, this ethnography of Bali Aga society will evoke a deep sense of recognition among those who have studied Austronesian societies in other parts of Indonesia and beyond.

For comparative historians, this study of ritual alliance systems in highland Bali may provide a useful model of how the first Hindu-Buddhist polities were established in Bali, and possibly in many other parts of Southeast Asia, by building on the foundation of and adding complexity to earlier and indigenous forms of regional organization. Some mountain temples (*pura*) and the domains (*banua*) attached to them have existed and evolved for more than a millennium. Several such temple networks appear to have been tied together in a larger ritual system at a time when the first Hindu kingdoms flourished on the island. Royal edicts written on bronze plates (*prasasti*) are found in many Bali Aga villages. Several ritual centers in the highlands are also graced by large collections of stone statues of early Balinese kings, hinting at their significance as former state temples.

The advancement of ethnographic knowledge about Bali Aga culture and about the place of the highland people in Balinese history and society is a worthy objective in its own right, and the first and longer section of this book (Part 1) is dedicated to the achievement of this aim. My main focus of analysis, however, is the different systems of representation that inform the regional status economy of highland Balinese society, that position the Bali Aga within a pan-Balinese landscape of identities, and that also position them and other Balinese within popular and anthropological Western discourses. That is, a specific ethnography is used to provide insights about representation in order to resolve the general problem of representation intrinsic to the project of ethnography itself. By beginning with an exploration of the highlands of Bali, however, the structure of this book inverts the course of its own history. A brief reflection on this history will help to clarify why such an inversion became necessary and why it may be fruitful.

Contemporary anthropologists no longer assume that their representations of other cultures belong or remain confined within a value-neutral sphere of scientific reflection. For many, the problem may first arise at the level of textual practice, as they begin to write an ethnography. For others, the problem of representation is encountered at the level of ethnographic practice, as a blatant and serious issue in the world at large. The political aspect of the problem, arising from popular (as well as academic) practices of representation, is forcefully brought to the awareness of researchers concerned with the study of a people like the Bali Aga, who are "marginal" not only in relation to Western power but also in relation to the wider societies and nations of which they are a part.

Politically naive or morally unreflective explorations of such marginal worlds at best would do little to address the practical concerns of the people who inhabit them and, at worst, could exacerbate their plight by falling into and deepening the very same discursive grooves that have circumscribed their marginality in the first place. Margins and centers are not natural phenomena; they are metaphorical constructs that, in the course of their pragmatic usage, help to articulate and facilitate specific patterns of power relations within a local, regional, national, or global politics of representation. Insofar as the people of highland Bali are indeed a marginalized people, rather than simply "marginal," any attempt to construct a politically neutral account of their society would have been impossible and irresponsible.

The issues raised by marginality studies in particular are vital ones within the social sciences in their current crisis of representation. The debate sparked by this crisis concerns the epistemology, ethics, and politics of cross-cultural representation, and it is not surprising that anthropology, the comparative study of human societies and cultures, for better or for worse, has been at the heart of the turbulence. A profound crisis of representation arose as postcolonial research revealed Western knowledge systems to have been integral to the establishment and preservation of international power structures in which Western nations occupied (and still maintain) a position of dominance. This and other evidence was interpreted in epistemological terms as the outcome of an underlying problem of subjective bias and as anathema to the notion that social science can provide accurate and objective representations of other societies and cultures.

Few contemporary scholars would deny that ethnographic or historical representations of other cultures have at times been severely biased. Read from a contemporary perspective, at least some of the portrayals of other cultures produced in the spirit of a nineteenth-century evolutionary anthropology and, likewise, some studies of colonized societies conducted by colonial scholars would seem obviously skewed. Unfortunately though, less obvious versions of the same representational distortions continue to affect the work of contemporary researchers, even though they may have absorbed some of the critical insights of postmodern theory and are operating in a postcolonial and rapidly globalizing world.

Among the undesirable continuities that have been identified in current anthropology, one of the most significant is the tendency to conflate concepts of geographical, cultural, and temporal remoteness (Said 1978; Fabian 1983; Appadurai 1988). This tendency could all too easily manifest itself in a portrayal of a people like the Mountain Balinese. Researchers in anthropology and other academic disciplines concerned with cross-cultural questions, however, cannot avoid an act of representation if they are to write anything at all about other cultures. A provocative question thus cannot be evaded: How can representations of other cultures be anything other than a subjective and inherently biased form of knowledge?

I commence my search for an answer to this question in the highlands of Bali. This is precisely because the Mountain Balinese are a people in whose history representation has been not just a philosophical but a highly practical issue and one to which they have had to find ways of responding. Approaching the topic of representation from within their lifeworld illustrates that representational bias is a general and existential human conundrum rather than just a special concern for the social sciences. An ethnographic analysis of representational practice also reveals how the scope for subjective bias is constrained by intersubjectivity within Bali Aga, pan-Balinese, colonial, and modern knowledge systems and, ultimately, how a focus on intersubjectivity may help to overcome the problem of subjective bias within the social sciences.

The distribution of status among Bali Aga communities within regional ritual domains involves a peculiar logic of mutual representation of its own. Social status systems, in this and other societies, are the culture-specific products of a history of collective representational labor.

Status relations are comparable to power relations insofar as both are negotiated within the context of the same fundamental paradox. The strategic pursuit of status and power involves an accumulation of "cultural capital" or "symbolic resources," and yet competing parties must rely on the manipulation of interactive, communicative, and essentially cooperative processes as their means of production. It is assumed, however, that status economies are focused more exclusively on symbolic resources. Symbolic economies therefore must rely more exclusively on cooperative processes of representation within a social system of voluntary association and free argumentation, at least for so long as they remain relatively undistorted by the influence (and, perhaps, help to prevent the occurrence) of glaring asymmetries in wealth and force within the economic and political economies of the societies concerned. In comparison to power, status may not, or not as readily, be derived from alternative sources, such as the exercise of coercive force or the strategic use of material wealth. By adopting a status economy rather than a political economy approach, this study aims to illustrate that the scope for strategic and biased representation in the competitive pursuit of symbolic resources (i.e., in the strategic construction of "knowledge systems") is significant but finite. Competitive interests and associated subjective biases among participants in a symbolic economy are constrained by a cooperative imperative inherent in the intersubjective nature of symbolic communication and associated processes of knowledge construction.[3]

As the focus of analysis shifts from the status systems of highland Balinese society to a broader and more political field of contestation in the second part of the book, to an islandwide politics of identity in which the "marginal" Bali Aga have played a surprisingly central role, the relevance of this imperative for communicative cooperation as a restraint on strategic bias in representation will be explored in a historical context of political and economic disparity.

Moving, finally, beyond the context of Balinese worlds and to a more global politics of representation, I will demonstrate how a communicative imperative for cooperation, though sometimes in the form of cross-cultural complicity, may have influenced the way in which the highlands and Bali as a whole have been portrayed by Western scholars working in a colonial or postcolonial setting.

It is in the following sense that the mountains of Bali may stand to fill the valleys of anthropological theory. If the analysis of status systems within Bali Aga society can lend strong support to the hypotheses that representation is an essentially intersubjective process and that cooperation is thus fundamental to the cultural construction and contestation of knowledge, it may be possible to extend the argument toward a more general intersubjective theory of representation and human understanding. In this book, then, an analysis of status systems in highland Bali is to provide the source of conceptual tools for a general critique of cultural knowledge as it is employed in the service of people's quest for status as well as power (insofar as both draw on communicative or interactive processes of representation). Looking at power and knowledge from the margins, this study aims to shed new light on the intersubjective play of human interests in processes of representation. This procedure may reveal how subjective biases and strategic interests affect popular or anthropological perceptions and portrayals *of* others, even within a single society or group, but also how a genuine intersubjective understanding may be gained in cooperation *with* others.

First Impressions

First impressions are powerful, deceptive, and often more durable than they deserve to be. Few could tell more about the fossilization of first impressions than the people of highland Bali. Unfortunately, the power of first impressions has not proved favorable for them. I found that some of the harshest realities in Bali Aga lives were a sediment of others' self-projective imagination, others to whom their lived reality had never been much of an issue. My own account of their culture must begin somewhere near the surface as well, inevitably perhaps, and not without purpose. In conveying a first impression of highland Bali, my aim is to illustrate how some of the established opinions about the Bali Aga were constructed and why they may need to be deconstructed.

First impressions are formed in the immediate context of personal experience and initially serve only to inform someone's private opinions about another people and their culture. Such isolated opinions are rarely of much consequence until they are voiced and discussed, and become widely accepted by others. The first evidence for a more permanent characterization is often a public act of labeling. How members of another culture are named may provide an indication of whether or not superficial impressions have hardened prematurely into opinions. The latter is likely to have occurred if the chosen name is a descriptive characterization.

The ethnic label "Bali Aga" is a perfect illustration (from Old Javanese *aga*, "mountain"). A popular Balinese term, it appears at first to be no more than a dispassionate and appropriate description for a people whose principal homeland is a vast highland region stretching across Bali's mountainous interior. The simplicity of the term, however, helps to conceal a deeper significance. This descriptive label draws exclusively on first and superficial impressions, isolates the visual characteristic of a people's location in physical space, and then transforms it into a value-charged metaphoric reference for the people themselves. As such, it must attract suspicion.

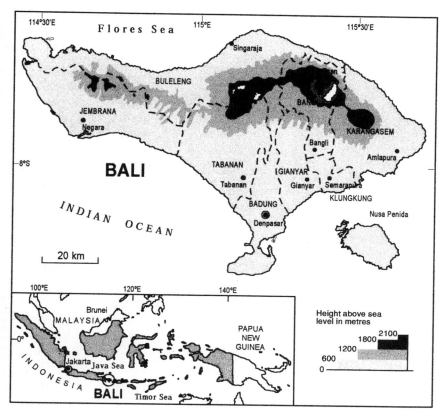

Map 2. The island of Bali

The topographic metaphor "Mountain Balinese" draws attention to the physical distance separating the people of the highlands from others living around the major urban and political centers of the island's southern coastal region (Map 2). As an element in the metaphoric construction of a cultural identity, however, it evokes a more complex notion of distance. This secondary and rather derisive connotation of the term arises because physical remoteness is employed in both traditional and modernist Balinese discourses as a trope for historical and cultural distance.[4] The term "Bali Aga" is a focal metaphor in a local discourse that has constructed its social referents as a remote and marginal people. Somewhat less common Balinese designations for this ethnic minority of mountain people are the terms *"bali mula"* and *"bali kuna,"* literally translated, the original or ancient Balinese. This choice of labels helps to confirm what has only been asserted until now. For other Balinese, an excursion into the distant highlands simultaneously signifies a journey into the past. It leads to a place where an indigenous people are assumed to maintain a cultural tradition originating from before the dawn of "Balinese civilization" (as southern Balinese define it).

For a number of reasons I retain the local designation "Bali Aga" in this text despite its somewhat negative connotations. A new label, on its own, could have provided no more than the illusion of a social change. Even if a replacement term were to become widely accepted, without a corresponding change of attitude among illocutors, it would all too soon acquire the same semantic character as the one it was meant to replace. In order to dispel the social prejudices that have haunted the Bali Aga, a more fundamental change of consciousness is required. This book aims to contribute by challenging superficial, selective, and misleading characterization of the highland people in popular and scientific discourses and by replacing first impressions with a deeper understanding of their culture.

The term "Bali Aga" was also retained because its meaning is ambiguous in any case, even as it is used by other Balinese and as the highland people themselves tend to stress. The mountains are, after all, the distant and sacred abode of the gods in Balinese cosmology. Furthermore, they are the distant water source of the river-irrigated rice-farming economy this island has depended on for a millennium. The alternative term *"mula"* is similarly polarized in its value implications. The notion of aboriginality is sometimes used to evoke an image of contrast, depicting a primitive culture and backward people who have been left behind on the path of social evolution by their supposedly more civilized and progressive fellow Balinese. In many other contexts, however, the notion of origin conjures up an image of Bali's mythical creation and sacred beginnings.

In the context of a modernizing society and in the discourses of Bali's new administrative and economic elite, the more positive value connotations of both terms are losing some of their earlier significance. By situating their cultural other at the opposite end of a temporal and topological scale on which they occupy the here and now, the apex of a cumulative civilization process and the center of power, prominent sectors of modern Balinese society are adopting a strategy of representation by contrast. The features of this strategy are remarkably similar to those identified by Said (1978) in his critique of Western orientalism.

Marginalizing portrayals of the highland people create an institutionalized invisibility rather than simply reflecting a natural invisibility and an innocent lack of knowledge about them. From the southern coast, the faraway home of the Bali Aga in the highlands of the island's interior is usually obscured by a milky ocean of cloud. Clusters of dark conical shapes sometimes appear in the east and west as Bali's majestic volcanic peaks rise from this land of mist. But the feature-less quality of an elusive highland world has not allowed its people to escape evaluation. Rather, the amorphous space between the faraway peaks has been shaped through the power of a projective imagination and fashioned into the shadow image of a dominant Balinese self. The popular image of Mountain Bali, constructed from the external perspective of a coastal civilization, has been clouded not by the steamy atmosphere of this tropical island but by opaque cultural lenses.

While it may have been a Balinese politics of identity that defined the Bali Aga in this way, local prejudices have also influenced pop-ular Western perceptions. Foreign visitors may occasionally explore an intriguing highland environment and gain glimpses of its people and culture. Their general impression of the island, however, is shaped by the powerful and exotic fantasy of a more "Balinese" Bali in the south: a fantasy in which southern Balinese themselves have a vested economic interest. Visitors arrive with expectations generated by travel brochures filled with romantic pictures of dazzling, palm-fringed surf beaches and elaborately terraced rice paddies, glittering in the benevolent light of a tropical sun. These prior expectations are difficult to reconcile with fleeting personal impressions of the island's less hospitable interior.

A set of even more pervasive "cultural tourism" expectations has been shaped by the pervasive image of Bali as the home of a refined courtly civilization. The exotic splendor of a Balinese high culture, commonly associated with the island's aristocracy and their palaces in the south, has been marketed with great proficiency to the world, most notably through the sophisticated, colorful medium of a wide range of artistic expressions. In the panoptic arcades of the global culture market, where visibility and consumer demand are mutually reinforcing variables, southern Bali is displayed and displays itself on a glass shelf at eye level. By contrast, the equally rich history and traditions of the mountain people are hidden and stowed away, for better or for worse, in the darkest recesses of Bali's dusty storeroom of cultural resources.

Superficial appearances have become all-important in the frenetic world of a global consumer culture, where difference is acknowledged and marketable only if it can be favorably recognized at a glance. Nevertheless, the physical characteristics of a highland environment do have a significance apart from their use as a trope for the cultural construction of its people. Bali's mountain economy is subject to a number of genuinely natural constraints relating to physical elevation, a cooler climate, and local demographics.

Most Bali Aga communities are located at elevations ranging from 800 to 1,700 meters, a climatic zone where intense wet rice cultivation is not feasible.[5] Highland Balinese have thus historically lacked the population density and surplus of material resources characteristic of the more productive agrarian economy of lowland Bali. Environmental conditions here are more amenable to the cultivation of slow-maturing dry rice varieties, maize, sweet potatoes, bananas, and vegetables, and to the raising of domestic pigs and cattle. A modest surplus could be gained by trading, in the past most notably by controlling the passage of goods through the mountains on their way from the important harbors of northern Bali to the south. More recently, a growing livestock export business (cattle, chickens, and pigs) and a move toward cash-crop agriculture (particularly coffee, citrus, and clove trees) have helped to augment the incomes of mountain farmers.[6] Where there is poverty in mountain villages nowadays, this is mainly due to a shortage of agricultural land emerging in the wake of recent population growth.[7] More and more young people fail to inherit or acquire sufficient land to remain agriculturists and are forced to seek alternative sources of income elsewhere.

The stark realities of limited economic opportunity in the highlands, however, are not determined by ecological factors alone. Access to new employment and business opportunities in the modern sector of the economy has often been denied the Bali Aga on account of their image of backwardness and lack of relevant connections. At the time when a cultural tourism industry came to dominate Bali's economy (Picard 1990), for example, the Bali Aga were poorly positioned to claim a significant stake in this new and highly profitable enterprise. Cast as a rather cultureless people by comparison to the glamorous courtly civilization of the south, their disadvantaged position could be attributed once again to the "natural" resource poverty of their highland economy.

A trickle of tourist dollars is reaching the highlands nonetheless, though this may not be because of a serious interest in highland culture. The promise of clearer skies and sometimes splendid views during the brief interlude of a relatively dry season, from May to September, attracts a modest influx of foreign and domestic tourists to Kintamani and other highland districts (*kecamatan*). Kintamani occupies the more elevated northern part of the land-locked regency (*kabupaten*) of Bangli.

Even as locals suffer the recurrent and acute water shortages of this season, streams of tourist buses and hired cars, interspersed by a more regular flow of trucks and vans, add traffic to the road winding up from the regency capital of Bangli in the south to Penelokan. As they follow this ancient trade road farther, through Kintamani Town, Sukawana, Bantang, and Dausa, on their way toward the northern coastal city of Singaraja and the black beaches of Lovina, visitors pass along the tall rim of the caldera that encircles the still active volcano and lake of Batur. Many pause to enjoy the scenic panorama and to catch a breath of cool air—a temporary but welcome relief to those who, their tropical island fantasy transformed into reality, suddenly find themselves suffering under the claustrophobia and relentless heat of the coastal plains.

The transportation needs of foreigners have had some historical impact on the development of mountain infrastructure. In the first decades of this century, Dutch administrator and keen traveler W.O.J. Nieuwenkamp reported with some satisfaction on the "path-breaking" contributions of a new colonial government to Balinese civilization: "In 1906 I traveled the path from Bangli to Batur on horseback, in 1918 by automobile!" (1920:99). Incidentally, 1918 was the year when Bangli, as the last of Bali's former principalities, came directly under Dutch colonial control. A more comprehensive network of smaller, partially sealed roads has been added since then, mostly during the last two decades. This time it was the Indonesian government's turn to claim the building of roads as a primary achievement and symbol of its power and administrative penetration.

The new network of secondary and poorly sealed local roads was designed more to meet the aims of national rural development plans than those of a tourist economy. While at the time of my research a majority of mountain villages were at last becoming accessible by road, in most of them the arrival of a white foreigner (*bule*, literally an albino or a person with a skin-discoloring disease) was still a rare, sensational, and sometimes unprecedented event. Significant tourist exposure and revenue has been obtained only in the village of Batur. The territories of this community include the scenic lookout Penelokan on the crater rim and the small settlement Toyabungka at the shore of Lake Batur. Construction projects currently under way in both locations aim to provide luxury facilities where only limited and modest budget accommodation has been available until now. With the majestic beauty and natural wonders of the volcanic highlands becoming more thoroughly commodified, the foremost attraction for the expected guests is assumed to be nature rather than culture.

Nearly all villages (*desa*) in Kintamani and in the wider region of the island's mountainous interior are Bali Aga communities (Figure 1). The only one to be recognized as such and to attract a measure of cultural tourism on account of this, however, is Desa Trunyan, on the far side of Lake Batur. Together with the famous Tenganan in the Karangasem regency, the Bali Aga village Trunyan is one of the few token emblems of a more archaic Bali on the island's cultural tourism trail and is known in particular for its "primitive" sky-burials.[8] The piles of skulls in the local cemetery attract only a modest number of visitors, however, owing to Trunyan's other and equally somber reputation as a village of begging children. Travelers' testimonies warn that local men may extort money from passengers by rocking their shaky boats as they ferry them across the lake. Authors of tourist guide books, who generally propagate romantic visions of smiling Balinese, have propagated the image problem of the hill people by characterizing them as "hostile, scruffy hustlers" (Winterton 1989: 157–158) and as a potential "hassle" to those wishing to enjoy the natural beauty of their mountain home (Darling 1990:156).

The highlands periodically witness another brief invasion by outsiders as southern Balinese visitors arrive suddenly and in great numbers. The timing and purpose of their pilgrimage to the mountains differs fundamentally from that of foreign tourists. Unlike Western visitors, Balinese are rarely attracted to the mountains during a meteorological and ritual dry season of relative ceremonial idleness lasting from May to October. Each year at the two liminal times of transition in the alternating cycle of the two seasons, however, it is an ancient religious tradition to undertake the once arduous journey into the mountains. These moments, marked by the appearance of the full moon in the months of April (end of wet season) and October (end of dry season), are times set apart for spectacular harvest or fertility rituals in a number of ancient Bali Aga temples. Of crucial importance in the articulation of a long-standing relationship between the people of the mountains and other Balinese, these ritual interactions will be discussed in detail later.

During a wet season of rain and blood sacrifices, lasting from November to March, the mountains recede behind a shroud of perpetual mist and endless chilling rains, and are avoided by tourists and pilgrims alike. Local farmers are mostly left alone to appreciate at first hand the descent of the heavenly precipitation from the realm

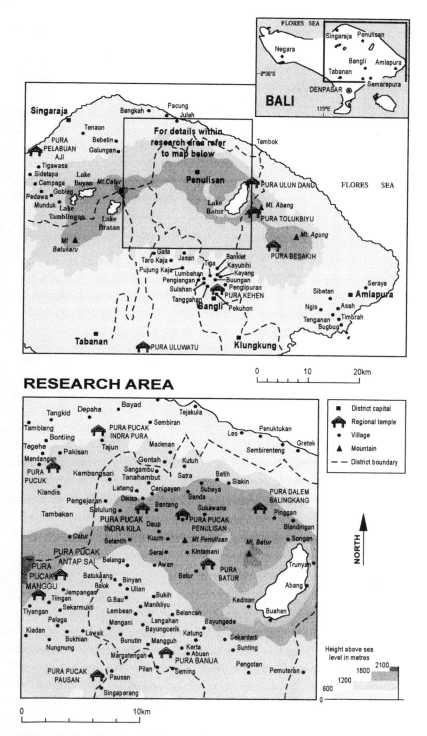

Figure 1. Distribution of villages with Bali Aga traditions in contemporary Bali

of the gods, on which the entire island has traditionally depended for its economic survival.

Identifying the Bali Aga with the mountains is tempting and not altogether inappropriate. Many of their communities are indeed located on and together dominate the most elevated central part of the island. Nor can it be doubted that agricultural practices in these communities are adapted to survival under the specific conditions of a tropical mountain environment. As Appadurai (1988) has suggested, however, the cultural discourses that localize an ethnic group in a confined and distant physical space are based on more than an innocent and unmediated metaphoric transferal of environmental features onto the level of social classification.

As the Bali Aga were allotted a place on the conceptual map of the island, through the speech acts and in the cultural representations of their fellow Balinese, anomalies and contradictions between an idealized social topology and actual settlement patterns had to be dismissed. It is conveniently ignored that a number of "Aga" villages are not in the mountains at all. The majority of villages along the arid northern coast of the regency of Buleleng, from Pacung to Penuktukan, are Bali Aga villages as well, and others are found in a small cluster along the southeastern coast of Karangasem, from Tenganan to Seraya. Although the ecology and economics of villages along the northern coast are very different from those in highland villages, the same cannot be said of their culture. Indeed, there would be no empirical grounds for suggesting a cultural divide between a "coastal" and "mountain" people in Bali if one were to define the northeastern coast as the island's most significant shore. The Bali Aga appear as a separate "people of the mountains" (*wong aga*) only when viewed from the perspective of the southern plains and foothills, as has been their fate for many centuries.

An understanding of other cultures inevitably begins with first impressions. These are often sufficient to illustrate that there are ways of life different from one's own. As such, they draw attention and may awaken a genuine sense of curiosity. But first impressions also tend to be riddled with contradictions, as are the kinds of discourses about other cultures that rely on them. Fleeting encounters evidently raise more questions about others (and ourselves) than can be answered on the basis of the superficial information they themselves can provide.

Such questions can only be answered by exploring cultural difference in more ethnographic detail, without allowing the resulting ethnographic knowledge to serve as a vehicle for constructing an even more pervasive and permanent sense of distance.[9] In order to reduce a prevailing popular sense of subjective distance toward a particular culture, it may be necessary first to deconstruct subjective and biased portrayals of that culture by other and presumably more prejudiced outsiders, but it is not sufficient. A greater quantity of information in itself is not a guarantee of greater objectivity when it comes to its interpretation. Given the apparent subjectivity of all knowledge and the inevitability of raising further knowledge claims in writing an ethnography (even if a pure deconstructivism approach is adopted), what is required instead is a solution to the fundamental problem of representation.

In the interim, the dismissal of ethnography as yet another form of biased representation should be suspended temporarily on the basis of a critical humanist assumption: Cultural differences (real or imaginary) are relative to a higher-order similarity among people on the grounds of a shared anthropological (lit. "human") condition, and hence, at least in principle, there is a potential in anthropology for a self-critical interpretation of cultural difference. Though this may be a somewhat uncertain foundation in that it assumes a capacity for critical intersubjectivity in advance of exploring its character and contingency, this uncertainty may provide sufficient rationale for granting this particular ethnography the opportunity to address ethnography's general dilemma of subjectivity.

In this book, therefore, I will consider Bali Aga ways of living initially as an unfamiliar set of cultural responses to the familiar challenges of human existence. The underlying problem of subjectivity in representation, of having the power to misrepresent and experiencing the agony of being misrepresented by others, constitutes just such a challenge. I will first explore how the Bali Aga people respond to this general dilemma where it is first encountered by them—within their own highland society.

Part I

Banua

Ritual Domains and the Status Economy of Highland Bali

Chapter 1

THE *BANUA* AS A CATEGORY
AND A SOCIAL PROCESS

The social landscape of highland Bali is patterned by regional networks of ritual alliance among groups of villages. Such networks are locally referred to as *banua,* or "ritual domains." How these regional associations are conceptualized and maintained, and how they generate a sense of shared identity among the mountain people and set the stage for a regional status economy will be explored in the following chapters. The study of regional social interaction among the Bali Aga leads to a magical world where human beings, ancestors, spirits, and gods share a sacred landscape and timescape, brought to life in an intricate pattern of narrative and ritual performance. The present chapter commences this exploration by introducing some underlying themes and variations in the conceptual and social organization of ritual domains.

Ritual Domains: Themes and Variations

In popular accounts of the ethnic history and composition of Balinese society, the Bali Aga are often classified together as the island's original people, to be distinguished from the descendants of later immigrants from the Javanese empire of Majapait. The study of their ritual domains reveals, however, that the Bali Aga draw further distinctions among themselves in similar terms. Internal relations within and among the *banua* of the highlands are articulated in narrative histories that trace an ancestral path of origin back through time and space. These "origin narratives" distinguish sacred places of origin and their founders from the newer villages and temples founded by their emigrating descendants or by foreign immigrants. Highland Balinese thus envisage contemporary society as the product of a historical sequence of migrations and village foundations that has its beginning in a mythical time of original settlement. The ritual status of a particular village depends on its position relative to others within a social order of "precedence." In an order of precedence, rank is indexed on proximity to the beginning of a temporal sequence of related, socially pertinent, and collectively remembered events. A value focus on origin and a distribution of status in terms of precedence is paradigmatic for Bali Aga social organization in general, as it also appears to be for other societies in the Austronesian-speaking world (Fox and Sathers 1996).

In a three-page exposition representing, to my knowledge, the only explicit reference to *banua* in the ethnographic literature on Bali, C. J. Grader mentions that participation in a *banua* may entail a shared responsibility for the maintenance of an important regional temple and for the celebration of its festivals (1969:134–137). Referring briefly to examples from the Kintamani district, Grader further suggests that the villages who cooperate in this fashion may be affiliated through the cult of local deities, linked by myths of their nuptial relation, as well as sharing a common history. The meaning of the term *"banua"* and the organization of the regional social association it refers to, however, are much more complex and variable than Grader's tantalizing hints reveal.[1]

From one perspective a *banua* can be said to consist of a network of voluntary association among a group of locally autonomous villages. This association is accompanied by a considerable degree of asymmetry in the relative status of participating villages, which immediately raises the paradox of status. What would motivate a politically and economically autonomous village to submit voluntarily to the superior ritual authority of another in the context of a regional association?[2]

This question touches on a fundamental conflict of social life. Human beings everywhere tend to display a strong interest in cooperative association within loosely bounded intersubjective fields of social and symbolic interaction. An element of competition is almost immediately introduced into such fields, however, by the irreconcilable strategic interests of particular subjects or groups of subjects. In a status economy, these strategic interests are irreconcilable, given that social status is a resource that cannot be significantly expanded, though it can certainly be redistributed (see Milner 1994:29–35). For example, a symmetrical attribution of "exceptional" status to all participants in a status economy would cause a symbolic inflation whereby the exceptional would become ordinary. If one group's status is to increase relative to others, it must necessarily be at the expense of others. Changes in the distribution of social status within a symbolic economy thus can be viewed as shifting currents in an asymmetrical flow of social approval. The value of such approval, however, in whatever form it may be conveyed (e.g., by offering or bestowing gifts, paying respect, or offering services and voluntary cooperation), is ultimately measured in terms of relativity and in the course of social comparison.[3] In this sense, status must always remain a finite resource.

How can one investigate a status economy in view of the paradox of having to cooperate in order to compete? An analysis focused exclusively on strategic interests and competition would reveal little about what holds a *banua* together as a culturally specific field of social interaction and a status economy. This perspective does provide an appreciation of the basic odds against which a status game in a context of voluntary association must be sustained: Those who voluntarily cooperate in order to be able to participate and compete, but who meet with little success, may well withdraw their cooperation. In the case of *banua* participants, for a number of reasons, this is not usually the case. Insofar as cooperation is generally a precondition for competition, I begin this analysis by exploring what it is that holds a *banua* together.

Banua participants themselves do not portray their mutual involvement as a form of voluntary association or as a field of strategic interaction, particularly at times when the organization and the distribution of status in their domain are comparatively stable. Following a recent shift in the status order of their alliances or after a group of villages has decided to withdraw their support altogether, they may concede to the effects of subjective choice in private discussions. Such cases, however, are relatively rare and even more rarely spoken of in public.

People participating in a *banua* discount the voluntary and negotiable character of their alliances by characterizing their joint ritual practices as the fulfillment of ancient and collective religious obligations. A sacred site of origin lies at the heart of every *banua*, and people's religious obligations are to the ancestral deities enshrined at these jointly maintained temples or temple complexes. In other words, the benefit of sheer participation within a sphere of ritual cooperation beyond the village, in a larger and more sacred social whole, is experienced and depicted as so compelling that it diminishes one's awareness of having made a voluntary choice and with it the relevance of questions about whether or not one's own competitive strategic interests are served well by this choice. While there may be a hidden scope for making choices concerning the how and with whom of ritual cooperation beyond the village, the local characterization of *banua* participation as a sacred obligation is nevertheless appropriate in some ways. It illustrates the general desirability of regional participation as an end in itself. Indeed, to be part of a regional world of ritual interaction is valued so highly that almost all Bali Aga villages belong to a *banua*. Even in the event that they withdraw their support from one network, they will allocate it to another immediately.

When asked to elaborate further, participants tend to describe a *banua* as a ritual association among groups of people from a number of related villages (*desa*) in fulfillment of their shared religious obligations toward the domain's founding ancestors and their temples. This description does not imply, however, that *banua* are necessarily conceptualized in terms of the common ancestry of their congregations. *"Desa"* and *"banua"* are terms referring to places as well as communities, and it is the more inclusive notion of sharing a common performance space that delineates their scope as spheres of social cooperation.

This privileged focus on place can be illustrated by looking at the way ritual obligations are justified in a *banua*. In villages whose founding ancestors are believed to have been the migrating descendants of the domain founders, the local population may include a large proportion of later immigrants, people who have no genealogical relationship whatsoever to the village or domain founders. These foreign immigrants must participate in the ritual life of both *desa* and *banua* nonetheless. Even where a village is said to have been founded by foreign immigrants in the first place, within the territories of a preexisting domain, the people of that village are expected to contribute to the maintenance of the relevant regional temples in full and to participate in the ceremonies held there in honor of the domain's founders.

The concept *"banua"* therefore evokes an image not so much of a network of ancestral connections as of a stretch of ancestral land, in other words, a domain. The spatial limits of a particular domain can be imagined as a line separating member villages from others belonging to neighboring domains, given that the villages of a *banua* tend to form a cohesive block and are not scattered or interspersed by nonparticipating neighbors.

Ancestral and spatial dimensions in the conceptualization of a *banua* tend to converge, together with an implicit or practical knowledge of the transformative power of agency or choice. Member villages are only those whose inhabitants actively and continuously acknowl-

edge, in the course of their ritual practice, that the deities of a particular *banua* temple are indeed the original ancestral founders and
spiritual protectors of a domain of which their own agricultural land
is a part.

The term "domain" is useful as a point of departure in that it captures the salient territorial connotations not only of the Balinese
word *"banua,"* but also of its cognates in related Malayo-Polynesian
languages.[4] Reflexes of the Proto-Austronesian reconstruction **banua*
in these languages usually convey the idea of a bounded territory: a
domain, village, or smaller settlement. For example, in Old Javanese,
wanua or *wanwa* connotes a village; in Iban, *menoa rumah* is the
domain of a longhouse; in Bidayuh, *binua* is a village composed of
several longhouses; in Ngada (Sara-Sedu), a *nua* is a village or ritual
territory; in Lio, *nua* is a ritual territory, domain, or polity; and in
Palué, *nua lua* refers to the island of Palué. Similarly, in Goodenough
manua connotes a village or dwelling place, while in Vanuatu (East
Ambai), Tonga, and Fiji, *vanua* or *fanua* is a stretch of land or territory. In New Zealand (Maori), *whenua* is the land of a localized
extended-family group. More sporadically the term is used to refer
to a house or the land and people attached to it, as in Toraja *banua*,
Banggai *bonua*, Wolio *banua*, Molima *vanua*, and Wusi-Mana *wanua*.[5]

In Balinese, the reflex *"banua"* is best translated as *"ritual* domain,"
a necessary qualification, given that it denotes a sphere of relevance
circumscribed not by legal codes or political means but by social
interactions within a ritual setting and idiom. The idea of a ritual
domain as a shared performance space also reverberates with the
local belief that the fertility of all agricultural land within a *banua*,
and hence the economic survival or prosperity (*rahayu*) of its people,
depends on the disposition of the ancestor deities of a particular
regional temple and that their disposition is only favorable as long as
they receive ritual offerings produced jointly by all those who use
that land, irrespective of their affiliation by descent.

The notion of an ancient and evolving relationship between the
people and the land is of paramount importance to the conceptualization of a *banua* and warrants further discussion. *Banua* are not de-
finable as corporations, by the lands its members collectively own. To
the contrary, they are constituted on the idea that a domain and its
people are "owned" by one or a group of deified ancestors or gods.[6]
From another perspective it could even be suggested that the land
"owns" both the people and their ancestor deities. It is the produce
of the land that nourishes humans, and from this produce they in

turn prepare offerings to feed the ancestors. In yet another sense, people say they "own the responsibility" of looking after both the land and the gods.

Access to agricultural land in highland Bali is often governed communally by the village. The right to cultivate a particular plot of village land (*tanah ayahan desa*) passes from defunct households to the next eligible couple, who are (or were) not necessarily the personal heirs of the former users. Even where usage rights are passed on by inheritance, such rights are subject to ritual obligations. These obligations are explained by arguing that even very distant generations of previous users are still connected to their land long after their names and precise connection to the present users by ties of descent have been forgotten.

Land thus has the character of a timeless material reality upon which transient social realities are more permanently inscribed, in particular, through the construction of human dwellings and "temples" (the dwellings of ancestors). The beginning of history and the sacred origin of society is the moment when people and land became conjoined in a sacred covenant, the time when the founding ancestors first cleared the primordial forest.

While a historical relationship between human beings and the land is fundamental to the conceptualization of a *banua*, there are three categories of invisible participants who also need to be considered. The ancestors who first settled the land represent a point of origin in human (or posthuman) rather than absolute terms, as they are not believed to have found the land in a state of vacancy. Not only did they clear the land of a primordial forest, they also displaced an original population of "spirit people" (*wong alus*, lit. "subtle/refined people"). The *wong alus* are the epitome of aboriginality, a nameless ancient people who have been displaced and taken refuge in dark forests, ravines, old ruins, and caves. Like deified human ancestors they are thus associated with specific places. They are invisible and ageless citizens of a timeless world (*niskala*, lit. "no-time," from *kala*, "time"), contiguous with but distinct from the temporally contingent world of mortal human beings (*sekala*, divisible and quantifiable time, from *se-*, "one"). The phase transition between these two worlds is and needs to be fluid. Spontaneous sightings of spirit beings are reported frequently in the mountains, while ritual is said to open a gate between the two worlds in a more deliberate and purposeful manner.

The earth and the ocean are the abode of another class of *niskala* entities of bizarre shape and malicious intent, the *buta kala* (lit. "blind of time"). Informants learned in magic and matters of the invisible world unanimously explained to me that *wong alus* are not as essentially malicious as these *buta kala*. But when angered or neglected they, and even the gods, may choose to take the form of *buta kala*, a category or, rather, a state of being that can be described as destructive of life, good health, fertility, and prosperity. In several locally recorded myths it is explained that the *buta kala* themselves, insofar as they are conceived as actual beings rather than dispositions, originally had been fair spirits. They only acquired their ugly appearance and lowly position after and because of the creation of human beings, who eventually displaced them from the visible middle world. The gods cursed the *buta kala*, causing them to hide in the earth or eat human excrement in the form of dogs, for they had ridiculed the gods, wagering the gods would fail in their attempt to fashion the first ancestors of the human race (usually from earth or wood).

The people of the mountains recognize a need to offer blood to these spirits of the earth in elaborate and frequent animal sacrifices designed to protect the boundaries of the human world against their trespassing.[7] In some ways similar and almost as important as the rituals dedicated to the original human founders of a domain, these blood sacrifices (*caru*) are essential precautions to prevent earlier (in this case nonhuman) occupants of the land from exacting revenge on their thankless successors by withholding or ruining its fertility.[8]

While low-dwelling spirits may have been the original nonhuman inhabitants of the land, they are not regarded as its creators. In an interpretation that shows similarity to Balinese ideas about human conception, the world is thought to have been created by a further class of highly refined invisible beings who have their lofty abode in the rain-ejaculating sky rather than the receptive earth (or ocean/ lake) below. These deities, commonly referred to as *"bhatara"* and addressed as *"ratu"* (king/chief) in the mountains, can be of great significance within the mythology and cult of important *banua* temples.[9] Although they may display a refined behavior and beautiful humanlike form when all is well (to those few to whom they reveal themselves in visions), they are as dangerous as the *buta kala* when neglected. Their aid in moderating the forces of nature for the benefit of agriculture, particularly in ensuring the timely commencement of seasonal rainfalls, cannot be taken for granted.

The sky-dwelling *bhatara* are not clearly distinguishable from distant and deified human ancestors who have long ascended to the heavens, just as the earthbound *buta kala* are difficult to differentiate from the spirits of the recently dead.[10] The malevolent spirits of the latter are expected to linger low, near their corpses buried in the earth, until they are ritually elevated in the course of postmortuary purification rites. As Leo Howe (1984) has argued, the Balinese pantheon of invisible entities is ultimately part of a general conceptual scale of being that pertains also to the classification of human persons and their variable dispositional and social states. Unlike in southern Bali, however, the people of the mountains refrain from breaking up this inherently continuous scale into distinct "castes" (*varna/wangsa*) or other fixed person categories on the basis of pedigree. To them, a person's life, and life itself, is a passage from heaven to earth and back to heaven. The status of a living person is mutable and contingent upon one's momentary position on the path of life. Deceased human beings travel farther along this same path as they are transformed from dangerous spirits of the graveyard into purified and refined ancestors enshrined at a temple. The elevated status attributed to the most refined beings, the most distant ancestors, and the most widely inclusive regional temples, however, is accompanied by a process of disembodiment and by a shift of discursive emphasis and practical interest away from the distribution of material resources to that of symbolic resources. This means that a regional association like the *banua* is a field of interaction wherein any immediate concern for regulating access to land has been abandoned to create an open stage for the playing out of a symbolic interest in status.[11]

The spiritual embeddedness of the land, the people, the ancestors, and other invisible beings within the sacred community of a *banua* is expressed and reaffirmed by the regular ceremonies held at its regional temple. Temple ceremonies are performed as a cooperative effort involving the ritual participation of all who live within the "social relevance sphere," or performance space, of the *banua* concerned. From a local perspective, these regular ceremonial activities are the acknowledgment of an a priori spiritual condition, rather than reflecting the free choice of a group of people to define and maintain a shared world of social interaction.

This explanation, however, does not address the sociologically more interesting questions of how a *banua* is established in the first place and how it is maintained or changed. The same questions are also of importance to participants, insofar as they have an interest not only in cooperating to create the stage for a symbolic economy, but in competing for the symbolic resources it makes available. The notion of a *banua* as a unified and self-evident social entity therefore must be reconciled with the fact that internal distinctions are drawn among different categories of persons, leading to an asymmetrical distribution of status. At this point, my aim is to show how such distinctions are drawn in the terms of a shared idiom of status reckoning, rather than to illustrate how processes of negotiation unfold with the strategic application of this idiom in specific situations.

Participants in a ritual domain seek answers to questions about current social arrangements by looking at the past. The very existence of a *banua* is based on an assumption that all contemporary participants are united by their orientation to a common origin and that each domain has grown from an original community into the larger, more differentiated social entity that it is today. *Banua* are thus viewed as the unique result of a unique mythohistorical process of settlement, expansion, and migration. This uniqueness is a testimony to the power of agency in shaping the past and provides considerable scope for accommodating the effects of human agency in the historical present, as contemporary people continue a process of inscription through action.

Local interpretations of ritual domains in terms of their historical origin and development must be taken seriously in that they constitute a representation and explanation of local social practices and, as such, exert a reciprocal influence on the experience they seek to represent and explain. They should also be taken seriously as a mode of understanding that has considerable analytic merit, whereby *banua* are appropriately portrayed as the product of specific and continuing processes rather than generic and timeless institutions. In addition, and in contrast to local discourses, *banua* may need to be recognized as products of historical processes that entail more than a mechanical cultural reproduction of the ever same and more also than the "natural" process of differentiation and growth hinted at in the historical and botanical idioms of the Bali Aga (below). *Banua* are produced and reproduced, changed, and maintained by people in the present as they engage in specific social practices and discourses designed to "read" as well as "write" history. Even insofar as the interactive performances of agents in the past have become objectified as the given cultural conditions of an inscribed present, the interpretation of that past in the present may still be manipulated. The Bali Aga, although they attribute great importance to the faithful commemoration of their path of origin, are able to shape the way history is traced and made to continue, much more so, perhaps, than they are willing to admit.

Banua participants in countless conversations proclaimed that ritual traditions are immutable, suggesting the contemporary ritual order of their domain was a mimetic reflection of a past that can no longer be changed or negotiated. This attitude is reflected in the expression *"mula keto,"* it has been like this from the beginning. *"Mula keto"* was the most frequent, seemingly vacuous response to my initial inquiries into the rationale of *banua* participation. Only after I had gained trust did informants concede that significant changes in the membership and organization of their domain had indeed occurred, even in the recent past, and that similar upheavals could recur in the future. This confidence suggests that they are well aware of their own agency, even though they publicly discount its relevance.

In general, my observations have tended to confirm local claims about the continuity of ritual traditions. Ritual ties can be altered in active response to internal conflicts, external challenges, or gradual changes in social and material conditions, and they often are. Nevertheless, the sheer force of inherited social conventions, combined with an added moral imperative to honor these conventions as religious obligations, has a powerful conservative effect. In this sense, the one-liner *"mula keto"* is a pithy explanation born out of participants' lived experience of culture as something that evidently precedes and often outlives them. Social conventions and normative principles, however, do not spell out how individuals should act under specific circumstances or how they may realize their personal ambitions.

In the terminology of a performance-oriented social theory, the members of a *banua* could be described as active social agents positioned within the constraints of a particular moment and scenario, set within the dynamics of an ongoing cultural history, a process that involves their appropriation, manipulation, and transformation of cultural knowledge as well as their contributing to its perpetuation. This dialectic of cultural reproduction and change is acknowledged partially in local "social theories" concerning the rationale of participation and status distribution in a *banua* and more strongly in the logic of associated local practices.

The interface between local "social theory" and "social practice" has been rightly problematized in the work of practice theorists like Anthony Giddens (1979) and Pierre Bourdieu (1977, 1998) and will be explored further in relation to the present ethnographic context. I shall propose that Bali Aga theories of society (e.g., in the context of the *banua*) draw on a number of different idioms to construct a totalizing vision of society as a unified entity with a durable structure. Such theories are totalizing representations of society to varying degrees, depending on the particular idiom they draw upon. In other words, they also may contain a variable potential for the acknowledgment of society as a set of transient and evolving arrangements among people whose practical conflicts of interest, in this case, may precipitate the fission or reorganization of a domain.

Many of my informants argued that the fulfillment of regional ritual obligations is not just an exercise of religious piety but a matter of life or death. A priest from Sukawana once explained this to me by evoking a physiological metaphor: "If the hands no longer want to feed the mouth, if the stomach refuses to digest the food, if the heart decides to stop beating, what kind of choice is that? It is to choose death, and who would be so ignorant as to choose that?" (Jero Bau Gusing Almarhum 1993). He portrays cooperation as a prerequisite for ensuring the practical survival of the domain as a totality made up of interdependent parts. This local representation of a set of social relations as a living system is oddly reminiscent of the functionalist interpretations of culture that at one time dominated anthropological theory. The flaw in such theories of society is their failure to acknowledge that the hands may rebel against the rest of the body nonetheless and that the malfunction of one social body simply gives birth to another.

Organic metaphors are evident not only in the statement of this informant but in a general symbolic logic of sacrifice among the highland people—a logic that does not venture to deny the possibility and indeed the inevitability of death. The ritual order of a *banua* is also a sacrificial order. At least one four-footed animal is sacrificed at the annual festivals of *banua* temples, and its symbolically resurrected body (*wangun urip*) represents the domain in the image of a whole that is and can be alive in an idealized sense only.

The idea of a limb severed from the social body of a *banua* and living on as an incomplete entity, at least in theory, would be regarded as an abomination to a "natural" order of things.[12] In a local cosmology of incorporation, every part of a ritual and social body is depicted as an integral component essential to the welfare of all others. The local expression for having a ritual obligation (*kena*, lit. "to be struck with") may further indicate that the task of playing a specific part in the remaking of the domain's past in the ritual present is to some extent existentially thrown upon each participating group. Nevertheless, with the acknowledgment of death in sacrifice, as an inevitable and perpetual challenge, society is ultimately depicted as a fragile whole—a system that will inevitably malfunction and disintegrate unless it is perpetually re-created. The idiom of sacrifice thus allows for meaningful expressions of human agency within a process of actively resurrecting (*wangun urip*) or beautifying (*wangun ayu*) sacrificial or social bodies.

The Bali Aga may employ body metaphors to articulate and characterize differences in social status, but they do not use them to justify such differences. In the ritual division of a sacrificial body, for example, particular body parts of the victim may sometimes signify that the human recipient has a high status (e.g., the head), while others (e.g., the tail) may signify a lower status. This and other practices help to articulate a local theory of society in which status differentiation is regarded as a necessary precondition for a stable social life, just as a differentiation among female and male bodies is a precondition for the continuity of life itself. Categorical patterns of status distribution, however, are not regarded as permanent with regard to their occupants. While it may define a permanent set of intrinsic symbolic relations between particular parts in relation to a social whole, the body-focused logic of sacrifice does not spell out the extrinsic rationale by which certain persons come to be associated with certain parts of a sacrificed body in the first place, nor does it comment on the transient nature of this association.

Readers may have noted a logical potential in metaphors of the body (e.g., head/tail) for theorizing a permanent or hierarchical model of social differentiation and a similar one in metaphors of spatial location (e.g., uphill/downhill). In terms of social practice, status differences in Bali Aga society are often articulated by establishing a metaphoric association between particular persons and particular body parts or places. These status differences, however, are initially constructed and subsequently explained in the terms of a much more pervasive idiom of time and action. This is extremely important. Rather than pursuing these possible visions of a permanent array of social body components or of a motionless social topography of fixed places to their hierarchical conclusion, Bali Aga models of society are focused on a history of human agency as it manifests itself in a dynamic process of expansion, migration, and social change. The body and the land are the media to be inscribed by human action or read and reinscribed by acts of recollection, but they are not the means of inscription. Indeed, from a Bali Aga perspective on personhood, "tails" can and do become "heads," just as newly settled places can and do become places of origin.

The history of human action, in the context of a *banua*, is captured in multiple and variable narrative accounts of how the domain was founded and how it developed through time. These origin narratives typically establish a temporal sequence of original and subsequent settlement foundations in a ritual domain, which serves as an index for the construction of a social order of precedence among the communities concerned. This focus on precedence institutionalizes a view of social status as a changeable condition contingent upon the unpredictable course of a continuing history of human action.

A village whose ancestral founders originated from another, older village may itself be the source village of the founders of even newer villages and so on, in a course of historical expansion. Moreover, once a relatively new village becomes the origin point for a large group of even newer villages, the link and obligation to its own source village may be forgotten. The status of villages within a regional ritual context is thus intrinsically relative and temporally contingent even in theory, and more so in practice, given that the origin narratives themselves are forever open to contestation and revision.

Ritual interaction is perhaps the most prominent stage for articulating status differences. An example is the division of ceremonial labor. The ultimate ritual authority over a *banua* or, more precisely, its principal temple usually rests in the hands of only one of the member communities. The priest-leaders who orchestrate the rituals of a regional *banua* temple often are selected exclusively from among the elders of this village. Most commonly, the village in whose territory the *banua* temple is located is also considered the oldest and hence occupies a position of ritual precedence. Its people are the *pangamong* or *pangempon*, the ritual and organizational custodians of the domain, while other communities may adopt an often very specific supportive role.[13] Other ritual expressions of precedence are the seating order of the gods and people of visiting villages, the order of ceremonial processions, the amount and form of offerings contributed to a temple festival by different villages, or the distribution of sanctified water (*tirta*) and leftover food offerings among them. The degree of differentiation and asymmetry in the distribution of ceremonial functions and privileges can vary from one domain to another, but the distribution of ritual authority and status is always deemed important enough to trigger strategic manipulation and organizational change.

It is best to avoid narrow binary interpretations of the *banua*—as a conceptual construct or a field of practical social interaction, as a place or a community, as an encountered reality or a world in the making. In my observation of its pragmatic usage in the highlands, participants themselves also tend to use the word *"banua"* to emphasize very different dimensions of what a ritual domain is or can be depending on the speech context. Such semantic nuances are also reflected in a wide range of composite terms. For example, a *desa banua* is the origin *village* (*desa*) of a domain, a *gebog banua* is a *set* (*gebog*) of villages who recognize a common origin and ritual responsibility, a *pura banua* is the principal *temple* of a domain that marks its point of origin, and *keraman banua* is the congregation of individual *heads of households* (*keraman*, from *rama*, "father") who finance and participate in the ritual of a domain temple.[14] A specific act of participation in a domain is described in the verb form *"mabanua,"* and a general state of involvement with a domain is called *"bebanuan."* Note that the terms *"banua"* and *"gebog"* carry similar meanings, except that *"banua"* is more suggestive of the domain as a composite reality with material, human, and spiritual dimensions, whereas *"gebog"* refers only to the social association among the people of a set of villages.[15]

The breadth of this semantic field suggests, as is indeed the case, that the term *"banua"* carries a broad range of meanings and may be used to designate similarly what are in fact a wide variety of different social arrangements. Of particular importance from a status-economy perspective are variations in how the relationship between "original" and "subsequently founded" communities is conceptually structured and articulated in the origin narratives and ritual life of different domains. Such variations as well as underlying similarities are most effectively illustrated by example cases from among the *banua* of the highlands. I discuss four types of domains, though I must stress in advance that these typologies are merely analytical devices for distinguishing among different ways of conceptualizing and actualizing a *banua*. In effect, different concepts and idioms of relatedness are often combined within the narrative and ritual traditions of a single network.

Some *banua* are small clusters of villages, one of which is regarded as the first and original "village of the domain" (*desa banua*). The senior status of the source village often finds metaphoric expression in the notion that a parent-child relationship links the ancestral deities in the local temples of the origin and branch villages. An example is the domain around the ancient mountain village Bayung Gede. In this *banua* and in others of its kind, a mythohistorical relationship between villages is reactualized within an idiom of mutual visits between deities during temple festivals. Visits to and from the village of origin are distinguished. The deified founders of the branch villages "return home" (*mulih*) to honor their parent(s), and far less frequently, the parent deities "go forth" (*lunga*) to visit and acknowledge a child. The festivals that entail such ritual visits are those of the villages' Pura Bale Agung (temple of the great pavilion) and/or Pura Puseh (navel temple). The idiom of traveling forth or returning along a path of origin implies a temporal ranking among generations of divine predecessors and successors inscribed upon space.

A similar spatial mapping of temporal and generational distinctions is evident in local interpretations of the past as a history of explicitly human action. Communities within *banua* of this type regard themselves as linked by a series of migrations. Subsidiary villages are said to have grown from a number of temporary dwellings in garden plots (*pondok*) too distant from the village for its occupants to return daily after completing their work. An example is Penglipura, one of several downstream *pondokan* founded by ancestors from Bayung Gede. Penglipura is now a separate village community (*desa adat*) with its own set of temples, but it still has a ceremonial obligation to attend (*mabanua*) at the temples of Bayung Gede during major festivities. On these occasions, the people of Penglipura will deliver "village-level prestations" (*atos desa*). *Atos desa* is a key marker of relationships between whole village communities within a *banua*, in distinction to links between other, smaller social associations.[16]

The visitors' delivery of offerings to a *banua* temple is not recognized as an asymmetric gift exchange among people belonging to a set of ranked status groups. Offerings of food or cash are exchanged instead between humans and divine beings. After the deities have consumed the invisible essence (*sari*) contained in the offerings, the paying guests may receive a symbolic share of the divine "leftovers" as a blessing as well as some sanctified rice and water. The large remainder of rice and other consumables is kept by the hosts, not to speak of the "leftover" cash donations. The small amount of sanctified rice and water received as a religious token of the visitors' reciprocal exchange with the deity thus conceals the economic potential in asymmetric ritual exchange transactions among human agents.

The articulation of exchanges among groups of people in a ritual idiom cannot be explained, however, as a form of material resource accumulation concealed beneath a cloak of religious justifications. The expenses incurred by the hosts of a temple festival can be as great or greater than the value of the resources obtained from visitors in the form of ritual gifts. A better explanation for the religious characterization of exchanges among villages in a domain may be that it defuses some of the competitiveness and conflicts in their asymmetric status relationships. Since the status of a group is vested in the opinions of others, there is a tendency for patrons to seek the approval of clients. This approval may be expressed in the form of ritualized exchanges as long as the flow of gifts overtly marks the association as asymmetric. The clients, however, while their own status may benefit from a close association with high status patrons, will seek to minimize displays of status asymmetry as much as is possible. By introducing a third, invisible party as the ultimate recipients in a flow of exchanges, this conflict of interests is prevented from becoming a bone of contention. With the invisible deities established as ultimate patrons, the relevance of differences between their human clients is reduced. Many informants from visiting villages also argued that the offerings they were delivering, rather than being their own gifts, were gifts from the junior deities of their village to the parent deities in the origin village. In this interpretation, the human agency of both givers and receivers is played down.

Exchanges between ranked groups also need to downplay the economic aspect of gift exchange so as to avoid any implication of buying or selling social approval. In agreement with the definition of symbolic capital proposed by Murray Milner (1994), I would argue that status is a relatively inalienable resource in most cases, perhaps with the exception of those societies in which status itself is defined predominantly in terms of wealth.[17] In his reflections on the nature of symbolic capital and status, Milner develops a critique of Bourdieu, taking objection in particular to his "reductionist tendency to see symbolic forms of capital ultimately as ways of disguising and legitimating material forms of power." He continues: "While I certainly agree that people often attempt to convert various forms of symbolic power into material power, I reject Bourdieu's assumption that this is always the disguised and 'misrecognised' motive" (Milner 1994:11). As far as *banua* participants are concerned, Milner's hypothesis seems to be confirmed. Ritual status has the potential to exert an influence on a person's access to material resources and vice versa. But the fact that such a possibility for resource conversion may exist and may need to be disguised does not mean that material and symbolic interests can be reduced from one to the other. At least in an ideal sense, status is regarded as an inalienable attribute of persons or groups in highland Bali and is valued as an end in itself.

In paying ritual visits to Bayung Gede, participants from branch villages are acknowledging the origin point of their village ancestors (*leluur*, lit. "the ones above") as well as the territorial encompassment of their village land, at least in a ritual context. Foreign immigrant groups who farm land have an obligation to honor the deified branch village founders in the temples of Penglipura and the domain or origin village founders in the temples of Bayung. In contrast to the exclusiveness of a local descent group ethos, the lack of an ancestral link to the founders of the origin village does not disqualify or excuse a descent group from participation. Nevertheless, in most cases a significant proportion of the branch village population is related to the source village by common ancestry, particularly those who claim the status of being its founder group. The visits to the source serve in part as a mechanism to commemorate that the ancestral source of the branch village founder group is also the ancestral origin of the village land and its divine protectors. This practice reinforces their privileged position and ritual authority as founders of the branch village vis-à-vis any later arrivals from elsewhere. Nonetheless, *mabanua* is an activity typically associated with villages, rather than descent groups, and it strengthens their unity as villages.[18] In a *banua* of this size, the often unspecified contributions brought by visitors are sufficient as a way of raising resources, since the scale of temple festivals is relatively modest.

In another type of *banua* the internal precedence ranking between member communities is not as obvious, since their common source village is said to have been destroyed or abandoned at some time in the past. The moment of original unity is thus represented by a socially vacant origin site rather than a living community. The origin narrative of Pura Tebenan and its *banua* exemplifies such a comparatively egalitarian arrangement.

> Once a group of people complained to the then king of Bali at his residence in Kuta Dalem [the oldest hamlet of Desa Sukawana, lit. "the fortified town of the king"] about their hardship in farming the steep slopes of Gunung Kauripan and asked leave to establish a new settlement downhill (*teben*). Since the realm was at peace and the population growing, the king granted their request for land but warned them that disaster was sure to befall them if their village council membership were to grow beyond the number of thirty-three heads of households. The village was called Tebenan to commemorate its origin from upstream Sukawana. Its dry-rice fields were fertile, people's lives were leisurely, and soon the population grew until the local council had a membership of two hundred heads of households (*keraman satak*).[19] It then happened that a ritual was planned in which a deer was to be sacrificed, offered to the gods, and divided among the council members. Much of the forest had been cleared, and deer were difficult to obtain. On the day of the ritual, the hunting party finally returned with a rather small animal. Once the deer had been sacrificed and divided, the food portions (*malang*) obtained were fewer than the number of eligible members. Arguments began, a fight broke out, brothers killed one another, and the survivors were scattered in the eight directions as leaves blown by the wind. They eventually founded

eight new villages: Ulian, Gunung Bau, Bunutin, Langahan, Pausan, Bukhi, Bayung Cerik, and Manikliyu, closest to the old Tebenan.[20] Their lives were short, their labor hard and fruitless. After some time the most senior elder and priest (Jero Kubayan) of Manikliyu had a dream in which he learned that their lot would improve only if they remembered their common origin and resumed the cult of the abandoned Pura Bale Agung [main village temple] of old Tebenan. He enticed people to search for the foundations of the old temple in the forest, but a rain quelled their enthusiasm, leaving the old priest to work single-handed. He uncovered nine [eight around a center] sacred xylophone leaves (*don selunding*) of the type used in temple music, indicating that he had found the precise site of origin, the old village temple of Tebenan. Work then continued with enthusiasm to rebuild it to serve as a new regional temple. Ever since, the *gebog banua* of eight villages, under the ritual leadership of a priest from Manikliyu [the temple is on their territory], has gathered there for a joint ceremony to honor their common ancestors with offerings and ask for a blessing on their crops. Although this all took place in times long gone, until today there may not be more than thirty-three core members in the village council of Manikliyu [*keraman desa nyilem,* lit. "councilors of the new-moon meeting"]. Before they take their ritual meal after a meeting (*sangkepan*), they first dedicate the food to the gods and allude to their origins with these words: "Insiders and elders of the heart, shoulder, elbow [titles in order of rank]! King's people! Assemble here. There are too many portions and not enough people!" (*Jero Bayan, Bau, Singgukan. . . . Wong Dalem! Mai sangkep jerone, lebihan malang kuangan jalma!*).

This origin narrative was conveyed to me by a group of elders from Manikliyu and neighboring villages gathered during a festival at the domain temple in 1993. Like other narratives of its kind, this is a popular tale and varies slightly with each telling. Only the versions told or recognized by village elders are in effect authoritative, since village elders also decide which obligations a community will honor in ritual practice. Knowledge of origin narratives tends to correlate with a person's age and ritual status. As is the case with all forms of spiritual knowledge, it is considered dangerous for the young and uninitiated to attempt an interpretation of such narratives, though they are not kept secret as such. At the most, some knowledgeable persons may choose to narrate only fragments to any one person or at any given time, preventing others from appropriating the story and challenging the interpretation of the narrator.

Bali Aga origin narratives are rarely written down, they are not formally recited in ritual contexts, nor are they told in a ritual language marked by distinct formal characteristics, as is the case in eastern Indonesia. Apart from their being offered as an explanation when I deliberately asked about the rationale of a particular ritual practice or intervillage connection, origin narratives are retold spontaneously during informal discussions among a group of priests, elders, and ordinary participants during the quieter moments of a festival at a *banua* temple. Frequently, they are recited at the request of younger men who have recently acquired ritual responsibilities.

These conversations can be described as discussions among representatives of participating villages insofar as there is room for polite disagreement about the content and interpretation of origin narratives. It is in such a context of discussion that most of the narratives reproduced in this book were recorded. As a product of living interaction, each narrative presented must be seen as a tentative consensus reached at a particular time and place rather than a monolithic text. Elders were sometimes visited at home at a later time if the festival had been too busy to allow for a lengthy discussion. In these cases several informants were always consulted in order to obtain a balanced view of a fluctuating consensus.

Origin narratives are not a genre that permits a free flight of the imagination. Deliberate and strategic modification of such narratives is regarded as a morally reprehensible or at least a dangerous act, insofar as they spell out religious obligations not to be neglected.[21] Slight variations in content and style among versions presented by different narrators are common and not necessarily of any significance. Wherever such recorded variations do reflect significant differences in content or meaning, I present the conflicting versions side by side and analyze them in terms of their pragmatic meaning and different intentions.

The Balinese respond to a major difference of interpretation in a similar way. When a disagreement surfaces in a discussion on origins, the different versions are simply tolerated and allowed to coexist for the time being. This practice avoids unpleasant arguments in a religious context where harmonious cooperation is deemed essential. Open criticism and speculation as to what may motivate others to have a different view on the history of a ritual relationship is only voiced later and in private.

When their usage in specific social contexts is taken into consideration, it becomes evident that myths cannot be interpreted as disembodied texts without reference to a world of practice. A structural analysis may reveal their intrinsic logic, the pattern of relations be-

tween the constitutive elements of a myth, but even these elements
have a contingent meaning. As Paul Ricoeur has argued,

> the kind of language-game which the whole system of oppositions and
> combinations embodies, would lack any significance if the opposi-
> tions themselves, which, according to Lévi-Strauss, the myth tends to
> mediate, were not meaningful oppositions concerning birth and death.
> . . . Beside these existential conflicts there would be no contradictions
> to overcome, no logical function of the myth as an attempt to solve
> these contradictions. Structural analysis does not exclude, but pre-
> supposes, the opposite hypothesis concerning myth, i.e., that it has a
> meaning as a narrative of origin. (1981:217)

The origin narratives presented in this book bear reference to a
cultural world per se but also to typical situations within that world.
Insofar as they refer to a world at large and to a culturally mediated
way of life, they contain nonostensive references that bear meaning
beyond the specific context in which the myth is told or heard. In
Ricoeur's view, myths are not only the focus of a conflict of interpretations but depict general types of "boundary situations" or existential conflicts in the world. In this sense, an analysis of the individual
intentions of particular narrators does not reveal all of the narrative's
significance.

By the same token, origin narratives are told and heard differently
by different interlocutors and in different situations. It is even typical
of their usage that the meaning of a narrative performance is negotiated by debating its content or silently questioning the speaker's
motivation. To the extent, then, that their content is adapted and
their interpretation shaped by speakers, listeners, and commentators
positioned differently in a specific situation, origin narratives also
cannot be just read, as texts or fixed inscriptions without authors. A
compromise approach toward the interpretation of myths of origin
may be to hear them as the spoken discourse of authors with specific
intentions and simultaneously to read them as the textual testimony
of a possible collective world.

The present origin narrative confirms Desa Manikliyu's role as
ritual leader among the member communities of this domain, even
though present-day Manikliyu is not the "village" of origin. The
origin point of the domain is identified as Pura Tebenan, a sanctuary
that is no longer a village temple even though it is located on the
wider territory of Desa Manikliyu.

All eight members of this *gebog banua* pay a proportional share of
the expenses incurred during the regular festivals at Pura Tebenan
according to local population size. This contribution in cash is re-

ferred to as *"peturunan"* ([paying for the cost of inviting the gods] to descend). The distinction between *peturunan* and *atos desa* contributions is not simply one of quantity or even one between contributions in cash and kind. *Atos desa* usually includes some unspecified amount of cash donations, while those who pay *peturunan* must also provide materials and food offerings for festivals. The principal difference is that, with the payment of *peturunan*, the people of the village concerned are officially classed among the hosts rather than the visitors. They are fully responsible for holding the ritual and for paying a fixed share of the expense (whatever that expense may be) rather than merely paying unspecified contributions. *Atos desa* can be regarded as a regular, obligatory ritual gift that may or may not be reciprocated, while *peturunan* is paid as a matter of fulfilling one's very own essential and primary duties. The latter is never reciprocated, because it carries no explicit connotation of exchange. In most smaller domains, *peturunan* is only paid by people in the host village, particularly where the *banua* festival is celebrated at a classificatory village temple, as in Bayung Gede. In larger domains, the *peturunan* is paid by all core member villages or, in other words, by those villages who belong to the *gebog banua*.[22]

The text reference to the higher authority of the ancient kings of Penulisan as the ultimate and now deified overlords of the land reflects the fact that all villages that *mabanua* at Pura Tebenan also participate within the larger ritual order around Pura Penulisan. This and other cases where one domain exists within another, larger domain illustrates that the *mabanua* relationship can operate recursively to some degree. A village may be simultaneously at the center of a smaller subdomain and at the social periphery of a larger encompassing domain.

The tale of Pura Tebenan, if it is read rather than heard, illustrates how the unity of a domain is generally contingent on the symbolic labor of recollecting and reenacting a common origin. The path of origin, in this case, is punctuated first by a lateral expansion by growing a new branch domain out of the unity of the Penulisan domain and again by the violent rupture of the village unity represented by what is now the Tebenan subdomain temple. Processes of lateral expansion or sudden fission both can establish relationships between parts and a whole embodied as a sacred origin point. With each progressive differentiation, the degree of social unity is diminished in the more immediate sense, as people no longer share the finite material resources within the reach of a single settlement, and simultaneously reintroduced at a broader symbolic level by bringing several villages together in the ritual context of the origin temple and its ceremonial order.

The idea that only a finite number of people can derive a reasonable share from a single sacrificial animal can be taken as a metaphor, suggesting that there can be a "natural" limit for sustainable solidarity on a material plane. This limit is often violated. The narrative thus proposes a golden mean, to be achieved by avoiding a practical condition of scarcity created by the togetherness of too many people in one place and an equally undesirable condition of social isolation that would arise if one were to define the small world of a single village as the only relevant sphere of social interaction. The problem of negotiating this balance is the archetypal boundary situation in the world this myth seeks to address. The proposed solution is to allocate material and symbolic concerns to separate levels of social interaction and relevance. Interpreted at this level, the narrative can be read as a commentary on a general dilemma of social cooperation and competition in agrarian communities with finite amounts of land and expanding populations.

Bali Aga origin narratives are not easily placed within a hypothetical body of Hindu mythology, although isolated narrative elements can occasionally be traced to Indian cultural influences. A project of comparative analysis would be more likely to meet with success if it were directed toward the discovery of similarities with the mythology of other Austronesian-speaking peoples. While such a project is not the aim of this book, an example relevant to the narrative of Tebenan illustrates its potential.

Robert Barnes has provided an account of how the people of Kédang in eastern Indonesia narrate their origins. One of their myths describes the dispersal of people from the first and now deserted origin village, Léu Rian, which was once situated near the peak of the island's highest mountain: "They [the inhabitants of Léu Rian] killed a pig for the feast associated with building this [the village] temple and divided it among those present, but because the villagers had become so numerous there was not enough. They then divided the teeth, bones and skin among those who had no meat, but this still was not enough. This led to a fight, and subsequently everyone fled down the mountain to found the present villages [of Kédang]" (Barnes 1974:35–36).[23] The similarities among the narratives of the abandoned origin villages Tebenan and Rian are obvious and striking.

A third variant of *banua* is based on a history of immigration and an associated notion of multiple ancestral origins. All highland domains include a number of newcomers as part of the populations of their member villages. In this type of *banua*, however, the immigrants are acknowledged not only as coresidents, but as the founders of subsidiary villages within the encompassing territories of a large original village. The idea of a temporal sequence of foundations, linking first settlers to different waves of newcomers, again serves as the index in a ritual order of precedence. The ancestors of the founder group in the original village were the first settlers of the domain (*wedan*, "people of the trunk," from *tuwed*, "the lower trunk, base, or stump of a tree"). Further settlements were founded by later arrivals (*pendonan*, "newcomers" or "people of the leaf," from *don*, "leaf") on the territory of the original village and later developed into separate *desa adat* (customary villages) after some time.[24] The temporal order of precedence among these villages is thus elaborated upon in a botanical idiom of trunk and leaf.

Desa Selulung is the core village of a domain of this type and is recognized as such in local and regional origin narratives. Newcomers are said to have arrived in distinct waves. These groups would "ask for a gift of land" (*nunas tanah*) from the legendary Jero Pasek (of) Selulung (still the title of the head of Selulung's founder group) and for permission to establish new settlements. It is narrated that the relationship was sometimes supplemented with an affinal tie. In these cases the land received was classified as a kind of marriage gift (*tadtadan*, the "things carried or brought" by the local bride), and the newcomer groom was incorporated into the village founders' origin house (*sanggah*) as the founder of a new branch house. This is an example of a mythical theme frequently found in the Austronesian world, whereby a stranger marries the sister or daughter of an indigenous ruler or chief.

The newcomers had to make a permanent commitment to pay homage to the deified spirits of the ancestral founders of Selulung's domain, who are the protectors of the land. They had to perform all rituals, even those relating to their own, separate village temples, in conformity with the Bali Aga "traditions" (*adat*) of the first settlers or their descendants. This commitment exemplifies the kind of conditions generally imposed on those who seek to be admitted into a status group. A status group must assume a degree of internal homogeneity, because the similarity among its members is the basis of its distinctiveness from other status groups. New members are therefore expected to conform to the behavioral norms and way of life of the group.[25]

While status groups may claim their members to be similar in some important respect, a degree of internal stratification can be maintained as well, namely, by restricting access to knowledge of more esoteric norms and associated symbolic capital to the core members of the group. For example, informants in the client villages of Selulung avoided commenting on regional origin narratives or matters of ritual procedure. Frequently, they would refer me to a prominent person in the origin village. In most cases their professed lack of knowledge of origin narratives and ritual procedures within the *banua* was genuine. Their conformity to the traditions pertaining to the domain as a whole equally identifies all participants as members, but not all members are regarded as equal in status.

Asymmetric patron-client-type relationships based on a history of immigrations appear to be less stable than those in domains whose members recognize a single ancestral origin. An obligation to the founding ancestors of the encompassing origin village is potentially contestable in the former case, because they are not one's own ancestors. The client villages may eventually try to claim ritual independence and a founder status for themselves by constructing their own village as a new point of origin and its foundation as the beginning of relevant history. The status relationships in all types of *banua* are far from being static, even where ancestry plays a role. There is usually a sufficient degree of historical uncertainty to justify a restructuring of origin narratives and associated ritual relations. For example, if immigrant clients wrest political control from the founder group of a subsidiary village within a domain, they may then decide to detach the entire village from the *banua* in order also to obliterate the ritual status claim of the founders. In general, a split within a *banua* is initiated by forgetting an earlier obligation to the source village or temple, since public expressions of strong mutual disapproval would only reduce the status of all parties concerned.

Finally, there are large *banua* centered on so-called summit temples (*pura pucak*), among them Pura Pucak Penulisan, Pura Pucak Tajun, Pura Pucak Indrakila, Pura Pucak Bon, and Pura Pucak Manggu. These large temples and their domains are associated with ideas of origin and relatedness that may transcend notions of common ancestry or shared ancestral land. Their sanctuaries and gods have likewise transcended the character of village temples and of ancestral deities. *Pura pucak* are often believed to have been prominent in the ritual order of earlier kingdoms and to be the abode of a paramount divinity whose persona incorporates the identity of former kings in deified form. Sometimes such temples are also loosely associated with such generic Hindu deities as Bhatara Siwa, Wisnu, or Indra.

Important regional temples in highland Bali are linked to myths of the creation or origin of the world and often not just the part of the world that constitutes their immediate domain. "Creation" (*pangawit*, from *wit*, "tree," or *ngawit*, "to originate, begin") is believed to be a process that must be reiterated in rituals so as to re-create an original harmony among the visible and invisible worlds. *Pura banua* of this type are the locus of rituals for the revitalization of the entire universe (*jagat*). They represent not only the source of human life, in the direct procreational sense of ancestry, but a source of life and nature writ large.[26] There are elements in the ritual and myth of several such temples that reflect an attempt to claim the entire island of Bali (*jagat bali*) as their domain. As far as this study has revealed, however, no temple has ever succeeded in monopolizing rituals relevant to Bali as a whole, or no more so than any single ruler has ever succeeded in controlling the entire island.[27]

The festivals of large *pura banua* are of such a grand scale that they cannot be supported from the resources of one village alone, even with the aid of customary and voluntary offerings brought by other communities. Instead, the festival is organized, performed, and paid for collectively by a group of core villages (*gebog banua*) who pay *peturunan*. This organization does not preclude visits from more loosely allied villages that only bring *atos desa* or from smaller groups of people who deliver private offerings (*nyasah/aturan pribadi*). Minor ritual connections of this kind are numerous and variable.

One notable exception to this trend toward direct regional funding of regional rituals are the festivals of Pura Batur. Although the temple forms the center of a large *banua*-like network, the idea of the paying guest has been extended here to a point where *peturunan* payments from outside the village of Batur are not required. Customary offerings of *atos desa* have been reinvented to become compulsory for visitors at the annual festival. The quantity and content of offerings is precisely specified and specifically requested in advance. Contributors are also encouraged to convert offerings in kind into cash payments so as to save temple officials the awkward task of selling tons of rice and hundreds of "sacrificial animals" after the festival. Batur's network is not called a *banua*. The local leadership nowadays prefer to construct their temple in terms of a more recent (and pro-Majapait) discourse as one of Bali's nine principal sanctuaries (*sadkayangan*). Nonetheless they still distinguish between a traditional core support network of forty-five villages referred to as "friends of the temple" (*pasihan pura batur*) and a wider web of other contributing parties, who are mainly irrigation societies (*subak*) rather than *desa*. There is no narrative of common historical origin or ancestry that would explain the ties among these forty-five villages.[28] The temple's special status rests on its association with Danu Batur, the crater lake recognized as the ultimate source of all irrigation water in much of southern Bali. Nevertheless, Pura Batur's relationship network shows sufficient structural similarities and historical connections to neighboring *banua* to allow for a fruitful comparison.

The pattern of connections that radiates from the centers of contemporary *banua* to their membership and also between their centers is of staggering complexity. The most important of these networks are represented graphically in Figure 2, while that of Pura Batur is shown separately (Figure 3), and some of the smaller *banua* are ignored. Omitted also are those that are part of a larger complex, such as the *banua* around Pura Tebenan or small domains formally classified as a single, large village (*desa*), as in the case of Tenaon.

Figures 2 and 3 provide an impression of the overall pattern of ritual ties among villages who adhere more or less to Bali Aga traditions. This is not to imply that *banua*-like patterns and concepts of regional ritual relatedness have no relevance in other parts of Bali. Southern Balinese temple networks sometimes rely on similar relationship concepts, narratives, and ritual practices for their maintenance.[29] In addition, there are also some direct ritual connections between southern Balinese villages and important mountain temples. The relevance boundary of the social construct *"banua"* is ultimately as intangible as that of the more general notion of a "Bali Aga culture."

It is important to note that many of the Bali Aga villages involved in these networks of ritual alliance are of great antiquity. Unless it is assumed that many of them were lost, it seems that most of the royal inscriptions (*prasasti*) that are the earliest written sources of Balinese history were issued to Bali Aga villages in the highlands and along the northern coast (see Figure 4; compare with Figure 2). In addition, inscriptions found in villages nearer to the southern plains tend to be the more recent ones.

The narrative landscapes, ritual activities, and social organization of the most important domains in the highlands of Bali will be described in following chapters. A first and prominent example is the *banua* of Pura Pucak Penulisan—the summit temple at the heart of the most far-reaching, elaborate, and, possibly, most ancient ritual

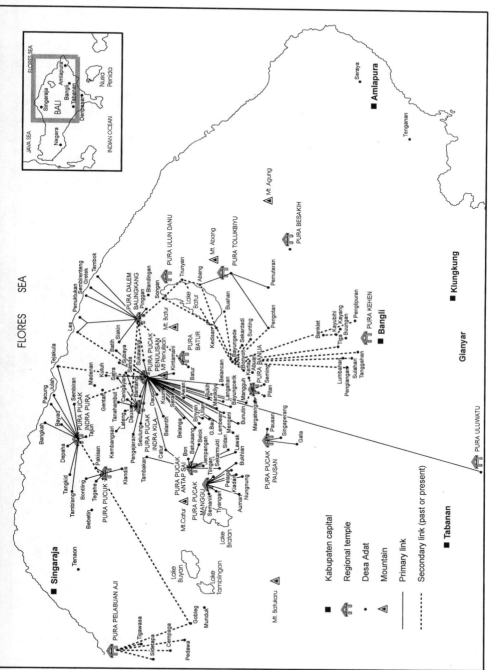

Figure 2. Ritual networks in the highlands of Bali

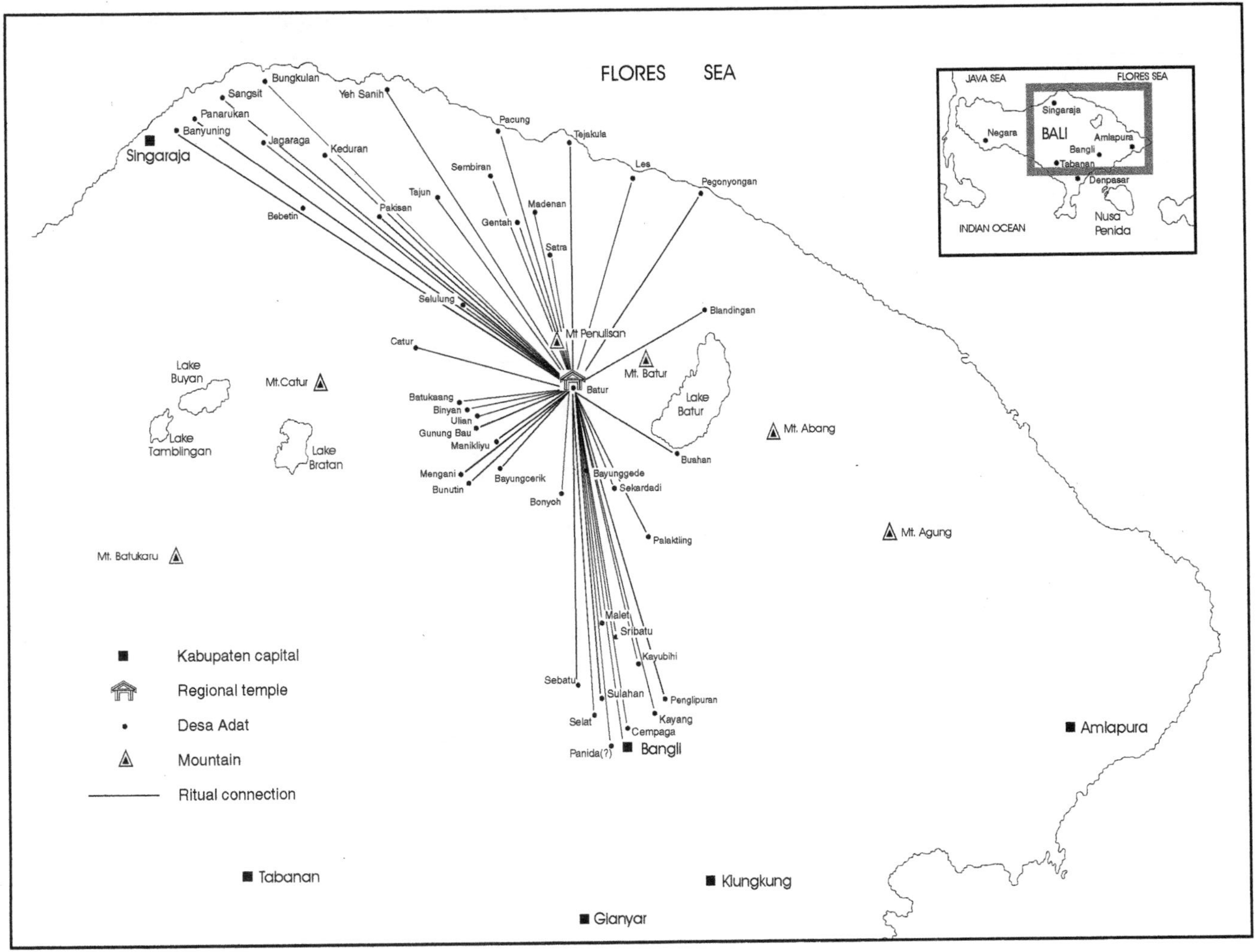

Figure 3. The ritual network of Pura Batur

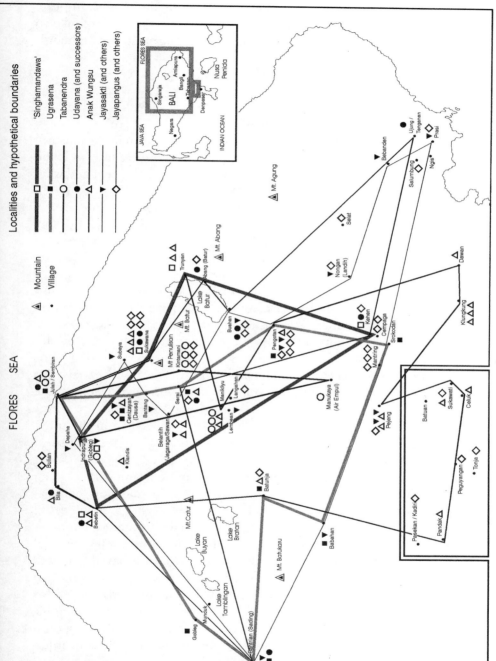

Figure 4. Royal inscriptions in Bali (pre-Majapait)

order ever established among the people of the mountains. In preparation for this ethnographic exploration, however, I would like to present a preliminary model of thought and society in the highlands by proposing a general theory of precedence.

Precedence: A Model of Bali Aga Society and a Theory of Status

Ethnographic knowledge is derived in the course of an intersubjective and cross-cultural encounter. This raises the question of who is the author of the knowledge presented in an ethnographic text and what kind of knowledge it is.

By frequent quotation from interviews with local people, it may be possible to associate particular expressions of knowledge with specific individuals who participated as informants in this study and to reproduce some of the dialogue of ethnographic research at the level of ethnographic writing. But no matter how much ethnography may rely on intersubjective exchanges among researchers and their informants, an ethnographic text cannot completely recount and reproduce such cross-cultural encounters and dialogues in the limited space of a written account. In writing a so-called dialogic ethnography, the ethnographer is compelled to select and orchestrate fragments of informants' voices into a textual composition. Unfortunately, this style of writing offers as much opportunity for the expression of the author's subjective biases as exists in writing a nondialogic ethnography. In short, all ethnographic texts are removed from the intersubjective worlds on which they reflect, or at least momentarily so.

There is another and more fundamental problem. The researcher's dialogic encounter with informants may not be as important for an understanding of the culture concerned as is the dialogue that happens between informants. This dialogue is also shaped by subjective biases, in that the statements of any individual informant will tend to reflect his or her strategic interests. At the same time, such individual knowledge or status claims are always addressed to a shared system of thought and phrased in a particular idiom of argumentation. This intersubjective space is where the possibility for knowledge arises, for both participants and ethnographers. In other words, an ethnographic representation of a society is secondary to and contingent upon a primary process of representation unfolding in the course of intersubjective encounters among people within the society itself.

When it comes to generalizing about how the specific utterances and personal knowledge claims of individual participants relate to a shared cultural idiom and a common way of conceptualizing the world, the author of an ethnographic text must accept full responsibility for constructing a subjective representation of an intersubjective process of representation. There is no pretending that ethnographic representations constitute a textual sphere of intersubjective understanding jointly produced by a foreign author and local participants. Given that all potential for knowledge or generalization is embedded in an intersubjective process, we as anthropologists cannot simply ask specific informants to draw the generalizations for us. Anthropological texts and theories may build on knowledge gained in the intersubjective space of encounters in the field, but they are written in a temporary solitude of subjectivity.

This is not necessarily problematic in view of another possible world, a world beyond narcissistic preoccupation with the personal dialogic experiences of particular ethnographers and their particular informants. Indeed, the moment of subjectivity in writing leads to the creation of a second, anthropological sphere of intersubjectivity, which would never be possible without the explicitly subjective contributions of specific subjects. This second sphere of intersubjectivity is inhabited by researchers writing on similar topics and by the readers and critics of their texts. It is from this second sphere that an ethnographic text must seek validation, rather than pretending to still exist within and draw legitimacy from the initial intersubjective sphere of the ethnographic encounter. The mechanism of validation is again dialogic, insofar as the knowledge claims raised in any one ethnographic text may coincide or clash with those raised in others and insofar as such knowledge can be negotiated freely and openly in the course of a critical debate.

My aim in presenting a theory of precedence in advance, in an attempt to capture the shared cultural idiom and logic used by highland Balinese as they raise and contest validity claims about social status among themselves, is thus to invite dialogue and facilitate contestation of my own claims in reference to a different world of anthropological practice. The theoretical model to be presented below is designed to meet the needs of a readership most of whom will have no prior knowledge of what it may mean to be Bali Aga and who must begin to understand a somewhat alien world in the terms of the worlds they are familiar with. This involves an act of translation and introduces a necessary element of distortion.

The proposed theory is nevertheless designed to remain as close as is possible to the mode of thinking and talking about social life that properly belongs to the Mountain Balinese people. A subjective portrayal of the intersubjective world of another culture should still be recognizable to participants, at the very least. It is my hope that as the world changes, and anthropology with it, the readership of this book will include more and more people to whom the highlands are home and that they in turn may conduct their own ethnographic research abroad. The anthropological project of creating a genuinely global sphere of free intersubjectivity and understanding can be promoted in the interim by drawing inspiration from ethnographic immersion into other intersubjective worlds, but it will never be realized properly without free and direct participation on a global scale at the anthropological level of textual representation and debate.[30]

Bali Aga people interpret their world and structure their relationships, in the *banua* as well as in other spheres of social interaction, by applying an ordering principle I shall refer to as "precedence." Just as the status of the Bali Aga in Balinese society as a whole is pivoted on a conceptual distinction between more recent arrivals and the original Bali Aga people who preceded them, so too are their own internal relations conceptualized by distinguishing between "predecessors" and "successors" in a great order of time, space, and life unfolding. Precedence is the primary notion evoked in order to establish, confirm, or contest the position and status of different persons or groups in highland Bali.

Although a notion of precedence is extremely salient in Bali Aga thought and practice, its full significance would have been difficult to recognize without the benefit of earlier ethnographic studies carried out by a group of researchers at the Australian National University, primarily among Eastern Indonesian peoples (see Fox 1980, 1990a; Lewis 1988; McWilliam 1989; and others). A tentative theory of precedence slowly began to emerge from a comparative analysis of the results of this empirical research. The initial aim was to convey a broader appreciation for a pattern of status construction and distribution frequently found among a large group of linguistically, historically, and culturally related Austronesian societies. Most of these societies turned out to be neither "egalitarian" nor "hierarchical."

"Precedence" is not merely another word for hierarchy. There are many culturally specific ways of conceptualizing and legitimizing status differences that can be broadly described as hierarchical, insofar as they do assume and legitimize the existence of status differences. For example, a conceptualization of status differences in terms of precedence is common among Austronesian societies, including the Bali Aga. This does not mean, however, that their status economies have anything in common with the status economy evident in the caste system of Indian society other than an obvious interest in status and status differentiation as such. James Fox (1990c) first stressed the need to distinguish between a recursive logic of "precedence" and a logic of encompassment in "hierarchical thought systems," as defined by Louis Dumont (1980:66).

More important, it cannot be assumed in advance that a society is hierarchical or egalitarian in practice simply because its system of thought lays a conceptual stress on difference or equality, respectively. A structuralist theory of hierarchy, or even a structuralist interpretation of precedence, would encourage the ethnographer to ignore this problem by focusing exclusively on the conceptual and dismissing practice as a topic unworthy or impervious to social theorizing.

As Jos Platenkamp (1990) has argued, much may depend on how hierarchy is defined in the first place. In this book, I reserve the term to refer to societies in which symbolic resources are distributed very unevenly, and more or less permanently so, not just in theory but also in practice. This cannot be said to be true of Bali Aga society. In agreement with Fox and Platenkamp, I suggest that Dumont's theory cannot be applied to this and other Austronesian-speaking societies unless one is willing to ignore local models of society or remove them artificially from their context of social practice. On similar grounds, some fellow Indologists (e.g., Dirks 1987) have even questioned the applicability of Dumont's theory to Indian society.

It is important to note that a tentative theory of precedence first emerged from empirical studies that paid specific attention to local models of society and associated local idioms. In one of the earliest of these studies, the word "precedence" was simply used as a translation of an important indigenous term (Lewis 1988). In subsequent studies the concept of precedence has begun to approach the character of an analytic device, and there have also been attempts to develop from it a more general theory for the interpretation of status systems in the context of comparative Austronesian ethnology (e.g., Reuter 1992). A major source of inspiration for this Comparative Austronesia Project to date has been a general method of comparative historical linguistics.

In its deliberate secondary intersubjective orientation, however, the somewhat more abstract theory of precedence I shall present is no longer a model *for* living but a model *of* another form of life. In other words, it is a general construct for describing the type of status economy one may expect to find in Austronesian-speaking societies, in the form of different and historically specific variants. While the present study retains a strong focus on language, a further innovation lies in a shift from a comparative linguistics model to a model based on a theory of communicative action. My aim is to flesh out the idea in comparative linguistics and ethnology that languages and cultures have evolved and become differentiated in the course of a broadly historical process. I do so by examining such processes directly, as they unfold in the course of representational practice in a specific inter-subjective world in the here and now.

In the English language "to precede" generally means to go or be before someone or something else in time, place, or rank. The term thus evokes an image of two or more distinct events or entities ordered in temporal succession (a, b). Precedence further implies an asymmetrical relationship between any two elements in such a sequence, provided that a superior value is attached to its origin point or end point ($a > b$, or less often, $b > a$). The direction of this asymmetry can be referred to as the valency of the relationship between the elements.

That such serial ordering can serve the purpose of ranking is reflected in the status connotations of the term "precedence" even in its common English usage. A principle of precedence operates also in some familiar social contexts, for example, in the forming of a queue in front of a bank teller machine. Nevertheless, I will use the term as an approximate translation of the similar terms or idiomatic expressions found in Austronesian language-speaking societies, which carry a far greater social significance than the English term does in English-speaking societies. Precedence can also be used as a term for the logic of local *practice* in Austronesian societies—where this logic is not fully or openly acknowledged as a primary organizing principle in local *theories* of society.

Many events are by their very nature recursive, and in a number of Austronesian societies recursivity is emphasized as a principle of conceptual and social organization. Pertinent classes of social events such as birth (a has a child b) or marriage (the persons e/f, who are children of the couples a/b and c/d, become another couple) are thought of in terms of paired person categories (parent/child, wife/ husband). The births or marriages of persons tend to be classified as recursive events in an ontological sequence in recognition of the fact that they presuppose the births and marriages of others who have preceded them.

An image is thus constructed of a potentially infinite temporal sequence of events in which each occurrence follows an earlier and precedes a later one of the same general class ($a, b, c \ldots$). For such a chain of events to become a social order of precedence, the events

must be used to define categories of persons who are related as pairs
(a/b, b/c) and whose members have an unequal status in relation to a
particular context ($a > b$, $b > c$, $c > d \dots$). The relative position of events
within such a sequence together with the valency of the asymmetric
relationship between them specifies the status information they carry
about the person categories they define. For a temporal sequence to
become cohesive over a period of time, the relationship between the
elements within it need to be transitive to some degree (see also Fox
1989). This means that if $a > b$, $b > c$, and $c > d$, then $a > d$ (but a and
n may no longer be recognized as connected in any way). In short, a
social order of precedence prevails in societies where the relative
status (or specific privileges) of persons or groups is indexed by their
positioning relative to others within the negotiable conceptual model
of a chainlike temporal sequence of "significant" and "historical"
events, the elements of which are logically connected through dualistic, recursive, asymmetric, and transitive linkages.

Usually, in the Austronesian-speaking world, to be situated near
the source or origin point of such a recursive chain is to have a status
superior to others who are further removed from it. It is thus a value
of origin that transforms a theoretical distinction in terms of precedence into a social status distinction. In this sense, a social order of
precedence can also be described as an "origin structure" (see Fox
1988:14–16). This attribution of value to origins is not entirely arbitrary and is even less likely to be portrayed as such. Since the birth or
marriage of an individual presupposes the prior birth and marriage
of his or her parents, for example, participants may portray a social
order of precedence not as a cultural construction but as an ontological order of things, a great chain of being. What maintains this vision
is a deep and not entirely inappropriate sense of indebtedness to one's
predecessors.

The historical or mythical knowledge required in order to trace
events back to a time or place of origin is crucially important in societies where precedence serves as an organizing principle. This knowledge is often preserved and contested in the form of origin narratives
and ritual performances, and in some societies it may also be preserved in writing.

Status within social orders of precedence is essentially mutable,
given that the concept of order on which it is founded already evokes
the notion of a dynamic historical process. Persons or groups gradually approach the origin or source with the continuation of the relevant sequence of events from the past into the present and the future.
For example, the youngest male member of an origin group may

become its most senior representative as his elders pass away and descendants multiply, even though any person senior to him will always remain his senior.

Irreversibility in the valency of social relationships may seem guaranteed in a chain of events with strictly recursive and asymmetric linkages, that is, where events follow one another in a predictable fashion, are clearly remembered or recorded, and appear to be causally related. This may apply to generational distinctions among close kin, for example. In other contexts the positioning of persons may be more open to negotiation. Information about sequences of events in the more distant past is hardly ever sufficiently reliable to rule out an alternative historical interpretation and subsequent rearrangement of the existing social order. For example, newcomers in a domain can be incorporated within an existing order of precedence whereby the founders of the domain remain ritually superior. But sooner or later, they may also usurp the ritual authority of the original settlers. The historical contingency of such courses of events can necessitate a realignment of cultural values in order to legitimize unanticipated status changes.

Social orders of precedence may draw on a cultural value of origin, but this value does not necessarily define a priori a specific order of precedence. More often, social orders of precedence are the outcome of a historical struggle of interpretation and action. Particular social outcomes may not be anticipated but certainly can be accommodated after the fact without introducing a fundamental contradiction. Such accommodation is achieved by a redefinition of origin (e.g., the newcomers are said to have founded the contemporary village after the original village was somehow destroyed, and hence they become the "founders") or a direct valency reversal (e.g., newcomers are simply classed as superior in status). The latter case may appear to be a transformation of the logical principle of preceding into one of "proceeding." The difference, however, is one of value orientation rather than logic. Furthermore, once newcomers are transformed into founders, and even though their outside origin may be stressed continuously, the event of their arrival in effect defines a new moment of origin, which will soon become an event of the mythical and sacred past.

Values in Austronesian societies generally tend to be flexible and contextually bound. The focal value that informs social orders of ritual precedence in the highlands, for example, has been said to be the notion of a sacred origin. In practice, however, the focal value placed on that polarity of a temporal sequence that points to its origin and to the past always evokes as its counterpart a second value placed on the new, on the pole of continuous growth that is essential for the sequence to be perpetuated into the future (e.g., the dead ancestors as original life givers versus the fertility of living human beings). This dualistic and reciprocal character of categories and values in Austronesian societies is often tied to a division among different value spheres. In a political context, for example, newcomers often wield greater authority than the original founders, whereas in a ritual context the opposite is usually the case.

Historical sequences of socially significant events are at least in part the sediment of intentional action. It would thus be incorrect to view orders of precedence as passively lived traditions born of a self-evident social history. A view of history as a product of action is reflected in the prevalent use of botanical idioms in the Austronesian world, whereby the active growth of plants serves as a metaphor for the active growth and gradual differentiation of social formations. Indeed, the notion of precedence in these societies is important not only to the interpretation but to the production of events. Individuals or groups generally act or produce events in such a way as to maximize their status and privileges, and in the course of these activities, they will employ strategies of representation that are generally informed but not specifically dictated by a shared notion of precedence.

Events and person categories in an order of precedence are elements of a constructed and hence deconstructable world of performance. Any particular claim to precedence can be contested at two different levels: first, whether and when a particular event has occurred and, second, whether such events are relevant for determining social status in the first place. This does not mean that socially constructed histories as such have no continuity or social efficacy. In order to communicate claims to particular privileges at all, a common set of concepts, values, and expressions must be evoked. These conventions provide at least partially standardized criteria for defining and interpreting the meaning of historical events and for communicating particular claims within a sphere of intersubjective action. If a particular argument does not appeal to an underlying cultural style and idiom of argumentation, it will not only be rejected, it will make no sense at all.

In this work the term "precedence" stands for a basic set of logical principles (duality, asymmetry, recursivity, transitivity) operating in conjunction with a cultural value of "origin," variously conceived. Participants must have a working knowledge of these principles and values, and evoke them in the context of negotiating status, before the society concerned deserves to be described as a social order of precedence. It is not necessary, however, that participants are able to articulate their knowledge and theorize about their society in such a way as to meet the conventional Western criteria of a social theory. In some cases, precedence may only exist insofar as a principle of precedence is applied in practice to mold particular classes of socially significant events and associated persons into a status economy with a characteristic pattern of conceptual and social relations. As for the Bali Aga, I shall argue that precedence to them is also a tool for theorizing about society and about the world in general. I will return to this question—whether Bali Aga theories of society and participant theories in general are indeed any more practice-oriented or any less disinterested than are sociological theories of society—at the conclusion of this book.

There is a danger of essentializing notions such as "social structure," "kinship," or, indeed, "precedence," of confusing what people do with what they are. As Mark Hobart recently pointed out in a discussion of Balinese social organization, "the kinds of schemes [traditionally] used to classify kin relations rely on Aristotelian metaphysical assumptions of particular things or people having essential properties, by virtue of which they may be definitively classified" (1991:35).

The replacement of one such classification scheme with another of the same kind can be avoided by insisting on a process-oriented social theory. Such a social theory must pay attention to local theories of society, both as general representational models of social practice and as instrumental models for achieving specific strategic outcomes. Local and sociological theories of society alike, however, should not be regarded as models that are able to specify human behavior in advance or even to describe it adequately in retrospect. A shared cultural knowledge and idiom may be important as a foundation for cooperative interaction, but even so, its particular expressions are creative and expert manipulations and adaptations of general principles for specific practical purposes set within specific contexts of performance.

Although they are underdetermined in this way, it is possible to capture some of the intersubjective orientation in the practices of individual human subjects within a heuristic and process-oriented model of society. Assessing the validity of such a model is a matter of asking whether and how it is socially performed and under what conditions, rather than asking whether or not it corresponds to an imaginary world of social objects.

The following chapters will explore in detail how the notion of "precedence" is, or can be, used in local practice and in analysis as a heuristic model of social performances in highland Bali. At the focus of my analysis will be the regional stages of a Bali Aga status economy, the *banua* and their temples of origin. By far the largest and most prominent among these temples, Pura Pucak Penulisan is introduced in the following chapter.

Chapter 2

PURA PUCAK PENULISAN
A Temple at the Tip of the World

The majority of villages in the mountain district of Kintamani (Bangli) and some further communities in the northern coastal district of Tejakula (Buleleng) take responsibility for the ritual and physical maintenance of a regional temple of great antiquity. This sacred location is colloquially referred to as Pura Pucak Penulisan, "the temple on the summit of Mt. Penulisan" (see Figure 2).

The temple complex is located on a peak that forms the northern part in a wide circular wall of mountains. This enormous crater rim is all that remains of the larger, primordial Mt. Batur that collapsed in the distant geological past. At 1,750 meters above sea level, the temple is more elevated than the summit of the new volcano that has grown once again in the midst of this ring of peaks. Pura Pucak Penulisan is indeed Bali's loftiest major temple and is situated within the territory of Desa Sukawana, the island's most elevated human settlement. This ancient sanctuary is the spiritual nexus of the largest ritual domain of the highlands. The exemplary character of Pura Penulisan and its domain qualifies them to serve as an introduction to the more general exploration of *banua* in the highlands of Bali that is to follow in later chapters.

On a clear day the commanding views from the hilltop of Penulisan extend to the neighboring islands of Lombok in the east, Nusa Penida in the south, and East Java in the far west. All the major peaks of Bali are visible, with the Batukaru group to the west and Mt. Batur, Mt. Abang, and Mt. Agung aligned in a straight line toward the southeast. The forested hilltop is shrouded intermittently in passing veils of mist on the best of days during the dry season and may vanish in a sea of cloud for weeks on end during the rainy season.

The island's broad central ridge, running from Mt. Batukaru and

Mt. Catur in the west (*kauh*) to Mt. Penulisan in the east (*kangin*), forms the watershed between northern and southern Bali. The structure of the island is locally defined in an idiom of cosmic anatomy. The ridge is referred to as "the spine of the world of Bali" (*tulang giing jagat bali*), with Pura Penulisan representing its "head" (*ulu*). Because of its superior physical and spiritual elevation, the temple is also considered *kaja* (mountainward) by surrounding villages, no matter whether they lie to the north or to the south of this ridge. All that lies beyond the temple boundaries, that is, the entire inhabited area of Bali, is considered *kelod* (toward the sea). Indeed, within the confines of this temple the term *"kaja"* becomes meaningless because it is already the ultimate mountain location.

Kaja is the most auspicious direction in Balinese cosmology, for it leads to the heavenly abode of the ancestors and gods. The inner sanctum (*jeroan*) of most Balinese temples, which normally have a rectangular layout, is thus located at the end facing *kaja*. In the case of Pura Pucak Penulisan, the layout is based on multiple terraces instead, a more ancient pattern common to Bali's oldest hilltop temples. The inner sanctum is located toward the east (*kangin*), which is also an auspicious direction, either on its own or more often in conjunction with *kaja* (*kaja-kangin*).

Though the temple is the embodiment of *kaja*, the logic of its internal spatial organization is still founded in part on a notion of relative elevation. There are several clusters of shrines distributed over a number of distinct terraces hugging the steep slope of the hilltop (Figure 5), and it is the highest (and simultaneously the most eastern) terrace that contains its inner sanctum. This internal differentiation among designated shrines is one of the reasons why the temple complex as a whole is known under a variety of different names.

Pura Tegeh Kauripan

Located on the loftiest terrace is Pura Tegeh Kauripan (or Koripan). The entire temple complex is often named after it as Gunung Wangun Urip or just Gunung Kauripan. The meaning of the three terms ("temple of upright life," "mountain of arising life," and "mountain of life") reflect the temple's association with the creation of life and the origins of civilization on the island in the minds of many Balinese and more so in the minds of its principal Bali Aga congregation.

Historical sources suggest that this temple may have been an important state temple of the Warmadewa and later dynasties of Balinese kings. Until today it features a large collection of stone statues

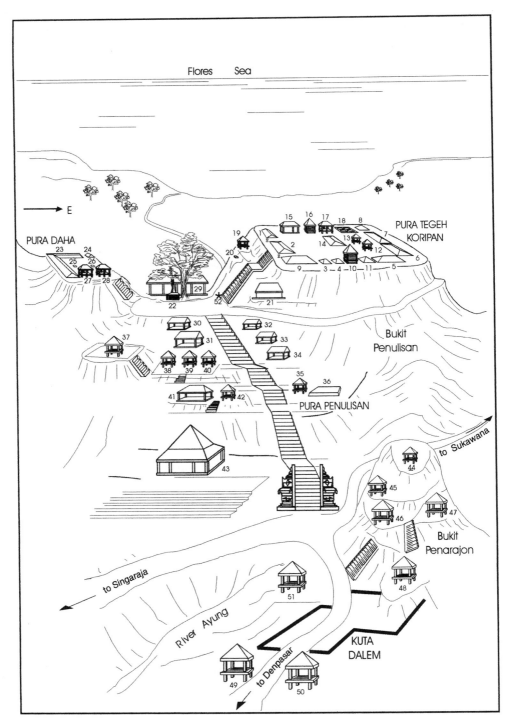

Figure 5. Pura Pucak Penulisan

Key

1–8	Gedong Arca: shelters for stone carvings and statues of kings and gods
9	Bale Gong Gede: place for the larger percussion group from Sukawana
10	Gedong Pusar Tasik (also known as Gedong Ayah or Gedong Petak)
11	Gedong Petirtaan: place for keeping ritually purified water
12	Bale Pecatu Tengen
13	Bale Pecatu Kiwa
14	Bale Pelik or Tajuk: location for placing the main *bakti* (complete group of offerings)
15	Bale Pajuruan (left, where visitors make cash donations) and Bale Gong Kamangkiran (right, for Sukawana's smaller percussion group)
16	Gedong Cemeng
17	Bale Dawa (Bale Saka Enem): place for Sukawana's head elders
18	Bale Pesamuan (Catur Desa/Catur Muka): with four separate platforms under a single roof
19	Bale Kulkul
20	*Bebaturan* (sacred stone)
21	Bale Gong (this and other *bale gong* serve also as shelters for visiting members of the *banua*)
22	Sacred *cemara* tree with offering platform (Pura Pengayatan, from *ayat*, "to create")
23	Bale Parantenan (temple kitchen): for preparing offerings *(makayangan/matanding)*
24	Gedong Pajuruan (for organizing committee)
25–26	*Bebaturan* (sacred stone)
27–28	Palinggih Ratu Daha Tua: the two shrines are symbolically male (28) and female (27)
29	Four *bale gong* in one building
30–34	Bale Gong
35–36	Palinggih and offering platform for Ratu Gede Penyarikan (Pura Penulisan)
37	Palinggih Ratu Sakti Bujangga
38–40	Bale Timbangan
41	Bale Pajuruan
42	Bale Dana
43	Wantilan: location for cockfights, *baris* and *rejang* dances, and other performances
44	Pura Gaduh
45	Pura Tengayang
46	Pura Puseh Batih
47	Pura Song Pasek
48	Pura Mas Melanting: a temple dedicated to the goddess of trade and the marketplace
49	Pura Dalem Sengkuug
50	Pura Lubak
51	Petirtaan Pujut Ayah at the source of River Ayung (here still referred to as Yeh Tipat)
52	Place where the sacrificial buffalo is killed

depicting royal personages of that era. Among the statues inscribed with names and dates are Queen Gunapriyadharmapatni with her consort Dharmodayana (carved in A.D. 991), the Indian saint Agastya (A.D. 1024), Bhatari Mandul (wife of King Anak Wungsu, A.D. 1078), Sri Aji Jayapangus with his queen (undated), and Astasuraratnabhumibanten (A.D. 1332), who was probably Bali's last indigenous king before the Majapait conquest (Stutterheim 1929). These statues, along with those of many other, unnamed kings, are revered by the local population, who dress them with festive sarongs during celebrations.[1] They formerly stood exposed to the elements, until the provincial Office of Archeology finally intervened in 1948 and suggested that shelters be created to avoid further deterioration. The early explorers Schwarz and Pleyte visited the temple in 1898 and 1899, respectively, and both complained that they were barred access to the sanctuary by fierce, stone-throwing locals. Nieuvenkamp was the first who managed to slip in, unofficially, in 1918 (see Bernet-Kempers 1991:165).

The temple is also regarded by many as the ultimate "fountain of life," a source of life-giving water. Located at the source of Bali's largest waterway, the River Ayung, its main ritual events are until today attended by many irrigation societies (*subak*) from Payangan and other downstream districts along the river. The temple also marks the source of a stream that flows past Puri Balingkang (in Desa Pinggan), disappears beneath the ground, and then reemerges in Desa Songan, where it feeds into Lake Batur. In local myths it is narrated how once, when the world was still dry, the "god of Pura Pucak Tegeh" (sometimes described as a manifestation of Siwa or Wisnu) meditated hidden below the ground until the mountain erupted with water, and a gigantic flood engulfed the villages now located along Lake Batur. The frightened inhabitants of Desa Mampah then gathered in what is now called Desa Songan (possibly from *song*, "a large hole"). They entreated the god to arrange for the waters to be channeled below the earth and gathered safely into a lake. The deity received their plea with kindness, and hence the source of Lake Batur's water came to be hidden. There is still a *pura patirtaan* in Songan, a shrine marking the location where the subterranean waters from Penulisan well up in a sacred spring within the lake.[2]

Among the most venerated shrines within Pura Kauripan is the Gedong Pusar Tasik, the "shrine of the navel of the primordial ocean."[3] The walled, wooden building contains a sacred well that marks the source of the water eruption described in the myth. It is said to be connected even now with faraway sacred locations by means of underground water channels. Evidence for this belief is presented in stories surrounding a "submerging" ceremony (*pakelem*) conducted here every ten years. A pure-white duck weighed down with a string of old Chinese coins (*pis bolong*, "coins with a small hole [in the center]") and tagged with an inscribed palm leaf (*lontar*) is immersed into the well inside the Gedong Pusar Tasik. On several occasions this duck is said to have surfaced sometime after the ceremony, alive and with the identifying *lontar* still intact, at the distant seaside temple of Uluwatu, in Lake Bratan, in Lake Batur, and at other places spiritually affiliated to Pura Penulisan.

Origin narratives from as far away as Desa Sembiran narrate how Pucak Tegeh Kauripan was the first mountain to be created. Lifted upwards by the creator Bhatara Guru (Siwa), the cosmic mountain of life arose from the navel or center of the primordial ocean.[4] The sanctuary atop its peak is thus often referred to as Pura Puseh Jagat Bali, the "navel temple of Bali," for example, in the Payangan district.

"Wangun Urip" is also the term used for a most important and intricate rite, performed as a ritual highlight during the annual temple festival and gathering of the *banua*. During most temple festivals in this region, a sacrificial animal, in this temple always a male water buffalo, is sacrificed, divided, and "resurrected" (*wangun urip*) in order to recreate and revitalize the domain that is represented on a miniature scale by the victim's body. The use of body metaphors in ritual imagery evokes the idea of a social order with the characteristics of a natural living entity. The diversity of interests among the participants of that order and the element of agency and contingency in their togetherness are deemphasized. But even the unity of a living organism is subject to contingency, mutilation, disease, and death. If nonconformity is the primary social evil, then it is the weight of this evil that must be borne by the ritual victim, whose death and physical deconstruction acts as a surrogate for the disintegration of the domain's social order. The unstructured and contingent aspects of the victim's body are removed, namely, the formless meat and fat. Only a select number of the bones that represent the essential structure of the animal's anatomy are carefully extracted and recombined to recreate a transmuted and idealized vision of a social unity, a body free of contingency. This is reflected in another designation. A very similar offering fashioned from animal carcasses is referred to as *wangun ayu*, "to arise [more] beautiful [than in real life]."

The practical and social boundaries of the temple's domain do not necessarily coincide with the wide boundaries drawn by local ritual and narrative discourses commenting on its supreme significance as the origin of life and the world. Nevertheless, the temple's rituals of renewal are certainly claimed to implicate the entire cosmos (*buana agung*). The largest, centennial ceremonial event at this temple, involving the sacrifice of twelve water buffaloes, overtly seeks to revitalize the entire realm of Bali.

The architecture of Pura Tegeh Kauripan and other shrines on this hilltop still diverges significantly from the standards imposed by the main government-sanctioned Hindu organization, despite repeated criticisms and threats directed at the local temple committee. There are no pagoda-like shrines with multiple roofs (*meru*) as there are in other Balinese temples, since it is deemed unnecessary to represent a mountain symbolically in a temple that is already located on a mountain peak. There is also no Palinggih Ratu Pucak (shrine to serve as the seat of the supreme deity at festivals), since this hilltop as a whole is considered to be the deity's permanent abode.[5] Nor is there a permanent stone shrine (*sanggaran agung*) to the sun god (Bhatara Surya) or a collective stone shrine for all the deities (*padmasana*). Instead, a temporary "sky-shrine" (*sanggaran tawang*) dedicated to the sun god is built anew each year in conformance to local ritual guidelines.[6]

The design of the mostly wooden shrines in Pura Tegeh Kauripan is an expression of an all-encompassing schema of dual classification. Paired cosmological categories such as "white-black" (*petak-cemeng*) or "left-right" (*kiwa-tengen*) are represented architecturally as pairs of shrines, like Gedong Petak and Gedong Cemeng or Pecatu Kiwa and Pecatu Tengen. Two pairs of categories can also be combined to create a set of four. An example is the directional system (*catur desa*, "the four locations [or directions]"), which joins a *kangin-kauh* (east-west) with a *kaja-kelod* (uphill-downhill) axis of orientation. This set of four is represented in the architecture of the Bale Pasamuan Agung (pavilion of the great gathering), composed of four separate raised platforms and sheltered by a single roof. The shrine is also known as *bale catur muka*, "the four faces," or *catur desa*.

Pura Daa

The second, less known and less elevated section of this terraced temple complex is Pura Daa, the temple of the "pure maiden" (*daa suci*) or "old maiden" (*daa tua*). The two temples form a complementary pair whereby Pura Kauripan is associated with a male and Pura Daa with a female deity. "Pura Daa," unlike the term "Pura Kauripan," is never used to refer to the temple complex as a whole. This does not mean, however, that the asymmetrical aspect of the relationship between the two temples can be described as a case of "encompassment" in the sense of Luis Dumont's classic theory of hierarchy (1980).

The paired symbolic categories of male and female are among the most fundamental elements of a complex and sophisticated form of thought among the Bali Aga that can be referred to as dualistic. Symbolic classification in terms of paired categories recurs in interpretations concerning all levels of the social and natural world, from the division of village society into ceremonial moieties to the pairing of components in an offering arrangement. The paired elements may be asymmetrically related, so that one is more auspicious than the other, but this is not always the case. Even where asymmetries are made obvious, the valency of the relationship between any two elements can change from one context to another, rather than being fixed by reference to a single, paramount value.

One possible explanation for the frequent use of paired categories, among the Bali Aga and many other societies, is that they provide a means for representing and symbolically resolving some of the ambiguities of life that are irresolvable in practice. The female and male deities of Pura Daa and Pura Kauripan, or the right-left polarity evoked in the architecture of particular shrines, for example, creates a symbolic image of unity in difference, a state of balance between "two that are different" (*rua bineda*). The Balinese consider balance as a highly desirable state of being, and the term *"rua bineda"* is often used to allude to this general philosophy of life. The symbolic representation of a whole conceived of as a complementary pair is synonymous with a religious concern for maintaining the social and spiritual unity of a domain composed of many different participating groups. The inevitability of divergent interests among the participants is temporarily transcended in a ritual moment of unity, and yet it is acknowledged, even at a symbolical level, as a dynamic tension among female and male deities, left and right sides of a shrine, or upper and lower terraces.

The ritual process that unifies a socially heterogeneous agglomeration of people into a single domain can be compared to the ritual processes that upheld the former Balinese kingdoms (*negara*). A prominent temple and its deity can "embody" the complex unity of a *banua*, just as a royal person embodies the realm in Hindu-Balinese models of kingship (C. Geertz 1980). In both cases, however, the embodiment of unity must contain an acknowledgment of diversity, which, in its simplest form, is duality. An underlying duality can be represented in temples in the form of male and female deities or paired shrines and, similarly, in a kingdom by a royal couple. Balinese inscriptions usually refer not just to male kings but to royal couples. Likewise, most statues of Balinese kings at Pura Pucak Penulisan depict couples. These representations of unity in duality can be interpreted as an attempt to redefine and reduce an irresolvable conflict of interests between those of higher and lower status or between rulers and followers into a symbolic tension between a male and a female deity or royal person, as embodiments of society as a whole.

Dumont's graphic representation of the notion of hierarchical encompassment, as a box within a box (1980:242, fig. 2), does not quite capture how the Bali Aga themselves picture the idea of unity in duality. One way in which unity is locally imagined is as two sides coming together at the "tip" or "peak" (muncuk or pucak/pucuk/mucuk), as in the triangular shape of a mountain or leaf, the body of the highest-ranking village elder and priest-leader ([pa]mucuk), or bodily gestures of greeting and prayer.[7] The tip represents the point of growth, the life (kauripan) that springs forth from a momentary coming together of male and female. The superior level of unity achieved in the tip is also associated with maleness. For example, the word "muncuk" (tip) itself is a common metaphor for male genitals, and, as has been mentioned, Pura Kauripan (life, male deity) is a label that can designate the temple as a whole. In addition, a new human life in Bali Aga society is most often classified as belonging to the origin house of his or her father.

Still, it can be argued that the maleness of the tip is not indicative of an encompassment of the female opposite. The predominance of men and of a male-focused symbology is not based on the assumption that a fixed and hierarchical unity can be achieved. When male priests celebrate the moment of unity with the ancestors and deities during a temple ceremony, by dedicating to them the offerings prepared by men and women together, they merely grasp a transient moment of unity in an otherwise unstable process of dynamic interaction between equal opposites. That the maleness of symbolic unity forever remains dependent on a state of rua bineda may be a perpetual paradox and a source of embarrassment for a male-oriented symbolic discourse, but this is freely acknowledged. In the ritual world, men must be married if they wish to hold office as priests. Husband and wife are also regarded as interdependent in a material sense, having to cooperate for the sake of natural reproduction and even more so on account of the very distinctiveness of their culturally constructed gender roles.

Human relationships in the world and the relationships between symbolic operators in discourses about that world are not fundamentally at odds in Bali Aga society. Practical interdependence among the social representatives of ranked categories is formally recognized in that the formal principle of ranking itself remains context-dependent and reversible. The authority wielded by priests at the ritual center over people from visiting villages, by male over female deities, and, more generally, by men over women and older over younger men is perpetuated through the periodic ritual practices at temples in which certain social privileges are "enshrined." But the actual preeminence of one over the other in a world of practice is limited and rather aptly depicted as such in a world of symbolic representation.

The pair of temples Pura Daa and Pura Kauripan can be regarded as a specific symbolic actualization of the conceptual polarity female/male (*luh / muani*). How the specific categories *daa* and *kauripan* have come to represent this conceptual pair in this context may be explained by considering the close relations among old Balinese kingdoms and polities in East Java, which, at their height, saw the Balinese prince Erlangga of the Warmadewa dynasty rule in Java, while his brother Anak Wungsu ruled in Bali. Erlangga's kingdom in Java, according to textual sources such as the Negara Kertagama and the Calonarang, was divided between his two sons, each taking residence in one of the two capital cities of his kingdom. These cities were named Daa and Kauripan. This genre of tale may not fulfill a Western definition of a historical text, but what is more significant here is their moral content.[8] The division of Erlangga's kingdom into two parts, female and male, is interpreted in this tale both as a physical split of what is conceptually inseparable and as a political disaster. As for the link between this mythical Javanese kingdom and the temple complex on Mt. Penulisan, some local informants speculated that Erlangga may have named his capital cities after the two main sections of his father's principal state temple in Bali.

In local versions of a pan-Balinese folktale about Rare Anggon and his beloved twin sister Lubang Kori, this fateful separation of male (*kauripan*, "life [essence]") and female (*daa*, "maiden") is elaborated on further. Swept away from Penulisan by a strong wind, they were transported to Java. He landed in the town of Kauripan and she descended in Daa. After much suffering, the divine twins were reunited as a royal couple.

A further reference to Daa and Kauripan is contained in the local version of the pan-Indonesian folktale of Bawang and Kesuna. In this case the central opposition is one between younger and older sibling (a metonym of female and male):

The king of Kauripan took a second queen since the first had remained childless. When this second wife gave birth to a daughter, the first wife became envious and solicited the help of a palace guard to have the child taken to the forest and killed. The guard took pity on the infant and merely left her deserted by the edge of a river.[9] There she was found by a widow with a daughter of her own, and this widow adopted the foundling. Her own daughter, who was the elder, was called Kesuna (white onion, i.e., garlic), and the younger she called Bawang (red onion). The two were similar in their physical appearance but not in character. Kesuna was lazy and cruel, ordering poor compliant Bawang around and forcing her to do all the chores.[10] When the two had become young women, it happened that the ruler of the neighboring kingdom of Daa decided it was time to retire. He thus sent a message to ask for the daughter of the king of Kauripan to become his son's wife. The messengers returned in dismay, having learned of the disappearance of the princess. So the prince of Daa went forth in search of her and eventually encountered Bawang in a forest without knowing her true identity. They instantly fell in love, and the prince returned home and sent messengers to her foster mother's house to ask for permission to marry her. But, alas, the messengers found two girls who fit his description and chose Kesuna, for she was dressed more beautifully than wretched Bawang. At the wedding feast the prince was served by Bawang and finally recognized the mistake. The widow then retold the story of Bawang's appearance, and a birthmark confirmed that she was none other than the princess of Kauripan. She was married to the prince of Daa, who thus became the son-in-law (*mantu*) of the king of Kauripan, as it had been destined all along.

The lost and adopted princess (female, red [onion], younger sibling) finds herself under the oppressive authority of an elder sibling, who is physically also female but has symbolically male attributes (the metonyms white [onion, i.e., garlic], elder sibling). Kesuna is rescued and betrothed to an idealized male figure. The prince obtains in her the means for securing the succession of the kingdom of Daa (female), yet, at a cost. As the son-in-law of Prabu Kauripan (male), the prince adopts a social position of subservience. The woman, as the female bearer of life, is structurally substituted by her father, as the male giver of the bride. In general, the story conveys a sense of value ambiguities and reversals, to be resolved in the end by establishing an enduring reciprocal relationship. This relationship is not ideal for being free of distinction. Rather, its sanctity lies in the fertility of the couple as a dyad and in their joint capacity to keep alive the social order of the realm.

The goddess of Pura Daa, Ni Daa Tua, should not be regarded merely as a symbolic counterpart to Ratu Pucak Kauripan. She is the central figure of many creation and origin narratives among the Bali

Aga people. *"Daa tua"* literally means "the old maiden," but the term is perhaps better translated as "the eternal maiden" or "virgin goddess." She is the protectress of the rain-irrigated rice fields that belong to the male creator deity Bhatara Guru (Siwa), just as in her manifestation as Dewi Danu (the [virgin] goddess of the lake [Batur]) she is the recipient and guardian of the waters issuing from the male deity Ratu Pucak.[11] In several myths of creation, it is she who protects and teaches the first human beings.

> The very first human beings in Bali, who were created by Bhatara Guru and Sang Hyang Licin, had fallen victim to disease and died, so that the island was left without human inhabitants for a thousand years. Then there lived a pregnant monkey who died in the course of giving birth prematurely. From her decaying body grew a *kastuban,* a fruit-bearing tree much frequented by monkeys until today. Like the female monkey in this story, the *kastuban* tree often drops its fruit before it is ripe when struck by the lightning from thunderstorms during the wet season. Hence it was cursed by Bhatara Guru that it should one day bear fruit in the form of human beings. This prophecy was actualized by Sang Hyang Licin, who descended to earth and became Ni Daa Tua. She guarded the pregnant tree so that the lightning did not dare to approach. Four fruits of human shape matured on the tree, and when they had ripened and fallen down, Ni Daa Tua protected them, until in the end two male and two female human beings emerged from their shells. It was Ni Daa Tua who raised them, taught them how to weave and grow crops, and gave them instructions on how to conduct their lives.[12]

Ratu Daa Tua is presented here as the protectress of life and a provider of nourishment. She is not the creator of life, but its preserver. The two natural female entities, the monkey and the *kastuban* tree, are criticized for being unable to shelter their offspring until maturity. Only a culturally constructed, ideal female, the deity Ratu Daa, is portrayed as capable of sustaining and nurturing life in the social sense.

In more practical terms, Pura Daa is the center for women's ritual work in ceremonial contexts. All the offerings made by women for the great annual festival are prepared by female elders from Desa Sukawana and a host of female helpers from all villages within the domain. The offerings are also purified at Pura Daa (by male elders) before they are taken up to Pura Kauripan. Offerings made by women consist mainly of food and are believed to serve as sustenance for the gods. Located within Pura Daa is also the temple kitchen (*pawaregan*), where cooked offerings are prepared and also the food to sustain those who are on work duty.

In some narratives it is told how Ni Daa Tua was subjected to (male) violence until she agreed to retreat to this temple kitchen belonging to Ratu Pucak. She is constructed as a socially marginal figure who must be overpowered before she can be recognized as a deity (Ratu Daa Tua), a deity who nevertheless remains confined to a symbolically female space. The violence she suffers in practice is mitigated in ritual, in an ideal context where she can be venerated without thereby questioning men's privileges within the public sphere of village life.

Sukawana version: Once an old unmarried woman (*daa tua*) came to live in the village of Batih. She was none other than the daughter of Ratu Tegeh Kauripan in disguise. Ni Daa Tua was diligent and frugal, and eventually became rich in land and gold. Her fellow villagers shunned hard work, preferring to borrow money from the rich woman, until most of them became deeply indebted to her. Finally Ni Daa Tua refused them any further loans, for they had failed to pay their earlier debts. So the men secretly began to devise a plot to murder the hated old woman. They gathered a large herd of cows in an enclosure, ushered her inside, and incited the animals to anger. Ni Daa was speared by their sharp horns, but before she died, she cursed the village that it should dwindle to seven households and remain poor no matter how hard they all worked (*sugih gae kirang pangan*). The spirit of Ni Daa Tua took its abode on Mt. Penulisan, in Pura Daa. Until today, Desa Batih will bring a miniature model of a plow for an important offering at the festival at Pura Pucak Penulisan.

Batih version: Ratu Daa Tua was the daughter of Ratu Pucak Tegeh and was sent to live in Batih, a large village of two hundred households (*keraman satak*). She was rich beyond measure, and the villagers were all too eager to borrow money from her. Once, twice, three times she obliged them, but at the fourth request she refused. Those who were indebted to her then began to devise a plan to rob and kill her. But others gave her warning, so the next day she took all her valuables and buried them at a place called Bukit Ambun. Her older brother, who still lived on Mt. Penulisan, heard of her troubles and came to speak to her: "Sister, why don't you come and live with me on Bukit Penulisan, where all your wealth will be safe. I will give you shelter as long as you are willing to stay in the temple kitchen (*pawaregan*)." To this she agreed, and henceforth she stayed at Pura Daa, where the temple kitchen is located. [The narrative continues with the arrival, murder, and curse of Teruna Camput Bagia, a marginal male figure (see Chapter 5)].[13]

The violation of an unmarried female, as in the story of Dewi Danu at Kehen (Chapter 5), is linked to notions about exchange among intimates (*baang ngidih,* "to give [and] to ask [for something]"). The men's demands are excessive in the context of their nonintimate relationship to Ni Daa Tua. Her demand for speedy repayments in turn prevent a relationship of that nature from arising, a relationship that would allow for and even depend on delayed reciprocation. Since her initial gifts are excessive, as in a potlatch exchange, the men also lack the resources necessary to reciprocate. This economic violence triggers a violent attempt to appropriate her female resources (rather than a marriage). But this violent act only leads to a curse of infertility, and the local society shrinks as it can no longer be reproduced adequately. It seems ironic that the descendants of her "murderers" should venerate her deified spirit, but this inconsistency in attitude only reflects the logical inconsistencies that stem from a simultaneous symbolic subjugation and dependence on a female principle. It is hardly surprising that the version from Batih reduces the verdict to attempted murder and reduces Ratu Pucak's status from that of a father to an older brother.

It is revealing that cows are chosen to become men's symbolic accomplices in a murderous plot. It is also cows that partake in the violation or cutting open of the earth's "female" body in the act of pulling a plow and are, in turn, killed in blood sacrifices to propitiate the *buta kala* spirits who dwell in the earth.[14] The plow (*tenggala*) is generally a male symbol and is paired together with the loom (*cagcag*) as a female symbol. For example, the miniature plow brought by Batih is paired with a miniature loom in the key offerings used at Pucak Penulisan's annual festival (Table 1), a set of offerings that accompany any form of buffalo sacrifice in Sukawana.

The relative value attached to symbols of maleness, femaleness, and unity is made conspicuous by the accompanying number of Chinese coins. While unity is grammatically defined as male (the male ending -*a* in *kerta* as opposed to the female -*i* in *kerti*), and while there is a greater number of coins in the male pula kedaton than the female pula kerti, the supreme value is the moment of unity. If the value of unity can indeed be counted in coins, it is here shown as greater than that of the two elements added together.[15] As new life is created, two becomes many, symbolically represented by a multitude of seeds.[16]

In the Batih version of the narrative, the father of Ni Daa Tua is

Table 1. Paired Categories in the Symbology of Offerings

Offering	Symbolic Meaning	Key Component	No. of Chinese Coins
pula kerti	female	miniature loom	2 × 33
pula kedaton	male	miniature plow	2 × 66
pula kerta	unity	a diversity of seeds (*sarwa wiji*)	2 × 225

replaced by her elder brother on her return to Penulisan. This shift reflects the marriagelike arrangement of common residence that is set up between the god and the goddess. Sibling marriage is common and not considered incestuous among deities, and corresponds with a moderate preference for endogamy in Bali Aga origin houses in the form of second parallel cousin marriage. Ratu Daa Tua's position in Pura Penulisan is paradigmatic of an ideal relationship between men and women. The female figure gains acceptance, even reverence, but at the cost of fulfilling her ascribed domestic role.

In sum, the temples Pura Daa and Kauripan are two of a pair. They reflect a gendered cosmos and, more generally, a Bali Aga view of an ideal world upheld by balances between paired categories coming together in a life-giving moment of unity. This is not a world maintained by domination and violence, though violence may sometimes be inflicted by men on women, by powerful newcomers on indigenous people, by ritual leaders on followers, or by the gods on humanity. It is a moral universe based on ideals of mutual respect and cooperation, even though these ideals are not always realized.

Pura Penulisan and Other Shrines

The temple complex as a whole is also colloquially referred to as Pura Penulisan, "the temple of the [royal] scribe."[17] More accurately, the name refers to a set of shrines on an even lower terrace to the east of the main staircase. The term is most frequently applied as a label for the temple complex as a whole in the context of discussing its role as the hub of the social and ceremonial network that forms the temple's congregation.

It may be surprising, at first, that a third and less elevated shrine should stand for the temple complex as a whole in the mundane context of its human support network. But the terrace of Pura Penulisan contains an important *palinggih* (seat) dedicated to Ratu Gede Penyarikan, "the messenger or secretary [of the gods or of a king]." This shrine is closely related to the nearby Bale Timbang (shrine of [the deity of] weighing or scales) and the Bale Dana (shrine [to the deity receiving] gifts of cash [on behalf of the gods]). A clue to the significance of these shrines is found in ancient royal inscriptions. In Prasasti Serai (A 1, 3b:3–4), for example, it is mentioned that villagers had to pay annually a variety of taxes in cash and kind that were received, measured, and recorded by the royal scribe, probably at a state temple or the palace.[18] Given that the villages belonging to this domain (including Desa Serai) still bring prestations to the "god" of this temple (*ratu*, also "a king") for the annual festival on *purnama-ning kapat* (the full moon of the fourth Balinese lunar month, or *kartika* in the inscriptions), it may be that these villages merely continue to fulfill their obligation to "the king" as the ultimate lord of the land. A once human king has been replaced by the divine king of the mountaintop (Ratu Pucak), as the temple's supreme deity is often called. The beginnings of a process of deification are evident in the inscriptions, where deceased kings are referred to as *"bhatara"* (gods). The very frequency of reference to regional temples in these edicts testifies to their importance in the statecraft of early Balinese kingdoms. Their rulers thus may have appropriated, refined, and expanded an earlier ceremonial order that, in some form, has far outlasted their own worldly kingdoms.

Important participants in the statecraft and ritual life of Balinese kingdoms from the beginning were priests, particularly those with a direct association to the royal household (*purohita*). After new kingdoms had been established by Javanese princes from Majapait, the existing priestly families in Bali were demoted. The original high priests were no longer referred to as *bujangga* ("dragon" or "snake") but as *sengguhu* (from *sengguh*, "to be believed"). This process of demotion is recorded in the Babad Brahmana, the origin myth of the current Brahmana clans, who claim a Javanese descent from Mpu Sakti Wahu Rahu. In this text the *sengguhu* is portrayed as no more than a skillful impostor (Rubinstein 1991).[19] In most of Bali these priests are still given some recognition, but only as specialists dealing with demonic forces. They are called upon for certain large purification rites, where they act as the third party in cooperation with a *pedanda siwa* and a *pedanda buda* (Hooykaas 1964).

The Bali Aga, however, refused to accept the new Brahmana priests (*pedanda*) and their claim to superiority. Most mountain villages still feature a Pura Bujangga, where people ask for *tirta pengentas*, otherwise only available from a *pedanda*. In the case of Pura Pucak Penulisan, there is not only a Pura Bujangga on a separate terrace, but also a specific family in Sukawana from which a new Bujangga priest is chosen by the village elders in every generation. Apart from producing *tirta pengentas*, the role of this Bujangga priest also relates to purification, such as the *balik sumpah* rite for the consecration of a new or repaired temple, as in other parts of Bali.[20] The Pura Ratu Sakti Bujangga at Penulisan is located beneath Pura Daa, but there is also a large branch temple in Banjar Kuum, where its local priest resides. The Bujangga's services are called upon by many nearby villages within the domain.

The shrines on Bukit Penerajon, finally, are also considered part of the temple complex, although they are located on a separate hilltop of lower elevation than Bukit Penulisan. The shrines on this hilltop are ritually maintained by the village of Sukawana alone, rather than the entire *banua.*

The shrines are of relevance to the domain as a whole nevertheless, given that the distinction between village and regional ritual in general is rather fluid in Sukawana. For example, the annual "village temple" festival in the Pura Bale Agung of Sukawana, celebrated on the full moon of the fifth lunar month (*ngusaba purnamaning kalima*), is attended by many member communities of the domain and in particular by downstream villages and their *subak* (from around Bangli, Payangan, and Kedewatan). The latter bring *suwinih* offerings (uncooked rice and some cash) and ask for *tirta wangsupada*, that is, holy water from the ritual washing of sacred objects (*pretima*).[21] The *pretima* belong to none other than the deity of Pura Pucak Penulisan, but they are kept and ritually cleansed annually in the Pura Bale Agung of Sukawana, which acts as its *pura penataran agung* in this context.[22] Only during the great decennial ritual of Pura Penulisan, the four-buffalo sacrifice Karya Catur Muka, are these objects of spiritual power taken out (*ngodal*) and walked in procession from Sukawana to Penulisan.[23] Distant villages also attend the festival of Pura Bale Agung Sukawana in order to "request revitalization" (*nunas pengurip*) for their sacred *barong* masks, though others will only go directly to Pura Penulisan. Thousands of visitors crowd the Pura Bale Agung during its annual festival, as I witnessed in 1994. Over a period of several days, the visitors had to be fed, and a task force of about 120 young people from Sukawana's organization of village boys and girls (*sekaa teruna teruni*) hardly left the temple kitchen. Drama and dance performances by the visitors, including an enactment of the Calonarang story, provided entertainment during the long chilly nights spent in guarding the temple (*makemit*).

The significance of *barong* masks and their entranced human carriers, chariots of village deities on their return journey to a point of origin (*kawitan*), will be discussed in more general terms later. In this specific case, each of the visiting village deities stands in a genealogically vertical and thus asymmetric relationship to the deity of Pura Pucak Penulisan. For example, the *barong* of Desa Bukhian and Desa Malinggih (Payangan) carry two sister deities, daughters of Ratu Pucak, who are believed to have been sent forth by their father to guard the rice fields of the two villages and who reside at their respective *pura puseh* (a village's "navel" or "origin" temple). The deity in Pura Puseh Sulahan (Bangli) is likewise Ratu Pucak's daughter, a connection that has only recently been "remembered."[24] Such kinship ties among deities are not necessarily embodied in a *barong*. The male and female deity of the Pura Puseh in Desa Selat, for example, have no *barong* as a vehicle and are simply "seated" on appropriate offerings, which are then taken to Sukawana.[25]

The *banua* and many other guests also attend during the peak of the lengthy purification ritual in which an elder from Sukawana is consecrated as a priest-leader and becomes able to officiate at Pura Penulisan, having achieved the rank of Jero Bau Putus.[26] Again this event takes place in the Pura Bale Agung. The visits are thought of as acts of witnessing and thus affirming the ritual authority that these priests exert over the congregation of Pura Penulisan.

The shrines located on Bukit Penarajon should also be considered at least marginally relevant to the *banua* as a whole. One of the shrines on this hilltop is said to be the Pura Puseh of Desa Batih. Others suggest that it was the Pura Puseh of old Sukawana (Kuta Dalem) until the temple was shifted to the upper end of the ridge on which the present village of Sukawana is situated. The link to Batih and Ni Daa Tua (female) fits in with the idea that the Pura Puseh of Sukawana is connected with the left (female, see below) moiety of the local village council. The claim that the Pura Puseh of Sukawana was shifted from here to its present location is also credible and has recently been acknowledged in ritual practice. When the new Pura Puseh in the village was reconsecrated after extensive repairs in 1994, a delegation of elders went to fetch *tirta* (holy water) at the old Pura Puseh on Bukit Penarajon.

Another shrine on Bukit Penarajon is Pura Song Pasek, which is related to the origin narratives of Pasek Kayuselem in Songan. Its festival, on the sixth full moon (*purnama kaenem*), involves a number of blood sacrifices (*caru*) but is not attended by outsiders. The same applies to Pura Gaduh and Pura Tengayang.[27]

Finally, there is a shrine at the base of the same hilltop, in Kuta Dalem, called Pura Mas Melanting. All over Bali temples of this name are usually found near a market. In this case the relevant market is Pasar Kintamani, which was relocated from Kuta Dalem down the main road to Kintamani proper in the 1930s by an initiative of the Dutch colonial government. The market was and is the most important trading center for the entire region and is held every third day (*pasah*). The temple festival (*odalan*) is held whenever Buda Wage

Kelawu (a date in the *wuku,* or Bali-Javanese permutational calendar) falls within the third to seventh lunar month. Private offerings are often made by those who seek material success in business or trade.[28]

Mt. Penulisan as a whole is a sacred location, a place where heaven and earth and all other polarities of the cosmos seem to meet. Past and present also merge in this temple complex as thousands of people gather to celebrate their common origin and to re-create their contemporary world in the image of a sacred past. It is these people and their notions of a common past that give meaning and continuing significance to this ancient sanctuary.

Chapter 3

GEBOG DOMAS
The Congregation of Pura Penulisan

Pura Pucak Penulisan is a popular place of worship among all Balinese Hindus. Pilgrims from the most distant corners of the island come here almost every day of the year, now that an age of motorized transport has made this temple easily accessible. But Pura Penulisan has a far deeper and more personal significance to the members of its principal congregation. Tens of thousands of people regard this sanctuary as the emblem of their sacred origin and the hub of their social and ritual world. This chapter will explore who these people are, what obligations they must meet, and why they regard themselves as related to one another in the context of a ritual domain.

I will begin by examining the principal membership of Pura Penulisan's support network, known as the *"gebog domas."* The temple's contemporary sphere of social relevance, however, represents no more than a momentary state within a dynamic historical and interpretive process. The current social and ritual arrangements in this domain, though they may be portrayed as the singular and true reflection of an immutable past, are a manifestation of a fluid system of shifting alliances.

The Contemporary Network

The *banua* of Pura Pucak Penulisan has at present a core membership of thirty "customary villages" (*desa adat*). The population size of these villages ranges from 36 to 740 heads of households (*kepala keluarga*). According to the temple budget reckoning, their populations together add up to a total of 4,901 contributing households. This is the official number of households who were required to pay the annual, pro rata contribution (*peturunan*) to the ritual and maintenance of Pura

Penulisan in 1992, but the actual number of households was much greater even then.[1] Since population size has increased, the amount payable by each village is simply divided by the current number of households to calculate individual amounts payable. The official figures are due for updating to match them with current population sizes. The number of principal contributors will then total 7,354 households, or about 33,000 people.[2]

All married couples who reside in a member village other than short-term visitors are expected to contribute in full, even if they are exempt from contributing to ritual events at the Pura Puseh or Bale Agung of that village for some reason. This rule presents an interesting parallel to the "membership" rules of Pura Dalem in the villages of this area, village temples to which all *banjar* (neighborhood) members must contribute financially and by participation in temple rituals.[3] Apart from paying *peturunan*, they will also bring *atos desa* as a village and private offerings as individual households at the time of Penulisan's annual festival.

The current core members of this domain refer to themselves as the *gebog domas* of Pura Penulisan. This organization is composed of four subdivisions, the *gebog satak* of Sukawana, Selulung, Bantang, and Kintamani. The term *"gebog"* refers to a set or bounded group, a totality made up of parts joined together (as in a length of cloth), but the significance of the numbers *satak* (two hundred) and *domas* (eight hundred, i.e., four times two hundred) is less transparent. The conglomeration of four times two hundred may reflect a "four or eight around a center" pattern common within the symbolism of Indonesian cultures (see Ossenbruggen 1977). A settlement of two hundred or more households also appears to have been recognized as a particular unit of administration by precolonial governments. Some claim that these units were *perbekelan*, territories under the authority of a *perbekel*, or village headman, during the reign of the Gelgel dynasty. This idea is supported by the fact that a *gebog domas* also forms the support network of the ancient Pura Kehen in the town of Bangli.[4]

The idea of *keraman satak* (two hundred households) appears in almost all of the origin myths of individual villages as an ideal population size, as in the origin narratives of Manikliyu (Pura Tebenan) and Batih that have already been presented. Such myths often focus on an early settlement and origin point that was abandoned or rebuilt after some disaster. The number of village council members (*keraman ulu apad*) in the original village is almost universally said to have been two hundred household heads, while the number of survivors tends to correspond to the fixed number of core elders in the current village council. A further example is the origin narrative of Desa Bantang, one of the four *gebog satak* centers in this domain:

> Long ago there was a village called Pengupetan, which consisted of two hundred households (*keraman satak*). At the time there lived among them a man named Kiayi Teruna Ajar. He was wealthy but unmarried.[5] Many villagers borrowed money from him and could not repay their debt when he asked them to repay it. So they thought of a means of killing him. First they felled a tree uphill from where Teruna Ajar was working, but to their surprise the tree fell uphill (*kaja*) [compare to the origin myth of Tangguan, Chapter 7]. Then they built a new temple kitchen from plaited bamboo (*bedeg*), and while he was cutting bamboo, they pushed the half-finished building from behind to collapse on him. Though he was killed, his spirit took the form of a quail (*kedis puuh*), which taunted the villagers until they all gave chase. Eventually the bird was caught, but when everyone asked to receive its head, a violent quarrel began. Many were killed and only seven couples remained. They fled to the top of the ridge and founded present-day Bantang, where until today the leadership of the village council consists of only seven ranks [seven pairs of elders]. They regularly pay ritual visits to Pengupetan and its old temples to propitiate the spirit of Teruna Ajar and to honor their point of origin.

The general theme of this and similar origin narratives is one of a golden age that comes to an end in a moment of conflict and destruction before the community is re-created in its present shape. The earlier and numerologically ideal order comes to an end because the rules of proper exchange are violated. The current social order is depicted as a compromise between a shattered ideal of sacred unity and the reality of conflicting interests and resource competition. In most of these narratives, the curse that befalls the original village is considered to be still active. The current social order will also meet its doom unless proper relations among human and invisible beings are constantly upheld and renewed with ritual performances.

The origin narratives of Desa Bantang, Selulung (Chapter 6), Kintamani, and Sukawana provide accounts of the origin of the four *gebog satak*. Each of the four divisions is named after its origin village and includes a variable number of younger and subsidiary settlements. The four subcenters are popularly associated with the Balinese directional system, with Sukawana located in the east (*kangin*), Selulung in the west (*kauh*), Bantang uphill (*kaja*), and Kintamani downhill (*kelod*).

There is no widely accepted origin narrative that would account for the number eight hundred in the designation *"gebog domas."* When pressed for an explanation, some informants offered fragmented reproductions of a story about the great Hindu teacher Maharishi

Markandeya as a possible explanation. Markandeya is said to have come to Bali with eight hundred followers from Desa Aga, a village situated at the foot of Mt. Raung in eastern Java.[6] These followers are said to have been the first to clear the forest and establish villages in Bali. But most of these eight hundred settlers died from disease and other misfortunes so that the saint was forced to return to Java and recruit a further thousand. With their help he then established a domain in Gianyar and founded Pura Besakih on Mt. Agung.[7]

The general ideological stance of this narrative suggests that it was either created or adapted by Majapait rulers, judging by the portrayal of the original population of Bali as survivors of a failed attempt to establish a stable civilization. Only the second wave of Javanese immigrants (from fourteenth-century Majapait) successfully established a stable order in Bali, in which Pura Besakih featured as the main state temple (Stuart-Fox 1987). Some Bali Aga versions seem to be more than reproductions of this popular southern Balinese myth with a different political slant. In Desa Julah, Maharishi Markandeya is said to have initially landed not in southern Bali, but at Ponjok Batu (just east of Julah), and in Batur some elders narrated to me that he eventually took residence not in Besakih but on Bukit Penulisan, under the name of Bhagawan Siwa Gandu. In any case, there is no certainty as to the origin of the term *"gebog domas,"* nor do its members feel a need for such an explanation.

The structure of the domain and its subdivisions is represented in Table 2. All of these villages are situated in the mountainous central highlands of Bali, and even the southernmost communities are still situated at an elevation of around one thousand meters above the sea. Pura Penulisan itself is located auspiciously at the highest point within the combined territories of these villages and at its northeastern edge. The roughly rectangular area covered by the *banua* measures about one hundred square kilometers.

On its southern slope the terrain of the *banua* is furrowed by increasingly steep gorges in the downstream regions. The lower part of the slope is thus separated into distinct ridges, connected only by small intersecting walking tracks. The major roads run along the crest of each ridge and converge on the main road that passes by Pura Pucak Penulisan. The northern edge of the area is formed by a rugged but broad saddle. From there the terrain falls with a dramatic drop toward the northern coast of Buleleng. The villages Kutuh, Batih, and Subaya are located on this northern slope, so that for them *kaja* equals south. From Sukawana, it is a mere four-hour walk (five kilometers) to the northern shore.[8] Until the 1970s there were no sealed

Table 2. The *Gebog Domas* of Pura Pucak Penulisan

Gebog Satak Sukawana	Gebog Satak Selulung	Gebog Satak Bantang	Gebog Satak Kintamani
Sukawana	Selulung-Blantih	Bantang	Kintamani
Kutuh	Pengejaran	(formerly also	Manikliyu
Subaya	Daup	Dausa and Satra)	Belancan
Batih	Catur		Serai
Kuum			Langgahan
			Mengani
			Awan
			Lembean
			Bunutin
			Batukaang
			Gelagahlinggah
			Ulian
			Bayungcerik
			Belanga
			Gunungbau
			Mangguh
			Kayukapas
			Binyan
			Bukih
			Pausan

Note: Binyan, Belanga, Batukaang, and Mengani were part of Gebog Satak Selulung rather than Gebog Satak Kintamani until 1943.

roads to connect these villages other than the main road from Bangli to Singaraja.

In terms of government administrative units, all of the thirty village communities except Desa Pausan fall within Kecamatan Kintamani, the northernmost district of the small landlocked *kabupaten* and former principality of Bangli. Despite a lack of complete correspondence between the boundaries of *kecamatan* and *banua*, government administrative (*dinas*) boundaries are of some significance. For example, along the periphery of the network are a number of villages that fall within other *kecamatan* or *kabupaten* but maintain traditions similar to those of the member villages. They often claim to have been connected to this *banua* in the past but are now no longer or only partially involved in its ceremonial order.[9]

In earlier territorial divisions, such as the precolonial *kerajaan,* or "principalities," these villages were not politically and administratively separated as they are today. It appears that such separation can eventually lead to a lapse in the maintenance of ritual alliances as well. An interesting case in point is Desa Pausan. This community was pressured by political leaders in Gianyar to leave the *banua*. The village had passed to Gianyar as a marriage gift when one of their princes was wed to a princess from Bangli, the principality to which the village had "belonged" until then. Existing ritual links may have posed a threat to the claim that this land was now a part of Gianyar. After the Dutch takeover, these considerations were no longer important, and Pausan felt at liberty to rejoin the domain, to which they were promptly readmitted. Generally, informants argued that ritually and politically defined territorial boundaries ought to match one another, at least in an ideal world.

Fluid Origin Histories and Shifting Patterns of Ritual Alliance

There is every indication that the ritual domain of Pura Pucak Penulisan as a social organization has a long history, marked by some remarkable continuities as well as significant and continuous changes. Participants pay much attention to this history in their attempts to legitimize how their relationships are defined or in reflecting on the way they could be or ought to be reshaped. In attempting to provide an impression of this *banua* as a dynamic process, I shall begin by reflecting on what is known from written sources and in living memory about its history, before considering how continuity and change arise as part of a negotiated system of mythical or "historical" narratives.

There are few reliable sources to reconstruct the membership history of Pura Penulisan's domain. The only available *lontar* reference is the Catur Dharma Kelawasan, which probably dates back to the early eighteenth century. The first version of this text mentions that there are ten members other than Sukawana but names only six (Dausa, Satra, Br Haa, Kutuh, Subaya, and Manikliyu), while the second version lists all ten villages (other than Sukawana), namely, the above six as well as Kintamani, Selulung, Balingkang (Desa Pinggan), and Bantang.[10] Many of the present members are not listed, but there is no indication that the list was meant to be exhaustive. Smaller member villages may well have been thought of as included along with their larger neighbors or may still have been incorporated within the administrative boundaries of the older and larger *desa adat* on this list. Together with the references to Pura Penulisan as a regional temple in early inscriptions, this source suggests that there has been considerable continuity in the membership of the temple's support network.

The same source also documents that some former supporters of Penulisan are no longer participating, most notably Pinggan and Dausa. Both villages are today the centers of other regional temple networks. The events surrounding the withdrawal of support by Desa Adat Dausa and its affiliates, and by the group around Pura Baling-kang (Desa Pinggan), can still be reconstructed from eyewitness accounts. Differently positioned reports could be recorded and cross-checked in order to gain a relatively balanced impression of this recent history. Both cases are very complex and will be discussed in Chapter 5.

The ritual and social arrangements between the *gebog satak* sub-centers and the central temple of the domain have also undergone changes within the span of living memory. Some earlier organizational functions of the *gebog satak* centers have been abandoned in favor of a more centralized system. The oldest generation still recalls that their cash contribution to Penulisan was paid to the Jero Mekel (*perbekel*) of the village heading their *gebog satak*, who would then surrender the money to the temple. This gathering of funds at a subcenter level apparently ceased following allegations of corruption. Another factor may have been that several of the smaller villages were gaining polit-ical autonomy by forming separate administrative villages, each with its own *perbekel* or, later, *kepala desa* (a village head incorporated within the modern Indonesian state administration).

There are interesting cases in recent history of villages shifting their orientation from one *gebog satak* to another for strategic reasons. For example, several small communities formerly attached to Selu-lung decided to transfer their allegiance to Gebog Satak Kintamani. The status relations between these villages and Selulung had been of a patron-client type, because their founding ancestors were newcomers and had asked for a grant of land within the territory of old Selu-lung. The founding (and leading) factions in these client villages were further tied to the core group of first settlers in Selulung by affinal ties and were more or less incorporated as branches within the an-cestral origin (*kawitan*) group called Pasek Selulung. Eventually the leading factions in client villages began to seek greater autonomy, a move supported by their own local clients, who were even later arrivals and thus not directly connected to Selulung. A shift to Gebog Satak Kintamani was seen as advantageous in a number of ways. It was preferred to be a new member village of a different *gebog*, with no specific status, rather than to continue to be ritually dominated by the core village within their original network. Kintamani was also the seat of an increasingly powerful colonial district administration, and the district head was able to protect them from possible acts of retribution and in disputes over land rights. Finally, the leading faction in Kintamani at that time was launching an attempt at usurping Sukawana's leadership in the committee of Pura Penulisan, a project in which they required as broad a support base as possible.

Although these events took place during the 1930s and 1940s, they are well remembered, not least for their later consequences. In two of the rebel villages, the leading faction attempted to eliminate all connotations of ritual dependence on Selulung. They rejected the origin narratives that described them as an in-marrying newcomer branch of Selulung's founding group. After "discovering" their genealogical origin to lie elsewhere, they ceased to attend their *pura kawitan* in Selulung. But no sooner had they cut all ties to this regional center than their own local clients began to flex their political muscle. In one village the founding faction has lost all local political and ritual control, and in another they are barely holding on. Without the link to Selulung, the legitimacy of their own leading position as recognized founders of a client village was open to question. Given their candid disregard for traditional ties, they found it difficult to appeal to traditional loyalties in order to retain their local privileges.

In view of the indisputable continuities and fluctuations in the domain's membership and in the pattern of relations among specific communities, it must be asked how relationships in this and other *banua* are legitimized and negotiated. It is a large body of orally transmitted relationship narratives of different kinds that establishes the ritual links among the villages or village clusters that are the core supporters of Pura Pucak Penulisan. The first type is a genre that can be loosely referred to as mythohistorical narratives of origin. A second type is a genre of legend, with ostensive references to specific artifacts or other elements of "historical evidence."

The most comprehensive mythical narrative about the domain's origins was recorded in Sukawana, and it recounts how the four sons of Ratu Sakti Pucak Penulisan founded the four *gebog satak*.

Ratu Pucak Penulisan had four sons. The three elder siblings were sent forth, while Ratu Pucak himself remained in Sukawana (east) with the youngest son. In this way all the four directions (*catur desa*) would be guarded. The eldest son, who had struck a path along the main ridge (*kaja*), decided to settle in Pengupetan [old Bantang]. But he did not wish to dwell in a temple on the ground. Hence he took his residence atop a tall *cemara* tree, a locality marked by a shrine where the *prasasti* of Bantang used to be kept. Until today their annual *ngusaba* begins at this tree, from which the gods will descend to attend the festival. The second son had traveled *kelod* to Kintamani, where he resides at Pura Tenten. He became wealthy as a sponsor of trade, and the gods themselves are believed to attend his temple festival to hold an "invisible" (*niskala*) market. The third son had traveled *kauh* (west) to Selulung, where he became the guardian of the rice fields. The area used to be called Desa Kauh in Sukawana and was the rice barn of the *banua* in days gone by.[11] Meanwhile the youngest became [the archetype of] a spoiled son. He complained one day that he was hungry but refused all the treats the servants would offer to him. When his father came to question him, he admitted that he longed for a "roast without a tail" (*guling buntut*), a metaphor for human sacrifice. Ratu Pucak was outraged to hear this request. He kicked his son with such force that he tumbled all the way down to Bukit Pengubengan, near Desa Subaya. There he lay and cried in dismay, pledging to change his ways if only he were given some *nasi cacah* [a crude mash made of sweet potato seasoned with salt and raw onion]. Until today he is given only *nasi cacah* as an offering by the people of Subaya.[12]

This narrative describes a process of expansion by outward migration from a point of origin. The sons of the deity at the origin point are sent forth to in order to establish their own, subsidiary domains. The birth order of siblings is reiterated by the temporal order in which they establish their domains.[13] Sukawana's status is ambiguous in that the village is the center of a *gebog satak* as well as being the sacred origin site of the domain as a whole. This explains why the fourth son, and the village of Subaya, cannot be portrayed in the myth as the origin of a *gebog satak*. The youngest stays at home with the father, as last-born sons often do, in the hope of becoming the principal heir. But, unlike human parents, deities do not die, and so the youngest son is eventually banished. His behavior indicates a discontent with received resources and an incapacity to access new resources. His unreasonable demands are contrasted with the agricultural and trading success of the dutiful elder sons, who have sought their fortune abroad and thereby expanded the resource base of the paternal domain.

Apart from such origin narratives, phrased in terms of divine kinship ties and the migration of ancestors away from a common source, the members of this domain often refer explicitly to a more familiar notion of "history" (B.I. *sejarah*). They speculate that the spatial limits of their ritual network and domain correspond to the boundaries of an old Balinese kingdom believed to have had its center at Penulisan. As an alternative to a more obviously mythological genre, such legends suggest the *gebog domas* was once a *negara*, that is, a political as well as ritual organization. Such legends often focus as a means of justification on a specific piece of "historical evidence" such as a *prasasti*, finds of antique objects, or ruins of ancient buildings. For example, many villagers in Sukawana believe that the site of the first king's palace (*kraton*) was on a hilltop (*bukit*) called Singawana, located two kilometers east of Penulisan (see Map 3). This belief ties in with the fact that Bali's first *prasasti* do not mention a king's name but do state that he held court at "Singamandawa." Archeological remains on Singawana are believed to be foundations of a palace, and countless antique objects have been found in the vicinity. Legend also has it that the Balinese kings later shifted from Singamandawa to Balingkang, a fortified hill about three kilometers downhill and farther west, which is surrounded by a moat and was formerly reached only by a drawbridge. Even nowadays, though it is used as a temple, Balingkang is referred to by the villagers as a *jero* or *puri* (palace) rather than a *pura* (temple). A third and final shift before the Majapait invasion, from Balingkang to Pejeng or Bedaulu in the south, is described in several local versions of the *lontar* Usana Bali.[14] Until today no archeological excavations have been attempted in the Kintamani district, and in the absence of reliable evidence, all reconstruction of the past must remain speculative. "Historical" narratives of kingship, however, are certainly significant as local explanations for the existence of this *banua* and as an alternative to origin narratives focused on the exploits of mythical ancestors and gods.

Both types of narratives are depictions of a current social order in the image of the past. As such they are important and sometimes fiercely contested statements about the distribution of status among the communities within the domain. Some examples will illustrate how accounts of the origin history of a domain are negotiated.

One important case involving "historical evidence" is Desa Dausa's withdrawal of ritual support from Penulisan. At the time, one of the *prasasti* of Dausa was reread, and the locals first came to understand (or pay attention to) its content. In the inscription (A.D. 1061), the king granted them leave from the worship of Bhatara Mandul in Sukawana since they already maintained a major temple of their own (Prasasti Dausa A 2).[15] This temple, Pura Bukit Indrakila, and its *banua* will be discussed in detail later, but suffice it to say for now that the split appears to be final, though there have been some half-hearted discussions about rejoining Penulisan. While they no longer pay *peturunan*, people from this group of villages still attend and bring offerings to Pura Penulisan's annual festival on a voluntary and

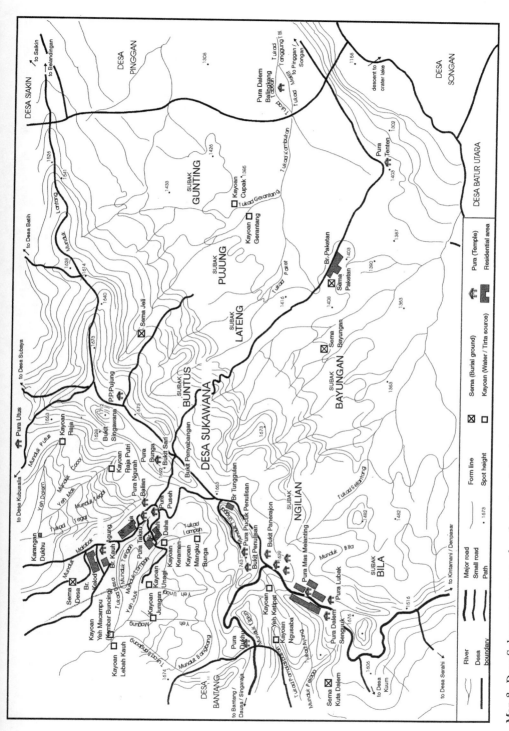

Map 3. Desa Sukawana: topography of a regional ritual center

private basis. They have also built a visiting shrine for Ratu Pucak Tegeh in their own regional temple.

Some time ago, Desa Awan presented a somewhat more ambitious, less convincing, and ultimately unsuccessful argument in order to improve its status within the domain. Villagers believe that in ancient times the original settlement was situated to the west of present-day Awan. About a hundred years ago, a man had discovered what seemed like the foundations of a royal palace or temple at the site, along with many antique objects such as Ming dynasty Chinese pottery, sarcophagi, stone carvings, and ritual implements. Locals speculated that this was a palace of Balinese kings before the shift to Kuta Dalem or Balingkang. A new temple was built on this archeological site and named Pura Kauripan (*sic*). Unfortunately, most of the remaining foundations were leveled for this purpose. In 1973, the gods of "Pura Kauripan" (Awan) were taken to Pura Tegeh Kauripan (Penulisan) in order to affirm the presumed connection. Since neither Sukawana nor Awan's other neighbors took any notice of their claims to a status of precedence, the narrative was eventually withdrawn from circulation, and few in Awan are willing to discuss the matter nowadays.

The events in Dausa and Awan illustrate how changes in a regional pattern of alliance may be brought about by creating or attempting to create a new ritual order in competition to the existing network. In many cases the ritual authority of a center is not questioned, nor is ritual support withheld. Rather, the competitors will attempt to create an alternative center and outperform the original one in terms of ritual display.[16] In such challenges, the main issue is not necessarily the legitimacy of established authority so much as its relevance and scope.

An appropriate example is the relationship between Desa Selulung and Desa Pengejaran, both of whom belong to the domain of Penulisan and have smaller domains of their own followers. The founding faction of Selulung claim that Pengejaran is a branch community (*pondokan*) established by ancestors who migrated from Selulung and that its population was later supplemented by the acceptance of immigrants. By contrast, the leading faction of Pengejaran claim that their village constitutes a separate and indeed an earlier origin point, in accordance with the following narrative:

(1) Ratu Pucak Tegeh [Kauripan] sent his daughter, Ratu Manik Penyalin,[17] to live on Bukit Pengalusan in a temple called Pura Nyuan. One day the son of the deity of Mt. Batukaru came by as he was hunting a bird [*kedis titiran*, a kind of dove]. Barely had they met when they fell in love, and no sooner had Ratu Batukaru departed than Ratu Manik

Penyalin realized she was pregnant. She gave birth to a son and named him Ratu Bagus Manik Mas. Often he played with the son of her neighbor, Ratu [Pura] Dalem. Because Ratu Manik Mas always won their games, the latter insulted him in retaliation, saying that he was someone who did not even know his own father (*bebinjat*). The young man then questioned his mother about the identity of his father, and she sent him to find Ratu Batukaru in the west. When he arrived at his father's court, no one took any notice of him. So he sat down with the groom of his majesty's fighting cocks and helped him to sharpen the spurs (*taji*). When the king received the spurs, he noticed that one was of different shape and far superior. He was told of the young man from Pengalusan who had come that day asking for his father. Ratu Batukaru immediately acknowledged his son. He gave him two heirlooms, a wand of *dapdap* wood [Indian coral tree, *Erythrina* sp.] and a magic stone, the one to mark his future residence in Pengejaran and the other to mark the boundary of his domain. But Ratu Bagus Manik Mas lost his way on the return journey and eventually took residence in Pura Kecagan in Desa Daup, where a large *dapdap* tree still grows as proof of his presence. To the east of his domain he planted the magic stone, which grew larger and larger until it became Mt. Agung. His domain included Desa Klandis, Selulung, Tegal, Catur, Tambakan, Blantih, and Daup. These villages still *mabanua* in Pengejaran, and each has its own pavilion in the Pura Bale Agung. The one exception is Selulung. Once, at the end of the *banua* festival, the people of Pengejaran started to sweep the garbage out of the temple before the visitors from Selulung had left. They felt insulted by this [regarding it as a hint to be on their way] and never returned thereafter.

(2) Long ago, before Pengejaran was established, a village already flourished there named Bukit Pengalusan [from *alus*, "refined"]. Its population of two hundred households lived in peace and order until a calamity befell them. One day, at the conclusion of a festival at the Pura Bale Agung, a cockfight was held that drew an enthusiastic crowd. Even the Jero Pasek joined in, but he was unable to find a match for his fighting cock. In the end he became hungry and returned home. He wanted to help himself to some shrimp paste (*terasi*) stored in a bamboo tube, but, alas, he could not pull his hand out again no matter how hard he struggled. Meanwhile, in the temple, a match had been found for his cock, and all was ready for the fight. So the Penyarikan was sent to call the Jero Pasek back to the cockfight. When he saw the Pasek from afar, struggling and waving a bamboo covered in shrimp paste, which looked like blood, he thought that Jero Pasek had gone berserk (*ngamuk*) and ran to warn the others. When the Pasek finally realized that he needed help, he returned to the temple, where he was attacked and killed by the suspicious crowd. When his family saw what had happened, they in turn attacked the others, until in the end only twelve survived [until today there are only twelve elders or core members on the village council] who had not participated in the cockfight but had been working in their gardens. They buried the Jero

Pasek of Pengalusan in the Pura Bale Agung, and on the grave a round
assembly pavilion was built [as opposed to the usual rectangular shape]
to express the sentiment that unity and harmony are more important
than rank and competition. Since the village was without leadership,
the Jero Pasek of nearby Selulung sent a priest named Mangku Mubai
to maintain their spiritual welfare. This priest became the ancestor of
the "western moiety" (*sibak kauh*) of Pengejaran's village council. [He
was a heroic figure and once saved Pasek Selulung from imprisonment
at the court of Raja Klungkung. The current *perbekel* of Pengejaran is a
descendant of his.]

The first section of the narrative establishes links to Pura Penulisan,
the paramount temple of the encompassing domain, as well as to
important neighbors toward the west (Batukaru). Selulung is not
mentioned as a way station or intermediate center, nor are their
counterclaims acknowledged or denied. The deity at Pengejaran is
portrayed as the mother of the deity at Daup, her son who became
the worldly ruler of her wider domain. Three of the villages in this
domain, Klandis, Tegal, and Tambakan, are located to the west, outside the *banua* of Pura Pucak Penulisan.[18] The failure to gain support
from their regional competitors in Selulung at present is traced back,
in a somewhat awkward adjunct to the actual narrative, to behavior
from which an insult was taken where none had actually been intended. While the competition between the two villages is thus down-
played as no more than a big misunderstanding, the narrative spells
out a claim to rival Selulung's ritual precedence claims as a *gebog satak*
origin point.

In the second section Pengejaran is established as a point of origin
in its own right, supposedly coming under the influence of Selulung
later, following the depopulation of the village and the death of its
leaders. The myth contains another example of the familiar theme
of calamity and subsequent population attrition from an ideal to the
current community size.

Pengejaran has had limited success in propagating this origin
account as a charter for securing ritual alliances. The attendance of
villages belonging to Pengejaran's own *banua* has been sporadic in
recent years, and certainly none of them are committed enough to
pay *peturunan*. Pengejaran also found a number of allies who have had
their own quarrels with Selulung. One of them is the leading faction
in Desa Blantih, who are tenacious competitors to the leading figures
in Selulung—despite or, perhaps, because of the fact that the two
desa dinas form a single *desa adat*. Complementary versions of the
above myth, recorded in Blantih, illustrate their position.

One of Blantih's founding ancestors named Ratu Bagus Nataria Kuta Waringin (who is the deity of Pura Bonsana) had a son, Prince Ki Bagus Alit. Once he met and fell in love with Ratu Ayu Penyalin, daughter of Ratu Pol Penyalin, who lived on the hilltop of Pengasepan [i.e., Penga-lusan] in Pengejaran. They married and resided at her home in Penge-jaran. The people of Selulung and Blantih did not know of the obliga-tion their own deity acquired when his son became the son-in-law of the deity at Pengejaran—that is, until one day when they were cleaning up at Pura Candi in Selulung after a festival. A man saw a small wild fig tree (*waringin*) sprouting in the temple yard, so he cut it down and threw it over the wall. To everyone's surprise the branch flew off like a missile and landed in Pengejaran, in the temple of Ratu Pol Penyalin. The elders held a meeting to discuss this, and finally some of them re-membered that their divine ancestor, Ki Bagus Alit, had been accepted by Ratu Pol Penyalin of Pengejaran as an in-marrying (*nyeburin*) son-in-law when he married her daughter Ratu Ayu Penyalin.

The first and principal ancestor of the people of Blantih, Ratu Gede Makarang [the great lord [who owns] the land], came from Java, and it was he who first cleared the land. He settled in the east (*kanginan*); hence his descendants live in Blantih. Later arrived Ratu Gede Kemulan [the great lord of (genealogical) origin], who originated from Batur. He settled in the west [*kawanan*, i.e., Selulung], where his descendants live until today.

These narratives from Blantih support Pengejaran's claim of senior-ity in a context of divine affinal relations and trace this connection through an ancestor from a temple located in and controlled by Blantih rather than Selulung. Nevertheless, the myth stops short of acknowledging either Pengejaran or Selulung as the source of Blantih's own ancestors.[19]

These competing narrative claims illustrate that there is covert com-petition for ritual precedence in this network. Indeed, the state of unity and harmonious cooperation assumed to prevail among villages within Gebog Satak Selulung, at least from the central perspective of Pura Penulisan and its leadership, is more an ideal than a reality. The notion that this major subdivision of the *gebog domas* is a fixed institutional and historical entity is also difficult to reconcile with the fact that several of Selulung's client villages have recently shifted affiliation to Gebog Satak Kintamani.

The case of Selulung illustrates that religious and historical dis-courses on the nature of *banua*, which picture villages tied in perma-nent allegiance to their common point of origin by the force of irrefutable sacred obligations born of an immutable past, may con-ceal a more flexible web of actual ritual alliances based on negotiated narrative and ritual traditions. Actual relations within a domain have permanence only in the more limited sense that a precarious balance is usually maintained between claims and counterclaims. What local people's idealizing religious discourses on the nature of relations in a domain deny is not that the present order has a particular history but that this history is constantly negotiated and reinvented.

The concealment of conflicts over the distribution of ritual status within a domain relates to a fundamental ambiguity in status-differentiated societies. In a highland Balinese domain, for example, villages evidently compete for symbolic resources. But, at the same time, status is also a product of cooperation. It would make little sense to raise a competitive claim unless there was a chance of having such claims accepted by others. Indeed, the very existence of these status-differentiated ritual alliance systems is testimony to the fact that, under certain conditions, people are willing to grant others a status superior to their own. The Bali Aga have their own way of negotiating this fundamental ambiguity.

One way of resolving this ambiguity is to create a shared and reliable procedure for the verification of specific claims about the origin history and status order of a society. As far as the participants of a *banua* are concerned, there is a certain confidence that no morally upright or at least sensible person would dare to deny a proven religious connection and thus neglect his or her obligations. Deliberately producing a fictitious origin narrative would most certainly incite the wrath of one's ancestors. One potential problem here lies in asserting at once that some others may be violating sacred obligations nonetheless and that one's own group would never do the same. This problem is generally resolved by suggesting that people often will in fact misrepresent their ancestry and origins but out of ignorance rather than social ambition. It would be highly problematic to recognize status competition as the source of the problem. A constructivist assumption, that the past is created in the image of contemporary concerns rather than the reverse, would question the very foundations of what is essentially a moral order. How then can specific origin narratives be verified or falsified without acknowledging the general problem strategic interests or sheer ignorance must pose for the truthful telling of such narratives?

Physical evidence may seem to play a role in the process of verification, considering the origin narratives from Dausa, Awan, and Manikliyu described above. In most disputes, however, such evidence is either unavailable or so open to interpretation that a resolution cannot be reached on the grounds of the evidence alone.[20] Even in the case of Dausa, the revealing text of the royal inscription did not in itself prescribe the particular course of action to be taken under the circumstances.

There are also some supernatural forms of verification that may be applied in the event of a dispute. People may receive guidance from their ancestors or from deities through dreams and signs, or may consult a trance medium (*balian taksu, tapakan*). The spirits of ancestors may be called on deliberately to comment on a specific origin issue in the case of a medium consultation (see Bateson 1970). And yet this too is a source of information seen as potentially unreliable.[21] The utterings of the medium are usually sufficiently ambiguous to allow for a wide range of interpretations. The process of trance consultation is thus not very different from more conventional means of reaching a consensus. It is effective as an aid in decision making only in cases where all parties are prepared to claim ignorance and genuinely seek an agreement in the first place. Trance merely provides an idiom that allows diplomatic negotiations among human agents to be constructed as responses to the demands of divine agents.

From an observer's perspective one could conclude that, in the absence of formal and binding standards for verifying its origin narratives, the shape of a ritual order is ultimately no more than the outcome of a number of decisions to grant or withhold, continue or withdraw practical support for the ritual enactment of a particular relationship. Private and sometimes public discussions of origin narratives are one procedure by which such decisions may be negotiated, culminating in a tentative consensus and a preliminary agreement on appropriate acts of regular ritual acknowledgment. Most often this is indeed how minor disputes are resolved. But discussion sometimes fails to dispel a lingering sense of disagreement based on underlying conflicts of interest. Silence and sometimes mutual avoidance are the strategies of choice for handling such a situation. Open verbal confrontations are considered unpleasant and are studiously avoided.[22]

The Bali Aga themselves would perhaps be prepared to acknowledge a role for human agency in that people are said to have a duty and an interest in creating a good society. But my informants also stressed that the truth about how a particular domain ought to be ordered does not emerge as the product of a human consensus, whether it is reached in discussions about origin narratives or by the interpretation of artifacts and trance messages. The truth is also not seen as a simple reflection of the way people agree to associate in their actual ritual practice. Participants readily conceded that past upheavals and arguments in their domain are evidence of a temporary misapprehension of the past, made possible by the general frailty of human memory and knowledge, or perhaps even by the blinding effects of ambition on a small number of individuals. But they would not concede that the way things are is the way they are meant to be simply because people have decided it should be so, and they are all reasonably content with their allotted role in the ritual order as it stands. Instead, local participants would insist that a false narrative of origin and the worship of the wrong ancestors (*salah kawitan*) would invite natural disasters and other causes of human misery. After all, worshiping at the wrong temple means that one's true ancestors and origin sites are forgotten and neglected. In short, the order of a ritual domain is seen as true whenever it accords with the will of divine forces.

In a less metaphysical interpretation of this Balinese attitude toward human agency, one could say that a ritual order must indeed meet not only the internal demands of a dynamic social system but the external demands of a reality beyond the liberty of human choices. This interpretation strikes at the heart of the matter. The appropriateness of the present social order, as a true image of the past, is revealed to the participants of a ritual domain in the form of "good fortune" (*rahayu*). A good harvest; harmonious human relations; the absence of unexplainable illnesses, deaths, and other misfortunes; and the capacity to meet the world beyond in confidence are the ultimate proof that a domain is organized as it ought to be.

Social ambition implicitly does have a place in this worldview. It is the driving force behind a necessary empirical process of trial and error, designed to approach an existential truth that cannot be established firmly on the basis of a priori knowledge about the past. If a group manages to redefine the order of a *banua* to its advantage and continues to prosper, then its very success is a testimony to the approval of the gods. If its members fail to secure support or bring misfortune upon themselves and their supporters, then they will be propelled to retract their claims. After the dust has settled, those who fail may even be criticized by others for having reached beyond their proper status in life. The material, social, and spiritual risks associated with a restructuring of the social and ritual order thus operate as powerful disincentives to radical change. At the very least, it is my impression that socially ambitious groups in highland Bali are more or less genuinely convinced of the legitimacy of their own claims. Actual behavior in the context of ritual association must therefore be seen in the context of a moral order that may seem difficult to accept from a rationalist point of view, in that its moral foundation rests on the empirical evidence of material and social success. The evidence of prosperity is a moral foundation nonetheless, insofar as it is never just the success of a privileged few that is at stake. A successful domain is one where all those who volunteer their support to a privileged party also share in the prosperity.

Prosperity may be taken as evidence that the way people conceive of the ideal order of society in their narrative models is correct, but it does not suffice to indicate a state of perfect knowledge about the past or about the proper order of things. Prosperity could always be greater than it is already, life could be more comfortable, the fields more fertile, people's lives even longer and less punctuated by times of illness. Knowledge of the proper order of the natural and social world is a project rather than a fait accompli to the Bali Aga. The sense of openness that permeates their narratives of origin has its source in this uncertainty, just as the tendency to remain faithful to proven traditions has its origin in the awareness that, no matter how much life may at times seem like a chain of disasters, things could surely be worse than they are under the present conception of the sociocosmic order.

Conflicting narratives and shifting ritual alliances are not peculiar to Gebog Satak Selulung. Similar examples could have been drawn from other parts of the *gebog domas* of Pura Penulisan. Nevertheless, it may not always be appropriate or justified to evoke a notion of conflict whenever there is a change in an existing pattern of alliances. The evident fluidity and multiplicity of relationship narratives and ritual practices in the highlands can also be interpreted as a readiness to embrace new sociopolitical opportunities. Individual villages may choose to partake in one or several new alliances without withdrawing their ritual support and reaping negative sentiments from their existing allies. Most villages in the domain of Pura Pucak Penulisan invest only a part of their social and ritual resources into maintaining a place within the *gebog domas* of Pura Pucak Penulisan or in their respective *gebog satak*. Many engage in additional bilateral ritual associations with specific neighboring villages or even with distant communities beyond the confines of this domain.

The people of Desa Serai, for example, are ardent participants in the *gebog domas*. Their participation in work parties during the festival of Pura Penulisan and their contributions in the form of offerings far exceed formal expectations. Serai borders on Sukawana to the south, and this proximity may in part explain their exceptional enthusiasm as supporters of Pura Penulisan. But, at the same time, Serai maintains close ties to its downstream neighbors in Desa Awan.

The biannual festival of Pura Bale Agung Serai on the fifth full moon is held jointly by the two villages. The temple even contains two separate assembly pavilions for the village deities (*bale pamaruman*) and two halls for the percussion groups (*bale gong*) of Awan and Serai, on the temple's western and eastern side, respectively. Serai reciprocates this visit at the festival of the Pura Desa in Awan, on every third Tumpek Landep (once every 630 days), but the relationship is slightly asymmetric. The deity in Serai requires a buffalo, while a pig suffices for the one in Awan. The argument in support of this differentiation is that several *prasasti* are kept in Serai's Pura Bale Agung. The potential for competition is curbed by mutual support for a compromising account of local history. It is believed that the inscriptions were formerly kept in Awan but later shifted to Serai because Awan's population was too small to finance the required buffalo sacrifice. The common origin point of the two villages, according to informants in Serai, is a third, but not entirely neutral site.

> Long ago some hunters settled permanently in the hunting grounds of Dalem Penulisan. The king ordered them to build a Pura Bale Agung as is proper for a permanent community. They decided to fell a large tree (*kayu lengung*) for the large assembly pavilion and supported its branches so that it would not come crashing down and break their houses. However, the force of the falling tree was too great, and many were crushed beneath it. The survivors ran off in confusion. Some founded Awan, others founded Serai, and others yet founded Desa Tiga. Hence the name Pura Belatanges [*belah* means "shattered"; *tanges* is from *tangeh*, "(to lose one's) composure"] was given to the temple that was later constructed at this origin site, which is located within the territory of contemporary Serai [*sic*].

Awan does not fully recognize this origin narrative, preferring to depict the bilateral *banua* relationship as one of mutual and equal support, in keeping with practical considerations. Despite these subtle disagreements, both parties recognize their alliance as valuable, as an incentive toward good neighborly relations, and as an acknowledgment of genuine historical ties.

Serai's major ceremonial events are also attended by people from a distant village in southern Bangli, Desa Tiga. This alliance is again a separate matter. The people of Tiga behold Serai as their ancestors' place of origin (*kawitan*). They are not a subsidiary settlement or *pondokan* of old Serai. Their Serai ancestors settled and founded a new village on the alien territory of Desa Buungan (Chapter 6), rather than in the confines of Serai's original territory. The founders of Buungan are hence patrons by merit of giving ancestral village land to the people of Tiga, while Serai is the place where Tiga's own ancestors originated. For the people of Serai, this ritual link opens up opportunities for establishing valuable personal relationships beyond their immediate surroundings. While Desa Serai's ritual alliances are thus evidently eclectic and arguably opportunistic, none of their multiple associations have precipitated a conflict of loyalty or initiated a competitive struggle for status.

A peaceful coexistence of different alliance systems, even among the same set of villages, is also evident in the rich pattern of smaller domains within the very large domain of Pura Penulisan. Apart from the division into four *gebog satak,* there are a number of other secondary *banua* alliances. Some among them have long since become established and well recognized regional institutions in their own right. Even though the villages concerned may fully participate as members of the *gebog domas,* these smaller alliances uphold separate and important ritual orders.

Often the presence of a recognized smaller *banua* within a larger domain is justifiable by the specific function attached to this additional layer of social organization. One such case, the small *banua* around Pura Tebenan in Manikliyu, was mentioned in Chapter 1. Another and closely related cluster of villages is the *banua* of the paired temples Pura Pucak Pausan in Desa Pausan and Pura Pengelimut in Desa Langahan. Both Pausan and Langahan are regular participants at some of the larger festivals celebrated at Pura Tebenan, and along with the other villages of the Tebenan group, they are also members of the *gebog domas* of Pura Penulisan.

Pucak Pausan and Pucak Pengelimut are regional agricultural temples whose geographical location coincides with a climatic boundary between downstream, irrigated and upstream, rain-fed rice agriculture in this part of Bali. Pausan's and Langgahan's upstream relationships (*mabanua*) are directed at Pura Tebenan and Pura Pucak Penulisan, but they themselves are the center in a pattern of similarly conceived visiting relationships with a number of downstream *subak* in the Payangan area. Among their periodic visitors are the villages Gata, Singaperang, Buahan, Susut, Sema (Payangan), and others.

The festivals at the two temples are both celebrated on the first full moon (*purnama kasa*) of the Balinese calendar. They are held in annual rotation, at Pucak Pausan in "odd" years (*saka ganjil*) and at Pura Pengelimut in "even" years (*saka genep*).[23] The timing of the festivals marks a turning point between two phases in the annual cycle of ritual and of rice cultivation. This pattern will be described later in relation to Pura Pucak Manggu (Chapter 6). Temple priests explained how the festival marks the end of the half of the annual cycle referred to as *"ring tengen"* (to the right, i.e., male) and the beginning of the half referred to as *"ring kiwa"* (to the left, i.e., female). The growth cycle in rice cultivation and climatic conditions at the elevation of Pausan differ significantly from those at Pucak Manggu, as does the timing of the festival.

Many of these *subak* relations of the two temples are accentuated by the visits of *barong*. Apart from relationship narratives based on the notion of family relations between divine beings, there are also a number of *barong* that physically originate from Pura Pucak Pausan. For example, the *barong* masks of Gata and Singaperang are both carved from "wood that was asked for" (*nunas kayu*) in Pausan. Consequently, these *barong* will return periodically to their place of origin for a revival of their life force (*nunas pangurip*).[24] Finally, there are also a number of visiting shrines in Pura Pucak Pausan for the deities of several related sanctuaries in the Payangan area as well as for Ratu Pucak Kauripan (Penulisan).

By contrast, the regional ritual activities in the *banua* of Pura Tebenan are focused on the still extensive dry (rain-fed) rice agriculture within its domain, an area that forms the only remaining rice-growing area of significance within the entire domain of the *gebog domas*. Because the pattern of ritual in the *banua* of Pausan/Langahan is synchronized with the cycles of wet (irrigated) rice agriculture and that of the *banua* of Tebenan with dry rice agriculture, both are seen as necessary and complementary ritual orders, and both are integrated within a larger whole by their association with the larger domain of Pura Penulisan. These and similar subsidiary ritual orders fulfill organizational functions no longer relevant to other members of the *gebog domas* who have ceased to cultivate rice. Yet, in terms of ritual precedence and sacredness, these smaller temples clearly acknowledge a subsidiary position in relation to the more ancient Pura Pucak Penulisan. They also function as important relay stations between the Payangan district and the mountains.[25]

The preceding description of alliance patterns within the domain of Pura Pucak Penulisan has illustrated some of the immense complexity of this flexible and layered regional institution. Beyond the group of villages counted among its core supporters, the temple is linked by specific narratives of origin and ancient ritual traditions to many other communities in the mountains and beyond.

Further Ritual Supporters of Pura Penulisan

Apart from the thirty villages of the *gebog domas*, there are a number of other communities who offer regular ritual support (*mabanua*) to

Pura Pucak Penulisan and are hence a part of its wider sphere of influence. These allied villages are commonly distinguished from core supporters on the grounds that they do not pay *peturunan*. Although they may attend the festival at Penulisan on a regular basis, they are classed as visitors. At that time they will deliver collective offerings as villages (*atos desa*) and may pay substantial amounts of cash in the form of temple donations. Although these donations are voluntary, they often match or surpass the amount of *peturunan* paid by "core supporters." How these villages are positioned within the *banua* as a whole is a matter of some complexity.

The outward expression, intensity, and explanations for these relationships vary considerably from case to case. For example, the ritual involvement of the villages Margatengah, Belog, and Sidan is minimal. The rationalization of the connections is broadly historical but not very specific, and the villages provide no essential and specified contributions.[26] By contrast, the involvement of irrigation societies (*subak*) from around Payangan and Bangli is extensive, and the offerings brought serve a specific purpose in relation to the fertility of their rice fields, although they are not seen as essential from the perspective of Penulisan's own ritual requirements. And yet, there is another category of villages—not counted among the *gebog domas*—that do bring offering ingredients that are required by the deity at Penulisan and are essential for the success of the festival. These offerings are known as "*cucukan*." Ritual associations with irrigation societies or with villages who provide *cucukan* offerings are common types of relationships and warrant further discussion.

Excellent studies by Stephen Lansing (1987) and I Gede Pitana (1993) have illustrated the general rationale and ritual expression of *subak* affiliations in Bali. *Subak* networks are based on a notion of retracing the flow of life-giving irrigation water back to its mountain source. This upstream passage is traced in several steps, marked by irrigation shrines or temples of increasing rank. However, the relationships between Penulisan and its affiliated *subak* appear to be somewhat different. They are phrased in an idiom similar to *banua* relationships.

The recognition of Pucak Penulisan as the source of the irrigation water used by its *subak* affiliates ought to be in itself a sufficient justification for their attendance. It is remarkable that there are additional relationship narratives and practices that link not only these particular *subak* but the entire villages from which these *subak* originate to Pura Penulisan or to the Pura Bale Agung of Sukawana. An example are the origin narratives and *barong* journeys described earlier. Village-level ritual ties of this kind are a paradigmatic form of relatedness among members of a *banua*. Nevertheless, none of the contributions delivered by *subak* affiliates are regarded as essential to the success of the general ritual process at Pura Pucak Penulisan. The visiting *subak* and their associated *desa adat* are thought to attend for their own purposes and benefit, rather than adopting the role of a ritual supporter.

A more explicitly supportive role (*mabanua*) is adopted by the villages of Tejakula and Les. This alliance relationship is substantiated by a narrative that tells how the deity of Pura Pucak Penulisan symbolically sold irrigation water to the ancestors of the two villages (see Chapter 6) and is accentuated by the periodic delivery of extraordinary offerings in the form of water buffaloes. These offerings are prescribed, and if no buffalo is brought by the two allies, it must be bought by the *gebog domas* members instead.[27]

In the case of Tejakula, the link is believed to be even more specific and intimate. According to legend, the village was part of a larger Desa Sukawana at some time in the not too distant past. This original village, spanning from Mt. Penulisan all the way down to the coast, is said to have had a council of elders (*ulu apad*) consisting of forty-five members (*keraman setimaan*) at that time.[28] The considerable distance villagers from the coast had to travel in order to attend fortnightly council meetings eventually led to a mutually agreeable fission. Twenty-three *keraman* remained in Sukawana and twenty-two built a new Pura Bale Agung in Desa Hiliran ("downstream"), now known as Tejakula. There they built a new temple modeled after the original Pura Bale Agung in Sukawana. Until today the *keraman setimaan* reunite temporarily during the annual festival at Pura Utus on the third full moon (from *putus*, "to break [of string]" or "to decide"). The temple is located on Sukawana territory, near the present boundary between the two villages, and is believed to have been the site where the amicable separation was formally ratified. Tejakula not only attends here but pays half of the *peturunan* for the festival.

Sukawana also intermittently visits a sea temple (*pura segara*) in Tejakula for certain rites of purification (*malaspas ring segara*), last occurring in 1994. Visitors from both Tejakula and Les in turn attend the festival (*usaba gede*) in the Pura Bale Agung of Sukawana.[29] One of their specific duties is to provide several varieties of saltwater fish used in offerings here and at Pura Penulisan. Tejakula is also responsible for repairs to the main gate (*cang apit*) of Pura Bale Agung Sukawana.

Extraordinary and essential offerings feature in another cluster of alliances, involving the coastal villages of Sembiran, Pacung, and Julah. The three villages share a common history. The *prasasti* of Sembiran are actually addressed to the "*keraman* of Julah," which suggests that the people of Sembiran at some time migrated from Julah to their present village, one kilometer uphill from the coast. The inscriptions suggest that they probably were fleeing from attacks by pirates. The specific offerings provided for the festival at Penulisan by these villages include mixed seeds of five colors (*bijaratus*), raw cotton (*kapas*), skeins of undyed cotton thread (*benang tukelan*), and bales of yellow and white cloth. All of these items are *cucukan*, "unique, essential, and indispensable contributions" to a ritual procedure.[30] The traditional robes specific to Sukawana's head elders and priest-leaders (Jero Kubayan or Jero Bau) are also specifically commissioned to weavers in Julah or Sembiran. These clothing items include black and white patterned sarongs (*kamben kotak geles*) and white waist cloths (*saput putih*).[31]

It is possible that these coastal towns were the source of imported textiles in previous times, or perhaps they maintained a small local textile industry as they do today. The cotton plantations that currently exist in that area are said to date back only to the Japanese occupation, so the cotton used by this local industry may earlier have been imported from the Kintamani area.[32] The choice of cotton and textiles as the specific contributions of these villages is sometimes also interpreted as a symbolic expression of their location at the "boundary" of Penulisan's domain and of the island of Bali, as by analogy textiles protect the periphery of the human body.

An example of an even more specialized and contextually limited contribution relates to the villages Madenan, Les, and Payangan. It is at one of these locations that the people of Sukawana obtain sacred coconuts required for an oracle at the annual festival at Penulisan (below). The coconuts must come from a tree growing inside a temple, and these three villages are the only known sites where such a tree can be found. Payangan and Les are connected to the domain in a number of other ways, but it is remarkable that Desa Madenan does not *mabanua* at Pura Pucak Penulisan at present.[33] Its current contribution of a ritual ingredient is not ritual but technical in essence, in that it no longer implies any alliance (*mabanua, masekaa*) between the two communities.

Perhaps the most distant ally of Pura Pucak Penulisan is the village of Pecatu. Desa Pecatu is situated on the Bukit peninsula at the southern tip of Bali. On its territory lies Pura Uluwatu, one of the island's most important seaside temples. As one would expect of such a distant connection, there is a narrative that explains why the people of Pecatu *mabanua* at Penulisan.

One night Jero Kubayan Nada of Sukawana passed by Pura Dalem Sengkuug, located on the ridge beneath Bukit Penarajon in Kuta Dalem. Suddenly he heard the cries of a child. He investigated and found a male infant inside the temple. Immediately he concluded that this child was of royal or divine origin, and decided to adopt him. When the boy had grown into a young man, it happened that a contest was held at the court of the king of Badung, Raja Pamecutan. A fight was to decide who would become the king's personal guard. For this reason, Kubayan Nada gave a magical kris to his protégé, who was keen to join the competition, and with the help of this weapon he soon defeated all others. Thereafter he lived with the king and eventually became his trusted protector and vassal (*patih*). For his services he was granted a large plot of land on the Bukit peninsula, where he founded Desa Pecatu. During the *puputan*, or "last stand," of Raja Badung against the invading Dutch army, this founder of Pecatu (or one of his descendants) was killed while protecting his king. The Dutch seized the kris and kept it safe in a prison [Kerta Gosa] in Bangli. From there the village headman of Bantang retrieved it by theft and kept it. He finally returned the weapon to Sukawana, because it was causing sickness in his own family [i.e., he was not the rightful owner]. Some time later a delegation from Pecatu arrived and asked to be allowed to keep the kris, arguing that the gift offered to their ancestor should not be taken back and complaining that misfortunes had befallen their village since the heirloom had been absent.[34] This request was accepted by the elders of Sukawana. However, it was also agreed that the weapon should be returned each year to be used in the sacrifice of the buffalo at Pura Penulisan.[35]

Until today, Desa Pecatu bring their gods to Pura Pucak Penulisan at the annual festival and formally surrender the magical kris in their keeping to a priest-leader of Sukawana, who then uses it (symbolically) to slay the sacrificial buffalo. It is also their task to purchase the buffalo itself on behalf of the *banua*, complete with its "dress" and associated offerings.[36] The members of Warga Tambiak, the direct descendants of the foundling and founder of Pecatu, now maintain a branch temple named Pura Penarajon in Denpasar, but they still come to pray at the descent group temple of Sanggah Kubayan Nada in Sukawana and come "to fetch their purified ancestors" (*mendak hyang*) from Pura Dalem Sengkuug at the conclusion of postmortuary rituals. The relationship between Sukawana and Pecatu is thus historically specific and characterized by Pecatu's substantial and unique contribution to the ritual process at Pura Penulisan. Nonetheless, this link of adoption has no direct bearing on the raison d'être of this temple and its *banua* as a whole.

The degree of involvement not only varies among different allies, but also for the same allies at different times. A case in point is Desa Songan, a village that has long had a number of mythological and historical ties to Pura Penulisan but that has not attended its festival for at least several decades, if it ever did.[37] However, in March 1994 I witnessed how a delegation from Songan unexpectedly arrived during a ritual at Pura Bale Agung Sukawana. They brought the typical offerings used to request the services of a priest (*bakti pangulem*), in this case the *kubayan* of Sukawana, since they wanted him to dedicate the offerings they had brought for Ratu Pucak Penulisan. The delegation was questioned by local elders as to the purpose of their visit to the temple. The subsequent discussion revealed both the occasion that had triggered the visit and underlying motivations. The visitors reported that without any apparent cause there recently had been several fires in Songan. Sometime thereafter, the *kubayan* of Songan had fallen into a state of trance and revealed that this misfortune had been caused by the failure to participate in the festival at Pura Pucak Penulisan. The offerings in 1994 were aimed to make amends temporarily. The topic of discussion then shifted to the recent rivalry between Songan and Batur over which temple was the authentic temple of the lake goddess, or Pura Ulun Danu. The leaders of Sukawana expressed their support for Songan in this matter. Pleased to hear this, the delegation inquired as to the possibility of joining the *banua* of Pucak Penulisan on a regular basis, beginning from the following annual festival. The locals responded with caution and suggested that a formal meeting would be required to decide this matter. After the visitors had departed, they expressed some reservations, fearing that ambitious elements in Songan could cause quarrels in their *banua* and wondering where Songan could be fit into the *gebok satak* system. Yet it was clear that the people of Songan would not be refused access to Penulisan. The outcome of this matter is still pending, but the case demonstrates how an allegiance may be revived after a long period of dormancy (actual or fictional).

In terms of financial support, about one-third of Pura Pucak Penulisan's income is derived from private donations (*dana punya*). About half of the donors are members of the *gebog domas* and other allied communities. Many other donations originate from residents of villages that have no overall link to Penulisan. Since the names of donors and the amounts of the donations are made public, local individuals or families can expect to gain some prestige by showing their generosity. The same applies to distant donors who are well known in all of Bali, foremost the households of the former aristocracy and political leaders such as the *camat* (district head) of Kintamani, the *bupati* (regency head) of Bangli, and the *gubernur* (head of the province) of Bali. However, a number of private donors are neither locally nor generally well known and have little prestige to gain from a donation. These donors are most often motivated by spiritual considerations, in the attempt to improve their personal fortune and well-being. The fulfillment of a promise, the lifting of a curse, and the lodgment of a request to the deity at Pura Penulisan are all occasions that may trigger donations of this kind. Such cash donations—small or large —are always accompanied by offerings.

A rather different group of generous donors are the ethnic Chinese population of the Kintamani district. Pura Pucak Penulisan and Pura Batur both feature statues or shrines that are considered "Buddhist" and are thus venerated by the Chinese in their own fashion. Their participation may be marginal but is well accepted. According to local legends, Chinese immigrants have been present in the district of Kintamani almost from the beginning of history. Some of the most established Chinese families maintain their own origin narratives, which describe their role in the establishment of temples and villages and in the political history of the area. One popular narrative focuses on the marriage between the king of Bali at Penulisan and a Chinese princess, who later resided at Puri Balingkang.[38]

In recent years there have also been a series of visits, at Penulisan and Balingkang, by descent groups who seek their genealogical origin (*kawitan*). These groups overtly express their wish to associate themselves with the old Balinese dynasties rather than claiming descent from Majapait. Instead of building a *pura kawargaan* (the main temple of a named clan [*warga*]) at Pura Besakih, as is the usual procedure for Majapait descendants, they wish to establish a shrine at Penulisan. The temple leadership has been hesitant, unsure whether to allow the temple to acquire such a novel function. Finally, in 1995, a first *pura kawitan* or *kawargaan* was built at Penulisan by Warga Pasek Bendesa of Sukawana and their relatives in a number of other villages. These trends are ongoing, and it is likely that other *pura kawargaan* will be added in the future.

These additional ties show Pura Pucak Penulisan's significance in relation to a wider domain and more generally as a major temple in Bali. The numerous relationships that form the foundation of its character as the origin temple of a domain are not only phrased in narratives of origin, but are made visible in the complex ritual interactions that take place during the annual temple festival. It is to this world of ritual processes that the following chapter is dedicated.

Chapter 4

THE RITUAL PROCESS
OF A DOMAIN

By far the most graphic and impressive display of Pura Pucak Penulisan's role as the regional ritual center of a domain is the celebration of up to eleven days that marks its annual festival. This festival is the most complex synchronized activity involving the entire *gebog domas* and wider membership of the domain. It is a ritual performance in celebration of the domain's sacred unity. It is also a stage for the enactment of internal distinctions of status in orientation to a common origin.

The symbolism and procedures of ritual in Bali Aga villages and ancestral origin houses warrant an entire volume of their own (Reuter, in press). The following comments form a preliminary introduction to ritual practices at a *banua* level, but seen in isolation, these rituals cannot be fully comprehended. The complex ceremonies at Pura Penulisan combine symbolic and procedural elements from a host of simpler ritual practices performed at a village or descent group level. Particularly significant are the rites marking stages in the life cycle of individuals. Among life-cycle rituals the ones most relevant to this ceremony—focused, as it is, on the death and resurrection of an animal victim—are childhood, mortuary, and postmortuary rituals. The latter are the most elaborate of all person-oriented rituals and can be described as paradigmatic of highland ancestor religion writ large.

Older informants stated that annual gatherings of the entire *banua* have only been held in the last few decades. Formerly the annual festival was conducted without a buffalo sacrifice and by Sukawana alone. This smaller festival was referred to as *karya muduh*, "the cooling ritual." The full congregation used to attend only the ten-yearly *karya catur muka* (the four-faced ritual), when four buffalo are sacrificed and when the sacred relics are "taken out" (*ngodalin*) of their shrine in the Pura Bale Agung and brought to Penulisan. This last happened in 1992. The explanation offered for recently increased ritual activity was that modern modes of transportation have greatly reduced the strains of such large ceremonial undertakings.

I had the opportunity to witness this festival twice, in October 1993 and 1994. This allowed me to make distinctions between rites considered obligatory performances and others more contingent to particular circumstances. One contingency is that, each year, some members will not attend because their village is "ritually polluted" (sebel) by the recent occurrence of a death or the birth of twins.[1] The visits of barong are also somewhat irregular, depending on the week in the wuku calendar into which the fourth full moon happens to fall.[2] More important still, there are many smaller, idiosyncratic ritual activities that are of a personal or contingent nature.

Still, the basic ritual process of the festival follows a fairly regular pattern each year. Indeed, rituals are held at the same localities and with such temporal regularity in Bali that one could be excused for misinterpreting them as repetitive, self-encapsulated processes. But although rituals may be temporally and spatially bounded events, they are also embedded in the lived experience of those who carry them out. This implies that the festival at Pura Pucak Penulisan is a routine for some people, in some years, but that it can also become imbued with personal meaning by transient and sometimes highly emotional issues. Those recovered from a life-threatening illness by the grace of the deity may show their heartfelt gratitude by offering a special sacrifice. Others struck by a bereavement or other fateful event may stay away. This is more than a matter of being categorized as sebel. A bereaved person's emotional state simply prevents that individual from appreciating the festival's mood of joyous celebration.

The following description of events is based on the festival held in 1994, except for some minor supplements as specified.[3] In view of the embeddedness of ritual events in everyday life, this rather schematic representation must not be taken for a full account of what the festival can mean to particular individuals or groups at different times.

The Great Annual Festival at Pura Pucak Penulisan

On 25 September 1994 some fifty elders from different villages, all members of the temple committee of Pura Pucak Penulisan, met in order to decide on a schedule for that year's festival and to discuss finances. The chairperson and Klian Adat of Sukawana, I Made Kaler, presented an annual report on income and expenses. The largest single expense had been the construction of the large new performance hall (wantilan) at Penulisan, where this meeting of elders took place. Further building and repair projects were proposed and approved. Because of existing savings in the temple's bank account (B.I. *kas pura*), the amount of *peturunan* for the following year was set at a very low 1,000 rupiah per household. A purification ceremony for the new buildings was scheduled before the festival.

A plan was devised in order to coordinate work parties of men and women from several member villages and determine their specific tasks in the preparation and performance of the ritual. A list of required basic materials was presented, including large amounts of bamboo, fresh and dry palm leaves, areca nuts, betel leaves, *penjor* (bamboo banners used as decorations during festivals), bamboo rope, flowers, and other ritual ingredients. Village representatives quickly volunteered to provide particular materials, depending on their availability in the respective community.

Several elders reported events relating to the *banua* or the festival. For example, the Jero Pasek of Selulung reported a trance occurrence in a village temple. The deity Ratu Daa Tua had spoken through the medium and requested that a specific offering (*suci petak*) be dedicated to her shrine on each day of the festival. This request was accepted on the condition that Selulung would provide the offerings.

The discussion was led by the chairperson, who, in turn, asked for approval from the head elders of Sukawana on any issues relating to tradition and ritual. Usually approval was given by a mere nod from the highest authority in these matters, the Kubayan Mucuk Sukawana (head elder of the right side). It was made obvious that the spokesperson had already consulted with him and the other elders of Sukawana on a number of issues before the meeting. The representatives of other villages silently accepted most reports and proposals but requested further information on several issues and pointed out matters that had been overlooked. In general, the elders of Sukawana were treated with deference. For example, they were the first to be served coffee and sweets, and no one would begin drinking or eating before they did. The language level used in mutual address was generally a cordial and moderately polite form of Balinese, with only slightly more refined language used for addressing senior elders from any village. The Balinese dialect spoken in Bali Aga villages generally differs from that used in other parts of Bali (Bawa 1990).[4]

On 13 October 1994, dozens of trucks began to arrive, delivering loads of materials. A composite work party of young men from several villages began to erect *penjor* along the stairways and to decorate the permanent shrines. Some temporary shrines were also erected under the supervision of elders, most notably the sky-shrine called "*sanggaran tawang*" and a number of temporary bamboo offering platforms in front of permanent shrines.[5]

When a person "dedicates labor" to a temple festival (*ngaturan ayah*), it is done not merely as an optional duty but as an act of devotion. To observe who does the ritual work (*ngayah*) is a means of distinguishing those who "own" the responsibility for the ritual from casual visitors.[6] The more polite term for work, "*karya*," is also the most common designation for a ritual celebration, and in this case people simply spoke of the festival as the "*karya pucak*." This terminology suggests that ritual practice is regarded as no more than an elevated form of labor in general. Technical labor, such as agricultural work, in turn, is never entirely devoid of symbolic content. It is thus unjustifiable to draw a sharp categorical distinction between symbolic (ritual) and technical (economic) labor or ritual and secular aspects of life in the mountains.

The following day, some two hundred married women (*kayangan*) arrived from all over the *banua* to join in the "preparation of offerings" (*makayangan*) at Pura Daa. Purchasing offerings or decorations in the marketplace, now common in urban areas, is a practice that alienates the sponsors of a ritual from its process, since half of all ritual activity and experience lies in the act of preparation. In this case, some women begin to prepare smaller components of large offering arrangements at home even before the official *makayangan* sessions, which extend over seven days. The gathering of women is also an important social event, in which participants find an opportunity to strengthen friendships with women from neighboring villages, many of whom they meet regularly at the Kintamani market. The atmosphere was busy, joyous, and informal.

During *makayangan* the women's labor is organized by the "wives of the twenty-three [highest-ranking elders]" (*telulikur istri*) of the village council (*ulu apad*) of Sukawana. These women are truly experts among experts in the preparation of offerings (*banten*), commanding a wealth of knowledge and skillful dexterity accumulated from a lifetime of practical experience and mimetic learning.[7] Some of the most important offerings, such as the *suci turunan* that facilitates the descending of the gods, can only be made by these female elders, and all others will be checked by them after completion.

The six most senior women are the female priest-leaders of Sukawana. They wear a special silver ring (*bungkung suda mala*) that is attributed with the power to purify the offerings. But in cases of uncertainty as to the proper "arrangement of components within a complex offering group" (*matanding*), even they will seek advice, from the wives of retired priest-leaders (Jero Salain Istri) who are no longer physically active participants. The mastery of producing *banten* is thus gradually passed on from one generation of women to the next. Male priest-leaders will only examine the finished product (*bakti*) in its entirety, to see whether all is complete. They will pay particular attention to the offerings they use as priests in the procedure of purifying the *bakti* (*malis, malukat*) and "lifting" or "presenting" it to the gods (*anteban, ngaturin*).

There are three major exceptions to the general predominance of women in offering preparation. One concerns a large tower-shaped arrangement called "*bebangkit*,"[8] which is assembled exclusively by male elders. Another is the *sayut agung*. This offering can be completed only by the six highest-ranking female elders, but a specific ritual song called "Kidung Aji Kembang" must be recited simultaneously by a male elder of specific rank (the Jero Pengelanan).[9] As a general rule, men are responsible mainly for impure, raw offerings dedicated to the female, chthonic deities and for all other offerings where a flow of blood is involved. In this festival, men are responsible for the killing and processing of the sacrificial deer and buffalo. Women prepare the purer offerings made from plant materials and cooked food for male, uranian deities.[10] In this predominantly heaven-orientated (*dewa yadnya*) festival, women's offerings are necessarily more prominent.[11]

One frequently offered explanation for the gender division of ritual labor evokes a comparison between ritual and the reception of guests in a domestic context. It is women who prepare the food by the hearth and men who sit in conversation with the visitors at the opposite end of the house. In ritual, people say, it is the same, only the guests are invisible.

As with any event that takes place in a temple, the *makayangan* is preceded by a brief rite of "informing the gods" (*matur piuning*) about the nature and aim of the activity. In this particular case, the rite comments on the central importance of Sukawana's female elders and their husbands. One pair of *banten tapakan palinggih* is placed into the *bale pecatu* at Pura Kauripan for each individual female elder from Sukawana and another for each group of women from other villages. These offerings serve as preliminary "seats" for the deities, who are believed to follow the women to the temple in order to witness and bless their work, and in anticipation of receiving offerings. As usual, further offerings were placed before the shrines dedicated to Ratu Daa Tua.

In the meantime, two pairs of special messengers from Sukawana had departed on a ritual quest to Payangan. These men are referred to as "*saya bunga*" (from *bunga*, "flower, youth") and are selected anew each year from among a specific rank category of younger members in Sukawana's village council (*sayan siap*). Each man had to gather two mature coconuts from a sacred tree inside Pura Dalem Maling-gih in Payangan.[12] These are known as "*nyuh titikan*" (from *titik* [Kawi], "to look out, observe, spy" or "to guess, seek a sign") and are used in a rite of divination later on. A six-pillar pavilion was built for the *saya bunga* on the western side of Pura Daa, where they performed a night vigil (*makemit*) on the eve of the opening ceremony. At evening the two *saya bunga* belonging to the so-called left or younger (*nyoma-nan*) ceremonial moiety of Sukawana's village council carried the four *nyuh titikan* that are to be used first, while those belonging to the right or elder (*tuaan*) moiety carried four reserves. All were surrounded by a host of (agnatic and affinal) relatives who not only support the men while they sit silent and motionless with folded hands during the night, but also each deliver a *banten palinggih* containing further reserves of (ordinary) coconuts. These nuts are only used if the actual *nyuh titikan* fail to be accepted.[13]

On Thursday, 20 October 1994 (*purnama kapat*), the actual festival began with the descent of all the deities (*bhatara turun kabeh*). This opening ceremony is conducted on the last Tuesday (Anggara), Thursday (Wraspati), Saturday (Saniscara), or Sunday (Redita) before the fourth full moon, unless the full moon falls on one of these days, as was the case this year.[14] The term "opening" is somewhat misleading, since it is actually the climax of a long period spend in elaborate preparation.

From the early morning the road intersection below Pura Pucak Penulisan was congested with countless trucks as the *banua* members started to arrive, all in festive attire. Each group carried its village gods in procession up the levels to Pura Kauripan, placing offerings (*nyasah*) at the shrines along the way, particularly at Pura Penulisan. The processions were accompanied by percussion groups (*sekaa gong*), and the portable seats of the deities were shaded and guarded by young men carrying parasols, ritual spears, and banners.

The first village deities to be seated were the gods from the source villages of the four *gebog satak*, each in their respective section of the *bale pesamuan agung*. The seats of the deities from Sukawana had already been placed early in the morning, and now the ones of Gebog Satak Bantang, Selulung, and Kintamani followed in that order. Once the gathering of deities was completed, however, the seats of the deities from Sukawana were immediately shifted to the central shrine (*bale tajuk, pamaruman*) on which all main offerings were also to be placed and in front of which all communal prayers were conducted. Only a single *banten tapakan palinggih* was left behind to mark Sukawana's section in the *bale pesamuan*.

The gathering of the village deities from the four directions of the domain under a single roof, on the four platforms of the *bale pesamuan*, is a powerful symbolic representation of their unity in diversity. The platforms are all of equal height. Still, the order of precedence among the four *gebog satak* is enacted in the order of seating. Particularly significant is the shifting of the god seats from Sukawana to the more elevated central shrine, which shows their significance both as a part and as representative of the domain as a whole.

Once the gods were accommodated, the numerous percussion groups settled into their respective permanent shelters (*bale gong*). Only the two groups from Sukawana remained inside Pura Kauripan to entertain the deities.[15] A large contingent had meanwhile arrived from Desa Pecatu, delivering a young, male buffalo and the sacred kris to be used to sacrifice the animal.

The first major ritual performance was the Karya Paneduh, a "cooling rite," which began at 8:00 A.M. with the slaughter of a deer (*kidang*) at Pura Daa.[16] The animal is referred to by the honorific title Sri Tutu, just as the sacrificial buffalo is referred to by the title Jero Gede. The bones of the fore and hind legs, the head, and the skin were used for an offering called "*wangun urip sri tutu*," the resurrected deer, the central item of the larger array of offerings for this rite (*bakti mubuh*). Once completed, this *bakti* was ritually cleansed (*nglukat*) before the two shrines at Pura Daa. Many of the female elders from the domain who had helped in preparing the offerings now gathered for this purification rite, with the senior women of Sukawana seated in front. Thereafter the offering collection was taken up to the *bale tajuk* of Pura Kauripan.

The most senior pair of male priest-leaders (*kubayan*) from Sukawana then formally dedicated the offerings to the assembled gods. Addressing the deities collectively, and naming only Ratu Pucak in particular, they enumerated and further purified the offerings with water, smoke, and cooling leaves before an enormous crowd of worshipers from all over the domain.[17] In the dedication of offerings, the priest-leaders from Sukawana had also included water from special springs around the hilltop as well as rice soaked in perfumed water. Once the gods had partaken from this, the sanctified water and rice were distributed to the congregation. The holy water (*tirta*) is sipped three times from the right hand, the rice placed on the forehead and some eaten. This act of communion was the conclusion of the congregation's prayers and was also led by the two local priests.

This session around 11:00 A.M. was the first communal prayer (*mabakti, muspa*) at Pura Kauripan, to be repeated many times during this and the following days of the festival. Only during the first session are the front rows reserved for the elders and priests of the *banua* and other visiting villages. All purified elders and temple priests are invited to participate in the distribution and sprinkling of *tirta* to the congregation. The elders of Sukawana will always receive *tirta* from their own *kubayan*, but otherwise there are no restrictions whatsoever as to who will receive *tirta* from whom. This *tirta* is ideally produced by washing the sacred objects (such as the *prasasti*) belonging to Ratu Pucak (*wangsupada*), but in practice this only occurs at the ten-yearly *karya catur muka*.[18]

The division of ritual labor, and particularly the function of priesthood, distinguishes the elders of Sukawana in this and all other rituals during the festival. However, since from whom a person will or will not receive holy water and rice is a significant cue about relative status in Bali, the working together of priests in their distribution constitutes a very strong statement. It reflects the pervading ethos of equality that marks all nonritual interactions during the festival.

The fourth full moon signals the end of the dry season, when farmers are anxiously awaiting the monsoon rains. The festival of Penulisan, and this first rite in particular, seeks to cool the earth and to invite rain. Locals are adamant that it always rains on at least one day of the festival or that a failure to receive such an omen signals a drought for the coming season. A sacred rock in Pura Taksu (Sukawana) is washed if it fails to rain, a rite that must be performed by the *klian adat* of Sukawana.[19]

All rituals were performed (*nganteb*) and concluded (*muput*) by the two Jero Kubayan of Sukawana or by their representatives, the four Jero Bau. Their prayer incantations are in (sometimes antiquated) Balinese. A pair of priest-leaders is required to conduct any major ritual, since there is a definite division of ritual functions between the priest of the left and right moieties (*kubayan kiwa tengen*). For example, the Kubayan Kiwa cuts the cord of the palm-leaf sprinkler (*lis*) before it is used by the Kubayan Tengen to splash the offerings with purifying water. Most "movements" in ritual are initiated by the priest of the left (female) and concluded by the elder of the right (male), just as activities at Pura Daa (female deity) precede those at Pura Kauripan (male deity).[20]

Immediately after the cooling ceremony and prayer, around 2:00

P.M., the *kubayan* and *bau* of Sukawana gathered in the six-pillar pavilion (*bale saka enem*) of Pura Kauripan for a rite of divination using a coconut oracle (*manitik*). The four *saya bunga* dressed in the finest of antique Balinese cloth but quite exhausted from their long vigil, were escorted from their guard pavilion behind Pura Daa to this pavilion in Pura Kauripan. The Kubayan Kiwa received the sacred coconuts (*nyuh titikan*) from the kneeling messengers and passed them to the Kubayan Tengen (or Kubayan Mucuk, "tip"), who then acknowledged that the *saya* had fulfilled their duty. The Kubayan Kiwa then proceeded to cut the coconuts and examined the white flesh for blemishes, using a bamboo skewer with a cotton wick soaked in coconut oil as a torch for additional lighting. To everyone's relief, no blemishes were discovered in the first four coconuts, indicating that the crops would be safe from pests and climatic disasters for this season.[21] The flesh of the coconuts was then processed by the elders using only traditional rattan grating utensils (*kikian penyalin*), later to be mixed with the minced flesh of the sacrificial buffalo.

Thereafter, individual food portions with the meat of the sacrificial deer were laid out on banana leaves in a double row in the same pavilion, two for each of the thirteen most senior pairs of elders from Sukawana. The elders sat down next to their portions in strict order of rank, with the most senior toward the eastern end of the pavilion. Their special share from the gods' leftovers marks Sukawana's elders as an inner circle of ritual leaders.

In the mid-afternoon of this day, the offering set for the forthcoming procession (*bakti papideh*) was assembled and purified at Pura Daa. The buffalo was led to the assembly area beneath the huge *cemara* tree, surrounded by elders and a crowd of onlookers, all eager to stroke the "Jero Gede." The victim was bathed in ritual fashion, using the same implements and procedure as in the bathing of a child at the age of 210 days during the *otonin* life-cycle ritual. The animal was then dressed, using several layers of textile with black and white checkered "protective" cloth (*poleng*) on top. The head and horns were dressed with a number of specific palm leaf and gold foil adornments (*bakang-bakang*).[22]

The purified victim, the accompanying offerings, and the seats of the gods were finally gathered between Pura Daa and Kauripan for a grand procession (*mapapada* or *mapapideh agung*). By 4:00 P.M. the procession set off, circling thrice around the hilltop of Pura Kauripan in a counterclockwise direction.[23] The long file was led by Gebog Satak Sukawana, followed by Kintamani, Bantang, and Selulung.[24] By this time the crowd had grown to at least ten thousand people, and the simultaneous clanging of dozens of percussion orchestras added to a general atmosphere of intense busy excitement (*rame*), as should accompany any large ritual celebration in Bali.

The procession eventually ascended up the stairs to Pura Kauripan, where the *bakti* and live victim were presented to the deities, who had been seated as before. After several sessions of prayer and receiving *tirta* (not all would fit into the temple in one session), many of the visitors departed for this day, while others remained behind to witness the "cutting" of the Jero Gede at dusk or to guard the temple.

As the sun was setting, the elders and *sekaa ebat*—the men responsible for processing meat during rituals—gathered around the buffalo, who had been "undressed" and tethered to a pole in the central assembly area. The Pemangku Gede of Desa Pecatu surrendered the sacred dagger to the Kubayan Mucuk of Sukawana, who, in turn, handed it to the Kubayan Kiwa. The latter twice stabbed the victim, first with a rolled-up betel leaf (*porosan*) and again with the ancient golden kris. The *sekaa ebat* then took control and actually cut the victim's throat, while carefully collecting the blood.[25] Bystanders were quiet and subdued. This stands in contrast to chthonic blood sacrifices, where the victim is killed more slowly and amidst great commotion, and where blood must spill onto the ground.

The processing of the buffalo carcass into an offering is a matter of great symbolic significance. The victim undergoes a process of symbolic reconstitution or resurrection, known as "*wangun urip*" (lit., "to arise alive"), and so does the entire domain. By means of the victim's death and transformation, the entire *banua* is said to be given new life and affirmed as an ordered whole. Death is the reciprocal gift of a life for the life received from the deity, a compensation for the fertility of the people and the land. This reciprocity of ritual interaction with the sacred is said to enable the continuous flow of life.[26]

A number of specific bones—including the sternum, a portion of the spine with ribs, the pelvis, as well as the skin, the tail, and the head of the victim—become the most important offering arrangement of the festival (called "*ukem*"). Each of these body parts is associated with a particular elder within the rank order of Sukawana's *ulu apad*, the ritual leaders of the domain.[27] This association directly links the social order with an anatomic ritual symbology, though neither may be reducible to the other. The finished *wangun urip* is placed in the center of the *bale tajuk* for the entire duration of the festival.

The amorphous flesh that has been carved from the bones is processed into a fixed number of *sate* sticks later to be arranged on square offering trays (*karangan*), several of which are placed on a temporary *sanggaran tawang*. The lower part of this shrine is structured like a hearth, with a fire and cooking vessel. It is worth noting that the meat from victims of sacrifices to demonic forces (usually cows) is all roasted on skewers over an open fire and must never enter a clay cooking pot. By contrast, a portion of the meat of the male Jero Gede is always boiled in an earthen vessel, a female symbol and a reminder of the immersion of maleness into the female domain of the impending wet season.

Over the next four days people who had not accompanied their village delegations on the first day arrived in small and large groups. Villages from the four *gebog satak* had been scheduled to attend on different days. This measure was an attempt to reduce the number of daily attendants to a manageable size and avoid a shortage of visitors on later days. The first day was allocated to Gebog Satak Sukawana, followed by Kintamani, Bantang, and Selulung. This ordering is variable, except that people from Gebog Satak Sukawana are always granted the first of these four days. Many groups of worshipers did not adhere to the official schedule.

Spectacular dance performances were held daily by *sekaa* (task-oriented groups) from the specific *gebog satak* attending on the day, and many were unique to that area. Despite the regulations on attendance, the audience always included many people from other parts of the *banua*. The dance groups thus found an arena for displaying their unique skills before the wider audience of the domain.

Rejang Daa dances are performed by unmarried girls and the Baris Teruna by unmarried boys. In all of the war dances (*baris*, "row") that are characteristic of Bali Aga performing art, such as the Baris Omang, Baris Perisi, Baris Gede, Baris Goak, Baris Jojor, Baris Ker, and Baris Dadap, the performers are adult men.[28] The nomenclature of these dances relates predominantly to the kind of weapon carried by the performers. The movements, costumes, and music vary. The Baris Dadap of Sukawana is the only dance accompanied by song (a piece called *panji marga*, "the path of the warrior"), and the Baris Goak of Selulung involves the dramatic enactment of a myth. All of these ritual dances are performed as an act of worship and are meant to provide entertainment for the gods.

Dozens of vendors had set up stalls around the great hall (*wantilan*), trading mainly in food, drinks, toys, and ornaments. The atmosphere was indeed that of a folk festival, and attendance was not entirely a matter of pious devotion. For most visitors there were many familiar faces in the crowd, and many used the opportunity to maintain and extend their social networks. Many also stayed overnight to

enjoy the more popular drama and dance performances that com-
menced in the late evenings and sometimes lasted until dawn. Though
these were performed by commercial performers, all were offering
their services free of charge or were sponsored by a donor.

On the sixth day, worshipers from the entire *gebog domas* were invited, specifically those who had been unable to visit earlier with their
respective *gebog satak*. Except for the main offerings listed above, all
smaller and perishable offerings were replaced each morning, and
the edible remains were divided each evening among representatives
from the *gebog domas* villages that had attended during the day. This
was an acknowledgment of their status as hosts rather than guests.

Visitors brought small offerings for the main shrines, participated
in a prayer session, received *tirta,* and then enjoyed the daily dance
performances at the *wantilan* during the afternoon. Many priests and
elders from member villages were involved in distributing *tirta,* an
exhausting task given that each time the crowded Pura Kauripan was
cleared by one assembly of worshipers, it would be refilled with new
arrivals within minutes. Worshipers who came as individual families
had first prayed in their house shrine (*pekaja*); larger groups also
prayed in their extended family temple (*sanggah*) or even in the Pura
Desa. These observances on the way are a reminder of the different
circles of their socioritual identity, wherein the *banua* is the widest and
most remote. The overall number of visitors during the festival was
in excess of fifty thousand people.

On the sixth and seventh day of the festival, there were also a
number of irregular visitors. One day a large delegation arrived from
Desa Buahan, bringing *atos desa* even though they do not normally
mabanua at Penulisan. In discussion with local elders, they revealed
their intention to restore a relationship that apparently had lapsed
for so long that none of them remembered it having been honored
during their lifetime. Shortly afterwards, a party arrived from Desa
Susut (Bangli) with their *barong* dancing up the stairs to Pura Kauripan and asking for a revival of its life force (*nunas pangurip*). Smaller
groups attended from all over Bali, as far away as Bugbug (a Bali Aga
community in Karangasem), Subak Pengemeng (Klungkung), Pecatu
(Badung), and Bengkala (Buleleng). To many individual visitors, Pura
Pucak Penulisan is simply one of Bali's most sacred temples, even
though government Hindu organizations largely ignore Penulisan
and do not mention its festival in the regular television announce-
ments of forthcoming religious events.

The seventh day had been reserved specifically for visiting *subak*
delegations (many had in fact arrived earlier). The main difference

between *subak* and *desa adat* delegations lay in the type of offerings they brought. *Subak* offerings (*suwinih*) mainly consist of dry rice and Chinese coins (*pis bolong*). Containers with *tirta* are taken home to be used in the local rituals of their rice fields. Not all *subak* attached to Pura Penulisan attended, since many preferred to wait for the holy water (*tirta wangsupada*) that would be prepared during the *usaba gede* festival at Pura Bale Agung Sukawana the following full moon.[29]

The final day of the festival, 27 October 1994, was a second climax in terms of ritual activity. This ritual revolved around the burial of the buffalo and the "putting away" (*nyimpen, nyineb*) of the gods and their symbolic representations.

The day began by offering a *bakti neduk* (from *teduh,* "cool"), an advance atonement for having to "open the earth" for the burial of the buffalo and for the planting of crops in the coming season. In this rite, attendance was compulsory for all men who were going to participate in the actual digging of the grave. The excavation took place inside Pura Kauripan, behind the *bale tajuk*. It was begun symbolically by the Kubayan Kiwa and the Kubayan Tengen of Sukawana followed by other elders in order of rank, before younger men took over. The remains of the buffalo (*ukem*) and other key offerings were lowered into the grave by the Singgukan Kiwa (fourth-ranking elder,[30] also responsible for the *wangun urip* process), along with four sprouting coconuts at the corners, symbolizing the growth of new life, the four *gebog satak,* and the four corners of the cosmos.

Many small, square palm-leaf boxes (*keben-kebenan*) containing a mixture of seeds were placed into the grave, one from each household in Sukawana. Like the male buffalo, the symbolically male seeds were said to be buried in the female earth so that they would bring forth new life and fertility throughout the domain. It is important to add that the bones of the sacrificial buffalo used at the festival of the Pura Bale Agung Sukawana on the following full moon were hung in a bundle from a rafter of the *pamaruman*. This arrangement was referred to as "*kebo bunga,*" that is, the "flower of the buffalo" (which had been buried or "planted" at Pura Kauripan a month earlier). It directly identifies the buffalo as a representation of the seed crops that are buried in the earth so that they may flower and bear new fruit.

The grave was lined with a plaited mat and white cloth as in a human burial, and the entire procedure was accompanied by traditional funeral hymns. Bystanders threw coins and small notes into the grave. Some were moved to tears, perhaps reminded by the songs of the funerals of close relatives or simply sad to see the end of this great festival. Each person threw a handful of soil into the grave with the left hand, as is customary, and then the hole was covered. The entire process was strongly reminiscent also of the postmortuary ritual referred to as "*nangun*," a term that in itself suggests parallels to the process of *wangun urip*. In this ritual the deceased are "awoken" from their graves. Each person is represented by an effigy (*ukur*) whose design emphasizes some of the same structural elements of the body as are chosen for the composition of a *wangun urip*.

Above the closed grave of the buffalo, the earth was heaped into a mound, symbolizing the "mountain of life" (Gunung Kauripan). Four parasols were planted around it in the cardinal directions to represent the four *gebog satak* whose members had gathered at this hilltop. Finally, a group of burial offerings (*bakti pamendeman*) was dedicated, facing toward the sunrise as usual. The *tirta* from this rite was poured over the burial mound, a gesture in hope of plentiful rains during the months to come.[31]

The final rite was the *ngluarang*, which means to disperse or scatter. The Kubayan Mucuk Sukawana seized the *penjor bunga*, a small bamboo tree with heavily decorated branches that had stood in the inner courtyard of Pura Kauripan throughout the duration of the festival. Carrying this symbol of the path that is traveled by the gods on their journey between heaven and earth, he led a procession to the hilltop toward the west of Pura Daa, where all had begun. Others carried a seat for the gods, along with ritual banners (*umbul, kober*) and spears (*tombak*). In a brief prayer facing the northern shore of Bali the priest-leaders asked forgiveness for any omissions in ritual procedure and bade farewell to the deities. The *penjor bunga* was tossed down the hillside toward the coast, and participants quickly dispersed.

Several days of cockfighting at the *wantilan* followed. Cockfighting is a traditional means of fundraising in that a proportion of all center bets are paid into the temple accounts. The performance of this bloody spectacle can also be interpreted in a ritual sense, as a blood sacrifice.

A large work party had also spent days sweeping the temple grounds and removing all decorations. After the *ngluarang* rite, village leaders had gathered to divide the huge piles of leftover coconuts and rice between all villages of the *gebog domas*. These shares by no means sufficed to compensate the members for the expenses incurred in the performance of this festival. I estimate that the festival's total cost to the core members of the *banua* exceeded thirty million rupiah (then about U.S. $17,000), not to mention the many weeks spent by work parties in unpaid labor during the preparation period and the personal offerings and donations contributed by individual households.

Ritual Interaction and the Struggle for Prominence

The image of Pura Pucak Penulisan, its domain, and its ritual order that has been conveyed by the preceding discussion is of a complex web of social relations and ritual interactions involving tens of thousands of participants. From a local point of view, it is in part the very complexity and magnitude of its web of ritual relatedness that lends Pura Penulisan the character of a major ritual center. Penulisan is the icon of a cultural ideal of intense sociality, just as it is a sacred origin point where the spiritual unity of local society is enshrined. At this point it may be fruitful to reiterate the question of what motivates so many people to participate in this and other *banua*.

That the Balinese partake in a wide array of ritual relationships cannot be reduced entirely to a quest for power or even prestige. While their social relations may be articulated in a formal ritual context, their motives do not necessarily differ all that much from a more familiar desire for an extensive network of friends and acquaintances. Being part of a larger social whole enriches the life and experience of a person. Participants of *banua* festivals have frequently stressed that a great ritual gathering of people and deities simply adds a moment of grandeur to their lives. Though an outsider perhaps cannot fathom the depth of this emotion, my own repeated experiences of festivals at Pura Penulisan and at other regional temples have provided a glimpse of what they may mean to local people.[32]

An elder from Batukaang once commented that there has to be more to life than working in one's gardens, raising a family, and ensuring economical survival, no matter how important these concerns may be. He explained that for those who follow in procession to the roof of the world, to the sound of dozens of percussion groups, banners whirling in the wind and all in festive attire, the troubles of daily life are forgotten for a moment, left behind with the soiled garments of the working routine. He also pointed to the dances performed on almost each day of the festival as a useful metaphor for the experience of moving gracefully together as a collectivity. Though participation is in one sense a shared experience, it does not presume homogeneity. In fact, this informant and many others stressed that the joy of it all comes from having succeeded against all odds to act in unison with many explicitly different others.

The desire to be embedded in a secure social network is perhaps intrinsically human and an end in itself. But the form of their association with particular others also defines the social identity of individuals and groups, and thus provides an index of their social status.

While participation in a web of social associations, as a form of communicative practice, may be a universal value in itself, it could be suggested that one particular person's positioning within a web of social relations is experienced as particularly valuable in a strategic sense only if it is a position of prominence relative to others.

Within the ritual domain of Pura Penulisan, the village of Sukawana and the origin villages of the other *gebog satak* clearly occupy a more prominent position than other villages. In part their prominence may be tolerated by others because of their desire to participate in a larger whole and to experience a ritual moment of socioreligious transcendence. In part they may also be persuaded to keep participating by a general ethos of equality among Bali Aga people. Indeed, in the absence of more compelling reasons, their less privileged participation will only be guaranteed as long as the status differentiation that does exist within the domain remains moderate. Status competition may be possible within *banua*, but it is hardly constitutive of their nature. It is for this reason that I would describe the status of Sukawana, for example, as prominent rather than encompassing, as it would be if ritual domains were hierarchies rather than social orders of precedence.

The dependence of prominent *banua* members on more or less voluntary expressions of deference from others is a powerful leveling factor for status ambitions, particularly in the absence of any underlying economical or political form of domination. Sukawana may be a wealthy village and thus have the disposable wealth required for costly displays of ritual prestige, but its leaders have no authority over the economic resources, political decision-making processes, and ritual life of other villages outside the context of the festival. This situation exemplifies what one might describe as a state of free social association.

There are none here with the resources to either buy or force others into offering their deference and ritual support, which merely simplifies matters, given that economic capital (wealth) and political capital (force) cannot be converted into symbolic capital (status) or, at least, not in an explicit manner. If the approval of others is bought or forced, it loses its intrinsic meaning, at least within the value system of traditional Balinese society.[33] The currently prominent villages in the *banua* have nothing to conceal in this respect; that is, they have little opportunity for hidden attempts to purchase or force the respect of others. This analysis leads to the question how even a moderately privileged status can be secured in the first place and, sometimes, as in the case of Sukawana, retained over a long period of time.[34]

The relatively free form of association at present may not be a historical constant that has always characterized *banua* organization. In the past the relationships between the founders of a domain and their clients, both in branch villages and immigrant-founded settlements, may not have been simply a matter of status, of ritual precedence in relation to a common origin temple, but may have entailed an element of economic and political domination. The "ownership" of the land, the primary economic resource, initially rested with the source village, and it is they who also dictated the standards of appropriate social behavior (*adat*) and ritual practice (*yadnya*) within the domain. This control over material resources has lapsed. Under contemporary conditions it would be ludicrous, for example, if the leaders of Selulung were to command the village of Batukaang to surrender the land that they once granted to their ancestors or if they were to try evicting individual landowners. And yet, it seems that this potential threat was still real enough, even until the time of Dutch colonial rule, to warrant Batukaang's shift of allegiance to another *gebog satak*. Thus, current status privileges may reflect an initially unequal distribution of wealth and power in the past.

The remaining question is how the logic of distributing symbolic capital developed once the present situation of mutual economic and political independence was established. One principle that needs to be recognized in this context is that the status value of a bilateral alliance relationship depends on the initial status of the two parties. It is "uplifting" to associate with those who hold an exalted position even if the interactions are not egalitarian, while it would be "downgrading" to associate with inferiors in the same way. In this paradoxical situation, one person's gain is another's loss. The prominent will therefore aim to maintain as many associations as possible as long as their superiority is made explicit within the form of the interaction. Nevertheless, they are under pressure to minimize the display of asymmetry or relegate it to a specific ritual context, so as not to discourage the association altogether. For this reason it is common for the leadership of Sukawana, for example, verbally to downplay their special status in public meetings of the temple committee and adopt a discourse of egalitarianism, while preserving their ritual privileges all the same.

Another effect of an initial-status-difference on a pattern of social associations is that it provides a certain stability to a given pattern of status distribution, even after the material and political conditions that may have supported the establishment of the initial status difference no longer exist. Symbolic capital is not unlike economic wealth, in that it is those who are rich in symbolic capital who have the greatest opportunities for accumulating more of the same. Their very prominence singles them out as the most desirable alliance partners. As a Balinese proverb describes it, "Many people will gather in the shade of a large tree," such as the huge *waringin* trees located at the center of many a Balinese village. The position of a privileged group will thus remain secure as long as they are able to maintain a balance between sharing and retaining their status, admitting similarity and yet denying sameness. This may seem like a formidable task to an outsider. However, the Balinese are socialized from an early age toward achieving mastery of complex social skills for managing status. Even a small child must learn to judge the status of another in order to be able to address that person in terms appropriate to his or her station. The first principle learned by a Bali Aga child is to distinguish persons by age, just as precedence is the first principle of status distribution in a domain.

The question of status is not confined to the negotiation of internal relations within a *banua*, such as the domain of Pura Pucak Penulisan, but also recurs in a wider context. The *banua* as a whole to some degree represents a status group in relation to other *banua*. Relationships between different *banua* are possible and common, and raise similar concerns about relative status and about a wider quest for regional ritual dominance. The domains of Pura Balingkang, Indrakila, and Batur, for example, are locally claimed to be subsidiary institutions to Pura Pucak Penulisan. These three networks will be investigated as a first step away from Pura Penulisan and its particular domain toward a wider field of cooperative and competitive relations among Bali Aga communities.

Chapter 5

BENEATH AND BEYOND PENULISAN
Three Related Domains

Even though the *banua* of the ancient temple of Penulisan is exemplary, outstanding in terms of both its size and its regional significance, it is only through a wider comparison among several different domains that the general conceptual and organizational features of *banua* can be established. With this chapter I begin a comparative exploration of several ritual domains beyond Penulisan, starting with its immediate neighbors. The study of other domains reveals that their participants are concerned not merely with relations within their own *banua*, but with a larger web of social and ritual relationships spanning the highlands of Bali and beyond. Although each regional temple is regarded as *the* center of its domain, it is really only one center of one domain among others of a similar kind. The following two chapters, therefore, are concerned not only with the relationship concepts, narratives, and practices that characterize the specific social relations within different domains, but with the cooperative and competitive relationships between *banua*. I will commence with a description of three independent ritual networks that are nonetheless intimately connected to Pura Penulisan. These domains are the *kanca satak* of Pura Dalem Balingkang in Desa Pinggan, the *gebog satak* of Pura Pucak Indrakila in Desa Dausa, and the *pasihan* of Pura Ulun Danu in Desa Batur. The analytical transition from the *banua*-internal structure of Penulisan to the ritual and political interactions between separate domains is by no means sudden or indicative of two radically different levels of relatedness.

The case study of Pura Pucak Penulisan and its *banua* has revealed that ritual activities among member villages are not all directed toward the paramount temple at Penulisan or controlled by the ritual leadership in Desa Sukawana. Many other alliances are simply bilateral ritual ties between member communities or are focused on subsidiary *banua* temples or minor origin villages and their ritual leaders. This flexibility may discourage the least privileged villages from deciding to disassociate themselves from the encompassing domain. Such a move would be resisted by groups with a vested interest both at the *banua* and the sub-*banua* level. When a fission does occur in a domain, it is more likely to take the form of a withdrawal of support by an entire subdomain, or *gebog satak*. While the ritual leaders of the encompassing domain may try to curb the ambitions of leaders at subsidiary centers, the coercive means available to them are limited. If their efforts to retain control prove futile, the withdrawal of support will lead to the establishment of a separate domain. Thereafter, the *banua* temple of the older domain still represents the paramount point of origin for the branch domains, but the scope of actual ritual interactions is greatly reduced and transformed. Sometimes the leadership of an older domain may continue to exert some influence over newer domains with nominal independence.

The following case studies present three temples and their *banua,* which are claimed to have been part of the domain of Pura Penulisan at some time in the past but have since become separate. I will describe how the Sukawana-based leadership at Penulisan gradually lost most of its control over these domains, while managing to retain a limited degree of ritual authority and a status of precedence for Pura Pucak Penulisan as a ritual "center among centers."

The Domain of Pura Balingkang

Mt. Penulisan forms the northwestern part of a large circular chain of mountains around the crater of Mt. Batur. Within this circle, below and to the east of Penulisan, lies a large flat shelf, several hundred meters above Lake Batur. A creek that has its origins on the slope of Mt. Penulisan has furrowed a deep gorge into this plateau. On a small hilltop secured by a fork of this gorge on both sides lies a temple that captures the imagination of many Balinese. Pura (also Puri or Jero) Dalem Balingkang (see Map 3) is associated with the dawn of Balinese civilization, a time before Majapait when mythical kings ruled the island. Many references to Dalem Balingkang (the king of Balingkang) are found in *lontar* texts such as the Usana Bali, Babad Bedaulu, Buana Mabah, and others.[1]

Usually the only historical information provided by these texts is that the powerful and virtuous Balinese king who resided at Balingkang, variously identified as Sri Jaya Sakti, Sri Jaya Pangus, or Masula-

Masuli, later decided to move his court to Bedaulu or Pejeng. There his evil and atheistic successor Mayadanawa was defeated by Gajah Mada, leader of the invading army from Majapait, with a helping hand from the gods. These accounts were written long after the invasion that marks the moment when Bali's "actual history" began. The name Balingkang therein evokes a mysterious, half forgotten, and half suppressed past, a time when Balinese civilization may have flourished all the better for lack of external political intervention.

The Balinese kings Sri Jaya Sakti and Jaya Pangus were historical personages and issued numerous edicts. A comparison of the geographical distributions of the bronze plate inscriptions issued by these two kings and their predecessor Anak Wungsu shows a gradual southward expansion in their political interests, insofar as these can be deduced from the issuing of royal edicts (see Figure 4). Both kings issued inscriptions in the district of Kintamani as well as in Pejeng, so that the historical question as to where their palaces (*jero, kraton*) were located is difficult to ascertain.

Some clues in support of the hypothesis that there was a royal palace in the mountains are found in a *lontar* text in the Middle Balinese language from Desa Les, issued by "Ida Paduka Bhatara Dalem Balingkang" (Budiastra 1993a). The king of Balingkang is named as Sri Aji Jaya Kasunu in the text, and his residence as "Pujungan" (plate 45.a3). A royal inscription from nearby Desa Subaya also refers to this location. It states that the villagers are freed from their duty to worship at the regional temple at "Pujung" (plate 7.a3). A "Raja Pujangan" is further mentioned in the story of the Baris Goak dance from Selulung. It is possible that this place lay on the southern slope of Bukit Singawana in Sukawana, just above Balingkang, which is still called "Pujung." The *subak abian* of Pujung still maintains a temple there, called Pura Pamantenan Pujung (*antenan*, "to be married"). The temple is believed to be the final resting place (*candi*) of the wife of "Sri Aji Jayapangus." According to local legend, the first Balinese kings resided in Sukawana, either in Kuta Dalem or on Bukit Singawana (which features an archeological site presumed to be the "Singamandawa" of the oldest Balinese edicts), before moving to Balingkang and finally to Pejeng. While the available evidence in support of this hypothesis may not satisfy a historian, it is sufficient to generate speculation among locals about kingdoms of the past and the relations of domains in the present.

Van der Tuuk and Brandes are the first and, to my knowledge, the last foreign researchers to mention Pura Balingkang. In 1885 they reported about a royal inscription kept at "Pekulem," a shrine attached to the temple of Balingkang. The promised publication of this text never eventuated, and the original plates have since been lost. The opening ceremony (*ngodal*) of Pura Balingkang's festival is still conducted at Pura Batan Tingkih, located in a nearby area called Alas Matahun. The shrine indeed belongs to a deity called Ratu Gede Makulem and marks the place where people remember the *prasasti* had been kept. The authors also mention in passing that Balingkang was "maintained by four villages in Buleleng [on the coast] and two in Bangli [in the mountains]" (1885:605, n. 1). These comments would suggest that Pura Dalem Balingkang has been the center of a *banua* of its own for some time, even though it is closely connected to Pura Pucak Penulisan.

The current supporters of the temple are referred to as the *kanca satak* (the two hundred companions). The core membership includes the mountain villages of Siakin and Pinggan as well as the villages of Les, Penuktukan, Sembirenteng, Gretek, and Tembok, situated on the northern coast below Balingkang.[2] Although all these communities maintain a number of traditions characteristic of "Bali Aga" villages, only Desa Les still maintains a full council of paired elders (*ulu apad*) as is typical of such communities.

Formerly, the villages of Songan, Batur, Bantang, Sukawana, and Dausa were also core supporters of Pura Balingkang, and they still participate in various ways.[3] Sukawana, in particular, fulfills a very important role in relation to the temple. It is the Jero Kubayan Kiwa of Sukawana, the head elder of the left moiety of their village council, who symbolically sacrifices the buffalo at Pura Balingkang, as he does at Pura Pucak Penulisan and elsewhere.[4]

The membership of the *banua* congregates annually in Balingkang for a festival and buffalo sacrifice around the fifth full moon (*purnama kalima*). Tradition stipulates that the festivities may only begin after the opening of the *usaba* at Pura Bale Agung Sukawana on the same full moon, so as to avoid a clash in the *kubayan*'s duties. Also worth noting is that the inner sanctum of Pura Balingkang is physically oriented directly toward Penulisan (*kaja*).

The core members of the *kanca satak* also (used to) assemble periodically at Pura Puseh Panjingan in Les and Pura Segara Pagonyongan in Gretek.[5] It is often stated that these three temples, along with Pura Pucak Penulisan and Pura Bale Agung Sukawana, are the principal sanctuaries (*kayangan*) of a single domain, analogous to the *kayangan tiga* (set of three essential temples) of a *desa adat*, but including also a mountain peak and a seaside sanctuary. The distribution of ritual functions and privileges is seen as a complementary set

Table 3. The Principal Sanctuaries of the *Kanca Satak*

Kayangan Category	Leadership Category	Location
Pura Pucak (Penulisan)	—	Sukawana
Pura Segara (Pagonyongan)	—	Gretek
Pura Puseh (Panjingan)	Jero Pasek (Les), Jero Penyarikan (Penuktukan), and a council of elders (Les)	Les/Penuktukan
Pura Bale Agung (Sukawana)	Jero Kubayan (head elder and priest-leader)	Sukawana
Pura Dalem (Balingkang)	Mangku Gede (temple priest)	Pinggan

as well, again in analogy to the customary leadership of a *desa adat*. These relationships are summarized in Table 3.

While it is problematic to establish the history of this temple or former palace and its domain, there is a rich tradition of oral origin narratives that reflect a local understanding of the past. These myths are often concerned with the general problem of how an ideal kingdom or social order can be maintained.[6]

Version 1 (Pinggan): Long ago King Jaya Sakti and his consort Sri Mahadewi ruled at Balingkang. Although the queen gave birth to a son, named Jaya Pangus, the king decided to take a second wife, by the name of Putri Pejeng. The latter was a widow from Pejeng who already had a son of her own, called Mayadrawa. Her influence over the king was great, and she hated the senior queen. The first son, Jaya Pangus, was disappointed by the king's actions and left to found his own kingdom on Bukit Indrakila [Dausa]. The second queen proved to be barren, but Sri Mahadewi gave birth again to the twins Masula [male] and Masuli [female]. Fearing for the life of her children, she fled with Masuli to Besakih, leaving Masula in the care of Mpu Siwa Narapetak at Alas Matahun. Not much later the evil Putri Pejeng and her son Mayadrawa assumed direct control of the kingdom, to the point of driving out King Jaya Sakti from his own *kraton*. During his exile, the old king met his son Masula at Alas Matahun but was unaware of his identity. Meanwhile in Balingkang, strange events marked the unjust rule of a usurper. Every time the royal household sat down to a meal, a giant *garuda raksasa* [a demon of eagle shape] swept down and took all the food. The angry Mayadrawa swore that whoever was able to kill the *garuda* would be adopted as his son and heir. This news reached Masula, and after practicing austerities, he was granted a weapon by Bhatara Pasupati. With its aid he was able to kill the *garuda* and was adopted by his stepbrother Mayadrawa. The latter disliked keeping the hero in his palace and thus ordered him to leave on the pretext that he needed to find a wife. Masula wandered far and wide until he met his twin sister Masuli at Besakih. They promptly fell in love, were married, and returned with their mother to Balingkang. But Mayadrawa's character had not changed. He was struck by Masuli's beauty and decided to kill Masula in order to fulfill his desire to possess her. The twin couple heard of this plan and fled. In the forest they met their father, and a voice from the heavens revealed his identity. Reunited, they gathered support and attacked Mayadrawa, driving him out of the palace and fleeing to Pejeng. Later he attacked Balingkang again, but with his magic weapon Masula caused a deep gorge to appear around the *kraton*, as there is today, and Mayadrawa's army was unable to enter.[7]

Version 2 (Batur): King Sri Jaya Sakti already had a queen, but he fell in love again with Kang Ching Wi, the daughter of a Chinese opium trader from the Kang clan. After she became his wife, she was known as Sri Mahardatta, and his kingdom was named Bali Kang or Balingkang. However, his royal priest and adviser at Bukit Penarajon, Bhagawan Siwagandu, had disapproved of the marriage and refused to conduct the ceremony. The angry king exiled his high priest, and thus he moved to Jung Les near Songan. Such a low place was not fit for a holy man, so Gunung Batur started spurting fire. He thus moved on to Kuta Dalem, but Gunung Penulisan erupted with water. Finally, he meditated on Gunung Penarajon until he was transformed into Wisnu Murti Catur Muka, whose shrine is the Gedong Puser Tasik at Penulisan, a well that reaches to the bottom of the *sapta patala* [the seven layers of the netherworld] and that is the origin of the waters of the Balingkang River. He then cursed Dalem Balingkang so that his rule would end and his own descendants would forget him. [The narratives continues, but the content is similar to the above version from Pinggan.]

Version 3 (Pinggan): During the reign of Raja Masula-Masuli at Balingkang, a magical being, half human and half bird (*garuda*), was once born from the trunk of a bamboo [*tiing tali*, the variety used to make ropes]. The bamboo split open with a loud bang, and out came a boy. He was adopted by Dalem Balingkang, and, in line with his strange birth, he was mockingly referred to as Dalem Keplogan [*keplog*, "to explode"].[8] One day, the men were busy chopping meat to make *lawar* [minced meat] for a ceremony when one cut his finger, so that his blood was mixed with the food. "Why is the *lawar* so tasty today?" asked Dalem Keplogan. When he learned what had happened, he developed an insatiable desire for human blood and flesh. Each time a *rejang* dance was performed by the village maidens, he caused a magical mist to appear and stole the dancer at the back of the row [the tallest] to take her to his secret cave and eat her. After several of these abductions, the people tied a white chicken to the girl and were able to follow the trail of feathers to his secret lair. Since they were too afraid to attack the monstrous ogre, they thought of a trick. At the *malaspas* ceremony for the consecration of a new meeting pavilion or longhouse (*bale lantang*), for the village council of elders, coins and leaves (*tepung tawar*) were thrown over the building. Afterwards they asked the Dalem Keplogan to fetch the coins that had fallen under the platform. Since he was too big to crawl beneath it, all joined forces to lift up the pavilion, only to release it and trap him as soon as he was underneath. But, alas, the ogre was still alive and immune to all their weapons. In the end, he proposed: "I shall reveal how I can be killed if you accept my curse, namely, that you will be reduced from nine hundred (*sepasatus*) households to only two hundred (*satak*). Also, you must adorn this and future *bale lantang* with my image." Dalem Balingkang responded: "Even if my kingdom is reduced to only fifty households, I will accept, as long as you perish." The ogre told them to first use a rolled up betel leaf (*porosan*) to stab him, to eliminate his magic protection. After he was slain, all came to pass as he had said. The kingdom fell apart, and only *kanca satak* [two hundred friends] remained, scattered in seven villages. Even these two hundred find it hard to remain united because of the king's taunt. Until today two hundred food parcels (*kawesan*) are prepared at the festival of Balingkang, each with a *porosan*. The base of the roof pillars (*tugeh*) of all *bale lantang* [among the Bali Aga] are still adorned with a carving of a bird with wings spread and sometimes with human features [called "*paksi*," "*boma*," or, if in the *bale pamaruman*, "*garuda*"]. Finally, a white chicken is still tied to the bamboo cover above the corpse or effigy of the deceased, and a bamboo cannon (*keplogan*) fired, to prevent evil spirits from approaching.

Version 4 (Les): Once there was a glorious kingdom ruled by the kings of Balingkang. Because these rulers created peace and order, they all had the title Jaya (triumphant, glorious, prosperous) as part of their name. After a disaster struck the kingdom, the survivors fled to Bukit Tingkih at Alas Matahun ("[to stay in] the forest for one year"). The king died after only one year of his rule. He had neglected his duty to conduct the obligatory blood sacrifice of the eleventh *wuku* week (*dungulan*) that is meant to protect the realm from demonic forces and epidemics. The new king and his people abandoned their temporary settlement and continued on toward the coast until they reached a place called Panjingan. Again the people became prosperous, following the rules of proper conduct set out by Dalem Balingkang [i.e., in the *lontar* from Desa Les mentioned above]. The first temple built at this location is still known as Pura Puseh Panjingan.[9]

These narratives reflect on the problems of maintaining the social order of a state or ritual domain. In mythical times, such an order was headed by a king, but the ethical principles of political rule are applicable also to present leaders. In any case, Dalem Balingkang's "kingdom" is defined more by the land and its people than by reference to the king himself. Even after the demise or departure of a king, the domain remains intact. The king is only the steward of a sacred realm, and although a virtuous rule is a prerequisite for prosperity, the absence of a living king has no influence on its continuing existence. The king, in any case, has religious obligations toward the divine founders and protectors of his domain. In short, the covenant between the ancestral deities and the land they first cleared precedes and outlasts any particular form of human government.

In his stewardship of the domain, the worldly ruler finds assistance from priests. His failure to recognize their authority is the cause of his downfall in version 2, which also establishes an asymmetrical relationship between Penulisan and Balingkang, or priest and ruler. The order of precedence is symbolized by the downward flow of water from the one to the other, as in ritual, where the priest gives *tirta* to the king. The king's failure to submit to spiritual authority results in a loss of power for him and his dynasty but does not destroy the domain as such.

The downfall of the ruler is also described in terms of inappropriate alliances, in this case, the contracting of an undesirable marriage. Jaya Sakti's lust for the beautiful daughter of an opium trader (version 2) provides a double image of intoxication and entails a neglect of dutiful action (*dharma*). The same applies to Mayadrawa (version 1), who desires the bride of his own (adoptive) son. Both unions entail a confusion of seniority ranking. Marrying Chinese is not condoned, since they are considered to be "older siblings" of the Balinese (at least in the Kintamani district), and marrying one's daughter (in-law) is equally despised. Jaya Sakti's second marriage in version 1, to a widow who already has a son (and heir), is a different kind of abomination. It presents a recipe for future conflict between the two sets of sons. These guidelines for avoiding inappropriate partners not only apply to royal households but pertain to the political and economic welfare of any family.

In contrast to these flawed marriages, the royal twins represent an ideal couple, destined for one another from birth and brought together against all odds by the forces of divine providence. The ideal king (or head of a household) is one who not only chooses his associates wisely but can balance the duality of male and female, of light and dark forces, as in a single body. However, people are aware that such a perfect union is merely an ideal. In reality, the opposing forces of life never reach a point of balance without a struggle, and even then only for a passing moment.[10]

The rule of the usurper, or unjust ruler, is marked by the physical incarnation of demonic or explosive forces in several of the versions. The kings by adoption, Mayadrawa, and more so Dalem Keplogan are representations of such wicked rulers. The physical image of evil is one of mixed shape, with human and animal features, indicating a violation of the categorical boundaries that uphold a social order. Their magical (illegitimate, female, left) power is contrasted to the legitimate (male) magical and political power of Masula, which is bestowed upon him by the gods or is his birthright. And yet, even under the rule of a rightful king, like Jaya Kasunu (version 4), the forces of evil are merely dormant and will manifest in the form of an epidemic or other disaster unless the ruler placates them by performing regular sacrifices. In the case of King Masula (in version 3), evil, in the shape of an ogre, is admitted into human society owing to a lack of discernment. The ogre's cannibalistic desires are triggered, however, by the contingency of a chance occurrence.

Here the demonic forces choose their own, human sacrifice to compensate for the absence of animal blood sacrifices. The victim is a maiden, a symbolic substitute for the female substance of sacrificial blood. The loss of a maiden is also linked to the loss of fertility that is believed to result from ignoring chthonic forces, particularly the fertility of the rice. The rice in turn is sown in the symbolic movements of the village maidens' *rejang* dance with its characteristic outward-sweeping arm motions.[11]

The contingencies of life can never be controlled in practice, even if negative forces are ritually placated. Many narratives of this kind thus introduce the notion of a curse (*pastu*) to signify the residue of evil and disorder that cannot be completely destroyed. The victory of society and the slaying of the evil or marginal figure are tainted with an element of guilt. Evil beings are, after all, only acting in accordance with their own nature and are an indispensable part of nature as a whole.

This theme of guilt and curse is made even more explicit in a narrative from Batih, the continuation of their version of the already presented Daa Tua myth. Here Ratu Daa is transformed into a male, Teruna Camput Bagia:

Some time after the departure of Ratu Daa Tua to Penulisan, a wealthy young man arrived in Batih. From whence he came and who his father and mother were he would not tell, so they called him Teruna Camput Bagia [*camput*, "without any family," and yet, *bagia*, "happy (because he was rich)"]. He became the youngest member of Batih's village council, and as such it was his task to bring *tuak* [palm wine] for the men at each meeting. Now the villagers, foremost the Klian Adat, had again been fast to ask money of the rich young man for cockfighting bets, but since they never repaid him, he began to refuse. The Klian Adat then decided to incriminate Teruna Camput Bagia, by putting an extract of the juice of a particular kind of edible tuber (*gadung*, poisonous unless it is boiled) into his palm wine collecting vessel. When I

Camput climbed the sugar palm tree the next morning to fetch the
vessel full of juice, he suspected no evil and faithfully brought it to the
meeting. Many of the men became intoxicated with the drug, and I
Camput stood accused of poisoning them. He was sentenced to death.
Although they tied him to a pole, none could kill him. He then revealed that he could not be harmed by ordinary weapons unless he
was stabbed first with the tip of a betel leaf. Before he was killed in the
outer yard of the Pura Bale Agung, he cursed them, saying that from
two hundred households they should dwindle to only seven. An epidemic broke out, and thus his curse took effect. His spirit later haunted
them in the shape of a woman dripping with blood until a shrine was
built in his (or her) honor.

Ultimately, the marginal, ambiguous, or demonic figures in these
myths are bound by society, as in a contract, and submit to male
dominance—"killed" symbolically with a *porosan*, a betel leaf (male/
tip), which envelops a betel nut within (female/fruit).[12] The killing
of Camput Bagia is also a separation of categories whereby an ambi-
sexual victim without a social identity reveals her female essence (the
blood-dripping female apparition). Similarly, the image of the half
human–half bird shaped ogre who is trapped by the unified force of
the social collective (version 3 above) marks and guards forever the
most pertinent social boundaries in the rank order of village society.
The wood carvings of this bird figure are located at the base of each
roof pillar in the ceremonial village longhouse (*bale lantang*). Their
location marks not only the lateral boundary between the left and
right ceremonial moieties of the village assembly but also the vertical
boundaries (*apad*) between sections (*rong*), that is, between categories of senior and junior members (see Chapter 7).

Likewise, the buffalo sacrificed at the festival of Pura Balingkang
(and Penulisan) represents a twofold ambiguity. Even though the
victim is an animal (*kebo*, buffalo), it is adorned and addressed as an
honorable human person (Jero Gede). Although it is a male, it must
be sexually immature, that is, the buffalo must not have reached a
life stage of sexual differentiation. This ambiguous victim carries the
burden of perpetual evil, of conceptual and social disorder, and is
first stabbed with a *porosan* by a symbolically female male (the head
elder of the left side) so that his potentially destructive magical power
(also left) can be controlled. The conflict is one of inseparable opposites and of mutual dependence even in contexts where the one
dominates over the other.

The narratives reveal the feeling of guilt and the logical blunder
in acts of domination. The resulting social order, tainted by a curse,
is only a shadow of the prosperity that could be achieved if these

opposites were to engage in an equal exchange in an ideal world rather than a world like the original Desa Batih, where men compensated for their natural poverty with social violence.

The origin narratives of Pura Balingkang are not simply abstract reflections on the nature of human social relations. On a more practical note, the recent political history of the *banua* of Pura Dalem Balingkang is so filled with internal conflicts and acts of external intervention that its ritual unity as a domain and the political unity of interests among its membership can no longer be taken for granted, if they ever could be. The present political scenario indeed mirrors the eternal state of tension and interdependence between duty and desire, or between the dominant and the dominated, as it is depicted in ideal terms in the above narratives.

Until around the time of Indonesian independence, Sukawana, Bantang, and Dausa not only regularly attended the festival at Pura Balingkang but contributed in full measure to the ritual and repair of the temple. They paid *peturunan* as did all other seven core members. Sukawana's elders were the ritual leaders at this temple. Their position was one of primus inter pares, similar to their current status in the *banua* of Pura Pucak Penulisan. The festivals of Pura Penulisan and Balingkang were simply different events in a ritual calendar held at different locations but with the same priestly leadership. Since Bantang, Dausa, Les/Penuktukan, and Pinggan also do or did *mabanua* at Penulisan, there is considerable overlap between the support groups of the two temples. In short, Pura Dalem Balingkang was a ritual center dominated by Sukawana and second to the summit temple of Pucak Penulisan in terms of its perceived antiquity, its elevation, its sacredness, and the timing of its annual ritual.

This intimate association came to an end following a dispute over labor contributions during a festival. People in Sukawana claim that they provided all the labor for the food preparations of the festival, while villagers from Pinggan simply came when it was time to collect their finished food parcels (*kawesan*). They thus decided to complete the preparation of their own offerings (*atos desa*) and those for the opening ceremony (*bakti ngodal*) at home in Sukawana, which then entitled them to take the food component they had brought back home again after the ceremony at Balingkang. Until this time, Sukawana had been the undisputed ritual leaders (*pangamong*) at the temple, and their priest-leaders accepted responsibility for opening the ceremony and dedicating the offerings to the gods. Many people in Pinggan agree with this account.

In the 1960s, a much more serious dispute arose over the temple land (*tanah laba pura*) attached to Pura Balingkang. This land, about 125 hectares, had been quietly occupied by farmers from Pinggan as if it were village land. But eventually, the Penyarikan of Penuktukan obtained evidence from administrative sources that it was indeed classified as temple land. He then demanded that the land be divided among all members of the *banua* or that the proceeds from leasing the land to individual farmers be used exclusively for the financing of the temple festival. Pinggan refused, and the case was brought to the court (some say the *bupati*) in Bangli. The court decided to allocate the land to Desa Pinggan, since the other members of the *banua* were too distant to utilize it effectively. This reclassification of land was made on the condition that the people of Pinggan henceforth be responsible for paying the entire cost of the annual festival on their own. This decision may have been a just solution, but it effectively destroyed an essential aspect of the *banua*, namely, their shared financial responsibility for Pura Balingkang.

As another consequence of this dispute, Siakin and Pinggan ceased to be a single *desa adat* (in 1965). All *banua* members stopped paying *peturunan* at Balingkang, although some kept on contributing a reduced amount in the form of *atos desa*. Sukawana, and with it Bantang and Dausa, stopped attending altogether. Only a small delegation would accompany the Kubayan Kiwa of Sukawana to the festival each year, for he still had to sacrifice the buffalo at Balingkang. They no longer brought the *bakti ngodal* for the opening ceremony, which was henceforth provided by Sembirenteng,[13] nor did they contribute any village offerings (*atos desa*). At that time the people of Pinggan also shifted the festival at Balingkang forward to the fifth full moon, while earlier it had always been celebrated on the sixth.

In 1969 a further rift about finances occurred, this time among the coastal villages. Les and Penuktukan lodged a protest after they had been asked to pay a share of the cost of repairing the domain's sea temple at Pagonyongan in Gretek. Their complaint was that there had been no meeting or other formal disclosure of the expenses incurred in the project, nor was it taken into account that Gretek had received government funding (under the "village help" scheme, Bantuan Desa, or Bandes for short) for projects such as this repair. When a disclosure was refused, Les and Penuktukan ceased to *mabanua* at Pura Pagonyongan. Some time after, they were in turn refused entry to conduct a bathing ceremony (*melasti*) for one of their village deities at Pura Pagonyongan. Pinggan, Siakin, Sembirenteng, Gretek, and Tembok still attend at this sea temple today.

Soon after, Desa Tembok also ceased attending at Pura Puseh Panjingan in Les. Apparently, members of the branch of Warga Satria Taman Bali in Tembok were offended by the fact that the people of Les refused to address them in the refined Balinese (*basa alus*) due to them in accordance with their claim to aristocratic status. The group believes that their ancestors were Satria Taman Bali, a branch of a former ruling house of Bangli, and had been sent to Tembok to guard the border with Karangasem. Most positions of authority in the village of Tembok are occupied by members of this family, so their decision to cut ties with Les applied to the *desa adat* as a whole. In addition to this dispute, the attendance at Pura Puseh Panjingan was further decimated following a violent quarrel at the temple between the hosts and some visitors from Pinggan and Siakin, who have since ceased their visits (or have ceased to be invited).

This process of internal division was accompanied and amplified by increasing external intervention. From around the turn of the century a *cokorda* of Bangli (Puri Semarabawa) began to act as a financial sponsor. As the ruler of the kingdom of Bangli and on behalf of the paramount ruler at Klungkung, he lay claim to a shrine with an eleven-tiered roof (*meru tumpang solas*). Such tall shrines are usually reserved for kings, but this one had been associated only with the deceased Dalem Balingkang until then. The *meru* in question had traditionally been maintained by Desa Songan, whose residents still bring a substantial amount of *atos desa* for the annual festival. However, they ceased to consider themselves core supporters (and co-owners) of Pura Balingkang from the time of this interference. Bangli's sponsorship ceased with the death of the *cokorda* in the 1940s.

From the 1940s onward, the now vacant role of "royal sponsor" was filled by the *cokorda* of Petak (Kabupaten Gianyar), a small *puri* that belongs to the Pemayun branch of Satria Dalem and, apparently, is not related to the *cokorda* of Bangli. The present ruler, Cokorda Mayun Petak, claims that a descendant of Dalem Balingkang became king at Pejeng and that the last king of Pejeng (Dewa Agung Mayem Suda), his own grandfather, was defeated in a war with Puri Ubud in 1893. He thus fled to Balingkang to recover his strength through meditation while gathering military support for a return. Around A.D. 1900, he established a small realm for himself in Desa Petak, but he never managed to reclaim his position in Pejeng. He and his son continued sponsoring Pura Balingkang, as does his grandson today. For example, the sponsors paid for the building of a containing wall around the sanctuary in 1948. Individual leaders of Desa Pinggan also benefited personally from the association and in turn supported the *cokorda* in his attempts to appropriate the temple ritually.

The *cokorda* eventually began to interfere in the ritual process, for example, by suggesting that the ceremonial circumambulating of the temple (*mapapideh*) should proceed in a clockwise direction rather than the traditional "turning toward the left." Finally, in the 1970s, he demanded the right to sacrifice the buffalo (symbolically) in place of the Kubayan Kiwa of Sukawana. Pinggan supported this demand, and Sukawana cut all ties with Balingkang in response.[14] The general sentiment within the *banua* silently turned against the *cokorda* and his group of clients in Pinggan. Rumors spread that he was responsible for the theft of Balingkang's *prasasti*, and some even allege to have seen these sacred objects during a festival at his descent temple (*merajaan*) in Petak. Rumor also has it that the first two *cokorda* of Petak died soon after sacrificing a buffalo at Balingkang, providing evidence of divine retribution for their presumptuous behavior. The present *cokorda* eventually stepped back (in the 1980s), allowing the Kubayan Sukawana to reclaim his traditional duty. However, the dispute still remained unresolved and resurfaced during the festival at Balingkang in 1993. Only after a heated debate did the *cokorda* withdraw his earlier demand to sacrifice the buffalo.[15]

Apart from the attrition suffered because of conflict among the congregation of this temple, there have also been rather different changes to the composition of the *banua* membership due to an influx of new supporters. During the last few years visitors from the villages of Krobokan, Menasa, Sangsit, and Tianyar (all located in Buleleng) have regularly attended and brought *atos* at the annual festival. The rationales offered as explanations for their sudden support vary. However, one example narrative was recorded when a group from Desa Pacung arrived for the first time during the festival in 1994. The visitors were all members of a large descent group who recently had been told by a trance medium that they are descendants of Dalem Balingkang. They intend on becoming regular participants, but this decision may not affect other descent groups in Desa Pacung.

My informants often attributed the upheavals in the recent political history of the *kanca satak* to the actions of a number of influential individuals, and the same is true of conflicts in other *banua*. It is indeed under the influence of informal rather than official ritual leaders that most changes of ritual alliance are brought about. These informal leaders are usually holders of a public office, a *klian adat*, *klian banjar*, *penyarikan*, *pemangku*, or *kepala desa dinas*, but their office as such only provides them with the initial courage to voice an opinion. More crucial to their wielding of influence is the power (*kesaktian*) of their personality, manifested in their willingness to argue their case in a debate until the opposition is silenced out of embarrassment. Most individuals refrain from such assertive behavior for fear of social resentment or even magical retribution from the silenced opposition. Even more than their courage, their resilience to public verbal disapproval and private magical retribution testifies to their *kesaktian*. The duration of the influence of such individuals is closely linked to their private fortunes and those of their opponents. For example, the accidental death of a close relative can be interpreted as a weakening of his magical defenses, while the death of an opponent can signify that the opponent's magical attack was deflected and struck its instigator instead.

External interference in the affairs of this *banua* is only partially responsible for its current state of disarray. The fundamental problem is rather that Sukawana's earlier ritual predominance at Pura Balingkang lacked an adequate political and economic basis and was supported solely by reference to local origin histories. Since the temple was located within the administrative territory of Desa Pinggan, Sukawana's claims to leadership were effectively those of an external sponsor, not unlike those of Cokorda Petak. The predominant sponsor, however, is the one who is able to pay the most significant economic support, along with being able to present a passable justification for his attendance. Given its already extensive commitment toward Pura Pucak Penulisan, Desa Sukawana did not have the resources to compete with the *cokorda* in feeding the gods and, indirectly, in feeding its clients in Pinggan. Its recent comeback was perhaps made possible by a growing political self-awareness among the Bali Aga and an associated desire to retain the right of ritual self-determination. Sentiments similar to those that precipitated an anti-caste movement among Balinese "commoners" (*jaba*, lit. "outsiders") in the 1930s are beginning to lead the Bali Aga toward resenting figures like Cokorda Petak, who stand for the former aristocracy and for attempts at outside intervention.

Despite Sukawana's limited control over the *banua* of Pura Dalem Balingkang, the ritual and historical precedence of Sukawana or Pura Pucak Penulisan is undisputed. The domains of the *gebog domas* and the *kanca satak* are indeed difficult to distinguish or separate from the perspective of their history, their membership, and their interconnecting ritual practices.

The Domain of Pura Pucak Indrakila

Pura Pucak Indrakila is a regional temple located within the village territory of Dausa, a mere four kilometers west of Penulisan. Apart

Table 4. The Membership of Gebog Satak Indrakila

Desa Dinas	Desa Adat
Dausa	Dausa
	Lateng
	Cenigayan
Satra	Satra (includes Banjar Tanah Gambir and Kembangsari)
	Sanda
	Tanah Ambut

from this current designation the sacred location is also still known as Bukit Humintang, its original name in Dausa's royal inscriptions. It has been mentioned that the group of villages that support this temple until quite recently belonged to Gebog Satak Bantang and were thus part of the *gebog domas* of Pura Penulisan. Their separation from this larger alliance may become a permanent state of affairs. However, none would deny, even now, that the two *banua* are closely related in terms of their origin history.

The membership of Gebog Satak Indrakila consists of two large *desa dinas* or six *desa adat*, as listed in Table 4. All of these are Bali Aga villages with a bipartite council of elders (*ulu apad*). The total population of the *banua* amounts to about 1,300 households (or 5,800 individuals), all of whom are core supporters who pay a share of *peturunan*.

The annual festival at Pura Bukit Indrakila is celebrated around the fourth full moon,[16] and it is often simultaneous with the festival at Pura Penulisan. The ritual is led by the three Mangku Gede (head village priests) of Dausa, Satra, and Cenigayan, who rotate the function of ritual leadership among themselves on a daily basis during the festival. However, the Mangku Gede Dausa has precedence over the visitors when it comes to making decisions about the temple. The head of the temple committee (*panitia*) is likewise from Dausa, though it includes representatives from all member villages.

There is some uncertainty as to the position of Gebok Satak Dausa within the internal organization of the *gebog domas* before the split in 1962. Informants in Dausa and Cenigayan simply denied that they had ever been a part of Gebog Satak Bantang, while others supported this claim with the help of specific origin narratives. For example, it is believed that the male deity of Pura Simanganti in Desa Sanda is the son of the Bhatara Puseh Pengupetan in Bantang, mentioned ear-

lier, and that before the conflict began, Desa Bantang used to participate in the festivals of this temple. Furthermore, people from Dausa,
Cenigayan, Lateng, Satra, Tanah Ambut, and Kembangsari still attend
the *usaba gede* in Desa Bantang as visitors (last in 1993).[17] Informants
in Bantang, in turn, argued that their leadership over this group of
desa adat was related to the fact that these villages were administered
by the *perbekel* (administrative village head) of Bantang until 1968,
when Dausa became a separate *desa dinas*. This administrative split is
said to have set the scene for a simultaneous ritual disassociation.

The initial split with Pura Pucak Penulisan occurred in 1962, when
the content of Prasasti Dausa A 2 was deciphered and translated into
Indonesian. The inscription mentioned a regional temple on Bukit
Humintang to be maintained by the "*keraman* of Percenigayan (Cenigayan)," a duty that had been forgotten for so long that only a few
ruins remained at the site. An origin narrative is often referred to as
an explanation for this long lapse in the temple's maintenance:

> Long ago Pura Indrakila was a domain temple jointly maintained by
> the ancient village of Cenigayan and the younger Desa Dausa. At the
> annual festival it was customary to blindfold the sacrificial buffalo for
> the procession. One year the blindfolded buffalo was seen by a royal
> emissary of Dalem Klungkung. He strongly objected to this custom,
> claiming that the animal was unable to see the obstacles in its path.
> He also reported his observations to the king and was sent back with
> orders to forbid the blindfolding. However, the messenger was only
> taunted and beaten by the villagers. Seeing this insolence, Dalem Klung-
> kung cursed them, that they should dwindle from two hundred to only
> seven households, and thus it came to pass. Soon after, a drought set
> in, and water needed to be rationed. Some women from Cenigayan
> stole the water allocated to the women of Dausa, and a heated argu-
> ment began among the women. When men arrived from Cenigayan,
> some lent support to the women of their own village while others criti-
> cized them for breaking the water distribution agreement with Dausa.
> Bitter words led to blows, and soon everyone was fighting indiscrimi-
> nately until most were killed. Seven survivors moved downridge from
> Indrakila to present-day Cenigayan, taking the temple's *prasasti* along
> with them. Henceforth they were politically dominated by the much
> more populous Desa Dausa, though they still held the sacred inscrip-
> tions as proof of their ritual precedence. For fear of losing this final
> privilege, they buried the *prasasti*. Eventually their joint ritual duties
> were forgotten. The *banua* temple was gradually abandoned and fell
> to ruin. Much later, in 1960, when the inscriptions were to be retrieved
> for a village festival in Cenigayan, none could remember where they
> lay buried. The *kubayan* at the time went into trance and directed them
> to Alas Belong. But when the villagers reached the location, they found
> that the *prasasti* had already flown away by itself and landed in their
> Pura Bale Agung.

The narrative tells how a civil war and population attrition in the origin village Cenigayan led to a takeover by the relative newcomers of Dausa, who later became the leaders of the rediscovered ritual center Pura Indrakila. That the king of Klungkung is said to have criticized Bali Aga customs and cursed the people indicates that the domain's collapse may be attributed to outside intervention as much as internal strife.

When the content of the inscriptions became known in 1962, the people of Dausa and their supporters "learned" that their distant ancestors in the eleventh century had been freed from contributing to Pura Pucak Penulisan on the basis of their existing duties toward "Pura Hyang Api" (Pura Indrakila).[18] A meeting was held, and it was decided to rebuild the ruined temple and eventually to cease supporting Pura Penulisan. There was much debate over which individual shrines ought to be built, but eventually it was agreed to include shrines dedicated to Ratu Pucak Tegeh (Penulisan) and Ratu Dalem Balingkang. Within one year, the constructions were complete and the first festival was held. However, in the following year (1963) Mount Agung erupted and the temple was destroyed yet again. For some years the separation venture faltered, and support of Penulisan resurged for fear of further disasters. Much conflict of opinion surrounded the future fate of Pura Indrakila. When the temple was finally refurbished for the second time in 1968, the split was complete. Although most villagers from this *banua* still attend privately at the festival of Pura Penulisan, they only deliver minor offerings rather than *atos desa*, and they certainly no longer pay *peturunan*.

A degree of resentment is still felt among several factions, particularly in Dausa. Often the split is attributed to the private ambitions of their leadership in the 1960s.[19] The present leaders in Dausa are well aware that the *lontar* Catur Dharma Kalawasan testifies to their obligations. In particular, it is believed to be the responsibility of Desa Dausa to maintain the main staircase of Pura Penulisan. The committee of Pura Penulisan have allowed the steps to deteriorate as a reminder.

One influential descent group from Dausa sent a delegation to the annual meeting of Penulisan's temple committee in 1994, asking for their group of households to be readmitted as full, *peturunan*-paying members of its *banua*. The request was granted, and their leader was even allocated a seat on the committee. It is possible that others will follow suit, but a number of obstacles make a future merger of the two *banua* seem unlikely. It is unthinkable that Pura Pucak Indrakila could be abandoned once again or that ties to Penulisan could be completely forgotten and denied. It is possible in principle that the members of this new domain will accept a dual loyalty in the future.

The Core Network of Pura Batur

The extensive network of ties of ritual affiliation connecting Pura Batur to its supporting villages are shown in Figure 3 above to reduce the density of information conveyed in Figure 2. More serious reasons for setting Pura Batur apart from other temple networks in the highlands are that its relations with supporters do not follow the same organizational pattern and logic as in a *banua* and that supporters themselves do not describe their network as a *banua*. However, these differences in organization and classification are limited and may be the result of comparatively recent developments. In any case, Pura Batur is of such great significance to ritual life in the mountain region that it cannot be ignored in this study.

Pura Batur nowadays has gained recognition as one of Bali's *sadkayangan* and has become Bali's most powerful irrigation source temple. The *sadkayangan,* or "nine temples," are promoted as the principal pilgrimage sites of the new, devotional Balinese Hinduism promoted by the Brahmana-dominated, government-sponsored, modernist religious institution Parisada Hindu Dharma Indonesia. The role of Pura Batur in pan-Balinese religious politics was recently commented on by I Gede Pitana (1995), and its apical position in a hierarchy of irrigation temples has been described in detail by Stephen Lansing (1991). My own research is complementary. It is predominantly concerned with Batur's other and probably more longstanding status as a regional ritual center among Bali Aga villages.

That Pura Batur's sphere of influence as the apex of a network of irrigation temples has been greatly expanded in recent times is demonstrated by the fact that even some irrigation societies (*subak*) from distant Sulawesi, established by transmigrants from Bali, come to ask for *tirta* at Pura Batur nowadays. The temple's gradual involvement in the wider contexts of provincial and national religious life has a long history, but the process accelerated dramatically in the 1970s. At that time Pura Batur was renamed Pura Ulun Danu Batur, "the temple at the head of Lake Batur." Beyond its undisputed status as a principal sanctuary of the goddess of Lake Batur (Dewi Danu), Pura Batur was now claimed to represent the very source of the lake's water. This concept was not new. The same status and function formerly had been associated with Pura Ulun Danu Songan. Bitter disputes arose as Songan began to lose its local and southern Balinese clientele of *subak* to Pura Batur.

Desa Batur is nowadays located above the lake, on the ridge of the surrounding caldera, a few kilometers south of Desa Kintamani. Throughout the disputes with Songan, which is located on the northern shore of the lake, much emphasis was placed on providing evidence that Batur had been relocated from its former position by the shore of the lake following its utter destruction through a volcanic eruption in 1926. Lansing mentions the dispute and his own role in providing documentary evidence of the shift (1991:106–108). However, the argument about Batur's relocation was perhaps both unnecessary and irrelevant. Everyone in the district of Kintamani remembered the up-hill shift clearly. An example are the people of Bayung Gede, with whom residents of Batur took refuge until their new village was established. The crux of the matter is that even old Batur was never located at the source of the lake but near its middle, that is, "downstream" of Songan.

In numerous interviews, informants from several supporting villages lamented their confusion subsequent to the dispute. Many became uncertain about where to perform the ritual duty of paying *suwinih* prestations (from *winih*, "seeds"), consisting predominantly of rice and brought by irrigation societies. Some recounted anecdotes of *subak* delegations arriving at the crossroads in Penelokan still arguing about where to go, with the older generation insisting that they always went to Pura Ulun Danu Songan and the younger generation preferring to support the now more glamorous Pura Batur.[20]

The recent status increments achieved by Pura Batur are part of a historical process that may have begun with the establishment of a close association to the rulers of Klungkung in the eighteenth century. Most of the mythology recorded in the written charter of the temple, the *Raja Purana Batur* (and also in the charter of Pura Besakih, the *Raja Purana Besakih*) date back to this period. A key motif of the origin narratives contained in this written collection is the relationship between the daughter and son of the creator god Bhatara Pasupati (who resides on Mt. Sumeru in Java). His daughter is Dewi Danu of Pura Batur and her older brother is Bhatara Putranjaya of Pura Besakih, the principal state temple of the Javanese-descended Bali Majapait dynasties of Gelgel and Klungkung.

For the ruler of Klungkung, the alliance with Batur provided some limited degree of control over irrigation and, perhaps, over the revenue from *suwinih* payments. The incorporation of a more ancient, autochthonous, and symbolically female authority added legitimacy to the king's political power in the context of the cultural ideal of dual authority, to be discussed in Chapter 9. The king's link to Batur also was in fulfillment of his royal duty to act as worldly sponsor for rituals aimed at maintaining the fertility of the land, the perpetual flow of water, and the welfare of a predominantly agriculturist people.

Most probably the male counterpart of Pura Batur was once Pura Penulisan rather than Pura Besakih. A ritual reorientation may have followed in the wake of a shift of power from earlier Balinese kings, for whom Penulisan was a state temple, to Majapait kings with their principal state temple at Besakih. For the leadership at Pura Batur, the new alliance provided continual access to state sponsorship and promotion. The same kinds of considerations may apply to their current involvement with a provincial government that is gradually replacing traditional feudal lords as the principal sponsor of temples.

Batur nonetheless has maintained its own Bali Aga traditions to a considerable degree. Village elders and priest-leaders may no longer achieve their office by moving through a traditional temporal rank order, but some aspects of the formal organization of a ranked village council that are typical for the mountains are still retained in Batur. The temple's highest priest or Jero Gede Duuran (from *duur,* "on top") is always a local. More precisely, he is selected from among the village founder group Pasek Kayuselem, "the black tree clan." The Jero Gede wields all ritual authority that is specific to Pura Batur, even though some visiting parties have increasingly brought their own Brahmana priests to this temple in recent years.

If this authority had been stripped from the people of Batur early on in the process of a reorientation toward Klungkung and Pura Besakih, their legitimizing value in a partnership with the later Balinese kings would have been diminished. It may also be that no serious attempt was made to appropriate their ritual authority insofar as it is seen as an inalienable attribute of those who first settled the island. The embodiment of this origin status is the female deity of the lake and the Jero Gede of Batur as her human representative.

Complaints have been voiced by many of Batur's more recent clients about the coercive tactics employed in expanding the temple's ritual support network. Supporting villages receive a letter each year, written on traditional *lontar* leaf, which specifies exactly what they are to pay at "the festival of the tenth full moon" (*usaba purnamaning kedasa*). Such letters also have been sent to irrigation societies and villages that never before regarded themselves as obliged to Pura Batur. Some of them have refused these novel demands, and others have brought only such quantities of offerings as they thought appropriate and sufficient. However, when the delegations arrive at the great temple festival at Pura Batur, the offerings are charted and a ticket is issued for the collection of *tirta*. Those who bring less than the specified amount of offerings and cash may be criticized or even refused holy water for their gardens or rice fields. Unwilling allies are threatened with the curse of the deity in the temple charter: "If the followers of the goddess fail to deliver the specified contributions (*pakenan*), their crops will fail and they will be struck by the curse (*pastun*) of the deity . . . they will suffer immediate disasters, their works will fail, and all that they plant will perish" (Babad Patisora, 28a–b, transcription by Museum Bali, my translation).

Such strategies are regarded as indicative of greed among some of Batur's leaders. Critics argue that the establishment of ritual relationships through forceful demands and threats is not in keeping with either tradition or religious sentiments. Indeed, Batur would not be able to wield such coercive powers if it were not for the political support it receives from government institutions and traditional political leaders such as the *cokorda* of Puri Ubud. However, what is of interest in the context of a discussion on ritual networks in highland Bali is not the moral interpretation of these practices, but Batur's place in the ritual map of this region.

The Babad Patisora is perhaps the single most important among the several *lontar* texts that form the charter of Pura Batur. The manuscript outlines a twofold social division within the congregation of the temple. The irrigation societies from southern Bali who attend the festival of Batur are explicitly distinguished from the temple's forty-five traditional "friends" (*pasihan* or *pasyan*). The forty-five *pasihan* of Pura Batur are almost all Bali Aga villages from the central highlands, Buleleng, and around Bangli. The *pasihan* are not referred to as *subak* in the text, but as villages (*desa*). Their classification as irrigation societies would be incorrect in any case. Even today, a large proportion of these villages have no local *subak* association whatsoever, since they have no irrigated rice fields.[21] The *pasihan* villages themselves also unanimously describe their contributions as village-level offerings (*atos desa*) rather than mere *subak* contributions (*suwinih*).

While it may be appropriate to portray Pura Batur as an important apex in Bali's system of irrigation temples (*pura subak*), as Lansing has argued, the *pasihan* relationship between the temple and nonirrigating mountain villages must be taken into closer consideration. To suggest that Batur is a center of a village alliance in the style of a *banua* is not to deny Batur's importance as a regional agricultural temple, a function that it holds in common with all other *banua* temples. Rather, it suggests that the participation of *subak* is only one aspect of Pura Batur's ritual order and arguably one that became more momentous with the relatively recent establishment of ties with Klungkung and southern Bali in general.

The relationship between Pura Batur and its *pasihan* is sometimes reflected in specific oral narratives that account for the origins and character of a specific link. For most villages in the Kintamani district, however, visits to Pura Batur and Pura Pucak Penulisan are simply part of traditional ritual practice. The festivals of both temples mark the turning points in an annual cycle of local agriculture. No special justification is required for their participation. If it were not for the pretentiousness attributed to its current leadership, the participating villages in the Kintamani district would not hesitate to exclaim that Pura Batur is *their* temple.

"Owning a temple" refers to the responsibility for its maintenance. The revenue Pura Batur collects from its *pasihan* and other clients is more than sufficient to cover the cost of the annual temple festival.[22] But only the contributions paid by residents of Desa Adat Batur are formally classified as *peturunan*. The payments are negligible and more or less symbolic at a mere Rp 200 and one kilogram of rice per household per year. The leadership of Batur nevertheless regards the *pasihan* villages' annual contributions as ritual offerings, rather than financial assistance, and stresses that they are classified as *atos desa* rather than *peturunan*. This interpretation is particularly tenuous given their recent encouragement of a conversion of ritual gifts, such as pigs or goats, into a cash payment. *Pasihan* villages instead regard themselves as the temple's traditional core congregation. They often complain when there is evidence of a lack of recognition from Batur, as, for example, when they are asked to pay an additional fee for special requests for *tirta* during the year. One group of informants explained their feelings with a play on words. They suggested that their relationship to Batur had acquired a bitter flavor (*pait*) ever since its leaders had started to pay more attention to *bali majapait* than to those with whom they have maintained a common set of traditions and histories form the beginning of time.

Although their connection to Batur is a matter beyond questioning for many nearby villages, a desire for mythological justification is displayed by some of those who carry an additional responsibility or hold a special status in relation to the temple. Local origin narratives state, for example, that the people of Desa Bayung Gede and Desa Batur are classificatory "siblings" (*sameton*, "same-generation collaterals") owing to their common ancestry. Weddings are prohibited between the two villages, since it is incestuous to marry a sibling. This rule is sometimes violated in practice. While there are no direct sanctions against them, these marriages are said to be doomed to failure. In the origin narrative of Bayung Gede, it is specified that a marriage with someone from Batur is permissible only if the couple provide enough precious Indian *patola* cloth to stretch the entire distance from Bayung to Batur, which is, virtually impossible. The demand simply evokes the image of two individuals or families so rich and powerful that they can do away with conformity to official rules. Ironically, a couple capable of sustaining such a marriage would be admired for their resistance to supernatural retribution.

This narrative claim to a special bond of ancestry is supported by the fact that Bayung Gede performs a number of specific and unique ritual services for Batur. Visitors from Bayung Gede are the only visitors at the great festival of the tenth full moon who bring their own percussion and dance groups (*sekaa gong, sekaa baris*) to Pura Batur. They also deliver a complete set of offerings without which the great procession (*mapapada agung*) cannot begin. The people of Bayung further provide a symbolic amount of spices used in preparing food portions for the many thousand visitors. Finally, they supply the offerings that are thrown into the mouth of the volcano (*bakti pakelem*) at a ritual held every five years (*panca wali krama*) at Pura Jati Batur. A somewhat different kind of responsibility is that the people of Bayung will carry the funeral tower (*bade*) of the Jero Gede of Batur to the graveyard. For providing these essential services the *banua* of Bayung Gede is often referred to as the foundation (*sendi*) of Batur or as its *pakandel* (*kandel*, "area surrounding a palace or temple," also "[those who are] trusted"). Some informants in Bayung even suggested that the people of Bayung are Batur's elder siblings, because theirs is the more ancient of the two communities.

In the *pasihan* village Pakisan (Buleleng) a similar ancestral link is articulated through the symbolism of a body metaphor. Desa Batur is here said to be the head, Bayung Gede the neck, and Pakisan the shoulders of the alliance network. The people of Pakisan believe their village ancestors to have been members of the Pasek Batur clan. An origin narrative is often cited to explain how they arrived in Pakisan.

> In ancient times there was a village called Pakwan, which was located near present-day Pakisan. One day Jero Pasek Batur came along and challenged Pasek Pakwan to a gamble using fighting crickets (*jangkrit*). Pasek Batur's cricket was victorious, but, unwilling to concede defeat, Pasek Pakwan used his land as a wager for another game. Again he lost, and so his land passed on to Pasek Batur, whose descendants established

Desa Pakisan. It is always one of the direct descendants of the Pasek
Batur ancestor who is chosen to become the highest-ranking temple
priest (*pemangku gede*) in this village. Pasek Pakwan was forced to move
farther up the mountains and founded Desa Klandis.[23]

The people of Pakisan explicitly accept the temporal precedence
of Batur in the context of establishing their own local position as
founders. The idea of a victory in gambling rules out any precedence
claims from the people of Klandis, the former owners of this land.
The potential for continuing disputes with Klandis arises particularly
in relation to an ancient temple situated on Pakisan's territory (Chapter 6). While most *pasihan* villages only send a small delegation of
elders to visit briefly at the great festival in Batur, the villagers of Pakisan attend Batur's festival in full and always stay overnight to guard
the temple (*makemit*). In their perception, the visit is an obligatory
return to their ancestral origins.

Desa Selulung also maintains more than a general *pasihan* connection with Batur. Its version of a widely known myth explains the
origins of the relationship and its unique character.

> In ancient days Selulung was a prosperous village of two hundred
> households. Intervillage warfare was common at that time, and even-
> tually Selulung was to be destroyed by marauders. The enemies were
> led to the village by the sound of Selulung's sacred wooden slit-drum
> (*kulkul*), which had been struck as is usual during a temple festival.
> Only seven households survived the attack. They decided to forbid
> henceforth the beating of a *kulkul* in Selulung, in order to avoid the
> recurrence of attacks. The sacred *kulkul* was given instead as a gift to
> Pura Batur. There the drum was used as a warning signal for all the
> villagers of Batur and other Wintang Danu communities in the event
> of an attack. Its sound would rally their warriors to the community's
> defense or allow them to go into temporary hiding before a superior
> foe. Several attacks led by Panji Sakti [some say Raja Gelgel] were cur-
> tailed in this manner, until at last he realized how the warning was
> broadcast. He stole the drum, burned it, and was then able to ransack
> these villages. In the end, however, he repented for having destroyed
> a sacred object and possession of Dewi Danu. As an atonement he be-
> stowed a golden *kulkul* on the temple that has been kept in its posses-
> sion until today.

The myth shows a transition in the function of the slit-drum, from
attracting enemies in Selulung to becoming a warning device against
attack and a symbol of unity in Batur. Selulung's gift of a ritual slit-
drum is a metaphoric surrender of some measure of ritual independence to Batur. The narrative reflects on the problem of isolation, a
predicament that can only be overcome by forming ritual alliances.

Isolation invites dangers from the outside, whereas unity provides strength and protection.

As in the cases of Bayung Gede and Pakisan, the presence of a specific origin narrative coincides with special ritual obligations and rights. The offerings Selulung (also Blandingan, Satra, Abang, Pacung, and Julah) brings to Pura Batur each year include a deer rather than the more common gift of a sacrificial pig. In turn, Selulung lays a claim to Pura Petak Cemeng, the section of Pura Batur where the golden *kulkul* is kept. Deer heads are a symbol commonly used in the origin temples of descent groups who claim a common ancestry. The deer offering may thus be a hint that the relationship to Batur is in part based on common descent. Even though this origin narrative does not comment on matters of ancestry, such a link is widely believed to exist. My comparative data on village organization support the idea that the two villages may have a common historical origin.[24]

The special emphasis on a common origin history evident in these three cases is exceptional. Most of Batur's *pasihan* indeed regard Pura Penulisan as their common point of origin, and this applies also to Selulung. For villages in the district of Kintamani, the goddess and their ritual observances at Pura Batur are simply a complement to the male god and festival of Pura Penulisan. Batur is not normally relevant to the tracing of ancestral origins in that all genealogical reckoning is biased toward male links. This leads to the question why and under what conditions such special relationship narratives are maintained at all.

Social relationships frequently reconcile an official with a practical agenda. Making a relationship official may be useful in that it curtails the possibility of choosing to disassociate. But such added security will only be sought in a relationship that is regarded as desirable in the first place. If this is correct, then the tendency to legitimize a ritual relationship formally should be most evident with regard to those ritual alliances that are the most beneficial to a particular member village in its relations to a third party or beneficial to a dominant part of the domain as a whole (in this case, to Batur).

The special contributions in goods or services from the three *pasihan* villages discussed above may partially explain Batur's willingness to support their narratives of origin. The link to Batur is, in turn, a source of legitimization for their own special local status in relation to their own ritual clients. But these factors alone do not explain what may qualify another village as a useful ally in more general terms.

One limiting factor for the practical usefulness of an intervillage alliance is the physical and social proximity of the alliance partners.

It is the most proximate allies with whom a regular exchange of material goods and practical services is the most likely. It is also their opinion that is most determinative of one's own status in day-to-day interaction. If this interpretation is correct, one would expect strong evidence of relationship formalization among proximate allies. The relative scarcity of narratives legitimizing the ties between Pura Batur and its local allies in Kintamani seems to contradict this hypothesis, unless it is accepted that ties to Batur are indirectly justified in terms of the villages' simultaneous obligations to Pura Penulisan. As illustrated earlier, Penulisan's relations to proximate allies are indeed officialized in narrative form.

Another factor contributing to the usefulness of an ally is the possibility of trade. Since the resources of distant allies are more likely to differ from one's own than the resources of one's immediate neighbors, the possibility of trading with the former becomes particularly enticing.[25] However, interactions with distant and less familiar others harbor a potential for danger. In relationships between distant alliance partners, one would thus expect a similarly strong desire for the added security of narrative officialization, in which case the narratives might adopt a somewhat different idiom than those pertaining to proximate allies.

It is indeed observable that ties to important *pasihan* who are located at a great distance from Batur are frequently legitimized by elaborate relationship narratives. Even where they emphasize Dewi Danu's role as the guardian of irrigation water, these narratives regularly evoke trade as the most relevant idiom of social interaction. Another recurrent theme is an initial state of hostility and distrust among the trading parties.

One such myth refers to different trading behaviors as an explanation for the unequal distribution of irrigation water among *pasihan* villages situated along the coast of Buleleng:

Dewi Danu once took a journey disguised as a water seller. After some time she became tired and rested for a while near Batih [from *bateeh*, an exclamation indicative of fatigue]. There she tested her powers and brought forth water in the form of a creek [Yeh Kunyit near Batih]. Downhill she continued her journey to the arid coast of eastern Buleleng. When she arrived in Panjingan, no one approached her. Dewi Danu then spoke to them: "You are visited by a deity, and yet you ask for nothing. Thus I will give you water anyhow." And she created a spring referred to as "temelesan" from which the village's current name of Les is derived. Westward she wandered until she met some people from Subaya who were outcasts and in a state of impurity. Dewi Danu offered to sell them water, but they felt embarrassed and complained about their condition. She then purified and healed them with holy water (*tirta parisuda*). Thus cured, they were able to establish a village called Tejakula [*teja kula*, "the radiant group of people"]. Both in Les and in Tejakula she asked for one buffalo in return for her services, and miraculously she was able to carry the animals hidden in a *tirta* vessel [*bungbung*, a holy water container made from one section of bamboo]. When she reached Bondalem, she was insulted for none there believed that she could produce water. So she cursed them, declaring that their village would be arid, and said: "If you ever come to ask for my holy water, your offerings will perish before you reach Batur."[26] In Desa Julah she was received with similar skepticism. After she had built a water fountain, the residents taunted her, saying that they would gladly pay if only their money had not been buried [just like her water was still buried]. Again she cursed them so that there would never be any running water in their village. On she went trying to sell her water without success, and she took a rest at Pura Ponjok Batu. Farther west, around Desa Bukti [proof], people said that they would be content if only they had a productive well, as it has "proven" to be until today. Tired and angry, Dewi Danu threw away her water vessel in Air Sanih—near the beach so the spring that arose from it would be useless for irrigation.

In this narrative the trading efforts of Dewi Danu are much frustrated by initial distrust. The bone of contention is the order of exchange. In some cases the goods are delivered before they are requested, let alone paid for (as in Batih and Subaya). Repayment then follows out of gratitude for a favor that already has been granted. In other cases her ability to provide the goods is questioned and payment is demanded in advance. The trade fails because of insulting behavior, and the cargo is cast away and lost.

There are other versions of this myth, most notably one in which the deity is not Dewi Danu but the male god of Pura Penulisan.

Once Ratu Pucak Penulisan took on a human form and began a journey as a water seller. He walked along the northern coast, from Tianyar in the east to Penyusuan [Air Sanih] in the west. Few were willing to buy his water, and hence the area is generally arid, lacking running water for irrigation. He was ignored in Penuktukan, but in Les people bought one *kepeng* [a Chinese coin] worth of water, and in Tejakula they bought two *kepeng* worth. Both villages still have a relatively plentiful supply of running water, which they use for irrigation, but Tejakula more so than Les. In Bondalem and Julah none were willing to make a purchase, and finally the deity cast down his earthen water vessel at Air Sanih, where there is still a freshwater bathing pool by the beach until today. As an expression of gratitude, Desa Les offers a buffalo to Ratu Pucak Penulisan every twenty years and Tejakula every ten years. [In recent times the villages of Les and Tejakula also have been asked to bring a buffalo to Batur every so often.][27]

In this version, trade is partially frustrated by a lack of interest, but it does not end in an exchange of insults and curses. The goods are openly displayed and immediately paid for, setting the stage for regular and repeated exchanges. The continuing ritual payments to Pura Penulisan are proportional to the water supplied by its deity.

Both versions of this relationship narrative equate an unwillingness to trade with a refusal to acknowledge a ritual connection to the temple of the deity. The relative shortage of irrigation water on the northern coast is not accepted as a natural condition but is attributed to a failure to recognize the spiritual potency of one or the other of the two deities. The two versions represent rival claims as to the irrigation water's source. This rivalry would not eventuate if one were to regard the two deities and their temples as complementary components in the cosmology of a single domain.

Distant allies from the northeastern coast are not likely to have been truly necessary as providers of ritual support to the two mountain temples. It is rather the practical relations to coastal communities, as gateways to interisland trade, that must have preoccupied the people of the Kintamani district from an early time. Such ties were vital particularly for Batur traders, who traditionally dealt in imported cloth such as Indian *patola*.[28]

A further relationship narrative from Batur that tells of the initial difficulties in establishing trade links with distant communities is concerned with villages farther west in Buleleng.

> Once Dewi Danu took the form of an old trading woman and went to the market of Desa Kubutambahan. She met with traders from six villages in Buleleng, namely, Sangsit, Jagaraga, Panarukan, Bungkulan, Banyuning, and Kluncing. She offered the villagers buffaloes for purchase, claiming that she carried the animals in her water vessel.[29] The people of Buleleng found her claim incredible and taunted her. But when she pulled the plug of the bamboo vessel, six buffaloes jumped out and quickly ran away. The villagers ran in pursuit. When the old woman caught up with them, she found the greedy villagers had already captured and slaughtered the animals for a feast. Dewi Danu then revealed herself and fined them the payment of two buffaloes for her festival at Pura Batur on the tenth full moon. Until today two of the six villages must take turns each year to deliver a pair of buffaloes.[30]

A recurrent theme in this and the other narratives is how a lack of trust can threaten or prevent a transaction. The ideal situation is one where the buyers are ready to pay for goods that are not visible to them or where the trader advances the goods without demanding instant payment. In both cases a delay occurs between payment and delivery. In the practical process of a traditional barter system (*murup-*

urup), it often may have been necessary to surrender goods at the mere promise of exchange goods at the next meeting. Ironically, it is precisely this kind of delay that turns an economic exchange into a social relationship. Immediate payment leads to the termination of a context-specific transaction rather than allowing the creation of a perpetual relationship.[31]

The chosen method for establishing a lasting trust among trading partners is to engage simultaneously in the more regulated exchanges of a ritual order. Human agency and the strategic manipulations of traders are subsumed in a higher-order relationship situated in a religious context. The sacred obligation to a temple is the symbolic antithesis of the practical competition and subtle deceitfulness of behavior in the marketplace.

In trying to deal with distant allies, the establishment of an encompassing framework for social and economic relationships in the form of a ritual domain is not always feasible. A further relationship narrative from Batur illustrates a different strategy that can be used in interactions with people of a ritual domain other than one's own:

> Dewi Danu once went in disguise to the market in Bangli to trade maize [sometimes tobacco or betel nut] for rice. She took a copper bowl (*ceeng temaga*) along to measure her produce by volume. The male god of Pura Kehen (Bangli) also happened to be at the market. He beheld her in the radiant beauty of her true form and began to make passionate approaches to her. Dewi Danu rejected him, for she had decided to remain a virgin goddess forever. A quarrel arose, and Dewi Danu brought forth her power (*kesaktian*) to escape the assault but was forced to leave her goods behind. She created a hilltop between them, which was later called Bukit Sari or Bukit Bangli. The hill was also meant to divert irrigation waters from Bangli, but in response to this threat Bhatara Kehen rallied his power. Turning himself into an eel of iron, he bored through the hill in order to create a passage for the water to pass beneath it. In her hurry to depart, Dewi Danu had also forgotten her copper bowl, and loath to return, she sent her adoptive child, Ngurah Cempaga, to ask for its return. Bhatara Kehen was still disappointed that he could not marry Dewi Danu but agreed to a settlement. He proclaimed that if Dewi Danu ever again were to travel southward to the beach to hold a *melasti* ritual [a purifying ritual bath for a deity], she would have to pay a fine of 1,300 Chinese coins (*pananjung batu*). Dewi Danu, in turn, proclaimed that anyone practicing as a *balian* in Bangli and using a prayer bell (*genta*) would have to pay a fee of 225 Chinese coins to Pura Batur.[32]

Bhatara Kehen's attack and Dewi Danu's subsequent loss of cargo on one level exemplify the possible disasters that can befall a trader in a hostile situation. The narrative attributes the cause of the quarrel to uncontrolled sexual desire, on the one hand, and the refusal of a regulated relationship (marriage), on the other.

In this narrative the goddess not only encounters human beings but one of her own kind. She is unable to withhold her goods (her maize and irrigation water) but is still able to refuse a relationship. In refusing regulated marital interactions with Ratu Kehen, she escapes the danger of compromising her own status. The introduction of mutual sanctions represents a kind of compromise, whereby social relations are regulated only by mutual avoidance and formal exchanges are reduced to cash transactions.[33] The female deity maintains her aloofness by refusing to marry, but she fails to assert her authority beyond her own domain. The male deity in turn asserts his own local authority but cannot encompass the deity.

On a level of practice, direct ritual links between Pura Batur and Pura Kehen are thus rejected from both sides in order to avoid any status concessions. Whether this has always been the case is difficult to establish. Considering that Bayung Gede had a relatively close relationship to the rulers of Bangli, who were traditionally associated with Pura Kehen, and that Trunyan (like Batur a Wintang Danu village) maintains direct ritual ties to Pura Kehen, the existence of further ritual links between the areas of Bangli and Lake Batur during earlier periods should not be ruled out. In the past, Batur's trade network may have extended not only to the northern coast but also southward to Bangli, irrespective of the boundaries of ritual domains.

Batur's relationship narratives show that ties to distant allies may become precarious and characterized by studied avoidance when there is no possibility of claiming ritual precedence over the other or willingness to surrender to the other's ritual authority. A similar unwillingness to establish a bond of structured alliance prevails between Pura Penulisan (Sukawana) and Pura Batur, even though the two centers are separated by only a few kilometers. The leadership of the two temples prohibit any mutual ritual visits between the two villages except in the context of individual religious practice.

Most informants expressed a conviction that this current situation is the result of a conflict that terminated the unity of an earlier ritual order wherein the two centers were complementary parts of a single whole. Even a cursory comparison of the two networks reveals that many villages in the district of Kintamani and some along the northern coast maintain simultaneous ritual ties with both temples. Such dual affiliation is not normally perceived as a conflict of loyalties from the perspective of the villages concerned or as a matter of competition for clientele between the two temples even today. There are some exceptional cases where a degree of direct competition is visible. Those cases involve distant allies like Tejakula and Les, as indicated in the two versions of the water-seller myth, and a number of *subak* from the Payangan area.

Although there is considerable overlap between the two alliance networks, it is noteworthy that Batur still maintains a number of long-term clients in the Bangli area who have no connection to Penulisan at all. It is possible that the trading network that spanned from the northern coast across the mountains to the southern part of Bali has been dominated by Batur (and other Wintang Danu villages) at its southern extremities for a prolonged period. The content of Prasasti Kintamani E (see Chapter 10) supports this hypothesis given that, in turn, the Penulisan group, most prominently the traders of Kintamani, at one time held a monopoly over trade with villages on the northeastern coast of Buleleng. This situation also may have encouraged traders in Batur to extend their ritual ties to villages on Buleleng's western coast (see myth concerning Dewi Danu's buffalo sale, above) or to the south. However, while such different trade orientations and interests may shed some light on a contemporary divergence of interests and affiliations among the two temples, they cannot account for the considerable overlap in their clientele of villages.

The presence of a shared clientele among Batur and Penulisan must be considered from the point of view of the two temples' cosmological complementarity. The supporting villages' dual loyalties are in fact enshrined in an annual ritual cycle. The festivals at Pura Penulisan and Pura Batur are conducted at a precise interval of six lunar months, on the fourth and tenth full moon, respectively. These two lunar months (as well as the fifth) are considered pure and auspicious (*sasih suci*). Diametrically opposed in the annual cycle, the fourth and tenth full moons are generally the most important dates for regional-level ritual directed toward the uranian deities, while annual blood sacrifices to chthonic deities are a village matter in the mountains (sixth to ninth *sasih*). They also mark the turning points between the wet and dry seasons in the annual climatic cycle and related patterns in the cycle of dry rice agriculture.[34] Respectively, the fourth and tenth months are the beginning of the rainy season and planting, and the dry season and harvest. Theoretically both of these ritual occasions could be conducted at the same temple. In practice, however, most *pura banua* have only one major annual festival in which the entire group of villages participates.

Changes to material or economic conditions directly affect the regiment of mundane practices and may indirectly have an impact on the ritual practices that articulate a representation of the former. Ritual orders are thus unlikely to remain fixed in times of economic upheaval. It is conceivable that the gradual decline of rice agriculture and the introduction of cash crops in the Kintamani area was in part responsible for the collapse of the former unity between Pura Batur and Pura Penulisan, along with external influences. Batur's efforts to establish a clientele of distant *subak* still engaged in rice agriculture may well have been a response to the decline of these agricultural practices among villages in the vicinity of the temple. As a temple of ancestral origin, Penulisan was less affected by these changes and did not need to seek out new clients defined in terms of their agricultural practice of irrigation. In a local idiom one could say that Dewi Danu, unlike Ratu Pucak, did not have any children of her own to support her, unless she was portrayed as the wife of Ratu Pucak and his children as hers. The latter option would not be acceptable in view of Pura Batur's contemporary status claims.

The villages in Kintamani that are affiliated with both temples see their function as broadly complementary in a cosmological sense. They suggested that their social links to Penulisan are (presently) much stronger than their links to Batur. One explanation lies in the elitist stance of the current leadership of Pura Batur, which prevents other villages from full participation and constructs their substantial contributions and hence their status as that of mere visitors. Another and perhaps related factor is that Pura Batur and its female deity do not represent a point of origin to them in the same way as Pura Penulisan and its male deity. This distinction reflects a similar patrifocal bias in the official ideology of kinship, whereby a descent-based group traces its connection to ancestral origins along a male line of predecessors and successors rather than a female line. Pura Batur's preeminent role in the maintenance of fertility is also reflective of the gender imagery in this cosmology. Women are associated with the receptive fertility of the earth, but it is men who plant the seeds of life.

In short, the support network of Pura Batur does not constitute a separate and independent *banua*. It is not inconceivable that two *banua* could occupy the same territory.[35] Far more likely is that the two temples were once paired and integrated within the ritual order of a single domain.

How and when the relationship between the two temples became one of avoidance is difficult to ascertain in historical terms. But there are several myths that focus on this event and on the origins of the present state of affairs, such as the following two versions from Penulisan (Sukawana):

(1) Once the deity of Pura Penulisan wanted to go forth and visit his relatives in Bayung Gede. When the people of Sukawana passed in solemn procession through Batur, they were invited to rest and take a meal, as was customary at that time. When all had eaten, the leftover food was thrown to the dogs. The following year the residents of Batur attended the festival at Pura Penulisan as they always did in those days. They too were received with a meal, but the remainder of the food was kept by the hosts for later consumption. The people of Batur then realized that their own behavior had been insulting and arrogant, for they had refused to keep the leftovers of their guests. Out of shame, they never returned to Pura Penulisan. Likewise, Sukawana does not pay ritual visits to Batur. They claim this to be unnecessary because they are the keepers of a sacred object (*pretima*) that represents the goddess.

(2) Dewi Danu once visited Ratu Pucak Penulisan, and her leftovers were kept for later consumption. But when she invited him for a return visit to Pura Batur, she threw the leftovers to the dogs. Ratu Pucak felt insulted, and the relationship was cut off. Since then, marriages between the two villages have been officially prohibited and are considered to be inauspicious.

Eating together or from the same source, and even more so the mutual consumption of one another's leftovers, is an expression of a very intimate association, reminiscent of the relations between a man and woman who form a household (*kuren*, lit. "hearth"). The literal meaning of their local designation defines households in terms of the day-to-day commensality of the group who share a single hearth. It is common that members of a household eat during the day when they return home from the fields, helping themselves to food that has been prepared in the morning. In a way, those who take their food later are thus eating the leftovers of those who have eaten earlier.

In this relationship narrative, Batur is accused of breaking the code of commensality and thereby ending a formerly intimate association. By discarding the food that was left unconsumed by their guests, the hosts from Batur rejected this kind of intimacy. Marriage between the two villages, another important form of intimate association, was thus forbidden as well. Batur's version of the event displaces the social relationship to the level of divine actors, and a refusal of marriage becomes the central issue:

(1) The deity of Pura Penulisan is the four-faced Bhatara Wisnu Murti, but when deities still had a human form, his name was Bhagawan

Siwagandu. Some say this great teacher was none other than Maharishi Markandeya, who changed his name after reaching *moksa* [spiritual liberation] on Gunung Agung.[36] In any case, a promise was once made by Dewi Danu that she would marry him if only he could raise a small mountain with his yogic power, tall enough so that her hair would no longer touch the ground.[37] Bhagawan Siwagandu put forth his powers, and Gunung Batur grew fuming in the midst of the crater lake. However, Dewi Danu's hair grew longer at the same rate, and finally her suitor gave up exhausted. In anger he tried to grab her, but the mountain had become so tall that she was out of reach. Thereafter their relationship became chilly indeed.

(2) When Bhagawan Siwagandu sought a new domicile after his dispute with Dalem Balingkang, he first moved to Jong Les [near Desa Pinggan] and then to Batu Magantung [Desa Songan, by the lake]. But each time Mt. Batur erupted, because a holy man should live at a high place. So finally he settled on Bukit Penarajon [Penulisan], which is higher than Mt. Batur.

Again it is Batur, or Dewi Danu, who refuses the intimate association offered by Sukawana, or Bhatara Pucak Penulisan. As in her relationship with Bhatara Kehen, such a marriage would have compromised her status and thus the status of her temple and its leadership. Still, the portrayal of Bhagawan Siwagandu shows a considerable degree of respect for both his power and his status. He is prevented from settling at the lake beneath Mt. Batur—the seat of the goddess—by means of volcanic eruptions, and his final position is higher than her own. Physical elevation is understood as a symbolic indicator of a person's status in Bali, and the sacredness of the mountains is just one aspect of this larger scheme.

The subtle acknowledgment of Penulisan's somewhat higher status is not just expressed by the references to relative elevation in this narrative. In contemporary ritual practice, such tacit acknowledgment is expressed by Batur's annual visit to Pura Balingkang. At the end of Pura Batur's great festival of the tenth month, the village will pay its respects to Bhatara Dalem Balingkang, the deified Balinese king whose ancestors are said to have lived in Kuta Dalem and whose state temple was Pura Penulisan. The area around Pura Balingkang is so closely associated with Sukawana and Penulisan in local history that it is often referred to as Sukawana II. As was noted earlier, a priest-leader from Sukawana also performs the crucial buffalo sacrifice at Balingkang. One could therefore say that to acknowledge Balingkang is to acknowledge the ritual leadership of Sukawana. Batur's visit to Balingkang is referred to as "*mapiuning*," which means "to [politely] inform the gods of an undertaking" in order to secure their approval and blessing. In this case, Batur informs the deity or king "Ratu Balingkang" that its duty of holding the festival of the tenth month has been completed and delivers a share of the offerings received to illustrate this.

It may be that Batur, in the past, collected *suwinih* and *atos* from the *subak* and *pasihan* and then delivered the king's share to Balingkang, at the time possibly still a royal residence (*puri*) rather than a temple (*pura*). When I asked several visitors from Batur in Balingkang whether they had stopped on the way at Penulisan to make their intention known to its deity (*mapiuning*), they became extremely embarrassed and conceded that they certainly should have done so, but that "frankly, the arrogance of our own leaders prevents us from showing such open and obvious deference to Pura Penulisan." It is often the case that feuds or competitive relationships between temples are frowned on by those who are not themselves ritual leaders but only followers at the temples concerned and who therefore benefit little from the increase in status that can be achieved by disassociating their own temple from the authority of other temples.

Given that any reconstruction of the previous relationship between the two temples is probably doomed to remain speculative, it may be more fruitful to explore instead the still functioning relationship between another pair of temples and their *banua*. These temples are Pura Pucak Antap Sai, with a female deity and a festival on *purnama kedasa* (like Pura Batur), and Pura Pucak Manggu, with a male deity and a festival on *purnama kapat* (like Pura Penulisan). This pair of sanctuaries is discussed in the following chapter. Another extension of the present image of ritual life in the highlands yet to be discussed is Batur's traditional ties with two other groups of villages, the *banua* of Desa Bayung Gede and the network known as the "Stars of the Lake Batur," or Wintang Danu. These groups of villages are clients of Pura Batur in one context but also form *banua* with their own ritual orders in which Batur is but a part. Still other domains in the highlands have a residual link to Pura Penulisan.

The domains of Pura Balingkang and Pura Indrakila can be described as branches of the older and perhaps once encompassing *banua* of Pura Pucak Penulisan. Pura Batur, in turn, may well have been Penulisan's female counterpart in a wider framework of ritual action, spanning a good part of the entire island, defining the rhythm of agricultural practice for many Balinese, and establishing important links of trade between the northern coast and the southern hinterland.

The observation that there can be regular ritual interactions across different domains is of the utmost importance for the wider question of Bali Aga identity. This study of ritual networks in the highlands has revealed so far that Bali Aga villages are not isolated but have always been organized within complex domains. If it is also true that these domains are in turn linked in an even wider, though perhaps more tenuous, web of relations and narrative histories, then a solution may be near to the enigma of Bali Aga unity over a period of six centuries of Majapait rule in Bali.

The process of differentiation that has led to a partial separation among the domains of Penulisan, Balingkang, and Indrapura is comparable to a similar process within domains whereby new independent villages are established on the territory of a large origin village. In both cases the new branch institutions may recognize that they are a part of a larger whole in some ritual contexts, while asserting their independence in other contexts. A similar logic of relatedness, based on a notion of origin, seems to permeate relations both within and between *banua*.

The main difference in relations within and between *banua* is that, at the present time, there is no wider social institution that would formally regulate the ritual relationships among original and branch domains. Penulisan may be the center among ritual centers in the highlands, but it is not the center of a distinct and named institution beyond the *banua*. The fact that the king of Bali granted the people of Cenigayan leave from their obligations to Pura Penulisan indicates that such an institution did exist in the past. The realms or polities (*negara*) of early Balinese kings may have provided the higher-order institutions that could regulate relations among *banua* and their temples within an overarching ritual order.

The origin narratives of Balingkang reflect a certain local disappointment with the old kings for having allowed their realms to dwindle. Mountain people resent that they have been stripped of the central position in the political life of Bali they claim to have occupied in the past. Where the old Balinese kings had acted as arbitrators in religious matters, the new Majapait-derived kingdoms were unwilling to provide a new umbrella for the many ritual domains of the Bali Aga or, at least, would have demanded modifications to Bali Aga ritual traditions in return.

The Bali Aga know that they have paid a price for this lack of full mutual recognition between Balinese Majapait kings and themselves. When asked to explain the blindfolding of the buffalo in the origin narrative of Cenigayan, some informants suggested that it represents how the Bali Aga people had closed their eyes to the world beyond and thereby threatened their own sense of unity. Without an external power of arbitration, relations within domains became voluntary and precarious arrangements. The enmity of Majapait kings and their own lack of vision upset the proper order of things, with the original people (here Cenigayan) forced away from their rightful place as custodians of the point of origin (here Pura Indrakila). The strategy of ignoring the new realm centered on the royal court of Klungkung may have been flawed; however, it was not adopted without cause. Wherever Majapait kings and princes have been allowed to intervene in a domain, as in the case of Balingkang, the effect has been to the detriment of the local ritual traditions in the *banua* concerned.

Beyond the *banua* of Pura Pucak Penulisan and its branch domains, there are a number of other *banua* around regional temples in the highlands of Bali. Some of them are still linked to Pura Pucak Penulisan, the ancient temple on the "mountain of life," though less directly and intimately so than the temples of Balingkang, Indrakila, and Batur. Others have an origin history and ritual order entirely of their own. A number of these additional cases will be presented in Chapter 6 in order to further advance a comparative understanding of ritual domains in Bali and to unravel the wider relations among them.

Chapter 6

A RITUAL MAP
OF THE HIGHLANDS

The institution of the *banua* is of significance well beyond the geographical sphere of Pura Pucak Penulisan's direct or indirect influence. Several other domains will be described in this chapter in brief
comparative sketches. These case studies are designed to reveal similarities and variations in the conceptual and ritual organization of
banua without exploring the intricacies of social processes in each
individual domain. I aim to provide a ritual map of the highlands
rather than a detailed account, even of such local complexities as have
already been studied, and there is much room for further research
in this area.

The first case study is of the domain of the village Bayung Gede.
This network was mentioned briefly at the beginning of the discussion
on different types of *banua* (Chapter 1). Other networks to be examined include the Stars of Lake Batur (Wintang Danu); the domains
of Pura Tolukbiyu, Pura Pucak Tajun, Pura Pucak Manggu, and Pura
Pucak Antap Sai; and several smaller *banua* on the southern fringe of
the highlands.

Desa Banua Bayung Gede

The ancient mountain village of Bayung Gede was one of the first to
achieve worldwide attention, for it was chosen as the ideal site for a
famous study on "Balinese Character" by Gregory Bateson and Margaret Mead (1942). This privilege was not granted on account of the
remarkable traditions of the village. The choice fell on Bayung because
of the authors' belief that an iodine deficiency syndrome endemic in
this region had produced a very simplistic mentality that would be
more readable for foreign researchers than the ever so complex

character of other, more sophisticated Balinese. Unfortunately Bateson and Mead's work revealed only glimpses of the complex social organization and regional significance of this village.

The people of Bayung Gede and their affiliates in other villages refer to themselves as the *gebog satak* of Bayung Gede. The member villages of the *gebog satak* proper are Bayung Gede, Penglipura, Tiga Kawan, and Sekardadi. Ritual interactions are the most fervent among this core group. However, the wider membership of the *banua* includes the *desa adat* of Sulahan, Pengiangan, Tanggahan, and Lumbahan (one *desa dinas*); Pengotan and Sunting (one *desa dinas*); and Kedisan, Buahan, and Bonyoh.[1] These villages maintain a range of conceptually different origin ties and ritual connections to Bayung Gede.

One group of villages is said to be *pondokan* of the original Desa Bayung. They were derived from a cluster of garden dwellings (*pondok*) established at some distance from the mother village and have long grown into permanent settlements and independent *desa adat*. The founder groups of these villages still claim that their ancestors originated from Bayung. Among such *pondokan* are Desa Bonyoh, Penglipura, Sekardadi, and others.

There is some scope for evaluating the historical accuracy of such origin narratives. That local origin histories may not be entirely fictitious can sometimes be shown by a comparative study of social organization in the villages concerned. For example, the customary titles and the mode of succession in the council of elders of Desa Bonyoh are indeed much more similar to those of Bayung than to those of ritually unrelated neighboring villages. In a few other cases, this kind of comparative evidence may contradict local histories. Historical accuracy is thus not a necessary requirement for the social efficacy of an origin narrative in establishing a *banua*. However, it would be rash to suggest that such narratives are utterly unrestrained flights of local historical imagination.

One reason is that ritual behavior has a strong conservative element. A newly established ritual link is most often constructed as a rediscovery, as in the tale of Pura Tebenan. The creation of a new link between villages is depicted as the discovery of an old and forgotten obligation. There is no official admission that history can be constructed. To the contrary, human agency is discounted as far as is possible, and the deliberate construction of a false origin history or a ritual association with a false point of origin would be regarded as an invitation to disaster and divine retribution.

A more tangible caveat to the imagining of history is the need for general acceptance of the social link that this history is meant to justify. While a large social and ritual network is considered desirable in general, a restraint to free networking is created by the problem of status differences within domains. For example, if a village initiates a bilateral tie with a powerful neighboring community or joins an established *banua*, it usually has to accept a relatively subsidiary position within the relationship. This prospect calls for a careful weighing of benefits and costs. The consensus and support within a village that are required before such a step is taken can be difficult to achieve, especially if the new link negates existing beliefs about the past or only reflects the strategic aims of a minority.

While a degree of caution is thus advisable in the interpretation of origin narratives as history, it also should not be ignored that often these narratives are genuine memories. The village of Bantang, for example, has for centuries visited the site of the deserted village Pengupetan, which its residents have faithfully remembered as their sacred point of origin. They were both unable and loath to read the sacred inscriptions kept at the site.[2] But when the inscriptions were finally deciphered in recent years by an official from the Bali Museum, the content proved to corroborate their narrative origin history (Budiastra 1993b).

I have mentioned already that the relationship between people of origin and branch villages in a domain are reaffirmed by ritual visits. The most important gathering of members of the *banua* of the Gebok Satak Bayung Gede takes place at the *usaba gede* in Bayung, which is celebrated on the fourth full moon (*purnama kapat*) of every second year.[3] Other, less regular and frequent gatherings occur at the *usaba gede* in Sekardadi, Pengotan, Buahan, and other important member villages. Major purification rites (*balik sumpah*) represent more irregular occasions for a *banua* assemblage. They are performed in Bayung after the birth of opposite-sex twins (*kembar buncing*) or following a temple restoration.

The agency of these visits among villages is displaced onto the visiting relationships of sacred beings. The deities of branch villages are "children" of the senior deity in Bayung Gede, and it is their filial duty to visit their "parents." For example, a male deity of Pura Puseh Klan, in Desa Bonyoh, is believed to be the son of Bhatara Pura Dukuh Bayung Gede. On each day of *manis galungan* (a date in the 210-day *wuku* calendar), this deity descends into a sacred Balinese dragon mask (*barong*) and visits his father at Pura Dukuh in Bayung.[4]

The carriers of the gods are in this case said to enter a state of trance, possessed by the deity that the mask represents.

The displacement of social relations among villages onto the sociality of divine agents and the enactment of these relationships in codified ritual action in part relates to a local perception of the problem of individual and collective agency. When locals speak of villages as the participating agents in a *banua*, they construct the idea of such communities by reference to the divine individuals who are their founders. Local religious discourses thus solve the problem of communal versus individual action by discounting both and by introducing the notion of divine agents. The ancestral deities are transcendental individuals who stand for social groups. Communal action in the village and domain is simply portrayed as the outcome of common obedience to the will of superior beings. With the introduction of gods, the individual agency that has been taken out of communal action is reintroduced at a transcendental level.

The reconciliation of collective and individual action is also an important issue in the social sciences. Indeed, to speak of communities interacting as if they were individual agents is deeply problematic. An unreflective attribution of agency to institutions is a form of reification and also a mystification of the political processes that inform joint actions.[5] Insofar as I appear to attribute agency to villages in my own discussion of *banua*, this should be taken as a reflection of local discourses that similarly discount individual agency in favor of group identities and traditions. This is not an accurate portrayal of social realities. While individuals may act collectively as if they were one, based on a momentary consensus or a somewhat more stable notion of tradition, they are never actually in complete agreement about who they are as a group and how they should act collectively. Therefore, the term "village" is used here not as a reference to some monolithic institution but as a gloss for a socially negotiated and shifting reality unfolding within the fluid organization of the *desa adat*. The agency of individuals or factions in a village is not fused into the agency of a transcendental village in any simple or final sense. The idea of villages doing things is meaningful only insofar as the arena for the expression of free agency of individuals in Bali is heavily circumscribed. Agency is restricted by the social conditions that people inherit from their predecessors and by their participation in the set of institutionalized practices that tend to reproduce these conditions. These restrictions are limited but important as a model for social cooperation. It is this cooperation that is ultimately valued and considered sacred in Bali. Displacement of sociality to an invisible world of divine beings has an additional advantage. It helps to diffuse some of the inevitable status messages implicit in any formal association between groups of people. A relatively even distribution of symbolic capital among the human participants of a domain can be maintained as long as it is only the gods who are overtly ranked as predecessors and successors through asymmetric exchanges and visiting patterns.

The journeys of *barong* and of deities carried in *palinggih* are a major symbolic and ritual paradigm for the expression of relationships between temples not only in the mountains but in many parts of Bali. Visits that are articulated as *barong* journeys tend to fall mostly into the festive *galungan* period, generally a season for visiting one's relatives in Bali. At this time of the *wuku* year, people will return to their house of origin to see parents or grandparents and to pay homage to the ancestors enshrined in their ancestral origin temple (*sanggah kemulan*).

Once a deity has entered a sacred mask, he or she is usually referred to as Ratu Alit Tapakan Barong, "the little lord [on his] *barong* mount," an indication that this deity is somewhat junior. The title reflects a general notion that juniors ought to visit their seniors rather than the reverse. The orientation of *barong* journeys reflects the same status pattern in a spatial idiom. *Barong* tend to pay visits to sacred uphill (*kaja*) locations more often than they travel downhill (*kelod*). This upward orientation of visiting patterns may also explain why there are far fewer *barong* in the mountains than in southern Bali. A mountain *barong* would be forced to travel downstream or to remain at home. The few who do exist are found at the southern fringe of the area depicted in Figure 2. Instead, the mountains and their sanctuaries are associated with the ancestors whom one must visit periodically just as one must visit one's elder living relatives. At the mountain temples of Pucak Penulisan and Pucak Pausan, for example, downstream *barong* gather in large numbers even though there are very few *barong* within these temples' domains that could reciprocate the visits.[6]

Not all villages affiliated to Bayung Gede are regarded as former *pondokan*. The people of Desa Katung, for example, are regarded as "immigrant clients." Their ancestors migrated from Desa Kayubihi and established a new village on vacant land that belonged to Bayung. Bateson (1970), in his famous essay on "an old temple and a new myth," describes an incident in which the people of Katung attempted to redefine their relations to Bayung. Following the discovery of an old, abandoned temple, they consulted a *balian taksu*. The medium proclaimed that the temple's deity was a daughter of a village deity in Bayung and a sibling of deities in Peludu (see below) and Abuan (also a village of client newcomers).

Bateson did not consider that the case was already decided in advance of the consultation by the general regulations applying to immigrant clients. The rediscovered temple was one for which Katung had automatically accepted responsibility (no matter whether anybody knew about it) at the moment their ancestors received the piece of land from Bayung Gede on which the ruins were located. The association between the newly discovered temple and the old origin village of Bayung Gede was beyond questioning from the outset because land is spiritually inalienable. However, immigrant clients may be and often are entrusted with the care of old temples situated on the part of the domain that is allocated to them by their patrons. Bateson's case illustrates a renegotiation of an existing patron-client relationship and at best a new addition to an old myth.

That temple in Katung is nowadays known as Pura Gunung Sari. At each of its festivals, Katung must "inform the gods" (*mapiuning*) in Bayung before the ceremony can commence. In turn, the people of Bayung still relate to the temple in a fashion that reflects their own concerns. Often they visit Pura Gunung Sari to seek a blessing before engaging in an artistic project, for its deity is said to be a sponsor of the arts.

Both villages had been unaware of the existence of this "new" temple, but there was only one appropriate and obvious interpretation: the temple was the acquired responsibility of the client immigrants. What is interesting is the initiative by Katung and the cautious acceptance by Bayung Gede to have the deity of the "new" temple integrated into the web of divine family relations that are the conceptual foundation of this *banua*. Katung gained a kind of adoptive status in the *banua* that transcends and camouflages its status as client immigrants in ritual contexts. It must be noted that the new deity was considered to be female. This meant that Katung could now be construed as wife- (and land-) receiving affines (*mantu*, "son-in-law").[7] Bateson's interviews show evidence that this rethinking of the relationship with Katung benefited Bayung as well, as Bayung had experienced difficulties in securing perpetual assistance from these clients for temple ceremonies and repairs in Bayung Gede. However, since the people of Katung maintain an ancestral origin claim with regard to Kayubihi, their status in the *banua* remains ambiguous. As descendants of an in-marrying son-in-law, they should ideally renounce or at least discount their agnatic ancestry link to Kayubihi.

A counterexample to Katung's search for a closer association with the domain center is Desa Bonyoh, an established *pondokan* of Bayung. Bonyoh's founder group is claimed to be Pasek Bayung Gede. However, representatives of a powerful faction of immigrant newcomers in this village are currently propagating an origin narrative that does away with the Bali Mula origins of the ancestors of the village (and of the founder group). They are attempting to distance themselves and the village as a whole from the center Bayung Gede and to undermine the local founder group's status.

> Before the village of Bonyoh was established, there was already a settlement three kilometers to the south. The settlement was called Desa Klan and the inhabitants were Bali Mula [original Balinese] from Bayung Gede. Nearby grew a *waringin* [Banyan] tree whose fruits were ceremonial daggers (kris). Great crowds of visitors came from far and wide to see the miraculous tree and had to be entertained by the unfortunate villagers to the point that they were reduced to poverty. They were ashamed to be unable to accommodate further visitors, and when the next lot arrived, they fled to Badung, where there is still a village called Klan. The guests thus found the village deserted and only a faint fragrance of coconut [*bo nyuh*, or Bonyoh] remained to titillate their appetite. Where these visitors came from is not known, but they decided to stay and founded the present Desa Bonyoh.[8]

The tale depicts the peaceful takeover of a village by newcomers from shame-faced locals who had failed in their duty as hosts by not providing adequately for their guests. The material poverty of the legitimate village founders is construed in the narrative as a justification for a political takeover by newcomers. This is a reflection of a contemporary scenario. The more affluent newcomers of contemporary Bonyoh, who propagate this myth, are currently attempting to wrest ritual control from a poverty-stricken group of village founders. Understandably, this account of Bonyoh's origins, though it maintains many elements of a more traditional version, is not accepted by the indigenous faction.

Bayung's relationships to several other neighboring villages is also posited on notions of an affinal association between divine beings, similar to the one recently established with Katung. It is said that the male deity of Pura Puseh Desa Belanga, for example, married a daughter of Ratu Pura Puseh Pinggit in Bayung Gede. A further link, to Desa Buahan, is conceptualized as a marriage between Ratu Sakti Subandar (the mighty lord harbor master) of Pura Pengelepasan (in Buahan) and a female deity from Bayung Gede. In all cases, a male god in another village is the *mantu* (daughter's husband) of a deity in Bayung and hence of inferior status (in the case of Katung, the son-in-law's identity is not made explicit).

Buahan is an interesting alliance partner for Bayung. The village is often considered one of the Wintang Danu (stars of the lake) group of villages because of its location at the shore of Lake Batur. However, locals see themselves as distinct and separate from their lakeside neighbors, perhaps because the latter attribute Buahan with only a secondary status. Their most important bilateral ancestral connection is with distant Desa Bondalem (Buleleng) on the northern coast. The affiliation with Bayung, though it has connotations of servility, presents a welcome opportunity for Buahan to distance itself from its immediate neighbors without becoming isolated. Links to other lakeside villages are indirectly affirmed, because Bayung Gede and other communities in its domain maintain ties with members of the Wintang Danu, including Kedisan, Trunyan, and Batur.[9]

The notion that people should associate closely with their neighbors in the *banjar* or *desa*, even though they are neither agnates nor affines, is of general importance also at the level of intervillage ritual association. On the basis of their proximity, neighboring villages are often invited as witnesses (*penyaksi*) at important temple festivals, just as one would invite neighbors to a wedding or other large family ritual. For Bayung, such occasional visitors include Trunyan, Kedisan, Pengotan, Sunting, Padpadan, and Susut. These visits are sporadic but reciprocal, and the visitors will bring *atos* as a sign of respect. This paradigm of neighborhood help is in many cases strengthened by a recognized similarity of customs (*adat*) and a defensive unity toward outsiders. Many legends recall the cooperation of Bali Aga villages in defending themselves, for example, against the marauding armies of Panji Sakti (see Worsley 1972). The *penyaksi* model of intervillage relations is also advantageous in cases where both parties wish to avoid issues of status ranking.

Bayung Gede is connected also to the centers of other ritual networks, where its residents adopt the role of homage-paying visitors or supporters. One upward connection from Bayung Gede is to Desa Sukawana. Whenever the sacred sugar palm fiber (*duk*) that covers the roof of the *bale lantang* (the long pavilion [for council meetings]) of Bayung Gede's Pura Bale Agung is to be replaced, the head elder of Bayung must visit Sukawana in order to ask for a specific kind of holy water called *tirta pekulu*. Likewise, Bayung's branch village Sekardadi will ask for *tirta* in Sukawana when they repair the roof of their temple gate (*cang apit*). Roofs, particularly when they are made of *duk,* symbolically represent the realm of the (sky-dwelling) gods above. Bayung also attends and brings *atos* to the annual festival at Pura Pucak Penulisan in Sukawana and occasionally to the festival of Sukawana's Pura Bale Agung.[10] No specific origin narrative supports this relationship, but it effectively displays a degree of ritual deference on the part of Bayung Gede.

Bayung Gede also maintains a ritual link to Kintamani, a *gebok satak* center within the *gebog domas* of Pura Penulisan. The link is in part related to the legendary history of Desa Peludu, which is said to have been destroyed by Panji Sakti. All inhabitants were killed or taken away as prisoners, and the vacant territory was divided between Bayung Gede and Kintamani. The old Pura Bale Agung of Peludu had to be maintained, however, since the village deities did not simply disappear with the death of the inhabitants. Farmers who now use the land of Peludu would consider it dangerous to ignore the land's guardian deities. The two villages have in part divided these duties, and in part they also hold rituals jointly. Furthermore, Bayung Gede's *barong celeng* (a *barong* in the guise of a boar) visits Pura Tenten in Kintamani, a temple where the gods of the entire region are believed to gather "in order to go shopping (*mamasar*) for their perfume (*burat wangi*)" and whose deity is a child of Bhatara Pucak Penulisan. Bayung Gede thus maintains tentative ritual links to important allies of Suka-wana. It is possible that Bayung's close relations to Batur led to some estrangement, since there is considerable animosity between Batur and Penulisan (Sukawana). Likewise, their links to the Wintang Danu are tainted nowadays by open rivalry between Batur and Songan.

The Wintang Danu

The Wintang Danu, or Stars of the Lake, do not form a *banua* with a singular center. In this loose conglomerate of interrelated villages, each community maintains at least one temple of regional signifi-cance that attracts visitors from its allies at the time of its annual festival. The prevailing pattern of reciprocal visits is reminiscent of ritual practices within the *banua* of Bayung Gede, to which the Stars of Lake Batur regard themselves as related. Sometimes the lake vil-lages and Bayung Gede together describe themselves as *bali mula* (original Balinese) rather than *bali aga*, introducing a further dis-tinction into the generic indigenous status attributed to all mountain villages by southern Balinese.[11]

The question of which village occupies a position of precedence or may represent the point of origin of others is left unresolved in the idiom of ritual visits within this *banua*. This is reflected in the origin narratives of its member communities. Local origin myths can be divided into at least two major bodies of narrative that provide rather different accounts of the settlement history of the lake shore. One is a tale of four divine siblings and founders of villages and favors Trunyan as a senior regional center. Another is the origin narrative of Pasek Kayuselem. It describes the creation of the first human being (Mpu Kamareka) from the blackened stump of a tree and the subsequent migrations of his village-founding descendants. This second tale situates the point of origin in either old Batur or Tampur Hyang, "the place where the creator deity first descended to the earth," or in Songan, where the ancestors established the first human settlement. Considering the open conflict between Batur and Songan over the location of the true Pura Ulun Danu and their competition in securing a clientele, it is not surprising that the interpretation of this second narrative is complicated by the circulation of conflicting versions, including various publications of the *lontar* text Babad Pasek Kayuselem (e.g., Sugriwa 1968 and Budiastra 1989). In view of these struggles about defining the past, my discussion will be confined to the most significant ritual alliances within the region that were operative at the time of my research. This account of the Wintang Danu villages as a ritual domain serves a purpose of comparison rather than representing an attempt to unravel the puzzles of their ethnohistory.[12]

The first set of ritual relationships among Wintang Danu villages center on an oral origin narrative about four divine siblings who established themselves in Kedisan, Abang, Trunyan, and Songan (or Batur). Different versions reflect the varying perceptions of their status relationships in different villages.

> *Trunyan version:* Once the king of Solo sent out his four children to Bali to seek the source of a strange perfume that reached as far as his palace in Central Java. The three brothers and their younger sister followed the faint scent, which originated from a sacred benzoin tree (*taru menyan*) located in Trunyan on the far shores of Lake Batur. When they finally arrived at the lake, the younger sister decided to remain at the temple of the lake goddess, Dewi Danu, where she still has a shrine under the name of Ratu Ayu Mas Maketeg. The brothers continued their journey along the shore of the lake. The youngest remained in Kedisan, distracted by the sound of a bird, and the second in Abang Dukuh, distracted by an encounter with two women. The eldest brother was angered by their dallying and would not let them accompany him any farther. He alone continued the mission and finally reached the sacred benzoin tree in Trunyan that was emitting the tantalizing scent. He found living there a girl and her hermaphrodite elder twin brother, children of a goddess impregnated by the sun. The

prince was overcome with passion and asked the brother's permission to marry the girl. This request was granted on the condition that he remain in Trunyan [*nyeburin*, uxorilocal marriage] to become the founder of that village and the ancestor of its people. He is known to the villagers as Ratu Sakti Pancering Jagat and his wife as Ratu Ayu Pingit Dalam Dasar. (Translated and summarized from Danandjaja 1980:40)

In this version, the sister is the youngest sibling and thus the last in order of seniority. She is associated with Dewi Danu, in whose temple she takes residence. She is not explicitly identified as Dewi Danu, as she is in a second version from Desa Abang. This second version also locates the original twins and human ancestors in Abang.

Abang version: There once lived a goddess in Trunyan called Ratu Ayu Dalem Pingit. Attracted by the perfume that issued from her, four divine siblings came to the lake, a girl and her three younger brothers. First they arrived in Kedisan, where the youngest brother saw a colorful bird (*kedis titiran*) with an enchanting voice. He chased after it, but his siblings became tired of waiting and moved on, leaving him behind to found Kedisan [from *kedis*, "bird"], where he is enshrined at Pura Sang Hyang Jero. When they arrived in Abang, the second-born brother encountered a human brother-sister pair, the twins I Bang (or I Barak, "red") and Ni Kuning ("yellow"; sometimes Ni Petak, "white") as well as their divine mother Ratu Mentang Panah. He felt that this would be a secure place to settle, and so his journey ended in Abang. His temple there is called Pura Dukuh Sakti.[13] The others continued and finally met Ratu Ayu Dalem Pingit in Trunyan. The eldest brother fell in love with her instantly, and they were married. He became the principal deity of Trunyan, Bhatara Sakti Mancering Jagat. The older sister, however, continued walking to the center of the lake, where she achieved spiritual liberation (*moksa*) and became known as Ratu Ayu Tengahan Segara, "the goddess at the center of the lake," or simply Dewi Danu, "the lake goddess." Her shrine is Pura Ulun Danu in Songan.

Origin narratives often reflect on a local ideology of ideal kinship relations as well as hinting at the practical conflicts of interest that this official ideology often cannot curtail. The regulation of relations among kin represents such a pervasive model of human relations in general that it is not surprising that they also inform much of the conceptual framework for articulating relationships between villages.

In both versions of the narrative, the relationship between the villages of Kedisan, Abang, Trunyan, and Songan/Batur is represented as a collateral relationship between siblings. Sibling relationships are the ideological cornerstone of a *sanggah*, the patrifocal descent group who worship at the same ancestor temple. The ongoing unity of this group rests on the ongoing solidarity of brothers and their descen-

dants (usually to the limit of second cousins). The incentive for such
unity is both political, in that their solidarity defines their efficacy in
interactions with other *sanggah*, and symbolic, insofar as one's personal status is derived from membership in a preferably large and
respected *sanggah* group. However, as the heirs of a single patrimony
and patrifocal identity, brothers are also faced with a potential for
conflict. They tend to compete for a share in inherited material and
symbolic resources, or for the control of such resources if they have
not yet been divided. In the origin narrative, the problem of dividing
the paternal estate does not arise. The founding of new and separate
villages by each of the mythical brothers prevents such competition.
The symbolic patrimony of a royal ancestry, however, remains as a
bone of contention.[14]

The status and rank order of brothers is determined, in an ideal,
structural sense, by reference to their birth order or seniority. Trunyan's claim to superiority in part rests on this assumption. However,
in the actual practice of *sanggah* relations, the allocation of paternal
resources is not predictable on the basis of birth order alone. In the
Trunyan version, therefore, the seniority claim of the eldest brother
is supported by reference to his superior conduct. He is the only
one who carries the paternal mission that all the siblings initially
held in common to its proper conclusion. Together with a local deity
he also fulfills his duty by biologically reproducing the paternal *sanggah*, in that their marriage provides for the birth of lineal successors.
Hence, it is he who passes on the symbolic capital of his royal
descent status (Prince of Solo) to the people of Trunyan (who claim
to be his descendants).

In the Abang version the second brother remains celibate, a *dukuh*
or "hermit" who forfeits his inheritance, while the third seeks new
resources (unclaimed land) in the wilderness. The latter represents
perhaps the ideal solution for overcoming a potential shortage of
resources after the splitting of a single inheritance and an antidote
to disputes over its division. The solution, presented in this and many
other origin narratives, is territorial expansion.[15]

In the Abang narrative the superior position of Desa Trunyan, as
represented by the eldest brother, is partially challenged. It is conceded that the deity of Trunyan is the elder brother of the deity in
Abang and that he married a local goddess from Trunyan. However,
the original human beings are associated with Abang (as is the celibate second brother). These twins were the ancestors of the original
local people whom the brothers from Solo encountered on their
arrival, and it is they who define Desa "Abang" (derived from the

name of the male twin I Bang) as the most senior point of ancestral origin. Abang's claim complements rather than contradicts the claims of Trunyan.

In yet another competing version, from Desa Kedisan, the status of the youngest brother who stayed in this village is more elevated. Here the elusive bird that he chases is transformed into a goddess and divine spouse. Although he is the youngest, he is superior because he is the first to marry. Earlier marriage implies superior rank in the context of a Bali Aga village assembly, or *ulu apad*. Just as villages in a *banua* that were founded earlier have precedence over those founded later, rank in a village assembly depends on the temporal order of marriages or household foundations (rather than on the chronological age of individuals).

Unlike the relationship narratives of Bayung Gede and its affiliates, with their emphasis on stable and asymmetric vertical bonds between parent and child or parent and son-in-law deities, this body of Wintang Danu myth is pivoted upon a more egalitarian and fragile lateral bond between divine brothers. The relationship between human brothers is intimate and problematic at the same time. Relative status is a matter of contention, since the birth-order ranking of brothers is not nearly as salient and indisputable as the ranking between agnatic or affinal generations. First, although the eldest brother in a family usually holds some authority over his brothers, he is not necessarily the primary heir. The authority of the parental generation is in part guaranteed by leaving the issue of succession underdetermined. As long as any one brother can become the principal heir, brothers are under considerable pressure to comply with parents' priorities if they wish to be favored by them. Second, the ideologically favored outcome of *sanggah* unity is not the only one possible or even the most common. In reality, fission is an everpresent alternative to solidarity between brothers or more distant collaterals. Fission tends to become the favored option whenever the benefit of autonomous control over resources outweighs the benefit of political and symbolic unity.

The choice of fraternal ties as a model of alliance relationships within a *banua* has important consequences. In ritual practice the idea of a shared ancestry among Wintang Danu villages is expressed by mutual visits at the festivals of village-level origin temples. As in the case of an original *sanggah* that has split into several smaller *sanggah*, there is no obligation toward the maintenance of the branch temples that belong to one's collaterals, though mutual visits and support at major festivals normally continues. Likewise, the mutual visits

Table 5. Ritual Practices among the Wintang Danu

Village	Temple	Annual Festival	Ritual Textiles
Songan	Pura Ulun Danu	*purnama kepitu* (March)	(none from Abang)
Kedisan	Pura Sang Hyang Jero (a part of Pura Dalem Pingit)	*purnama kedasa* (April)	*kain lelancang, kain leluhu*
Abang	Pura Dukuh Sakti	*purnama karo* (August)	*kampuh putih polos*
Trunyan	Pura Gede Pancering Jagat	*purnama kapat* (October)	*kampuh puja wali, kain wulan matanai*

among the Wintang Danu villages are not accompanied by essential or compulsory material support. *Peturunan* is always paid by the hosts alone, while visitors deliver only a modest amount of *atos desa*. Nevertheless, there are also specific offerings from visitors that are considered ritually essential and suggest that there is at least a symbolic sense of unity. For example, weavers from Abang produce a number of textiles for the festivals conducted in the village temples of other Wintang Danu communities. These textiles serve as festive attire for the temple deities. The location of these temples, the temporal distribution of their festivals within the annual ritual cycle, and the use of specific textiles is shown in Table 5.[16]

The periodic reunion of divine ancestors, at different locations at different times, suggests a fluid center or a unity without a single focal point. When questioned about the center of their ritual world, most informants suggested that the lake itself is the symbolic hub of all their activities, a center symbolized by Ratu Ayu Tengahan Segara or Dewi Danu, the sister of the three founding brothers. In a *sanggah*, the sister represents the possibility of association with other *sanggah*. The outward marriages of sisters across the boundaries of the *sanggah* are an important aspect of the political cooperation and perceived unity of these patrifocal origin houses vis-à-vis the outside world. The fact that the newcomer brothers marry local women further amplifies the emphasis on affinal alliance. The lake with its female goddess is thus the symbolic center that represents the political and ritual unity of a *banua* defined by its boundary rather than its center. The ritual order also reflects that the villages' male ancestry is focused on Solo, a distant origin point that lies outside the island of Bali. In the absence of a tangible male point of common origin, it is along the boundary of the female lake that the shared ritual concerns of the Stars of the Lake are articulated.

The specific practices surrounding mutual ritual visits among these villages bear no clear indication of a fixed differentiation in terms of relative status, despite the somewhat elevated status of Trunyan in the myths. Similar to the case of the *banua* of Pura Tebenan, none of the villages represents an absolute origin point. The geographic distance of the brother's origin point (in Solo) can be compared to the temporal distance of the destroyed village of Tebenan, an ultimate point of origin that no longer exists socially as a village but only symbolically as a temple in the forest.

The predominant focus on sibling relations, and hence on the *sanggah* group, as a model for regional ties recurs in the second body of origin narratives among the Wintang Danu group, the Babad Pasek Kayuselem. Another recurrent theme is an ambiguity between creator deities and village-founding human ancestors as possible alternatives for deciding where an origin point lies. Despite these recurrent themes, there are a number of important innovations.

The Babad Pasek Kayuselem is no longer just an oral account of origins. It has become a fixed written text that ideally should never be altered (even if it needs to be transcribed). This rule is not always obeyed, as is illustrated by the difference in content among various "original" manuscripts of the Babad Pasek Kayuselem. There is also some flexibility because these texts are never such comprehensive accounts of the past that they would preclude competing interpretations. Nonetheless, the antiquity of some palm-leaf manuscripts (*lontar*) and the presumably even greater antiquity of their contents have led them to be associated with the sacred, though less so than royal inscriptions (*prasasti*). Such original manuscripts are treasured possessions, and access to them is often more restricted than is access to oral narratives.[17] Local people generally give greater weight to *lontar* manuscripts than to oral narrative concerning the same events. For example, while oral versions of the Kayuselem story are still known to many who have never read the text, the *lontar* version is regarded as a more accurate and credible source of evidence when it comes to settling a ritual-political dispute.

From the perspective of an anthropologist, the opposite could be the case. A truly ancient text may provide valuable hints about a former ritual organization within a domain, but it cannot be expected to reflect accurately on the present situation. At one time such texts may have been periodically adjusted to keep them in line with novel situations and current political interests, but this clandestine process of updating is no longer possible in the case of the Babad Kayuselem. Several of the "original" versions have been translated and published as books, which severely limits the scope for their modification in the present or future. This relative lack of openness, and sometimes the genuine antiquity of written texts concerning the origins of a domain, reduces their usefulness as an indicator of current social relationships. Even as a window on past relationships, their content must be treated with great caution. To study how such texts are interpreted and used in contemporary practice is perhaps the most fruitful approach.

The objectives of written origin narratives, often referred to as "*babad*," differ from those of oral narratives. Written texts of this genre tend to place greater emphasis on human genealogical relations within a named descent group than on relations between the nameless deified founders of villages. The following summary of a part of the Babad Kayuselem is designed to reveal some of its logical structure and the characteristics of *babad* as a genre, in contrast to the oral origin narratives described earlier.[18]

The divine creator, Sang Hyang Pasupati, sent his children to Bali to create the first human beings. Up until that time there had been no one to present offerings to the gods. The deities descended at Tampur Hyang [Batur] and cleared the forest with a fire to prepare agricultural land for human beings. One scorched stump remained and was roughly carved by the gods to approximate a human shape. While a number of attempts to fashion humans out of clay had failed, they finally succeeded in creating two sets of twins: first Ki Pita and Ni Jnar, then Ki Bang and Ni Barak. Their descendants were the Bali Aga. Bhatara Indra instructed them on how to conduct their lives and how to carve wood. Bhatara Guru later ordered some of his celestial followers [*widyadara/i* or *bidedari, dedari*] to dwell among them and teach them how to produce cloth (*kain*) and ceremonial daggers (kris). The Bali Aga implemented their new skills and tools on the blackened tree trunk (*tuwed kayu asem*) left by the gods. Its shape was refined and the figure dressed with fine cloth and a dagger. It was most beautiful to behold. On his journey through Bali, Mpu Mahameru encountered this statue and in his compassion brought it to life as a human being. The man was named Kayureka. Since there were as yet no priests (*mpu, jero gede*) among the Bali Aga people, he was initiated by the gods and was henceforth known as Mpu Kamareka. The gods then sent Bidedari Kuning to be his wife. Their first children were the twins Ki Kayu Ireng and Ni Kayu Ayu Cemeng, who were considered married even from when they were still in the womb. They took residence in Gwa Song [Songan]. Mpu Kamareka had three more sons, Made Celagi, Nyoman Tarunan, and Ketut Kayuselem [their wives are not mentioned]. Ki Made Celagi practiced yoga on Bukit Penarajon [Sukawana] and resided in Balingkang;[19] Ki Nyoman Tarunan took residence on Gunung Tolukbiyu [above Trunyan]; and Ki Ketut stayed in Songan. Ki Kayu Ireng had three sons and a daughter; Ki Made Celagi had a son and four daughters; Nyoman Tarunan had a son and three daughters; and Ketut Kayuselem had two sons [all named]. These first cousins then intermarried and produced many descendants. Finally, Mpu Kamareka achieved *moksa* on a hilltop above Songan (now Pura Kawitan Pasek Kayuselem), and a *kayu asem* tree (*Tamarindus indicus*) grows there as a reminder of their common origin (*kawitan*) from a tree (*wit, kayu*). Before he ascended to the heavens, he instructed his descendants to hold regular ceremonies to commemorate their common origin at this temple on each tenth new moon (*tilem kedasa*). [Balinese kings who ruled the Bali Aga people are mentioned in a later part of the text.]

This text is no longer just concerned with the relationships between villages and their divine founders but with genealogical relationships in a large and regionally dispersed origin group claiming a common ancestry. This ancestry is traced in the manner common to Balinese dynastic genealogies (*babad*). Even though much of the content of this excerpt is similar to that of an oral version I recorded in Bayung Gede, there are other passages in the Babad Kayuselem that indicate that it was written no earlier than toward the end of the Gelgel dynasty's rule in Bali. It is likely that after the installment of local agents to the king of Gelgel (Pasek Gelgel or Bendesa) in villages like Sukawana, Songan, and Trunyan, the distinction between different descent groups within a village became more of an issue than it had been earlier. The need to define such genealogical boundaries increased, since these newcomers had a claim to a distinguished status within the villages that was unprecedented. Local descent groups, such as Pasek Kayuselem, may eventually have followed the example of the newcomers in expanding their genealogical memory through written texts.

Mountain villages with mixed origins are differentiated into political factions that maintain links to related groups in other villages. These genealogically conceived factions are institutionalized as named *pasek,* or "commoner clans." Notions of genealogical origin also may have become more predominant as some village offices became hereditary. In Songan, for example, the Pasek Gelgel group has never participated in the temporal precedence order of the village council, but its members hold a number of prestigious hereditary offices outside the council. Although the adoption of a genealogical perspective and the practice of writing genealogical histories (*babad*) among the autochthonous population may well have been inspired by similar practices among the new arrivals, the situation in itself also favored such a development among both groups.

The former ritual ties between villages were supplemented by ritual relations between same-descent-group factions in different villages. While entire *desa adat* would visit Pura Ulun Danu Songan during its annual festivals, the Kayuselem descent temple (*pura kawitan*) in Songan would be visited also, but only by those who where members of the *sanggah gede* (extended-descent-group temple) of Pasek Kayuselem in Trunyan, Sukawana, and many other villages.[20]

The persistence of intervillage ritual ties among the Wintang Danu indicate that this transition was never complete.[21] Although it may be that royal agents in these villages had to some degree appropriated local authority, they were not able to disassociate village identity from the identity of its original inhabitants. An ongoing struggle among factions over the right to define village identity is particularly obvious in Songan. Several decades ago, the members of the Pasek Kayuselem clan in Songan were forced to relocate Pura Kawitan Kayuselem. The dominant Pasek Gelgel faction had claimed that the sanctuary was not an exclusive descent group temple but a general village origin temple (a *pura puseh*) to Desa Songan. They thus argued that it should not remain under the ritual authority of the Pasek Kayuselem clan.[22] The resentment among the original population (Pasek Kayuselem) for being incorporated within a Pasek Gelgel–dominated Desa Songan was still a potent sentiment until the 1970s, when the village finally split into two separate *desa dinas* (administrative villages) representing these factions. By contrast, the Pasek Bendesa of Sukawana were much more integrated into the local village organization and even took up a leading role in the perpetuation of the *banua* of Pura Penulisan as a regional institution. In other words, this group chose to adopt and promote local ritual practices rather than insisting on its own distinctness as a named status group with different ritual privileges.[23]

One factor that may have facilitated a shift toward a more genealogical idiom of origin among the Wintang Danu is that the initial oral origin narrative was posited on sibling relationships as a model of relatedness. Maintaining ties among siblings and more distant collaterals is a necessary prerequisite for creating a wider ramifying kinship network, which can also be made to include distant collaterals in other villages.

Batur's relationship to the Wintang Danu is nowadays a matter of much debate. Interpretations of the Babad Kayuselem vary significantly. While the people of Batur emphasize that their village marks the place where the gods first descended, their opponents in Songan focus on the statement that their village was the first settlement established by human ancestors. In 1990, in response to the conflict with Songan over the location of the true Pura Ulun Danu, the founder group of Pasek Kayuselem in Batur formally distanced themselves from the original Pura Kawitan Kayuselem in Songan and even from its branch at Pura Jati. They established a third *pura kawitan* immediately next to Pura Batur on top of the crater rim.

Political tensions made research among the villages around Lake Batur extremely arduous. The somewhat inconclusive account of the Wintang Danu provided here is nevertheless a testimony to the many kinds of conflicts that can beset a *banua*. The following case study will illustrate that fractures in a domain can also be repaired.

The Domain of Pura Pucak Tolukbiyu

The original Pura Penataran Tolukbiyu was situated in the ancient and long-destroyed village of Abang on the shore of Lake Batur (Er Awang in the royal inscriptions). The village is said to have been abandoned by its first inhabitants after an earthquake about one century ago. It was later resettled by people from Bangli (Pasek Tangkas), Karangasem (Desa Batudinding), and Songan (Pasek Gelgel). These newcomers had to abide by the traditions of the former inhabitants, who by then had permanently relocated to Penelokan (Desa Dinas Batur). After the temple and resettled Desa Abang were destroyed once again, by a landslide in 1963, the second inhabitants were forced to flee also, this time to the southeastern rim of the volcano. There they established three villages, Abang Batudinding, Abang Suter,[24] and Abang Songan, each representing one of the three descent group factions. Each new village built a branch temple (*pasimpangan*) of the original Pura Penataran Tolukbiyu. In the 1980s, the original refugees from the first Abang, now residing in Penelokan, established a fourth Pura Tolukbiyu in Batur, where the *prasasti* of Er Awang are still kept.

One reason such a proliferation of Pura Tolukbiyu could be established is that, like the original temple by the lake, they only represent the temple yard (*pura penataran*) of a remote summit temple (*pura pucak*) that has always been located on the peak of Mt. Abang. The establishment of *pura penataran* is usually justified by reference to the difficulty of holding a temple festival at such a remote location. But often enough the presence of multiple *penataran* is evidence of internal conflicts among the congregation of the summit temple.

In the 1990s, finally, the original Pura Penataran Tolukbiyu was rebuilt by the lake, as a joint venture by several factions in an effort to restore a sense of unity. The festival of this temple is on the fourth full moon (*purnama kapat*). The opening ceremony (*ngodal,* "to bring out") is held in Abang Suter, where the sacred objects (*pretima*) of the temple are kept. As at Pura Pucak Penulisan, no pigs may be offered at this temple. Both the timing and the restrictions on sacrificial animals testify to the temple's elevated regional ritual status. All villages within the *banua* pay *peturunan,* and the ceremony is conducted jointly by elders and priests representing the four communities.[25]

The *banua* of Pura Pucak Tolukbiyu currently includes an additional seven *desa adat,* namely, Pengotan, Palak Tiing, Landih, Buwayang, Langkahan, Penaga (all one *desa dinas*), and Pemuteran. The territories of these villages used to belong to Desa Abang. After the boundaries of principalities were redrawn by the Dutch, however, the land that Abang had leased to sharecroppers became the property of the latter, since it fell no longer into the same principality or "residency" as Abang itself.[26] The *banua* of Pura Tolukbiyu is thus focused on the people of Desa Abang as the current occupants of the original center of the domain, supported by their former sharecroppers in villages that are nowadays completely independent in administrative terms. The people of Penelokan may have been the first occupants, but they have severed their immediate relationship with the land.

It is remarkable that the process of fission, fueled by the diversity of genealogical descent groups and factions in Abang and amplified by the impact of natural disasters and political upheaval, has recently been reversed. The rehabilitation of the original Pura Penataran Tolukbiyu by the lake, in the former Er Awang, followed a period of "widespread illness and misfortune" in the separate communities that were once a unity. Informants have this as a dark period of civil war (B.I. *perang saudara,* lit. "a war among brothers"). Those who were prominently involved in this struggle for supremacy are retrospectively portrayed as having acted in contempt of ethical principles.

The growing sentiment that their mutual antagonism was causing misfortune was confirmed by a spontaneous trance occurrence. A message from the gods called for a revival of the ritual order of the *banua.* The reconstruction of the old temple was perceived as the appropriate response to these divine instructions and as a necessary step in restoring the good fortune of all the villages involved.

By this time the process of territorial separation had reached a stage where any disputes over the control of material resources had been resolved among the three Desa Dinas Abang and with their former sharecropping clients. Each of the villages had gained a sphere of political autonomy and the current land distribution had been accepted as final, even if some aspects of the arrangement still met with resentment. A symbolic and political reunion in relation to the outside was made possible only by the tacit acceptance of the internal status quo. The acceptance of a shared ritual authority over the temple further cleared the path for a resumption of joint ritual. This pattern of separation and reunification is reminiscent of fluctuations in the relations between the heirs of a single patrimony. Brothers may quarrel for years over the division of resources, primarily land. Once the matter is settled and resentments forgotten, they may re-affirm their unity, recognizing that no further significant gains can be achieved by continuing the dispute and that their common symbolic resources are in fact threatened by internal political and ritual division.[27]

The Domain of Pura Pucak Tajun (Sinunggal)

A solitary hilltop hugging the northern slope of Bali's central highlands is visible from a wide stretch of the coast of Buleleng below. The hilltop is known as Bukit Sinunggal, from *si*, "the most," and *tunggal*, "[to be] one or united" (as in *matunggalan*, "to have descended from one ancestor"). It is also referred to as Bukit Tajun after the largest settlement in its vicinity. On the summit of this peak lies the regional temple Pura Pucak Tajun. Its ritual domain covers the area to the west of the *banua* of Pura Indrakila (Dausa). It includes not only surrounding mountain villages like Tajun, Tegal, Tangkid, Bila-Bajang, Tamblang, Bayad, and Depaa (which includes Banjar Tunjung), but also a number of settlements on or near the coast, including Sembiran, Julah, Pacung, Bonkala, Bondalem, Bangkah, and (formerly) Tejakula. The majority of these villages maintain Bali Aga traditions, such as a bipartite village council.[28]

The cost of repairs and of the annual temple festival on the fourth full moon is shared proportionally among the membership of the domain, except that Desa Tajun's *peturunan* contribution is higher than that paid by other villages. Visiting villages do bring their percussion groups and village-level offerings (*atos desa*), but Tajun's leading role in regulating the affairs of the temple is undisputed. Both the head of the temple committee (*ketua panitia*) and the highest temple priest (*mangku pucak*) are selected from specific descent groups in Tajun.

The sanctuary is of considerable antiquity and has enjoyed a long history of regional significance. This is testified by several *prasasti* (Ginarsa 1979), the first of which was issued in A.D. 914. The inscriptions refer to the village of Indrapura (temple of Indra) at Air Tabar. They also note that "the *banua* at Air Tabar" had to attend the temple for an annual collection of taxes. Three of these *prasasti* are now kept in faraway Desa Gobleg, near Lake Tamblingan in western Buleleng. This suggests that an outward migration took place at some point in history.[29] As a consequence, Desa Gobleg attends the festival of Pura Pucak Tajun, as do groups from Jati Luwih, Apuan (Kecamatan Penebel, Tabanan), and others who believe that their ancestors came from this area. Oral origin narratives are nowadays given less weight than the content and location of the royal inscriptions.

Pura Pucak Tajun's relationships with other temples and villages are articulated in a variety of ritual practices. One example is an important sea temple (*pura segara*) in Desa Julah known as Pura Ponjok Batu. The people of Tajun visit this temple on the full moon of the first month for a purification ritual called "*makasangi*" (from *kasang*, a white cloth used in ritual). Some claim that similar visits were once paid to sea temples in Sangsit and Sinabun. On these occasions the gods are taken to the sea for a purifying bath. It is also common practice to bring offerings (*bakti penerus*) to Pura Pucak Penulisan at the end of the last postmortuary ritual (*matuun*, "to cause someone to descend"). At this time the purified ancestors are recalled from their heavenly abode so that they may reside in the family temple. Tejakula's link to Tajun (and Pacung) was similarly related to postmortuary ritual but has now been abandoned.

There are also architectural expressions of relationships among domain temples. For example, the Pura Bale Agung of Sembiran, a village in the domain of Pucak Tajun, contains individual shrines dedicated to Ratu Bukit Sinunggal (the deity at Pura Pucak Tajun), Ratu Ngurah Sakti (their designation for the deity at Pura Pucak Penulisan), Ratu Ngurah Balingkang (the deity at Pura Balingkang), and Ratu Ngurah Gunung Lebah (the deity of Pura Batur). Offerings presented at such visiting shrines invite the deities of distant regional temples to partake in the celebration of local temple festivals. The presence of these shrines illustrates once again the centrality of Pura Pucak Penulisan and its past or present subsidiaries in the ritual landscape of highland Bali.

There are also claims of close ties between Pura Pucak Tajun (male deity) and another and somewhat related hilltop temple nearby, but little more remains of this larger ritual network than a vague memory.

This regional temple is Pura Pucuk, situated in the mountains southwest of Tajun, between the villages of Bontiing and Pakisan. The deity of this temple is female, and she is the divine guardian of water for irrigation in nearby villages. Relationship narratives pertaining to Pura Pucuk describe the journeys of the deity as a water seller, similar to some of the narratives from Batur and Sukawana described earlier. The ritual activities at Pura Pucuk involve the communities of Bontiing, Pakisan, Klandis, Sangburni, and Tegehe.

There are two further ritual domains in central and western Buleleng whose organization is similar to the *banua* of Bali's central highlands. An alliance around Pura Bukit Bale Agung in Desa Tenaon will be discussed later, because it still shows a transitional pattern of organization and can be described either as a regional village or as a villagelike domain. I will not discuss the ritual network among villages between the sea temple Pura Pelabuan Aji and the mountain temple of Pura Ulun Danu Tamblingan (see Figure 2), since it is currently in a state of great turmoil and on the brink of collapse. Pura Pelabuan Aji was appropriated by Parisada Hindu Dharma Indonesia in the 1970s, and much of its earlier significance has been lost as a result. The temple was originally located on the territory of the Bali Aga village of Cempaga. Following the dispossession of their coastal land and temple, the people of Cempaga are no longer even invited to the festivals that were once their own. These events were difficult to reconstruct for lack of familiarity with local informants. Some of the following case studies from the southern fringe of the highlands are better suited for an analysis of the impact of external interventions.[30]

Banua on the Southern Fringe

A number of further ritual networks are located in the foothills on the southern fringe of Bali's central highlands. The traditions maintained in this area are not always consistent with "Bali Aga culture," and yet the similarity of organizational patterns in these domains justifies a brief description in the present context.

These *banua* represent transitional cases, both in a cultural sense, from Bali Aga to Bali Dataran, and in a historical sense, from relatively independent village alliances to temple networks that have consistently come under the direct influence of traditional secular rulers or contemporary government institutions. Some of the smaller *banua* in this area are also transitional in that they were more recently established and have barely outgrown the status of village-level organizations.

The Gebog Domas *of Pura Kehen (Bangli)*

Pura Kehen has been, and in part still is, a major focal point of regional ritual from ancient times. The temple, located in the town of Bangli, was first mentioned in one of Bali's earliest royal inscriptions (Prasasti Pura Kehen A, approximately A.D. 910). Its antiquity is thus comparable to that of Pura Pucak Penulisan (A.D. 882). Another similarity between the two temples is that each is supported by a *gebog domas* (see above).

The *gebog domas* of Pura Kehen is a large group of communities all of whom pay *peturunan* as villages in support of the regular rituals conducted at the temple. The most important ritual event is the triennial Ngusaba Purnama Kelima (festival of the fifth full moon, last in 1994). Smaller festivals (*odalan*), in keeping with the permutational *wuku* calendar, take place every 210 days on Rebo Kliwon Sinta (Pagerwesi). The members of the domain also bring *atos desa* at the time of a *ngusaba* and carry their village gods in procession to Pura Kehen, accompanied by their own percussion groups (*sekaa gong*). Those communities that have irrigated rice fields (*sawah*), and hence a *sekaa subak* (irrigation society), will also deliver separate *suwinih* offerings, namely two kilograms of rice per hectare of *sawah*. However, only villagers from Banjar Pekuhon (in Bangli), the origin village of the domain, provide obligatory labor service (*ngayah*) for the preparation and priestly services for the execution of ritual performances.

The *gebog domas* is formed by a total of nineteen separate *desa adat.* Some of them are grouped together into larger administrative units (*desa dinas* or *kelurahan*). The latter include Kubu, Tegal Suci, Penglipura, Sidan Bunut,[31] Cempaga, Bangli Kota, Bebalang, Tanggahan Peken, Penatahan, Susut (Banjar Pukuh), and Demule.[32] The traditional priestly leadership all originate from Banjar Pekuhon, located on the northern edge of the town of Bangli, near the temple. This group of sixteen priests (*saing nambelas*) is divided into a left and right moiety (*sibak kiwa tengen*) as shown in Table 6.

The twofold division of this group is reminiscent of the twofold division of Bali Aga village councils (*ulu apad*), groups of elders that often comprise sixteen core members. The titles Jero Gede and Jero Pasek are also known in Batur, Songan, Selulung, and some other Bali Aga villages. However, in contrast to the seniority system that is characteristic of Bali Aga village councils, succession to the sixteen ranked positions of leadership in this domain is by agnatic descent. Access is thus confined to members of a few families in Pekuhon.

Table 6. The Priest-Leaders of the *Gebog Domas* of Pura Kehen

Kiwa (Left)	Tengen (Right)
Jero Pasek	Jero Gede
Danka Pucak	Danka Gunung Agung
Danka Corong Agung	Danka Manik Tirta
Danka Pujung Sari	Danka Gede Pande
Danka Gunung Tengah	Danka Pasek Majembul
Danka Gunung Keloko	Danka Mas Ayu Nganten
Danka Gede Sema	Danka Kubu Suwe
Danka Nyarikan	Danka Sanding Bingin

The only village in the *gebog domas* of Pura Kehen that still adheres to a distinctly Bali Aga form of organization is Desa Penglipura (a *pondokan* of Bayung Gede), but it is likely that such traditions were once prevalent in the Bangli area as a whole.

The *gebog domas,* as the principal congregation of Pura Kehen, has been unable to maintain control over its own sanctuary. Unlike the *banua* of the highlands, this region and its temple have been located near the center of a Majapait kingdom, under the political leadership of Puri Nyalian, Puri Taman Bali, or Puri Bangli, for several centuries. The influence of these kingdoms persisted well into this century, given that Bangli was the last Balinese principality to come under Dutch administration. The rulers of this principality initially had lent their support to the colonizers.

It is difficult to establish with certainty to what extent the rulers of Bangli influenced the ritual practices and political processes surrounding Pura Kehen in the past. What is certain is that the temple did not escape their attention. Until today it is the ruler (*cokorda*) of Puri Bangli Semarabawa who officiates at the *wangsupada* ritual during Pura Kehen's major festivals. His task is to bathe the sacred objects representing the deity in order to produce holy water (*tirta wangsupada*).

Until the 1980s, this same *cokorda* and his family were major financial sponsors of ritual and more so of temple renovations at Pura Kehen, in conjunction with the *gebog domas*. His presence during the festival was described as essential, for he acted as a witness (*pesaksi*) to attest to the proper carrying out of the people's ritual obligations. All this changed when Puri Semarabawa lost the best of its power following a protracted and continuing period of rivalry with Griya Bukit, a powerful Brahmana house in Bangli. Their defeat was brought about when a member of Griya Bukit was appointed as the *bupati* of Kabupaten Bangli.[33] Since that time, the new *bupati* has appropriated the role of witness, or representative of worldly authority (*guru wisesa*).

Generous government funds have since been allocated to the maintenance of Pura Kehen as a modern-day state temple, so generous that the contributions of the *banua* villages have become irrelevant. Using his influence in Parisada Hindu Dharma Indonesia, the new *bupati* was also instrumental in introducing *pedanda* (Brahmana priests) as the leading officiants of Pura Kehen's festivals. Some rituals were henceforth conducted in conformance to Brahmana orthodoxy. The status of the original group of priest-leaders was downgraded accordingly. They continue to lead only in rituals that are specific to this temple and hence fall outside the sphere of Brahmanic ritual competence.

In short, the symbolic capital vested in this regional temple has attracted and continues to attract claimants other than the alliance of villages centered on it. While *banua* temples may have been associated with or been fundamental to state authority in the past, the nature of that authority has changed drastically, as have the social practices surrounding some of these sanctuaries.[34] The gradual displacement of village alliances as the material support and social substance of the sacred domain of a regional temple and the transformation of regional temples into state-orchestrated ritual centers led by a politicoritual national Hindu elite are a development that has progressed furthest at Bali's most promoted temple, Pura Besakih.

Situated on the slope of Mt. Agung, Pura Besakih has become the foremost symbol of modern Balinese Hinduism and a focal point of state-sponsored ritual, particularly the great purification rites of Panca Wali Krama and Eka Dasa Rudra. State sponsorship has been continuous from the times of the Gelgel and Klungkung dynasties of Bali Majapait kings.

Conversely, in his detailed account of the history and ritual of Pura Besakih, David Stuart-Fox (1987) mentions that the temple was, and in a minor way still is, supported by a number of nearby villages, which he refers to as "*desa pragunung.*" These villages were involved most intensely with the agricultural ritual held at Pura Banua, one of the oldest in the fast expanding complex of temples at Besakih. Foremost among this network of villages is Desa Adat Besakih itself. Stuart-Fox observes that each of the temple priests (*pemangku*) of the complex originates from a specific *banjar* of Desa Adat Besakih, the community whose members also contribute most of the labor for the preparation of rituals. This arrangement was eventually superseded by government sponsorship: "The inhabitants of the region's [western Karangasem] villages not only paid homage to the gods of Pura Besakih but gave contributions of cash and kind towards its upkeep, and participated directly in specific rituals. . . . [They are] a group of villages with special ritual rights and obligations . . . known as the villages of Pragunung Besakih. Then, from around the 1930's the role of the Pragunung began to diminish and erode." Concerning their present role in financing the performance of rituals, he states that "contributions from *pragunung* and other villages of the region are now largely a thing of the past" and that they amounted to less than 9 percent of the temple's total expenditure (1987:268). The proportion of the government's contribution had reached a staggering 83.4 percent in 1983. Large sums from government funds have also been devoted to building projects. Photographs from before 1930 illustrate just how much even the physical appearance of the temple has been changed by expansion and modification. Inquiries made in 1994 in the course of this research suggest that some of the original ties between the temple and surrounding villages are still operative. However, it would likely be futile to attempt a reconstruction of the temple's former role as the hub of their regional alliance.

While both Pura Kehen and Pura Besakih have long served the function of a state temple for Bali's precolonial rulers, their appropriation by modern government institutions in recent times may herald the end of their role as the centers of ritual domains. Earlier secular rulers had neither the financial resources nor the technology now available to the representatives and institutions of a modern nation-state. To the contrary, they may have depended on these networks in a number of ways. It was beyond their capacity to conduct the ritual affairs of such sanctuaries directly without the support of the local population.

One example of the effects of technological change is the impact of modern means of transportation. The availability of motor cars, trucks, and an extensive road network allows people to attend distant temples on a regular basis. Resources that formerly had to be provided locally can now be transported to temples from the outside. In the wake of such new possibilities, regional alliances among villages may be eclipsed by a broader and more homogeneous religious sentiment in determining the social relevance of many major Balinese temples.

Kayubihi

Located in the area that lies between Bayung Gede and Bangli are a number of smaller alliances that have not fully transcended the level of a village internal institution. These cases are particularly intriguing in relation to questions about the historical genesis of *banua* from smaller institutions.

One of these networks is focused on Desa Kayubihi. This village is one of the southernmost communities that maintain a council of ranked and paired elders (*ulu apad*), typical of Bali Aga villages, as was first noted by the Dutch researcher Boekian (1936). Desa Dinas Kayubihi consists of three separate *desa adat*, Kayubihi, Bangkled, and Kayang, all of whom join forces in celebrating the biannual festival (*usaba*) at the Pura Puseh of Desa Adat Kayubihi. The founders of Desa Kayang were immigrants from Pengotan and are thus considered as land-receiving clients of Kayubihi, with associated ritual obligations to the local deities. Bangkled is regarded as a former *pondokan* established by people from Kayubihi itself. Another village attending this ceremony is Desa Langkahan, the point of origin of Kayubihi's founding ancestors. Origin myths narrate how the ancestors from Langkahan took refuge in the Kayubihi area following an attack by Panji Sakti.

Although the communities who visit Kayubihi are distinct *desa adat*, their mutual ritual cooperation does not constitute a fully developed regional alliance, for they are members of a single administrative village (*desa dinas*). The principles of their association are nonetheless similar to those described for the *banua* of Bayung Gede. One special case is the visit from Langkahan. Informants explained that the people who resettled this village after its destruction by Panji Sakti have an obligation to the deified ancestors who first cleared the agricultural land of Langkahan. Those ancestors' shrines, however, are now situated in Kayubihi, the village founded by the refugee founders and inhabited by their descendants. Unlike the second settlers of Desa Abang, who took over a temple left behind by the first settlers, the people of Kayubihi permanently relocated their origin temple from Langkahan to the newly founded Kayubihi.

Buungan

Another small *banua*, to the north of Kayubihi, is the *gebog satak* of Desa Buungan. This small *banua* is composed of a group of seven *banjar adat* (or *dusun,* in administrative terms). Together they form a single customary village (*desa adat*) and also a single administrative village (*desa dinas*). The ritual center of this area is the Pura Bale Agung of Buungan, and the temple's annual festival is celebrated on *purnama kapat.*[35]

In describing the social configuration of this group, the term "village" is reaching the limits of its usefulness as a translation of the local term "*desa.*" Despite their administrative and ritual unity, these seven component units, namely, Buungan, Tiga, Tembaga, Linjong, Malet Gede, Malet Kuta Mesir, and Kayuambua, are widely dispersed and thus physically discrete settlements or villages. Their characteristics diverge from what is suggested by the term "neighborhood," an equally problematic translation of the Balinese "*banjar.*" In this case, the seven *banjar* are not simply adjacent parts of a larger town but distinct hamlets with a well-developed sense of separate identity. In terms of practical day-to-day social interaction, they are different communities. Each has its own and specific narrative origin history. Banjar Tiga, for example, was founded by immigrants from Desa Serai in Kintamani. Nevertheless, all seven *banjar* partake in the larger ritual community of the encompassing *desa adat* of Buungan. This larger unity is based on ritualized forms of interaction and more abstract notions of identity than one would normally expect of a *desa.*

A wide variety of sociopolitical arrangements are concealed behind the singular label "*banjar.*" Among the Bali Aga villages of the highlands, a division of the *desa adat* into several *banjar* is as rarely found as it is common in southern Bali. The *desa adat* and *banjar* in mountain villages are functionally and socially distinct institutions, with the *desa* clearly the more significant and powerful. The most salient social distinction lies in the different requirements for membership. Recent newcomers are frequently excluded from the *desa adat* assembly—which is led by the descendants of founders and earlier immigrants—and hence from ownership of village-owned agricultural land (*tanah ayahan desa*). By contrast the *banjar* is almost totally inclusive, with membership compulsory for all married couples and associated with the right to sufficient land to build a house (*tanah pekarangan*). Most often the group of newcomers (or *banjar*-only members) is a small and less affluent minority that is easily controlled in a political sense. Where this is no longer the case (e.g., Desa Bonyoh), several options arise. The most common is a fission into separate *desa.* Once fission has occurred, the different *desa adat* tend to maintain ritual ties in the form of a *banua* and often in relation to a regional temple. In the highlands it is uncommon to find a permanent division into physically distinct *banjar* each with a distinct social identity but still united in the worship of a classificatory village temple (e.g., a Pura Bale Agung), as is the case in Buungan.

Surprisingly, a process of fission into separate *desa adat* has not occurred in the Buungan group, despite the impression of inequity created by the fact that only 226 out of the thousands of households residing in the area are represented in the assembly (*ulu apad*) of the encompassing *desa adat*. Why is there an apparent lack of ambition for political autonomy among the people in Buungan's ritually dependent *banjar*? The explanation is that, although they are in formal and ritual terms mere *banjar*, Buungan's subsidiary communities actually enjoy rights of political self-determination to a degree that belies their humble classificatory status as *banjar*. A second factor is that—in order to maintain the unity of a *desa adat* of such size and diversity—the core group who claim descent from Buungan's original founders have orchestrated a set of ritual practices that have expanded the meaning of the *desa ada* to such a degree that it has become synonymous with the meaning of the term "*banua*," just as the *banjar* are expanded into social institutions resembling *desa adat*. As a consequence, ritual independence has lost at least some of its appeal as an indirect expression and vehicle for gaining political autonomy. It must also be considered that the rather recent settlement of this area places its development into a very different historical context from that of older alliances. Here the costs of ritual independence that accompany the formation of separate *desa adat* (with a full set of village temples) apparently outweighed the benefits. A village-style domain has indeed some added advantages. In Buungan there is no need to establish a rank order among deities from core and branch villages, since the entire domain is still ritually serviced from a central village temple, the Pura Bale Agung of Buungan. The encompassing efficacy of this ritual center operates in the formal absence of ranked parts. It does not stand for a more complex whole, it is the whole.

In general, the *desa* and *banua* are both founded on the common notion of an ancestral territory or domain bounded by shifting patterns of collective ritual action and social cooperation. The difference is that the *banua* presumes the existence of subsidiary but independent "village domains" within its boundaries. In a situation where a *desa adat* likewise admits, in nominal or practical terms, the existence of socially and spatially distinct subsidiary units, this distinction becomes rather intangible.

Panoramic view of the highlands of Bali. A view of the highlands as seen from the television tower on Mt. Penulisan, looking south on a clear day, with Mt. Batur, Mt. Abang, and Mt. Agung in the background.

Royal edicts. A young "flower priest" (*mangku bunga*) from Sukawana is holding a sacred bronze plate containing part of the ninth-century royal inscription of his village. At the annual festival of the fifth full moon (*usaba kelima*), these and other relics are taken out to be washed and oiled in order to produce a particular kind of "holy water" (*tirta wangsu pada*).

Statue of an early Balinese king and queen. This statue of a royal couple from the twelfth century is located inside Pura Tegeh Kauripan, on the upper terrace of the Pura Pucak Penulisan temple complex.

The *bale pasamuan agung*. During the great festival of the fourth full moon (*usaba kapat*), the gods of the four directions, from all the villages of the four *gebog satak* of Pura Penulisan, are brought to the temple in processions. The village gods are then seated on the appropriate one of the four platforms of the "shrine of the great gathering" (*bale pasamuan agung*).

Preparations for the great oracle. Special village messengers (*saya bunga*) deliver the sacred coconuts (*nyuh titikan*) that will be cut during the oracle ceremony at the annual festival of Pura Pucak Penulisan. These coconuts are from sacred palms growing inside a temple in a village allied to the domain. The messengers must observe a number of strict taboos while on their journey from the village and while handing over the coconuts to the domain's priest-leaders.

The great oracle. Village priest-leaders cut and inspect the inside of the sacred coconuts for blemishes, as a means of divination. Different blemishes indicate that the crops may be affected by pests or drought in the coming season. If the flesh of the coconut is white and flawless, then chances are there will be abundant rain and a bumper harvest.

Preparing the sacrificial buffalo. The sacrificial buffalo at Penulisan is ritually cleansed in a way reminiscent of the human life-cycle rituals of early childhood. This and other signs indicate a symbolic transformation of the animal victim into an honorary human.

Resurrecting the buffalo. The sacrificed buffalo is symbolically "brought to life again" (*wangun urip*) to be presented as a key offering to the gods of the domain of Pura Penulisan. The head and a number of carefully selected bones (*ukem*) are placed in a basket before being taken to the central offering platform within Pura Tegeh Kauripan. The remains are later buried as part of this particular festival. On other occasions the bones of a four-footed sacrificial victim are distributed to the village elders, with each bone corresponding to a specific rank.

Baris dancer at the festival of Pura Penulisan. *Baris* warrior dances are a part of every important temple festival in the highlands of Bali and are performed by male villagers. Different varieties of *baris* are distinguished by the type of weapon carried by the dancers.

Baris goak performer from Desa Selulung at Penulisan. The *baris goak* dance incorporates the dramatic re-enactment of an important origin myth from Selulung, the core village of one of the four sections (*gebog satak*) of the domain of Pura Pucak Penulisan.

The mountain of life. *Gunung Kauripan,* the mountain of life, is recreated in miniature as a mound on top of the "grave" of the sacrificial buffalo, with umbrellas indicating the four cardinal directions.

Pura Dalem Balingkang. Crowds of visitors arrive during the annual festival of the fifth full moon at the entrance of Pura Dalem Balingkang. This ancient temple is surrounded by a moat and is widely believed to have been a residence of Balinese kings prior to the Majapait take-over.

Ritual precedence between domains. The priest-leader of the left moiety (*kubayan kiwa*) of Sukawana's council of elders, who is the highest ritual authority within the domain of Pura Pucak Penulisan, is invited to sacrifice a buffalo and goat at the temple festival of the neighboring domain at Pura Balingkang. This practice is a reminder of Sukawana's special status of ritual precedence throughout the region.

Blood sacrifices of the rainy season. The head and phallus of a bull are displayed on a sacrificial pole in Desa Bantang during one of the spectacular rituals of blood sacrifice (here, *usaba posa*) that are typical of the rainy season.

The council of elders. As in all Bali Aga villages, the elders of Sukawana gather in the village longhouse (*bale lantang*) of the main village temple for a meeting on the new moon and on other occasions. The elders sit in two rows in order of precedence according to their rank and moiety affiliation. The head elder sits in the center only while summoning the ancestors to partake in the ritual meal that always accompanies these formal meetings.

A traditional house in the highlands. Traditional Bali Aga houses with their typical wooden frame, plaited bamboo walls, layered roof shingles, and characteristic interior layout are fast disappearing. This picture was taken in the small hamlet of Pangkung, Desa Blantih.

Margatengah

Located on the southwestern edge of the *banua* of Pura Penulisan and to the west of Buungan is a small alliance of five independent villages, namely Margatengah, Mangguh, Kerta, Pilan, and Seming. Ritual activity is focused on the Pura Banua of Desa Margatengah, situated at the geographic center of this domain. The arrangement of four (or eight) elements around a center is regarded as an ideal configuration and represents a recurrent motif in Indonesian cultures in general.[36] An example is the Monca-Pat pattern in Javanese classification and social organization first described by F.G.E. van Ossenbruggen (1977 [1916]). The members of this domain are explicitly designated as such a configuration with the term "*panca pradesa*," the five villages (*panca* is a cognate of the Javanese *monca*, "five").

The ritual participation of the villages Kerta and Mangguh in the *banua* of Margatengah has been reduced to a private and voluntary level in recent years.[37] Both of these former branch villages have since built their own Pura Banua. These nominal *banua* temples are functionally village temples. The persistent use of the term "*banua*" for ritual institutions now confined to single communities is an inversion of the Buungan case, where what is functionally a *banua* is described as a large *desa adat*.

It will be recalled that Desa Mangguh is a full member of the *gebog domas* of Pura Pucak Penulisan. Desa Margatengah participates in the domain of Pura Penulisan as well, by offering *atos desa* at the festival each year and by asking for *tirta pekulu* whenever it repairs its own Pura Bale Agung. The people of Margatengah also occasionally visit Pura Gunung Kunyit, a temple in Desa Kintamani, where they once sought and received refuge during a period of war. In Sukawana, the name "*marga tengah*" (the midpoint of the road or half of the way) is believed to refer to the position of this village halfway between Penulisan (or Balingkang) and Pejeng, presumably the first and second centers of old Balinese kingdoms. Margatengah is also mentioned as a way station in the origin narrative of Bayung Gede.[38] In terms of social organization, finally, all of the five villages except Kerta feature a council of paired elders and other practices typical of Bali Aga villages. All this suggests that Margatengah and its affiliates are part of a cultural and historical complex that is ultimately focused on Pura Penulisan.

The current popular version of Margatengah's origin narrative, however, is a variant of the Maharishi Markandeya myth. This confirms that there are indeed connections to the south as well as to the north, but to the area between Ubud, Taro, and Payangan rather than to Pejeng. In this region the Markandeya cycle of origin narratives is of paramount importance in local explanations of the origin of current ritual connections between villages (Macrae 1995). The following narrative is the Margatengah version:

> On his first journey to Bali, Maharishi Markandeya and his followers from Desa Aga [hence the term "Bali Aga"], on the slopes of Mt. Raung in Java, tried to establish a village in the forest of Srawana [Desa Taro]. They were struck by misfortune and perished. On his second expedition, he landed with eight hundred followers at Ponjok Batu near Desa Julah and went on to establish the village of Kerta and the temple called Pura Alas Angker. They then established villages in Taro, Payangan, and Pengaji, and finally founded Margatengah and the other villages of the *panca pradesa*.

Desa Taro is prominently featured in most versions describing the journeys of this great Indian saint and champion of civilization (Macrae 1995). I have noted that some consider him identical to Bhagawan Siwagandu at Pura Penulisan, that he is reputed to have founded Julah, and that Taro is regarded as one of several origin points in the myths of Bayung Gede. Furthermore, Desa Adat Taro Kaja still has a *kubayan* (the head elder of a Bali Aga village council) among its leaders. Finally, the people of Desa Blantih, key members of the *banua* of Pura Penulisan, consider themselves to be Pasek Taro.[39] Desa Taro Kaja, in turn, pays regular visits to Pura Batur and Pura Penulisan. This rather circumstantial evidence is inconclusive, but it is at least likely that the area between Taro and Payangan had close historical and cultural links to the highlands. In the case of other pockets of Bali Aga tradition in the southern foothills, such as Pujung Taleput, the link may be based on a specific history of migration.[40]

Another domain northeast of Margatengah, around the summit temples of Desa Tiingan and Bon in Northern Badung, shows even closer links to villages in the Kintamani districts. This two-temple alliance network may even shed light on the nature of the former relationship between Pura Pucak Penulisan and Pura Batur in the context of a global pattern of ritual and agricultural practice.

The Domain of Two Temples:
Pura Pucak Manggu and Antap Sai

The area toward the western end of a broad ridge spanning from Mt. Penulisan to Mt. Catur and Mt. Batukaru is occupied by a rather large *banua* centered on two temples, Pura Pucak Antap Sai (also known as Pura Pucak Bon) and Pura Pucak Manggu. In both cases, the actual sanctuary is a remote summit temple, while most ritual activities take place in the more easily accessible *pura penataran agung*. The two sanctuaries jointly form the ritual focus of a singular alliance of villages.

Most of the member villages of this twofold *banua* fall within the administrative boundaries of the regency of Badung, except for Desa Tambakan (Buleleng) and Catur (Bangli). Unlike their neighbors in Kintamani, the people in this area still cultivate dry rice as their major agricultural crop.

The contemporary relationship between the two temples can serve as a model of how Pura Pucak Penulisan and Pura Batur may have interrelated as two temples of a single domain in the past. There are some striking parallels in the characteristics and functions of the two pairs of temples that support this claim as well as a number of direct historical links that may explain the parallels.

Local informants in many villages of this *banua* were adamant that their ancestors and *adat* (traditions) originated from Bali Aga villages in the Kintamani district. Their traditions are indeed similar. For example, villages in this domain maintain councils of elders similar to those of their Kintamani origin villages. However, the domain of the two temples is believed to have been settled relatively recently.[41] Even though the villages consider themselves to be new villages, they believe that they have perpetuated the ancient ways of their Kintamani ancestors. Table 7 lists the ancestral origins of some of the villages in this domain.

In Desa Belok, Sidan, and other villages attached to Pura Pucak Antap Sai in particular, many of the older people still remembered that they had once taken part in the festivals of Pura Pucak Penulisan not just privately, as is the current arrangement, but as villages.[42] They repeatedly expressed their desire to revive this link. The connection to Penulisan is in part articulated by the maintenance of a shrine within Pura Pucak Antap Sai named Pura Pengubengan. The wife of the male deity of this shrine is said to originate from Sukawana. Informants remembered two occasions when the goddess was taken back to Sukawana "to visit her ancestors." There are also legends that the deity (or king) of Pura Penulisan often traveled west through this area on his way to Mt. Batukaru, where he would bathe in the hot springs. Hence the local etymology of the name Pura Pucak "Antap Sai"—"passed by frequently."[43] Finally, there is a visiting shrine in Pura Pucak Manggu dedicated to Ratu Gede

Table 7. The Kintamani Ancestry of Villages in Northern Badung

Present Village	Ancestors Came From
Tiingan	Ulian
Tingahan	Kutuh
Kiadan	Awan
Belok (left side of the *ulu apad*)	Selulung
Belok (right side of the *ulu apad*)	Pinggan

Catur Muka, a common pseudonym for the deity of Pura Pucak Penulisan.

There are further ties between the individual villages of the two *banua*. For example, Desa Catur and Tambakan also pay ceremonial visits to Desa Pengejaran, a member of the *banua* of Pucak Penulisan.[44] Among the villages of the Pucak Antap Sai group, Desa Catur is the only community that fully observes a dual loyalty in that it belongs to the *gebog domas* of Pura Penulisan simultaneously. This dual loyalty is metaphorically referred to as *negen*, "to balance two weights," or *mabanua ngarangkep*, "double *banua* participation."[45]

Table 8 summarizes some information on the ritual organization of the two sanctuaries and lists the membership of their respective *banua*. The symbolic, functional, temporal, and orientational relations between these paired temples is strikingly similar to the relations between Pura Pucak Penulisan and Pura Batur. Both Pura Penulisan and Pura Manggu have a male deity, a *kauh* (western) location, and a festival on *purnama kapat* at the end of the dry season, as opposed to Pura Batur and Antap Sai, with a female deity, a *kangin* (eastern) location, and a festival on *purnama kedasa* at the end of the wet season.

Until 1945, all sixteen villages in Table 8 formed a single *banua* and jointly paid *peturunan* for the festivals of both temples. Thereafter, the primary duties relating to the two sanctuaries were divided between two groups of eight villages. It is said that the reason for this change was an increase in population, which allowed each group to finance an entire festival on its own. Desa Adat Pelaga, for example, no longer pays *peturunan* at Pura Pucak Antap Sai, but only at Pura Pucak Manggu. However, the Pucak Manggu group of villages still attends the festivals at Pucak Antap Sai with *atos desa* and will ask for *tirta*, and the Pucak Antap Sai group still attends the festival at Pucak Manggu in the same way. Part of these residual responsibilities to the opposite temple is that one of the eight villages (in rotation) will

Table 8. The Organization of Pura Pucak Manggu and Antap Sai

	Pura Pucak Manggu (or Pucak Kauh) compare to Pura Penulisan	Pura Pucak Antap Sai (or Pucak Kangin) compare to Pura Batur
Location		
Summit temple	Mt. Bratan (Manggu)[1]	Mt. Catur
Pura Penataran Agung	Desa Tiingan	Desa Bon
Annual Festival	*purnama kapat*	*purnama kedasa*
Occasion	rice planting	rice harvest
	end of dry season	end of wet season
Deity	male	female
Tirta	*wangsupada*	*pekulu*
Member Villages	Auman	Belok (23)[2]
(desa adat paying	Tiingan	Sidan (72)
peturunan as well as	Tingahan	Lawak (22)
atos desa)	Semanik	Sekarmukti (26)
	Nungnung	Bon (24)
	Kiadan	Jempanang (23)
	Bukhian	Catur (24)
	Pelaga	Tambakan (24)

[1] Occasionally there are also ritual visits from Pura Pucak Manggu to the lake temple Pura Ulun Danu Bratan for a *pakelem* ceremony.

[2] The numbers in parentheses relate to proportional contributions of *peturunan* by villages in the Pura Antap Sai group, as will be explained later.

send its *sekaa gong* to the temple of the opposite group at the time of the festival.

Payments of *peturunan* are based on the ratio between a village's population size and the total population of the *banua*. As in the *gebog domas* of Pura Penulisan, these ratios were fixed at some time in the past. The total cost of performing the festival at Pura Pucak Antap is divided into 247 shares, the total number of households in the area at one time. Each village pays a fixed number of these shares, in accordance with the number of households that resided in this village at the time when the ratios were fixed. Desa Bon, for example, still pays for 24 households even though the village population has since increased to 138 households. The individual contribution of each household in Bon is thus calculated as Desa Bon's total of 24 shares divided by 138 (no households are exempt).

In addition to the *peturunan* paid by the *banua*, the temples have been receiving contributions from a number of aristocratic sponsors, particularly Pura Pucak Manggu. Until A.D. 1891, the major political force in this region was the royal dynasty of Mengwi and its various satellite centers (Grader 1960). The foremost leader of this dynasty, I Gusti Nyoman Mayun (1836–1871), extended Mengwi's control over the area during his reign, and some credit him with building part of the *penataran agung* of the two temples. Henk Schulte-Nordholt has claimed that "the three main temples of the negara Mengwi [were] the mountain temple Pura Penataran Agung in the desa Tinggan [Pura Pucak Manggu], the central temple Pura Taman Ayu and the sea temple Pura Ulun Siwi near Desa Seseh" (1988:14–15).[46]

This statement may reflect the vision of a larger ritual order espoused and promoted by the rulers of Mengwi. However, the part said to have been played by Pura Pucak Manggu in this network of state temples does not explain its significance as a *banua* temple. This significance may be more ancient in that the settlement of the area predates the creation of the state (*negara*) of Mengwi in the early eighteenth century. In a more recent publication, Schulte-Nordholt concedes that "the temple's features and the fact that brahman priests were not welcome there may well illustrate the intransigence of Balinese mountain culture" (1996:135).

That the appropriation of this twofold domain was incomplete is also reflected in the fact that Pucak Manggu's twin temple, Pura Pucak Antap Sai, receives no attention in this Mengwi portrayal of their ritual world, even though Mengwi had lent support to this temple as well. Even for some years after the fall of Mengwi, the ruler of Puri Belayu, a descendant of one of the satellite dynasties of Mengwi, continued to sponsor Pura Pucak Antap Sai. Eventually the support ceased. After a long lapse, the sponsorship was taken up again in recent decades by the ruler of Puri Carangsari, a relative of the national hero I Gusti Ngurah Rai and head of this branch of the former kingdom of Mengwi. This move followed the consultation of a trance medium (*balian*), who had advised the new rulers that their recent misfortunes were due to a neglect of their royal duties toward the temple as the heirs of Mengwi. Still, it is evident that the resumption of these duties also served to reaffirm their status, for an heir inherits rights and duties in equal measure.

In recent years, Puri Carangsari has started to bring along a *pedanda,* who officiates at what it perceives as the most significant rite during the festival of Pura Pucak Antap Sai. This rite is seen locally as a recent and unnecessary addition to the ritual process. In the last few years, the current Anak Agung of Belayu has also made a reappearance, but only as a passive participant and minor donor. More recently, the regency government of Badung has become a major sponsor at Pura Pucak Manggu, along with surviving descendants of the traditional rulers of Mengwi.

Developments similar to those that have occurred at Pura Kehen are thus beginning to affect the relevance of the *banua* in relation to the maintenance of the two temples, especially Pura Pucak Manggu. This state of affairs has already begun to affect the local appreciation of the temples as the symbolic focus of an origin structure that defines regional status relations. Informants in Bon, for example, obstinately refused to recount any of the origin and relationship narratives of Pura Pucak Antap Sai even though they were well aware of them. They argued that such narratives are not reliable historical information that an anthropologist would want to gather. They perceived their own mythical histories as inferior to the accounts given by the *cokorda*, who claims that history began when the two sanctuaries became state temples of the kingdom of Mengwi. It may also be that they were not sufficiently familiar with me or were uncertain about my political position. In the absence of information on such narratives and associated practices, it is difficult to assess forms of status differentiation and contestation among the villages of this *banua*.

Even though there has been some interference in the affairs of the two temples from the rulers of Mengwi, Schulte-Nordholt's analysis of the situation may not be correct. He claims that "large-scale direct mobilization caused [*sic*] the people to attend large periodical rituals which had to purify the *negara*, and the regular *odalan* ('birthdays') of the main *negara* temples" (1991:9). This may have been the case in some rituals and temples sponsored by the rulers of Mengwi, but it does not apply to these sanctuaries. The sponsors do not organize ritual, nor do they need to notify or mobilize the villages to perform, let alone attend, the festivals of the two temples.

In conversations with local leaders in Bon, I asked what the effect would be if all external sponsorship were to be suspended. The immediate and unanimous verdict was that the ritual at the two temples would continue as it always had. The long periods when the *banua* functioned equally well left to its own devices were referred to as evidence in support of this claim. Villagers commented with a certain gleefulness that the Anak Agung of Carangsari was showing signs of becoming "tired" or "exhausted"; that is, he was running short of the economic resources necessary for retaining his claim. They expected that the hypothetical situation of having no external sponsor might soon become a reality.

It would be ludicrous to suggest that the ritual domains of high-land Bali have existed in a kind of political vacuum beyond the influence of secular powers throughout their history. It is debatable whether *banua* as ritual institutions predate state formation in Bali or are in part a product of state formation, at least in their present form. The absence of reliable sources usually prevents a reconstruction of the historical interplay between political and ritual institutions as two important forms of organization that have shaped Balinese lives. The image of a *banua* that has been evoked by the discussion so far suggests that, in any case, the regularity and purpose of the social practices within a *banua* cannot be reduced to either politics or ritual or a combination of both. The activities at a *pura banua* are embedded in an agricultural cycle of production.

The symbolic organization of a domain is tied to the cycles and processes of material production. While agricultural practices may be regulated and reflected upon in an idiom of ritual practice, they are shaped also by regular events of an external nature, such as the cycle of seasons, and by irregular external events, such as intermittent crop failures and famines. Agricultural practices can also be transformed by the introduction of new crops or methods of cultivation. Ritual and political relationships can be expected to suffer adjustments in response to alterations in this changing process of material production.

The relationship between social expressions at the levels of ritual and politics, on the one hand, and mundane practice, on the other, cannot be described as deterministic in either direction. But it is reasonable to expect that shifts in one are likely to elicit changes in other domains of life. By taking this assumption as the foundation for an analysis of the complex historical relationship between *negara* and *banua,* some of the reasons for fluctuating degrees of interference in the domains of Pura Manggu and Antap Sai may become more transparent.

I have noted earlier that origin narratives, although they form part of a religious discourse, are challenged with increasing frequency as the perceived material and social prosperity of a domain decreases. One could say that reflexivity is called for in situations where the social or material conditions from which a logic of practice is derived fail to be reproduced by it. Such crises can arise in the wake of historical, social, and political changes; from the indeterminacies of nature; or from a combination of several factors.

Schulte-Nordholt has suggested that some of the most important ritual mobilizations in the *negara* of Mengwi occurred in response to natural disasters such as epidemics and crop failure (1988:13). Such crises threatened the reproduction of social and material conditions and even the very survival of the people. They called for extraordinary and innovative responses rather than an adherence to the established form of organization that was informed by a traditional practical logic and articulated in a local ritual idiom. It is precisely these moments of "questioning the given" that presented an opportunity for the ruler to prove his spiritual efficacy (*kesaktian*) and to interfere legitimately in the organization of a domain.

Anthony Forge (1980) has argued similarly that the extraordinary purification rituals held at Pura Besakih in 1963 (Eka Dasa Rudra), 1978 (Panca Wali Krama), and 1979 (Eka Dasa Rudra) were ritual mobilizations that marked periods of great social change and crisis in Bali. They provided an opportunity for reconstructing the established order of ritual practice at the temple to better fit the social conditions of a modernizing Bali. At the same time, they provided a legitimate occasion for advancing the appropriation of the temple by emergent religious state authorities.

On a smaller scale, the occasional need for a major repair to a temple represents a crisis to small communities unable to raise the necessary material resources. Numerous examples from among the *banua* temples of highland Bali illustrate that it is precisely these extraordinary occasions that call for financial contributions from external sponsors. In partial awareness of this situation, such repair crises have also been deliberately imposed on villages in recent times through the Parasida Hindu Dharma Indonesia–sponsored guidelines for temple design. To meet these guidelines, mountain villages are forced to hire tradesmen and import materials from the outside. Formerly, the materials and skills for the construction of traditional shrines had been locally available at little or no cost to the community.

Material and social crises can thus elicit specific responses at a level of ritual performance and invite external political interference. More permanent adjustments to the ritual order of a domain may result from fundamental changes in sociopolitical conditions and the means of agricultural production. One such lasting adjustment may await the domains of Pura Pucak Manggu and Antap Sai in response to the gradual extension of the traditional area of irrigated rice agriculture up into the mountains. This spread of irrigation agriculture was initiated by the rulers of Mengwi and by local hopes for a better crop yield. The production methods and temporal ritual order relevant to the process of irrigation agriculture differ significantly from those of the dry rice cultivation that has been the traditional livelihood of the villages in this twofold domain. However, most of the villages in the area were not yet affected by this change at the time of my research, and the ritual order of their domains still reflected the seasonal pattern of dry rice cultivation.

A further variable in the relationship between *banua* and *negara* has been the capacity of the ruler or government to enforce sanctions on local people in order to force them into altering the ritual organization of their domain or their agricultural system. In the absence of a fully developed state apparatus, as is at the disposal of the current national government, the rulers of Mengwi were unable to exert such force consistently on mountain villages. Instead they largely depended on discourses of kingship, that is, on claims to a legitimate right to rule and on their attractiveness as royal patrons.

From a local perspective, such discourses were taken most seriously in the event of a local crisis in which a king was able to provide aid. The state could be ignored as long as it had little effect on the material concerns of day-to-day village life. While locals would restrict the legitimacy of the ruler's authority to a context of crisis, the carriers of a discourse of kingship would have liked to see their authority extended beyond the occasion of need. Perhaps the threat of future natural crises and the permanent menace of raiders from other kingdoms were sufficient to give substance to this demand and to perpetuate a discourse of secular rule. But the continuous potential for crises did not automatically imply a stable flow of allegiance to any particular king. Villages were able to switch allegiance if their practical concerns were better met by another king (C. Geertz 1980). In general, practical interests in this domain were focused on local processes of agricultural production to which the rulers of Mengwi were of little relevance.

The temporal cycle of formalized ritual practices within the domain of Pura Pucak Manggu and Pucak Antap Sai derives part of its meaning from the cycle of dry rice agriculture. The domain of these temples is unique in this sense, given that most other mountain villages now rely predominantly on a variety of cash crops. It is an exemplary case that may help to elucidate the relevance of *banua* ritual to agricultural production cycles. The continuous adherence to rice agriculture in the domain of these twin temples may in part explain why male and female sanctuaries still coexist here, unlike in the case of Pura Pucak Penulisan and Pura Batur.

The timing of ritual, and indeed the perception of the flow of time in general, owes much to the alternating pattern of the planting, growth, and harvesting of rice in this twin domain. Natural weather patterns do not necessarily conform to an ideal temporal cosmology. Rains may fail when they are expected or required for ensuring adequate growth or may cause destruction when they occur out of season. The vicissitudes of nature call for human intervention or for divine intervention at human request. The regularity of the ritual cycle reflects a practical concern in that it compensates for a lack of regularity in nature. Not only does ritual provide people with a sense of control, it also supplies a practical time frame for estimating the turning points between the seasons and for synchronizing farmers' practices in a pattern of regional cooperation.

The patterning of ritual and agricultural activities is closely linked to other fundamental concepts of social organization. One example is a division of labor between men and women that is equally prominent in ritual and agriculture. This division finds expression as a gendered cosmology in the ideal world of ritual, which in turn helps to socialize men and women to perform their allotted roles in a practical universe of gendered labor. Another fundamental set of concepts relates to spatial orientation. Ritual activities mirror the movements of the rice, outward to the fields for planting and back inward (to the rice barn, *lumbung*) at the time of harvesting. Both of these movements are interpreted in relation to basic regularities in human experiences of space and time. The journey of the rice is analogous to the daily movements of people as they depart from and return to their houses (*umah*), and it is the experience of dwelling in a traditional house that provides the first experience of a code of spatial orientation. Just as basic as the experience and idiom of bodily movement in space is the experience and idiom of body histories. The body is subject to growth, decay, and death. When farmers say that "the rice is already pregnant (*beling*)" or is "dry like the body of an aged person" and when they conduct rituals to mark these growth stages, they are interpreting the cultivation cycle in terms of more basic embodied experiences. While agricultural practices are thus regulated by a symbolic ritual order, the patterns of both ritual and agricultural activities employ metaphors derived from other aspects of experience.

Figure 6 is a graphic representation of parallels between the pattern of agricultural practice in this domain and the cycle of ritual practices at its two regional temples. The shape of a sine curve was chosen in order to highlight the peaks of the rainy and dry seasons and the moments of transition between them. The organizational patterns of ritual and agricultural practice are presented in the context

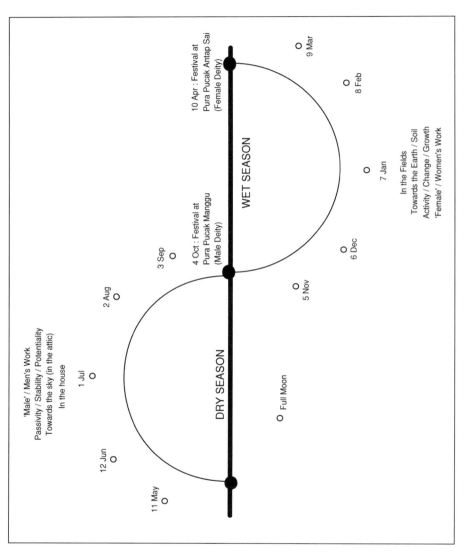

Figure 6. Cycles of agricultural and ritual practice

of a more general local cosmological framework. The numbers indicate Balinese lunar months and are followed by their approximate equivalents in the Julian calendar.

Two qualifications should be kept in mind in the interpretation of this graph. First, this diagram refers to more than just a symbolic schema. A symbolic framework of interpretation may influence the organization of ritual and agricultural practices, but it does not capture them in their entirety. People's experience of regularities in their environmental, embodied, and social condition gives rise to a practical logic that is not always subjected to reflection and symbolic interpretation. Symbolic frameworks and a logic of practice may be closely intertwined, but one cannot be reduced to the other. Second, the diagram represents only one of several possible ritual or agricultural calendars. The format of a calendar varies in accordance to its specific practical application. Some of the locally written calendrical texts (*wariga*) that have been transcribed in the course of my research may appear to provide a totalizing model for the appropriate timing of human actions. But on closer inspection, what is said to be appropriate action at a given time depends also on the characteristics of the actor, the situation, and the undertaking.

It would therefore be presumptuous to suggest that a single and universal Balinese calendar could suffice as a reference frame for the interpretation of all temporally structured local practices. The Balinese calendar alluded to in this graph is one based on the twelve lunar months (*sasih*). Occasional adjustments in the form of an additional thirteenth month are necessary in order to recalibrate this lunar calendar to the slightly longer solar year. This calendar reflects the annual growth cycle of dry or rain-irrigated rice with its comparatively long maturation period.[47] In contrast to the faster growing rice varieties used on fields irrigated by water canals, rain-irrigated rice will yield only a single crop in a year. The *sasih* calendar is thus relevant as a specific time frame for dry rice agriculture as well as for the cultivation of coffee and other cash crops with an annual harvest cycle that are nowadays grown in the highlands.

The life cycle of the rice begins in the dry season. The preparation of the fields for planting commences during the third Balinese lunar month (*sasih ketiga*). The treatment of the land, in particular the plowing, is the responsibility of men. In a spatial idiom, the seed rice is about to leave the domesticated spaces of the house and the village and to move outward into the fields. Both village councils (*desa ulu apad*) and ancestral origin houses (*sanggah*) are social spheres predominantly structured in terms of a succession of their male members. It is therefore men who prepare the earth for the male seed rice on its journey to the female fields. By contrast, it is women who fetch dried rice (*baas*) from the attic or rice barn for cooking.

On the last day and new moon of the third month (*tilem ketiga*), all agricultural tools made of iron are brought to the blacksmith (*pande*) for repair. This occasion is accompanied by a ritual called Nyeeb, from *seeb*, "to heat (the metal)." Heating is not only a means of repairing these tools but an act of purifying them after they have come into contact with the earth. All blacksmith work must cease for forty-two days thereafter.

Some time after the great festival of the fourth full moon (*purnama kapat*) at Pura Pucak Manggu, with its male deity, the male seed rice (*baas*) will be taken out from the rice barn or attic by the woman of each household in order to be planted. The men's work comes to an end as soon as the dry seed moves toward the symbolically female sphere of the earth and the female time of the wet season. The rituals of the wet season are said to be directed to the left (female) and those of the dry season to the right (male). Though the festival of Pura Manggu acts as a signal for rice planting, the exact timing is somewhat flexible. Farmers may wait for the actual arrival of the first rains of the season.

Although rains are eagerly awaited at this time of necessary transition, the change of seasons is regarded as a precarious time for the rice. The dry seed rice must be fortified ritually before becoming immersed in the moist earth. Villagers ask for *tirta wangsupada*. In order to produce this holy water, the sacred objects that represent the male deity at Pura Pucak Manggu are "washed" (immersed in moisture).[48] *Tirta*, like rain itself, is moisture from a heavenly, male source. Water as a symbol of life in general is ambiguous, as it incorporates both a male and a female aspect. Just as female moisture is represented on a macrocosmic scale by a lake and its female goddess, it is represented on a microcosmic scale by the womb that holds the amniotic fluid. *Tirta* is a substance that derives much of its potency from this very ambiguity.

The first task to be completed exclusively by women is the actual planting of the rice seedlings. The rice is from now on referred to as *padi* rather than *baas*. Planting is followed by the first weeding of the fields toward the end of the fifth month. This occasion is marked by the ritual of Melayakin (from *layak*, "to turn one's body backwards [in dance]"). The movements of the body can be regarded as the foundation of all categories of spatial orientation. In this case, the image of a body turning backward or inward suggests that the rice is beginning its long return journey from the fields back to the house.

Soon after the first weeding, the rice plant begins to emerge out of an initially asexual process of growth and is about to flower and "become pregnant." The rice has now grown upward from the earth to meet the sky. But it can ultimately reproduce itself only by fertilization and the forming of seeds over a period of "pregnancy" or gestation.

Between the sixth and ninth months, blood sacrifices are carried out separately in individual mountain villages, usually on a new moon. The sacrifices of this season are directed specifically toward the chthonic deities (*buta kala*) of the earth or netherworld. These entities are of a demonic disposition and pose a threat to all human endeavors unless they are appeased. The spilling of blood, a symbolically female substance, strengthens the fertility of the earth and protects the crops during the time of gestation or swelling. Just as menstruation must cease during pregnancy to prevent a miscarriage, the blood sacrifices during the gestation period of the rice may be interpreted as a symbolic substitute for menstruation, preventing the rice or the earth from "miscarrying." Reproduction—the successful union of male and female—represents a precarious negotiation of categorical boundaries at an intersection. This idea is represented in the location of the blood sacrifices of this season. They usually take place either at a village crossroads (*pempatan*) or near a cemetery, the crossroads between life and death, and are performed by men.

Other ritual activities during this period include the Neduh ceremony (from *teduh*, "cool") during the seventh month (*sasih kapitu*), which marks the time when the rice is fully grown and flowering. This cooling is the inverse of the heating of tools in the third month. The flowering rice has extended up to the male sky and sun, and is awaiting fertilization. Since it connects the earth with the sky, the earth must be cooled to prevent the rice plant from drying up before it has matured.

When the rice has become pregnant and the new seeds are beginning to swell in their panicles in the eighth lunar month (*sasih kawulu*), the ritual of Ngebekin (from *ngebek*, "to fill something") is held. Finally, the harvest is initiated by the ritual of Ngalamping. Harvesting commences during the ninth or early in the tenth month (*sasih kesanga, sasih kedasa*) and is predominantly carried out by women. At this time "first fruits" (*sesari*, lit. "essence") are offered initially at village temples. The synchronization of production cycles effected by these smaller rituals does not extend beyond a particular village, and the timing of rituals may differ from one place to another. Only the regional rituals of the fourth and tenth months are communally held by all villages in the domain.

It is thus on the full moon of the tenth month (*purnama kedasa*), at the festival of Pura Pucak Antap Sai, that the cycle closes. The rainy season has come to an end, and clear conditions are desirable around this time in order to dry the rice harvest. The ritual marks the safe return of the resurrected rice to the rice barn, where it is stored away from the earth as dry seed until the next planting season.[49] Addressed to a female deity, the ceremony is an act of thanksgiving to the female forces of nature that are the source of all sustenance.[50] It also helps to fortify the female aspects of the rice before it enters its male phase of desiccation. The festival is followed by two months in which no major agricultural rituals are conducted at all, a period during which the rice rests in its dormant seed state.[51]

The holy water that is produced at Pura Pucak Antap Sai is referred to as "*tirta pekulu*," a term derived from *ulu*, "the head, topmost part, or upper end," as opposed to *tirta wangsupada*, from *pada*, "feet [lower end of the body]." The direction of the feet is toward the female earth and marks the seasonal turn toward the wet season. The direction of the head is toward the male sky and signals the start of the dry season.

The partly cosmological and partly practical framework just described has an impact on the organization of all human activities and social interactions in the highlands. For a people who continue to depend on agriculture for their economic survival, the regionally synchronized ritual and cultivation practices within a domain count among the most pertinent practical and reflexive concerns. Although a diversity of cash crops have replaced rice as the economic mainstay in most other domains in the Balinese highlands and despite the diversity in the cycles of activity surrounding the production of these various other crops, most Mountain Balinese have retained their intimate psychological bond to the land and their appreciation for the livelihood it provides. Rice is still considered the ideal food, and the cultivation cycle of rice still serves as an ideal temporal blueprint for the ritual ordering of the relationship between people and land in most *banua*.

Origin and Precedence: The Organization of Ritual Domains in Highland Bali

The preceding chapters have drawn a sketch of a rich narrative and ritual landscape spanning the Balinese highlands and beyond, and have illustrated the significance of the *banua* as a prominent form of regional organization among Bali Aga villages. Despite a wide range of organizational variation among ritual domains, there are a number of features they hold in common. Some of these shared characteristics must now be identified and examined in the light of the general theory of precedence proposed at the beginning.

I think it is worthwhile at this juncture to reflect briefly on the utility of regional research. No isolated village study or even a combination of several such studies could have revealed the macropattern of regional social and ritual relationships among village communities in the highlands and along the northeastern coast of Bali. At the same time, there is no denying a great demand for continuing research. Detailed studies of domains other than that of Pura Pucak Penulisan would perhaps reveal local complexities that are as yet unknown. If the present study encourages further research on the people and culture of highland Bali by forthcoming generations of researchers, one of its most important goals would be accomplished. The more so if their results were to challenge or enrich the following conclusions.

Banua are ritual domains constituted on the idea of a shared and sacred origin (*kemulan*). Points of origin are marked by temples: the symbolic representations of the domain's sacred unity and the "houses" of their ancestral founders or paramount deities. The relation of individual member villages to a shared source is articulated in origin narratives and recognized by observing specific ritual obligations. The narrative and ritual practices of a domain are both focused on commemorating the mythical history of its expansion, from a large original village to a more complex regional network of separate but related communities.

Two distinct idioms of relatedness are observable in the origin narratives of different *banua*. One form of relationship narrative relies on the notion of a shared genealogical origin among the deities or ancestors of a domain. In an idiom of ancestry and marriage, the structuring principle is most often a distinction between generational levels (parent-child [in-law]) or between siblings in the order of their birth. The distinction is one of temporal precedence in both cases, in that the more senior party is attributed with higher status. A ranking of village-founding ancestor deities tends to elicit more pronounced status asymmetries among the villages concerned where the distinction is one among members of different generations rather than among siblings (by their order of birth).

The significance of ancestors in the context of a *banua* lies in their accomplishments as the founders (divine or "posthuman") of villages and domains with specific boundaries. Origin narratives always identify deified ancestors in relation to specific places, as founders of villages and occupants of their origin temples. The positioning of the ancestors' actions bears witness to a spatial idiom of relatedness within ritual domains, which is nevertheless secondary to a temporal idiom of precedence. The spatial proximity of a village temple to a domain temple as such does not say anything about its status. For example, the Pura Bale Agung of Batih is located closer to the domain temple of Penulisan than is that of Selulung, and yet the latter is a subdomain temple, whereas the former is an ordinary village temple.

To narrate the path and ancestry of origin in a domain is to trace its history of human settlement and migration. The temporal order of precedence among villages within a domain is thus constructed by reference to the time of their foundation. The first settlement represents the preeminent point of origin and marks the moment when a lasting covenant between the land and the people was first established. Successively founded subsidiary settlements are further ranked in the order of their foundation. Among later established villages, an additional categorical distinction is drawn between those founded by emigrants from the origin village and others founded by outsider immigrants. Immigrants are linked in a more precarious patron-client relationship to the original owners of the land or are integrated into their local web of ancestral relationships as in-marrying sons-in-laws and branch-house founders. In some cases immigrant outsiders succeed in redefining the previous origin histories and installing themselves at the inside of an existing or a new domain.

Myths and legends about the deeds and kinship relations of deified ancestors form the narrative charter of a domain. All human knowledge about the past, however, is considered to be incomplete. This view of history creates possibilities for contesting origin charters and for occasional changes in a given pattern of ritual association, which, in turn, bears witness to a considerable interest in the distribution of ritual authority and status within Bali Aga domains. Since *banua* are constituted conceptually on the idea of a temporal process that can only be apprehended with imperfection, in a process of retrospective historical reflection, it is implied that the internal structure of a domain must remain subject to negotiation and change.

The scope for contesting the given order of a domain is accentuated by the economic and political autonomy of contemporary branch villages. Some control over the crucial material resource of agricultural land in branch villages may have been retained by the origin villages of domains up to the recent past. This would have lent a degree of security to their position of ritual preeminence. In the current situation, however, a claim to ritual authority can only be successful if it meets with the voluntary and active social approval of others. The effect of struggles over the control of land can be recognized in the recent history of some *banua*, where land disputes have led to social disintegration.

One factor that may have prevented such disintegration in most other *banua* is the effect of an initial status disparity. It has already been discussed in relation to the *gebog domas* of Pura Penulisan that the advantage of occupying a position of relatively high status in the first place may be sufficient to maintain the status quo even if all other pertinent resources are now evenly distributed.

Whenever a given ritual order is challenged and renegotiated, the outcome depends greatly on how different parties perceive the social benefits and costs of their association. A loss of unity, for example, can be experienced as a negative outcome and trigger restorative efforts, as in the domain of Pura Pucak Tolukbiyu. This illustrates that such renegotiations are often accomplished in a process of trial and error, and that there are considerations beyond the need for a mutually acceptable form of association. The ultimate validity test of the ritual order of temporal precedence in a domain at any given time is the welfare of its people and the measure of satisfaction they enjoy in their engagements with each other and the quotidian world. In a religious idiom, the fortunes of human beings reflect the degree to which their behavior concords with the wishes of divine (non- or post-human) forces.

Ritual is perhaps the most powerful idiom for the articulation of social relationships within a *banua*. The inward gathering of villages during a regional temple festival is in part a symbolic inversion of the outward ancestral journeys reported in the origin narratives of the domain. But ritual practices are both less and more than reenactments of the origin narratives of a domain. Origin narratives are not generally designed as scripts for the performance of ritual. Some of their content may be expressed in the order of a procession or seating arrangement, in the distribution of offerings, in the allocation of shares from the body of a sacrificial victim, and, most important, in the division of ritual labor. Many details of an origin narrative, however, will never be enacted in specific rituals. Ritual practices can also be more than a mere enactment, by serving as the idiom of articulation for intervillage relationships many of which are not accompanied by a specific narrative of origin. This point is particularly obvious in the case of Pura Batur's network, where acceptance of a common origin history is not required. One reason may be that a relationship articulated in an idiom of ritual practice does not make the issue of relative status explicit to the same degree as an origin narrative would.

The great festivals of *banua* temples nearly always involve the sacrifice of a male water buffalo or other four-footed animal. These sacrifices are focused not so much on the death of the victim as on his resurrection (*wangun urip*). They are a celebration of life, of the unity of different parts working together to form a whole. This unity is ultimately conceived in terms of a pervading sociocosmic dualism: as a coming together of invisible and visible worlds (*niskala sekala*), female and male (*luh muani*) participants, visible offerings and invisible deities, left and right sides (*kiwa tengen*) of the sacrificial body, or left and right moieties of the village council with its elders and priest-leaders, in a spirit of unity and balance referred to as "*rua bineda*" (two that are different). This unity is temporary and precarious but highly valued. In a process whereby a natural and contingent body is dissected and culturally reconstructed, society defines itself as a complex web of relationships that require constant clarification and revitalization. The possibility of separation, disintegration, and death is not denied or despised but defined as the essence of fertility. Difference must reassert itself before new life can be created in a moment of coming together.

What then is the role assigned to social change in highland Balinese representations of their social world? I would suggest change is a fundamental assumption in Bali Aga thought even though continuity is highly valued. A social order of precedence presupposes that a process of expansion and differentiation has taken place and that this process must continue. The sacralization of the past in an idiom of origin is no more than an acknowledgment of the historical condition of society. History is at once a fait accompli and an ongoing process. Even sacralization itself is a process, evident in the gradual transformation of the ordinary human beings of today into the venerable elders of tomorrow and the divine ancestors of future generations. Status and sacredness are a matter of degree, to be measured on a continuous temporal scale of precedence. The ritual world of Bali Aga domains is thus not a timeless sacred universe or a fixed social hierarchy. It is a temporally contingent world shaped by shifting perceptions of a past that is alive in the present and continually expands into the future.

History, to the Bali Aga, is more than a set of inscriptions, an ideal text reproduced mimetically with each act of ritual reinscription. It is more akin to the texts of fading palm-leaf manuscripts, which have to be transcribed perpetually on fresh strips of palm leaf and whose content may be changed in the process. The people of highland Bali may symbolically return to their origin in ritual, but they know all too well that time is irreversible and history is a book never to be completed. What ultimately matters to them is that, as a people who are able to retrace the path of origin, they are able to maintain a sense of spiritual unity, purpose, and direction. Reflecting on their origins, they are reassured about their future path, wherever it may lead them. This perception of life as a process balanced between a respect for elders and time-honored tradition, on the one hand, and a deep appreciation of change and new life, on the other, provides the foundation for a model of society that is based on neither totalization nor atomization. One could say that culture, to the Bali Aga, is both a heritage and a quest, a cooperative venture and the site of a competitive struggle.

A comparison between different *banua* reveals local peculiarities in the conceptualization and enactment of relationships among participating villages. Some of these differences may be attributed to variable and external historical factors. While there is clearly some scope for such variation in external factors (e.g., the intervention of southern Balinese kings in some domains but not others), it is also true that some historical processes have had a similar effect on the entire highland region. The early development of trade, changes in the type and mode of agricultural production, gradual state formation, colonization, and modernity all have had a broad impact on material, political, and social conditions in this part of Bali and on the island as a whole.

What limited historical information is available illustrates that most domains have been transformed in recent times and that such changes unfold as the result of continuous negotiation of the past in the present. The case studies presented in the preceding chapters suggest that to negotiate, make choices, and change society is not only a possibility intrinsic to a logic of precedence. It is a reality made evident in social practice. This dynamic in itself is sufficient to explain why each domain is in some ways unique, though it may not account for every element of commonality or variation.

The *banua* has been instrumental in shaping and coordinating Bali Aga responses to the outside world. The complex web of linkages within and between the different ritual domains in Bali's highlands generates a widespread awareness of a shared cultural heritage and history among Bali Aga people. They have thus been able to relate to a changing Balinese society with at least a broad sense of shared identity as the island's original people and the custodians of the mountains with their ancient sanctuaries.

Regional interactions within the context of the *banua* may generate a sense of solidarity and a degree of cultural similarity among the Bali Aga and may facilitate a self-definition in contrast to other Balinese. *Banua*, however, cannot account for all that is cohesive about Bali Aga culture. For example, the very striking similarities in the internal organization of village communities seem underdetermined from the perspective of their mutual regional involvement, considering the high degree of mutual autonomy among them. In order to gain a more complete impression of Bali Aga society, a society in which regional ties intermesh with more narrowly localized and exclusive forms of association, it is necessary to look beyond the context of ritual domains.

The following chapter will briefly delve into the more narrow organizational spheres of *desa* and *sanggah*. Bali Aga villages (*desa*) could be described as ritual domains on a smaller scale. At the same time, the *desa* itself builds on organizational patterns derived from the even more basic social sphere of interaction defined by the *sanggah*, an origin group of "houses" related by kinship. One notable difference between domains and more local spheres of social interaction is that in the latter far greater emphasis is placed on individual persons, which gives rise to more precise and intricate social orders of precedence. The following comparison of the concepts and social practices that uphold *banua*, *desa*, and *sanggah* will indeed reveal that notions of origin and precedence are fundamental to all levels of social organization in the highlands.

Chapter 7

THE STATUS ECONOMY
OF HIGHLAND BALI
From the *Banua* to Smaller
Spheres of Social Organization

Exploring the lifeworld of the Mountain Balinese from the perspective of their regional alliances within ritual domains (*banua*) has relegated to the background the more immediate community and family settings that form the stage for many of their mundane and ritual activities. This chapter is concerned first with the internal social organization of Bali Aga communities, so far referred to by the gloss "village" or by the popular local term of Sanskrit origin "*desa*" (village or place). *Desa*, in turn, include even smaller and denser spheres of social interaction, among kin and affines, defined by their common worship at private ancestral "origin temples," or *sanggah kemulan*. A more complete impression of Bali Aga society and its multilayered status economy can be conveyed by tracing conceptual, social, and historical continuities from the *banua* to these two other dimensions of their social world.

I will accomplish this task in three stages. A first step is to describe and analyze *desa* and *sanggah* as independent social spheres, though they are also similar to the *banua* and to one another in their common appeal to notions of origin and precedence. I will explore these continuities in the conceptual and social organization of domains, villages, and kinship-focused groups further by examining situations where the nominal boundaries between these different spheres of social interaction are crossed in practice. Finally, there are a number of historically informative cases with transitional organizational features where the local categorical distinctions between *banua* and *desa* or between *desa* and *sanggah* reach the limits of their usefulness. Underlying logical similarities, practical boundary crossings, and transitional cases together illustrate the fluidity of nominally different levels of social organization normally distinguished, by Balinese and ethnographers alike, for the purpose of reflection and representation.

Desa Ulu Apad and *Sanggah Kemulan:* The Ceremonial Order of Villages and Ancestral Houses among Mountain Balinese

The Desa Ulu Apad

Although embedded in the *banua,* the *desa adat* of the highlands are significant social and ritual worlds in their own right and also significantly different in every respect from the social patterns these same terms may designate in southern Bali. Indeed, an appreciation of Bali Aga society in all its idiosyncrasy and local intricacy cannot be complete without at least a brief description and comparative analysis of village organization.

A much more detailed exploration of Bali Aga society from the perspective of *desa* and *sanggah* is the topic of another volume (Reuter, in press). The purpose of the outline that follows is to illustrate the broader significance notions of origin and precedence have in Bali Aga society beyond a context of regional ritual alliance.

The project of a comparative exploration of Bali Aga village organization was first envisaged by the Dutch explorer C. J. Grader, who compared the social organization of a small number of "old Balinese villages" in a very brief essay, first published in 1937. Written in the theoretical tradition of Dutch ethnology at the time, Grader's comparative study is focused on the task of abstracting a structural model from ethnographic snapshots of a variety of organizational forms and fails to explore the dynamics and practical intricacies of the *desa* as a living community. My own research in more than fifty Bali Aga villages suggests that their conceptual and social order is characterized by precedence distinctions in relation to a shared and sacred origin and cannot be reduced to any conceivable set of timeless, structural relations.

Much of the ceremonial, social, and political life of Bali Aga communities revolves around an assembly or council of land-owning, married villagers that is structured as a very intricate temporal order of precedence. This assembly is known as *"krama desa ulu apad."* The term *"ulu apad"* is a spatial metaphor and refers to the process of incremental rank increases by which an assembly member (*keraman,* from *rama*, "father") may rise to the status of a village elder or priest-leader (with the generic honorific title *jero*, "insider"). Literally it means "[to climb] the steps (*apad*) to the head (*ulu*) end [of the rectangular platform of a village longhouse (*bale lantang*)]." In relation to the architecture of the ceremonial village longhouses found in all Bali Aga villages, the term "*apad*" refers to the planks of wood between the several pairs of pillars that divide the elongated rectangle of the *bale lantang* into sections. The section where the elders are formally seated is always located at the head end (*ulu*) of this rectangular open pavilion. This end is oriented upward toward the shrines of the village ancestors located in the temple's "inner sanctum" (*jeroan*). The shrines themselves are positioned "toward the mountain" (*kaja*) and ultimately toward the sky. Changing one's seating position in the direction of *ulu* (or *kaja* or *jeroan*) thus signifies an increase in rank, understood as a greater proximity to a sacred origin.

An alternative term for this ranked village council in several other villages is "*dulu dapuh.*" Here the metaphoric reference is to the uphill movement through ascending ranks along the two long planks (*dapuh*) at the sides of the platform on which the elders (in small villages the entire assembly of men) are seated. Again it describes a process, common to all traditional Bali Aga villages, by which any "eligible" person can gradually rise in rank from the bottom (*teben*) to the topmost (*ulu*) rank position in the village assembly.

This fluid order of relative rank distinctions is expressed visually in the seating order of men at customary meetings (*sangkepan*), usually on a full or new moon (*purnama/tilem*). These meetings are held in the ceremonial longhouses (*bale lantang* or *dawa*, lit. "long pavilion") located in the village's Pura Bale Agung and other temples.[1] The highest-ranking elders sit at the upper (*ulu*) end of the *bale lantang*, hold a rank-specific title, and are each allocated a specific set of ritual tasks and privileges. The lowest-ranking (pair of) members sit at the lower (*teben*) extremity of the platform, that is, at the end pointing downhill (*kelod*, "toward the sea").[2] Rank is also expressed by the order of eating the rank-specific individual food portions (*malang*) that are laid out in the longhouse for the communal meal that marks the conclusion of the regular lunar meetings of the *ulu apad*. During temple festivals, when there is an animal sacrifice, these *malang* include rank-specific body parts of the victim.

A member of the assembly rises one position upward each time a position of higher rank than his own (on his side) is vacated by the death or retirement of a more senior member. A man will eventually

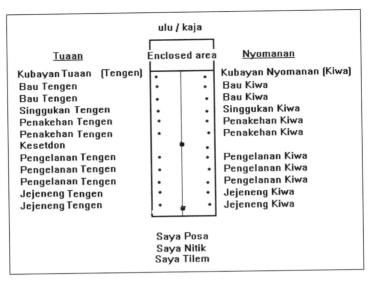

Figure 7. Rank order of elders in Sukawana (seating positions at new moon meetings)

become an elder or initiated priest-leader unless his circumstances force (or allow) him to retire prematurely.

Figure 7 depicts the *ulu apad* of Desa Sukawana as an example. This assembly had 740 members at the time of research, but only the elders meet regularly, as shown in this figure. A list is kept by the *keset don* in order to record the relative rank of the many younger council members.[3]

This and all other *desa ulu apad* are further divided into two sides (*sibak*) of approximately equal size. About half of the men belong to the "left side" (*sibak kiwa*) and will sit on the left *dapuh* of the *bale lantang*, whereas the others belong to and sit on the "right side" (*sibak tengen*).[4] In Sukawana and many other communities, it is a matter of paternity whether a man belongs to the left or right of these ceremonial moieties (*sibak*). That is, people belong to the *sibak* of their fathers. Married women, however, will have shifted to the *sibak* of their husbands. In a few other villages (e.g., Bayung Gede) the moieties of the assembly are entirely symbolic, since there is no relationship between *sibak* affiliation and descent. In such cases succession often follows a single order of rank, and as one's rank increases, one moves uphill in a constant zigzag (rather than linear) pattern alternating from the left *sibak* to the right and back to the left (and so on). In this less common pattern of succession, the rank positions immediately above and below one's own belong to members of the opposite moiety.

The members of the right side in Sukawana are also commonly referred to as Tuaan (*tua*, "old[er]") and those of the left as Nyomanan (*nyom*, "young[er]," or *nyoman*, "third-born child"). By implication the Tuaan are considered symbolically male (right) and the Nyomanan female (left).[5] In the origin myth of Sukawana, the third and youngest (*nyoman*) of the three newcomer brothers who founded the present village married a local girl from Tanah Daa (the land of the maiden), the part of the village where most contemporary Nyomanan families live. The Nyomanan are the indigenous affines and their descendants, while the Tuaan are the descendants of the three newcomer brothers. The former are associated with ritual relating to ancestral land and the Pura Puseh, while the Tuaan are outsiders who installed themselves as political leaders in the village and now dominate in the rituals of the Pura Bale Agung. While similar narrative histories explain the origin of descent-based *sibak* in many other villages, this kind of explanation is not always or necessarily offered.

All *keraman* are ranked and seated in order of their seniority. The assembly is headed by a core group of elders and priest-leaders with individual titles (the highest-ranking elder is always called *kubayan;* other titles vary), whereas lower-ranking men are generally classed within broader rank categories. Seniority does not refer to the chronological age of individual men. A man's rank relative to others is fixed by the time when he "became married" (*makurenan*) or, more literally, when he founded his own "household" (from *kuren*, "hearth"). People must be married before they can "ascend to [become members of] the village assembly" (*menek madesa*), and they cease to be members when they are no longer married.[6] The constituency of a *desa ulu apad* thus consists of the households of married couples ranked in the order in which they were founded, rather than of individuals.[7]

The dualism of the two *sibak* entails that all elders are conceived as complementary pairs of equal rank (e.g., Kubayan Kiwa Tengen), and the left-right distinction is often associated with a further, lateral division of ritual labor. The pairing of left and right sides, or symbolically "female" and "male" men, emulates the pairing of women and men within the households that are the social elements of this rank order (and mirrors the more practical gender-specific division of labor between them). Ritual knowledge is passed down from preceding to succeeding pairs of elders. Each pair is a link in a continuous chain of cultural reproduction, a social process that, in turn, would be inconceivable without simultaneous biological reproduction. Hence at least a nominal capacity to produce socially legitimate off-spring (being married) is a precondition for retaining one's membership and rank.

Most Bali Aga communities are further stratified along a divide between *desa ulu apad* members and other residents, who are excused from the duties and excluded from the prerogatives of membership in this assembly. The duties include attendance at regular meetings on a full and new moon (sometimes also on the *wuku* calendar day called Anggara Kasih), financial contributions to *desa* rituals and temple festivals (*peturunan*), and contributions of unpaid labor (*ayahan desa*), mostly in a ritual context. The rights in many Bali Aga villages (but not in Sukawana, Bantang, Dausa, and a few others) include access to village-owned agricultural land (*tanah ayahan desa*), which is redistributed from retiring members to newly married couples (nowadays plots of land pass from a man to his heir, but formerly they were reallocated at random in at least some villages). Where pots of village land are available but no longer subdividable, a young man may have to wait for an allocation of land until his father retires. Other rights include participation in decision-making processes during *ulu apad* meetings, which often affect the entire community.[8]

Local residents excluded from the *desa* nevertheless do participate in the almost completely inclusive *banjar adat*, with associated rights and obligations. This participation includes attendance at informal *banjar* meetings where secular community issues are sometimes raised and discussed, later to be considered and decided by the *ulu apad*. *Banjar* members are also fully involved in all activities relating to the Pura Dalem of their village and pay *peturunan* for its festivals. They are usually entitled to receive communal residential land (*tanah pekarangan*) sufficient for building a houseyard as well as a place in the village's burial ground. *Banjar*-only community members are most often newcomers or "people of the leaf" (*pendonan*), as opposed to "people of the village trunk" (*wedan* or *tuwed desa*). This precedence distinction is again relative and flexible. Many newcomers are eventually admitted to the council or, as in the case of Sukawana, may even acquire a prominent position in the end. This process of redefining eligibility to membership may occur quickly or only after many generations of local residence. Much may depend on the status of the village within its *banua* (in an origin village like Sukawana, full admission to the *desa adat* is not usually granted to newcomers for a long time).

Bali Aga villages and their assemblies are clearly organized as social orders of precedence. A higher-ranking individual is literally said to precede (*maluan*) those who follow in the ranks below, and the logic of ranking in general is evidently based on a temporal succession of socially pertinent events (marriages or household foundations). This local rank order is associated with a very intricate division of individual ritual labor (e.g., the *singgukan* are responsible for dissecting sacrificial bodies into *wangun urip*) and is hence necessarily more precise and personal than the rank order of villages within a regional domain.

In spite of the similarities among Bali Aga communities, their comparison inevitably raises once more the familiar problem of variation (the same applies to *sanggah*). While it can be argued that the similarities are striking in this case, there is no justification for constructing an ideal type of a mountain community and treating all particular cases as more or less imperfect realizations. The more productive approach is to treat variation in local organization as the variable outcome of a flexible generative scheme embodied in a finite but expandable set of concepts, idioms, and organizational options. This schema is one of precedence distinctions and is relevant not only to the *desa ulu apad* but to all aspects of Bali Aga society.

The Sanggah Kemulan

Similar to the *desa*, the basic social components of *sanggah* groups are households (*kuren*) rather than individuals. The practical manifestation of social ties among members of households, coresidence in a single dwelling or house and day-to-day commensality, anticipates the symbolic function of the ceremonial longhouse and of communal ritual meals as the markers of a broader sense of social unity in the *desa*. The additional requirement for households to be considered part of a *sanggah* group is that their occupants are expected to be related by bonds of common ancestry in a more immediate and exclusive sense than is the case in most villages.

Each house (*umah*) is home to a married couple, their children, and sometimes an elderly and dependent parent. Such households are called "*kuren*," the term for both a hearth and the group of people who share the food cooked on it. The *kuren* is the basic socioeconomic unit of production and consumption in highland Bali. Each house contains a small ancestor shrine (*pekaja*) located at the sacred uphill extremity, which also marks those who dwell beneath its roof as the most basic worship group.

Bali Aga houses are clustered together in larger houseyards

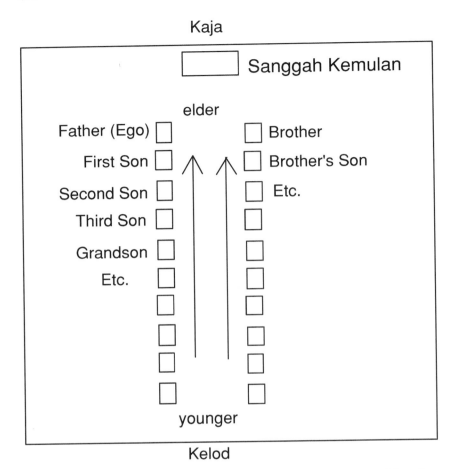

Figure 8. The spatial ordering of domestic houses in relation to *sanggah kemulan*

(*banjaran* or *pakarangan*) enclosed by an earthen wall or hedge
(see Figure 8). At the sacred uphill end of each houseyard is a
sacred house or temple, the *sanggah kemulan*, literally, the "shrine of
origin." This house-temple accommodates the common ancestors of
the human occupants of residential houses within the houseyard.
The patrifocal descent group who occupy a houseyard and their
temple are both called *sanggah,* and the unity of the group is primarily conceived in terms of jointly held religious obligations.

The houses within a compound are arranged in one or two rows
oriented along an uphill-downhill axis. A singular row is often believed to indicate a houseyard established by a single male ancestor,
whereas two parallel rows are said to originate from a set of two or

more brothers. As the male children of older couples marry and form their own households, new houses are added at the downhill end of the row, and likewise for their grandchildren. Bali Aga houses are sturdy and therefore outlive their first occupants. As the older generation passes away, the dwellings at the uphill end become vacant. Hence the younger couples who inherit them must repeatedly move house in an upward direction. This ideal pattern of spatially encoded precedence is not always adhered to because of a variety of practical constraints. It is obligatory in several villages, however, that the most senior couple dwell in the house at the uphill extremity of the appropriate row within their compound once they have become village elders.

It is important that the oldest house in a row, occupied by the most senior household of the group, is spatially positioned at the upper end of the house row. This end points toward the group's sacred origin temple (*sanggah kemulan*). The dwelling of the deceased ancestors is a logical extension from the house of the oldest living predecessor, just as ritual obligations to ancestors are an extension of practical obligations toward living kin, particularly one's elders.

The house rows of the Bali Aga reveal a pattern of uphill to downhill succession and sometimes a right-left dualism that mirrors the structure of Bali Aga village councils. The members of village councils are also seated in parallel rows in order of seniority during meetings and communal meals in the ceremonial village longhouse. Each male council member again represents a household. The village longhouse could be described as a superlative houseyard, emulated in a single open structure, in which the entire *desa* community is represented.

The arrangement of Bali Aga houses in rows and in a temporal order of precedence, oriented toward a point of common origin, has a striking resemblance to the design and temporal logic of longhouses in Borneo, Sumatra, and other parts of the Indonesian archipelago. It is common for such longhouses to contain a row of household compartments under a single roof, each representing a married couple or household within a larger kin group.[9] The obvious difference between the two designs is that the Bali Aga houses within a row no longer form a single structure. The spatial logic, however, is very similar indeed. The major Bali Aga innovation is the invention of the houseyard (*sanggah*) as an encompassing space and an alternative social category to the residential longhouses of their neighbors on other islands.

Bali Aga houses also make for an interesting comparison with those of southern Bali, where the houseyard concept is taken a step further. A seminal article by Leo Howe (1983) illustrates a further innovation. Whereas Bali Aga houses are integrated and complete dwellings with multiple functions, southern Balinese houseyards contain diverse buildings that are functionally specific: a house for sleeping and living, a granary, a pavilion for ceremonies, a separate cooking house, and so on.

When the residential space in a houseyard is exhausted and no more houses can be added, a new houseyard needs to be built. In this event, the ancestor temple of the original houseyard is upgraded to the status (and design) of a "great *sanggah*," or *sanggah gede*. Residents of the new houseyard, though they will also build a new *sanggah kemulan* of their own, will usually continue to participate in the ceremonies of this older *sanggah gede*.

More often than lack of space, this process of fission is triggered by conflicts among *sanggah* members, usually relating to matters of inheritance. A *sanggah kemulan* is not normally expected to be maintained by a worship group extending beyond an ideal four-generation limit, whereby the most distant relationship is one between second cousins (*mindon*). Indeed, the unity of a *sanggah kemulan* may collapse much earlier. At the same time, there are also cases where a cluster of related *sanggah kemulan*, or even several *sanggah gede* spread over different villages, remain united by their common ancestor worship at a regional ancestral origin temple, or *pura kawitan*. The latter often has as regional a following as a *pura banua*, though its constituency is several *sanggah* rather than several *desa*. The main distinction between *banua* and *kawitan* temples is one of place and name. This difference has become more salient in recent times, as increasing emphasis is being placed on written origin histories with pretensions of genealogical accuracy and exclusivity with regard to *kawitan* connections.

The houses within a houseyard are not necessarily the houses of agnatically related men. It is common practice for a couple to adopt a male child if they lack a lineal successor altogether or to contract an uxorilocal marriage if they have only daughters. The primary social value of house groups is to maintain an unbroken continuity between a sacred ancestral origin in the past and ever new generations of successors in the present and the future rather than to obey an agnatic principle of descent (in which case a collateral successor or brother's child would be chosen as a substitute male heir instead of an adopted child or a stay-at-home daughter).

Bali Aga people also acknowledge the *sanggah* of their affines as socially relevant origin points. While they may not pay *peturunan* for financing the rituals held at the *sanggah* of their (grand-)mothers and sisters, they do attend and deliver small offerings (*nyasah*). Again resorting to a botanical metaphor, the temples of wife-takers are referred to as *akah* (root) and those of wife-giving affines as *muncuk* (tip). The affinal relationship is asymmetric, with the tip ranked above the root. The debt entailed in receiving a spouse is most obviously reciprocated by the son-in-law (*mantu*), who must render many services and always show deference to his father-in-law (*matua*). Subsequent marriages that lead to immediate reciprocation (sister exchange or the return of a bride to the origin house of her mother or grandmother) are discouraged, because they would invert the status distribution pattern of an existing affinal precedence relationship. This and other practices imply that there is an asymmetry that extends beyond the *mantu-matua* relationship, but not indefinitely. There is no fixed ranking of clans in a fixed pattern of marriage exchange and asymmetric alliance. What is held to be important are historical sequences of exchange that precipitate obligations only within the range of the approximately four generations of a *sanggah*'s living occupants.[10]

Sanggah can thus be described as social orders of precedence, both in their internal organization and in their relations with the *sanggah* of affines. The common orientation of houses or households in a *sanggah* is to a shared ancestral origin, though ancestry may be conceived in a more immediate and narrow sense than it is in the context of highland villages or domains.

Boundary Crossings: The Conceptual Interface between *Banua*, *Desa,* and *Sanggah* in the Context of Social Practice

The preceding discussion has provided a brief and preliminary introduction to forms of social organization in highland Balinese society other than the *banua*. My aim has been to explore continuities in the construction of status across different contexts of social interaction. A further task is to assess how significant *banua* in fact are for Bali Aga society as a whole, in conjunction with and in comparison to the *desa* and the *sanggah*.

The social significance of regional ritual domains needs to be assessed in relation to that of their constituency of *desa* and the significance of *desa* in relation to their constituency of *sanggah*. At the same time, the *banua* is an important means for relating to a world of lesser social intensity but greater social scope than the *desa*, and likewise the *desa* performs the same function vis-à-vis the *sanggah*. Rather than attempting to fix the importance of contextual boundaries or discounting them, the most appropriate approach is to examine how these different organizational patterns intermesh and how the hypothetical boundaries between them are crossed in social practice.

Banua *and* Desa

Imagine for a moment that it is a full moon in October, *purnama kapat* in the Balinese solar-lunar calendar. The elders and residents of numerous highland communities are returning to Pura Pucak Penulisan, the temple of the largest Bali Aga domain. Picture the Jero Kubayan and the Jero Bau of many villages—wearing their characteristic white head cloths, seated in front of a huge congregation, and facing the ancestral deities of the domain in fulfillment of their duty as priest-leaders. This image of a regional ceremonial gathering of village priest-leaders from many communities is conveyed by a popular allegorical poem.

> *Bebeke putih jambul—makaber ngaja-kanginan*
> *Teked di kaja kangin—trus ditu ya menceg*

> The white crested ducks fly toward the northeast,
> They arrive in the northeast, and there they land together.

Why should numerous local communities, each entertaining the idea of forming a complete sacred-social whole, find it conceptually necessary or socially desirable to participate in a larger sphere of regional ritual practice? Are the white crested ducks drawn together each year by a higher purpose, or do they gather out of a natural affinity toward others of the same kind?

Local interpretations of the poem say that both theories are true, that interlocal similarity is the basis of regional unity and vice versa. The *banua* of Bali's highlands do not artificially unite villages that, in term of their local organization, have nothing in common with one another. Bali Aga communities share very similar patterns of local association and status distribution unique to their society, foremost among them the *desa ulu apad*. The variations among individual villages may testify to the autonomy of local communities in regulating their own affairs, but their similarity is also celebrated and thus reinforced in the *banua*. In this case, at least, cultural identity seems to percolate up and trickle down at the same time.

Just as a *banua* is dependent on cooperation among mutually independent villages, so are the origin and status of individual villages and their local temples vis-à-vis the outside world determined by their positioning within the regional context of a domain. This interdependence of *banua* and *desa* is not a coincidence. It reflects an underlying similarity in how the two institutions are constituted and upheld. Both *desa* and *banua* are associations based on a cult of deified ancestral founders enshrined at an origin temple. Both cultivate an ethos of a unity embracing all people who depend on the land first cleared by their founders, irrespective of people's different kinship-based affiliations. Both are conceived as localized fields of relatedness or places, even though the relevance boundaries of the *desa* and *banua* may carry different degrees of significance in relation to actual land usage rights. Domains and villages are also similar in that they deemphasize social divisions along the lines of *sanggah* affiliation, while at the same time borrowing ideas from this more exclusive sphere of social life. Finally, both *banua* and *desa* are ritual orders of precedence whose participants are ranked by their relative proximity to a shared and sacred origin.

Desa are, however, much smaller and more intimate spheres of sociality than *banua*. Coresidents of a village engage in face-to-face social interactions with one another on a daily basis. People are propelled toward practical cooperation and confronted with conflicts of interest far more frequently as villagers than as participants of a domain. Village organization is therefore concerned with the allocation of tasks and the cultural regulation of encounters not just among large groups who rarely assemble but among individuals who meet in many routine contexts of their daily lives.

One procedure for analyzing the *banua-desa* interface is to consider the relationship between the two organizations from a conceptual perspective. It has been remarked that villages in a domain are joined in a train of mythohistorical events. A new community of people emerges from a parent village by fission and emigration or as outsiders become immigrant clients of such an original village. It may also be that a group of villages is founded simultaneously by fellow refugees after a disaster destroyed their common origin village. All of these connections employ narratives of place and movement in order to establish a relation between parts and a whole, signified by a common point of origin. The territory of a domain composed of several villages is a whole in a spiritual sense, and its people are one in their dependence on the founding ancestors who perpetuate the fertility of the land. It could therefore be proposed that, conceptually, the ceremonial domain of a *banua* encompasses the smaller ceremonial domains of all *desa adat* that lie within its spatial boundaries.

The narrative origin histories and symbolic ritual performances of a domain, however, articulate a conceptual ordering of settlements in the image of a path rather than emphasizing bounded physical spaces and fixed relationships of encompassment. *Banua* are based on spatiotemporally conceived event sequences rather than on hierarchies of immutable spaces with fixed concentric boundaries, as in a mandala. The notion that *desa adat* are encompassed within the spiritual territory of a *banua* may be enticing from an observer's perspective, but it is not a prominent theme in local representational discourses and practices. The interrelations among *desa* in a domain are conceived and enacted as a fluid order of precedence in an expanding time-space continuum.

The relationship between *desa* and *banua* can also be explored from an ontological perspective. Each domain is said to have been born with the establishment of a single and original *desa.* This suggests that the necessary precursor of every *banua* is a village, and, indeed, in the Old Javanese and Old Balinese inscriptions (of both Java and Bali) the word "*wanua*" indicates a single village (Supomo 1995). While the organization of domains may be anticipated in that of villages, *banua* have a distinct form of organization designed to fit the demands of a much looser and wider social setting. This issue will be explored further in the discussion of transitional cases.

It is groups of people who interrelate, rather than their places of residence, even if those groups conceive of themselves in terms of the land they jointly depend on and identify with as members of a ritual community or domain. At a level of social practice, the issue of their relative significance can be explored by asking whether the leaders of one of the two institutions have the capacity to lend approval or impose sanctions on the other.

If one considers the *banua-desa* interface in terms of representational practice, as a flow of social approval, it could be argued that the prestige of ritual leaders in a domain's origin village is dependent on the willingness of several other villages to cooperate with them at a regional level. Any participating community can impose a passive sanction on the domain and its leadership by withdrawing support. In turn, the autonomy of villages is limited by their inclusion in the ritual life of a domain, and divine punishment may fall upon those local communities who choose to dissociate themselves from a *banua* temple. On a more positive note, association with a domain may lend a village the opportunity to gain acceptance, influence, or even prominence in a regional context. The domain as a whole, in turn, gains interregional prominence by having a large constituency.

Much depends on whether villages' lending support and surrendering a measure of their ritual autonomy to a domain is interpreted as voluntary or compulsory. Perhaps there is an intrinsic element of compulsion insofar as a social or ritual convention gives rise to a shared sphere of communication, knowledge, and practice.[11] For a mountain village to detach itself from higher-order traditional organizations means to relinquish its access to this sphere. I am unaware of Bali Aga villages that do not entertain ritual and social ties with neighboring communities, and locals have commented that such a state would be highly undesirable.[12]

A series of examples will better illustrate how practical considerations cut across the *banua-desa* interface. To begin with, the relationship of a village to a domain may influence the internal order of precedence within that village. The special status of "village founders" is often supported by origin narratives that link the community as a whole to a wider domain. The order of precedence in a village assembly in turn influences the affairs of a *banua* whenever that village supplies the domain's ritual leaders from among its elders. Sukawana is such a case in which the men who are its highest-ranking village elders or priests at the time will conduct all important ceremonies at the regional temple Pura Penulisan.

Formal and informal leaders of the *gebog domas* have no authority to intervene in the political or ritual affairs of individual villages within the domain. Nor was there ever during my research an informal action, by either the elders of Sukawana or the committee of Pura Pucak Penulisan, that would have compromised the autonomy of a *desa adat* in regulating its internal rituals, let alone its political affairs. There are no rules that prescribe to the constituent *desa* what forms of local organization they must adhere to or reject, or what traditional rules of propriety (*adat*) or village charter (*awig-awig*) they must abide by as *desa*.

Insofar as they wish to remain a part of a *banua*, however, member villages must perform their individual duties (or exercise their rights) toward the domain temple in conformity to certain regional traditions. In all matters relating to the ceremonies and maintenance of Pura Penulisan, for example, the participants must accept Sukawana's prominent status and ritual leadership. But while specific mistakes may precipitate fines, none are imposed on those who neglect their duties altogether. The only indirect mechanism of imposing sanctions is gossip about derelict members and wishing the wrath of the ancestors upon them. Refusal of holy water (*tirta*) and a formal and public curse (*sumpa*) are perhaps the most extreme measures for eliciting compliance available to the priest-leaders at Penulisan, but these are rarely resorted to or even considered.

In contrast to the *banua*, the *desa adat* is a community that imposes rather strict and explicit rules of propriety on its individual members. These rules may be written down or are simply common knowledge.[13] They form a discourse about local *adat*, "the traditions of Desa X," and stipulate the behavioral expectations associated with being a member of that community. "To impose a rule" is a rather emphatic expression. It suggests that villages have a degree of formal jural authority over people's behavior, a capacity for law enforcement, and high expectations of individual conformity. That is precisely the way it is. Even nowadays and more so in the past, *desa adat* in the mountains have had the power to impose severe religious, economic, and social sanctions on individuals who fail to respect local traditions, ranging from exclusion, fines, and physical punishment to dispossession and expulsion from the community.[14]

Local *adat* can thus be described, at least in part, as a set of prohibitions and prescriptions. In Sukawana, for example, it is prohibited to bring a cow into the village, and perpetrators will be fined. A prescriptive rule is the duty to attend customary meetings. Again absentees are in the first instance subject to a fine. In contrast, a domain has no comparable authority over its member villages, though on rare occasions an individual (rather than a village) may be fined for an offense at a *banua* temple.[15] Generally, however, socialization is so effective that both local and regional *adat* rarely require codification let alone enforcement.

Even a cursory examination of the social organization and traditions of mountain villages reveals that each village is in some way unique. This variation alone is ample evidence of the autonomy of customary villages in legislating and enforcing their own local regulations. It is the village council of a *desa adat* that amends, abolishes, creates, or enforces normative codes of behavior and propriety. Thus, the power of maintaining and reconstructing "tradition" rests in the hands of elders and officeholders at the village level. Most studies of Balinese culture are therefore drawn to focus on social regulations at the village level, and rightly so. It is crucial, nevertheless, to balance such a portrayal by exploring how both higher- and lower-order organizations place limitations on the *desa adat*'s role as the maker of tradition.

There are a number of limitations placed on a village by its involvement in a *banua*. Specific beliefs and traditions pertaining to the *gebog domas*, for example, may indirectly affect member villages. Some are connected to the ritual regulations of Pura Penulisan. One such restriction is that its deity will not accept pigs as sacrificial offerings. The prohibition may have no bearing at all on ritual practices at sub-*banua* or village-level temples, but this belief was brought to the foreground recently in a conflict with a government-sponsored and *pedanda*-led delegation who violated this rule. Another such belief, and one of much broader relevance, is that the smoke from a cremation would offend the deity who resides on Mount Penulisan and that the dead should be buried instead. This argument is raised frequently to explain to outsiders why cremation is rejected as a means of disposing of the dead among the villages of this *banua*.

The issue of cremation is revealing in other ways. Over the last few decades there have been sporadic attempts to introduce cremation. In most cases, requests for permission to cremate came from newcomer kin groups or local upstarts who had begun to claim *triwangsa* (upper caste) status. As *triwangsa* people, they argued, it was their duty to cremate the corpses of their dead. In most cases the *desa adat* categorically refused to allow this.[16] In this pressure situation it became obvious that the decision to allow or forbid cremation rested with the individual *desa adat* rather than the *banua*. Nevertheless, it was their regional obligation to honor the deity of Pura Penulisan that was evoked in village council discussions as the main argument to counter the demands of the kinship faction seeking the right to cremate. While adherence to the broader traditions of the *banua* is a matter of choice, regional affiliations do have an impact on local practices. Fear of outside disapproval or ridicule and respect for time-honored regional conventions combine to impose considerable strictures on villages' ritual autonomy.

Perhaps the relationship between *desa* and *banua*, though they are different sites of social practice, is best characterized as one of mutual and conditional support. For one, unity among the people of a *desa adat* is not strengthened by their ritual responsibilities toward local temples alone. They are propelled to cooperate as a group when they participate in a *banua* by the competition they must face from other, similar groups. This is a disincentive to factionalism within the village in that it creates a demand for unity located outside the context of its internal politics. It is also a great comfort to know that there are dozens of other villages within the *banua* with traditions similar to those of one's own, even if these are not always valued by other sectors of Balinese society. Awareness of this similarity is one of the foundations of a shared cultural identity among the Bali Aga in relation to Balinese society as a whole.

Shared regional traditions and regionally similar local traditions together create a buffer zone where individual *desa adat* are shielded from the impact of outside critique or interference. On this wider stage, choosing to depart from the norms of mainstream Balinese society is thus again a matter of having sufficient numbers as well as a substantial pool of symbolic and material resources, both of which would be unavailable to an isolated village. While the Bali Aga may be a marginal section of Balinese society over all, the situation is tolerable because their regional alliances are large enough to provide an arena for the meaningful pursuit of status.[17]

Desa *and* Sanggah

While it is undeniable that the logical distinctions that inform the internal organization of a *desa* anticipate the principles of precedence that structure a *banua,* they themselves are anticipated in the conceptualization of ancestral origin houses (*sanggah*). The two larger institutions may lay more stress on place, an ethos of practical kinship that unites all coresidents within their sphere of relevance. Kin within a *sanggah,* however, are also linked by the land and common ritual obligation they have received from their personal ancestors, and are ranked by their positioning within shared residential time-spaces.

The borrowing of kinship imagery within the *desa* and the *banua* can be considered from two historical vantage points. An earlier, *sanggah*-derived concept of precedence among generations of kin may have informed a subsequent organization within *desa* and *banua,* even though the latter do tend to suppress kinship-based internal divisions by stressing a more inclusive idiom of place. Alternatively, the two idioms may have coexisted and complemented one another from the beginning. Rather than juxtapose these interpretive options, it may be more instructive to note that the logic of Bali Aga kinship itself is not adequately captured by a universal anthropological category of patrilineal descent. The local kinship system is based on a logic that combines a notion of genealogical ancestry with a broader notion of spatiotemporal positioning pertaining to the houses of the living and the temples of their ancestors, who may in fact have been maternal relatives to many of the group's members. *Sanggah* are not patrilineal descent groups but house-based origin groups. Their unity rests on the joint worship of common ancestors remembered by their origin houses and temples rather than relying on the memory or written records of specific names and genealogical connections. It is, after all, by reference to a sacred locality, the temple of family ancestors (*sanggah*), that such origin groups are categorically defined.

Temples in general are the idealized houses of idealized beings in the highlands.[18] A case could be made that Bali Aga society, to use the terminology of Claude Lévi-Strauss (1983, 1987), is a *société à maisons*, as has been argued recently by James Boon (1990) for southern Bali. Rather than being a universal category in the Lévi-Straussian sense, however, house societies with characteristics similar to the Balinese case are generally found within the Austronesian world (Macdonald 1987; Fox 1993).[19]

Not unlike domains, *desa adat* and *sanggah* are ultimately voluntary associations. Although village councils are a primary force in shaping and regulating people's behavior and access to land, their powers operate within certain constraints. If individual members of the *desa adat* do not abide by local rules of propriety, they may indeed be fined and, if they refuse to pay, may even be dispossessed and expelled from the village. But in most cases the authority of the *desa adat* is not systematically challenged by individuals. It is groups or factions that constrain its power from below. If a minority group of *adat* offenders is large enough, their wishes must be accommodated in some way unless the majority is willing to face the possibility of a permanent and formal division.[20] Authors of studies that portray the *desa adat* as a highly normative and powerful institution may have been misled by viewing it through Western eyes, from the perspective of a single individual, an angle from which it displays a formidable ability to exercise social control and even physical force. This perspective must be tempered, however, with an awareness that the unity of the *desa adat* becomes fragile whenever there is widespread dissatisfaction and organized dissent among its membership.

Similar restrictions also apply to the *sanggah*. Common descent may not even be a necessary condition for membership, and it is certainly not sufficient.[21] Individuals may find it very difficult indeed to escape the close bonds and obligations of kinship and may be disinherited if they try to do so. But again, entire branch houses may rather easily detach themselves from a senior origin house and need not fear many practical repercussions other than a shrinkage of their sphere of social participation. The same principle of critical mass applies to *banua*. A singular village community may find it difficult and rather undesirable to become detached from its *banua* and isolated from its neighbors. In the recorded cases of fission within the *gebog domas*, there was always a departure (*nunas pamit*, "to ask permission to leave") not of one village but of a group of villages or sub-*banua*, such as the *gebog satak* of Dausa and its associates.

However, the organizational structure of the *desa ulu apad* acts as a

check on the ambitions of politically influential *sanggah* and in most
cases successfully maintains an embracing unity among them. It is
true that the highest-ranking elders sometimes may all belong to one
faction, but such a temporary advantage is quickly lost as these elders
retire. There are some strategies for delaying retirement, such as
the adoption of a child to prevent *baki*, but their effects remain temporary. Even during the limited time when one faction may indeed
control key ranks and offices in the *desa adat*, it is not permitted to
dictate how matters concerning the village are decided. Its power is
restrained not only by an ideal of consensus in decision making. Dictatorial attitudes would contradict the ethos of the village as a moral
community and only lead to a permanent split into two or more separate *desa*.

A large and politically dominant faction must also eclipse the power
of the *desa adat* at the risk of finding its own unity threatened by
internal divisions. While a large *sanggah* and its allies may exert a dis-
proportionate informal influence on the management of village affairs
for some time, observations suggest that these alliances often tend to
suffer instability in direct proportion to their size. The forces keeping
a cluster of *sanggah* or a faction together are certainly no more and
probably less effective than those uniting a *desa adat*. No matter how
much *sanggah* networks may impact the micropolitics of village life,
it is the opportunities available within the wider political forum of
the village that largely define the purpose of *sanggah* unity. Networks
of house-based origin groups also have a major disadvantage in the
exclusiveness of their genealogical focus. Extended kinship networks
cannot encompass the diversity of personal ancestral origins in a
typical Bali Aga village, let alone a domain.

Transitions: The Interface
between *Sanggah, Desa,* and *Banua*
as the Site of a Historical Process

There is further evidence suggesting that the interface between
sanggah, desa adat, and *banua* is more like a gateway than a solid
stone wall. The following two case studies are of social associations
that defy any simple classification. The tiny hamlet of Tangguan and
the very large village of Tenaon may perhaps be described as the extremes of what a village can be. The former consists of the house compounds of an extended *sanggah* group on their way to becoming a
desa, whereas the latter is large and complex enough to be classed a
banua.

Tangguan: The Sanggah *and the Birth of a* Desa

Tangguan is a distinct settlement on the territory of Desa Blantih, a tiny conglomerate of a few compounds occupied by members of a single extended kin group. This minute settlement has been incorporated within Desa Adat Blantih-Selulung for as long as anyone can remember, and its inhabitants participate as members of the *ulu apad* of Selulung. But Tangguan is on the way to becoming a separate village. Its people have constructed (or remember) a separate origin narrative reflecting their past and present ambitions.

> In the distant past the people of Tangguan were more numerous and prosperous than they are today. When their number was two hundred households, they decided to build a village assembly hall (*bale lantang*) as part of a proposed Pura Bale Agung [an emblem of separate *desa* status]. They felled a large tree to obtain the timber. This proved to be fatal, because their priest-leader had forgotten to propitiate the spirit of the tree. The giant tree fell on top of and killed most of the two hundred residents [literally squashing their hopes of becoming a separate *desa adat*!]. Only a few survived the disaster, and their number has remained small until recently.

Present-day Tangguan represents the prototype of a village in its infancy. Most interesting in the present context is the spatiotemporal logic of Tangguan's settlement pattern (as in Figure 8). The same pattern can be identified in larger villages such as Blantih and Sukawana. However, the original layout of many older villages has been obscured, in part by an increasing shortage of residential space and also by irregular residential arrangements following intermarriages between different compounds or *sanggah*.

Each compound in Tangguan consists of a fenced area with one or two rows (*leret*) of adjacent houses (*umah*) oriented along a *kaja-kelod* axis in an order of precedence as described earlier. At the *kaja* end of the row(s) is the *sanggah kemulan* (shrine of origin). It is also the *kaja* end of each individual house that is considered sacred and contains a house shrine (*pekaja*). Despite recent changes to traditional architecture and settlement patterns in the mountains of Bali, part of this basic arrangement remains intact in many villages. The most senior male member of a *sanggah* ought to dwell in the house at the *kaja* end of the *leret* in his compound. If for reasons of convenience he does not dwell there already, he must shift to the most mountainward house when he becomes a village priest-leader.

The settlement pattern depicted in Figure 8 is founded on a spatiotemporal idiom of precedence. The positioning of houses in order of seniority, in one or two "vertical" rows, creates a pattern almost identical to the double (or sometimes single) row seating order of an *ulu apad*. Given that each of the men seated in the ranked rows of a Bali Aga village assembly represents the house or household of a married couple, it becomes evident that the *ulu apad* emulates and re-creates the spatial organization of residential space among kin residing in a shared compound on the level of a more complex localized community. Historically, this re-creation may have become necessary in cases where the spatial arrangement of houses no longer sufficed as an index of social relations. Two possible causes are that the residential pattern lost its function as a symbolic expression of the social order as it became obliterated by the forces of residential convenience and necessity, or that growing settlements came to include the compounds of affines and immigrants with different ancestral origins.

Even the terminology for describing the members of a house compound and an *ulu apad* are similar. The members of a *sanggah* temple are referred to as "*rama ngarep*" (*ngarep*, "directly confronted, primary; i.e., in the first line of duty"), while the participants of an *ulu apad* are referred to as "*keraman desa*" (from *ke-rama-an*). In some villages the members of the core village are even referred to as "*keraman desa ngarep*." In the highlands the word "*rama*" is used as a respectful term of reference for all relatives.[22] The same term in Old Javanese and High Balinese means "father," indicating the male head of a household.

Tenaon: *A* Desa Adat *and the Birth of a* Banua

Similar to the case of Buungan described in Chapter 6, Desa Adat Tenaon (in western Buleleng) is a single village and at the same time a regional institution. This *desa adat* is composed of eight separate communities (*banjar*) located within the watershed and irrigation network of Tukad Buwus. Each of the *banjar* is by itself a virtual *desa adat* with its own leadership and traditional charter (*awig-awig*). However, none of the eight *banjar* have built a Pura Bale Agung, a situation that they explain by reference to their affiliation to a regional temple known as Pura Bukit Bale Agung. This "Pura Bale Agung" is shared among the eight communities. The eight *banjar* all hold their community gatherings (*sangkepan*) in this temple separately on a rotational basis.

The eight subdivisions of Desa Adat Tenaon do not simply represent an equal number of distinct settlements or *banjar*. Because these settlements vary in population size, they are also divided into eight *tempekan* as follows: Banjar Tenaon (one *tempekan*), Banjar Alas Anker (two), Banjar Poh (two), Banjar Bengong (one), Banjar Pendem and Banjar Benkel (one), Banjar Juruk Manis, and Banjar Pumahan (one). Informants explained that the purpose of this secondary eightfold division was to prevent any one *banjar* from becoming dominant by virtue of its larger population.

On the fourth full moon the entire congregation holds an annual joint ritual at Pura Bukit Bale Agung under the leadership of four *kubayan*, who are said to represent the unity of communities in an "eight (2 × 4) around a center" pattern (compare this to the eight villages around Pura Tebenan, the four *gebog satak* of Pura Pucak Penulisan, and the *panca pradesa* of the Margatengah group).

The sense of common purpose among the eight communities is strengthened by their participation in a single regional irrigation system. *Subak* organizations from these and some other villages participate in the great festival on *purnama kapat* as well as in another held on *purnama kasa*, and pay a special contribution called "*puwini*" (raw rice and *kepeng*). Furthermore, the nearby villages of Pengalatan and Jinengdalem attend as visiting *desa adat*, bringing *atos desa* for the deities of Pura Bukit Bale Agung. Unlike the eight core villages, they do not pay *peturunan*.

In sum, Pura Bukit Bale Agung is well on the way to becoming a temple of great regional significance, and different grades of participation in its domain are already structured in terms of different contributions as in a regular *banua*. Yet its very name suggests that this sacred origin site still maintains some characteristics of a village temple. If each member community were to establish its own Pura Bale Agung and to hold its village assemblies locally, the professed status of this temple would change. It is unlikely that a process of increasing local autonomy would destroy the larger unity of the temple's regional congregation. The network around Pura Bukit Bale Agung clearly has the potential for becoming a *banua,* considering its relevance as a symbol of shared identity and its importance as a ritual system enmeshed with cycles of agricultural production.[23]

These two cases of *sanggah-desa* and *desa-banua* hybrids illustrate the limitations of fixed categories in the discussion of different levels of social organization, even if the categories are local ones. Not all of the characteristics of the social phenomena classed within a particular category are shared or even typical, let alone necessary. The global distinctions implicit in the use of such categories may be quite realistic and useful for some cases, but they become inappropriate for other, transitional cases.

One possible explanation for this fluidity, following a Durkheimian or Weberian model, would be to assume a hypothetical developmental process whereby ideas were taken from simpler and older forms of social organization and applied to the construction of more complex and recent institutions. Some contemporary anthropologists would probably still support a moderate version of this argument, given that human societies do appear to have developed in the direction of increasing organizational complexity. Others would rightly argue that larger and more impersonal spheres of social life are not necessarily governed by principles more complex than those operating in spheres of smaller scale but featuring more intimate or dense interactions. A historical argument may be rather compelling in this case, particularly in the light of the evidence provided by transitional cases. However, it is also a sobering thought that—no matter in what order they were invented—regional, local, and kinship-oriented institutions have probably coexisted in highland Bali for a millennium. Moreover, the direction of this hypothetical process of historical change could be reversed. A *banua* can become a mere *desa* if its origin village loses all its external support, just as a *desa* may split into smaller units (though they may still be called *desa*) following a serious dispute among *sanggah*-based factions.

The Status Economies of Highland Balinese Society

The preceding discussion of Bali Aga society as a whole reveals some striking conceptual and organizational similarities across different contexts of association. The *banua, desa,* and *sanggah,* as fields of intersubjective knowledge and action, are all based on the same pivotal concepts of origin and precedence, concerned with the distribution of status and socially maintained through narrative and ritual performances. The social significance of each of these fields is defined and constrained by the others, and their relevance boundaries overlap. Participation in a *banua* requires association in villages, and village councils demand of their members that they must first be householders. Transitional cases hint at the possibility of a historical transformation of *sanggah* into *desa* and of *desa* into *banua*. In consideration of these important conceptual continuities and practical connections across different aspects of Bali Aga thought and experience, this society may be described as a multilayered status economy with a common sociocultural foundation. The following is an attempt to capture what constitutes this common ground.

The social status of Bali Aga persons and groups is defined in terms of precedence, that is, by relative temporal proximity to a shared and sacred origin point.[24] This time-oriented idiom has a tremendous impact on the status economies of highland Bali in that it is process-oriented and irreconcilable with the notion of a hierarchical social structure.

The division of a village community into *wedan* and *pendonan*, for example, may be described as a form of social stratification that entails the construction of immigrant newcomers as persons of lesser status than village founders and their exclusion from the ceremonial order of the *desa ulu apad*. This distinction, however, is not always made and not necessarily permanent, and exclusion is always partial and costly. The *ulu apad* of a village (including newcomers no longer regarded as such) itself is also not a permanent body, because its members are likewise ranked on the basis of the temporal sequence in which their households were founded, just as the villages established by emigrants from an origin village (and the villages of socially integrated immigrants) are ranked in the temporal order of their foundation. A similar logic of precedence in the *sanggah* context stipulates that genealogical predecessors by descent or marriage have moral and ritual authority over their children or children-in-law, whereby changes in personal status occur naturally as older people pass away and their successors acquire successors of their own. The underlying notion of status entails an emphasis on people's time-space position in relation to a historical sequence of predecessors and successors and their movements through an evolving material and representational landscape. In this sense, Bali Aga status economies are not hierarchical, though they may encourage differentiation and shifting patterns of stratification.

Notions of time, place, and person become intricately intertwined in a Bali Aga cosmology that depicts life as a path of origin. From the perspective of local representational models of society, the path of origin may seem to be permanently inscribed on space, but it is laid down by a continuous process of plantlike growth and differentiating expansion (a discourse of common ancestry and emigration) or additive fusion (newcomers of multiple ancestry are integrated through a discourse of common ancestral land or by marriage). From a more critical and practical perspective, the path of origin is also a history of human agency and competition, marked by many organizational changes, transformations, and sometimes permanent fission. Even though participants discount the significance of competition and the voluntary dimension of their social cooperation, local discourses about society do anticipate change in the present and can accommodate changing perceptions of the past.

The negotiable character of a past that must be reconstructed from the present is necessarily deemphasized in theory in order to legitimize the outcomes of status negotiations in the present. The effect strategic interests in the present have on representations of social history and contemporary society is recognized, however, when ideas about the past do suddenly change and, more generally, in stressing the need to limit this effect. The people of highland Bali concede that their ideas of origin can be mistaken (*salah kawitan*) and that some people may question their "religious obligations." Hence they emphasize a need to counteract human "forgetfulness" through deliberate and frequent acts of ritual commemoration. Life, to them, is never free of struggles over the representation and regulation of difference. At the same time, difference also inspires cooperation insofar as difference and unity (*rua bineda*) are recognized by the Bali Aga as the joint preconditions for knowledge and for life itself.

The most pertinent example of how time is employed in representations of society and brought to bear upon social practices and spaces are the markers or way stations on the path of origin: the private, local, and regional temples that are so central to Bali Aga ritual performances and narratives.

Ritual performances in highland Bali involve elaborate exchanges of offerings and other markers of approval and are in this sense economies. Ritual has an economic character, because it is about symbolic resource accumulation, as is clearly evident in the asymmetrical nature of ritual exchange. While the offerings exchanged are material and often consumable objects, and are ultimately exchanged between and consumed by human beings, Bali Aga ritual is rarely an exchange venture profitable in monetary terms to its organizers. Ritual is designed to exchange symbolic information about relationships between people, and between people and the (nonhuman) world, relationships that constitute a primary value in their own right by satisfying a fundamental human interest in cooperation and survival. Ritual association may entail a possibility for competitive resource acquisition, but the currency in this exchange is social approval, and its resource context is a symbolic economy concerned with status. Indeed, it can be argued that Bali Aga society, at least at a level of regional interaction, is held together almost entirely by its symbolic economy.

This rather strong assertion requires some qualification as well as an explanation. How, where, and to what extent is the symbolic economy of Bali Aga society connected or disconnected from its political and economic economy? And if it is only weakly connected, as far as *banua* are concerned, why does Bali Aga society display this exceptionally strong focus on status acquisition and a symbolic economy at the regional level?

Ritual domains (*banua*) are sites of ritual association that regulate a regional flow of social approval and hence establish a regional distribution of symbolic capital. They are concerned with knowledge and mutual representation in an intersubjective game in which the stake is social status. It is evident that *banua* are not directly concerned with the control of land and other material resources. Nor are they political organizations that would exert coercive control over the local political affairs of their constituency or produce the knowledge to legitimize the exercise of such power. This is not to deny that Bali Aga society has an economic and political economy, as it certainly does, or that economic and political economies lack an important symbolic dimension. I am arguing only that politics and economics do not operate very strongly in this society at a regional level and that regional ritual organization has very limited significance as a supporting knowledge structure in the more local settings where they do operate.

Access to land, the primary economic resource in this agrarian society, is regulated by the *desa adat* (communal land) or *sanggah* (inheritable land) rather than the *banua*, though the situation may have been different in the past and may change in the future.[25] At a level of material resource exchange, the regional sphere of the *banua* is also of little relevance. The agricultural products available for trading are similar ones in most Bali Aga village economies, and hence local products are exchanged predominantly with people and for commodities from outside the highlands rather than within the same region.

The control of coercive force, as a political resource, is likewise vested not in the *banua* but in the *desa* and *sanggah*, where individual nonconformance with the mostly informal norms of the group can still precipitate severe social, economic, or physical punishment. The more general monopoly for legislation and the execution of force beyond a local and informal context lie not in the hands of the *banua* but again outside the highlands, in the hands of the Indonesian government and its Balinese representatives.

Unlike the *banua*, the *desa* and *sanggah* are indeed concerned with the local control of material as well as symbolic resources and are thus fields of interaction on which people's competing economic and political interest can be played out. If it is generally possible for people of high status to use their symbolic capital in order to increase their wealth and power (given that these material forms of capital do have a symbolic component as well), it is appropriate to examine to what degree such a transfer occurs in Bali Aga society at this local level.

Knowledge systems based on a cultural idiom of precedence negotiate an underlying paradox of status, the paradox of having to cooperative in a process of mutual representation in order to be able to compete (assuming there are no coercive opportunities due to disparities in the material economies of the society concerned). Even though the villages and origin houses of the Bali Aga are concerned with a local political economics and some moderate disparities are observable therein, the demands of their highly developed symbolic economies create a powerful preventative for coercion to occur. To begin with, the temporary nature of status in Bali Aga society has a general effect on local politics and economics, insofar as the latter also contain a symbolic component. The status of a person within the precedence system of the *ulu apad*, for example, is relative and temporary, and it is difficult to translate a temporary status advantage into permanent material advantages.[26] But what of founder-newcomer relations, a status stratification that could provide a more durable foundation for economic inequality? Informants frequently explained that many newcomers were eventually admitted to the status of *ulu apad* membership in their villages and given access to the associated economic privilege of receiving village land because of a need to share more broadly across the local community the often enormous economic burden of the village's ritual performance obligations. Similarly, while divisions within a *sanggah* may be precipitated by a quest for political or economic independence, a division again entails an additional ritual burden, as houses in a branch houseyard must bear the economic cost of building and maintaining a new *sanggah gede*. There is also a political cost, because the group may lose its symbolic unity and hence some of its power as a cohesive faction within the *desa*.

From another perspective, social status is of such intrinsic importance to the people of highland Bali that it provides them with an alternative outlet for their competitive interests. The importance of this avenue for economics is evident in a tendency, particularly at the level of the *sanggah*, to dispose of accumulated wealth by staging a ritual performance more elaborate or more public than what is prescribed for a particular occasion.[27]

While the people of highland Bali clearly have economic and political interests, and while these interests cannot be separated from their positioning within local symbolic economies, theirs is a society where gross disparities in wealth and power are the exception rather than the rule, even at a local level. The generative schema of representational and practical knowledge that informs the distribution of symbolic capital within Bali Aga society, in its focus on time and change, its openness to contestation, and its many built-in checks and balances, is designed not only to allocate symbolic resources differentially but to reallocate them continuously. Status remains negotiable in a society where symbolic capital is generated on the basis of relatively free association and voluntary cooperation. Representational knowledge, under these conditions, is unlikely to become a docile and reliable servant of power. Furthermore, a state of relative equality in material terms within a given society, often considered accidental, should be recognized as an active and significant cultural achievement, an achievement that is in part the outcome of a particular logic and the practice of mutual representation within that society.[28]

The *banua* does exert a limited influence as a status economy on the smaller status economies of the *desa* and *sanggah*, and these local status economies do have a limited impact on local politics and economics. It is therefore necessary to concede that the *banua* too may carry residual traces of political and economic relevance within Bali Aga society. Apart from this qualification, an explanation is still required to account for the predominance of a symbolic economy at the regional level of the domain, precisely the organizational level where one would expect a localized micropolitics to end and "proper politics" (in the classical sense) to begin. While it is important to remember that the internal checks and balances of a precedence order are still relevant at this regional level, as a means of preventing the rise of a more rigid and oppressive hierarchical status structure (in the Dumontian sense), precedence in itself does not explain the apparent lack of a regional political economy in the highlands.

It could be argued that the Bali Aga are to some degree fortunate in being able to interact and compete with one another for ritual status at a regional level in a spirit of relatively free association and argumentation, constrained only by the desirability and intrinsic value of social cooperation. Fortunate, that is, in the limited sense that they have been allocated a specific and rather unusual position within the broader context of Balinese society and its origin history.

A more explicitly political form of association or even a pattern of domination might well have developed in Bali Aga society at a regional level if it had not been that any such larger political formations would have attracted violent opposition from lowland Balinese kings. These kings maintained at least a nominal claim to political power over the highlands, though they exerted only a moderate degree of tangible political control. In short, the power of these kings (or nowadays the Indonesian government) may have been sufficiently distant to allow for a degree of political autonomy and a proportional degree of internal political competition at the local level of the *desa*, and yet close enough to ensure a highly cooperative and rather apolitical form of organization at the regional level of the *banua*.

The people of highland Bali and their notion of precedence illustrate, however, that history is always more than just a string of accidents. It may be true that the possibilities for using regional symbolic capital for political purposes in Bali's highlands were restricted by economic and political conditions on the island as a whole. Nevertheless, the Bali Aga themselves have also helped to shape these conditions. In Part 2, I shall argue that the power of southern Balinese kings was held at bay not just by accident or by a lack of interest in the highlands on their behalf, but as the result of the long and persistent struggle of the highland people to retain their ritual and political independence in which the *banua* played a crucial role.

The Bali Aga have been able to maintain a regional status economy of their own and, on the basis of this unity, a specific position of ritual status and authority in relation to Balinese society as a whole. In this wider societal context, the ritual authority of the indigenous people of the mountains has come to serve as a conceptual counterpart to the political power vested in Bali's kings, who are said to be the descendants of relatively recent immigrants and conquerors from across the sea. At the same time, one need only to recall the prominence of warrior dances in Bali Aga ritual to gain a sense of how this representational schema may also be the sediment of a mutual political engagement. Even though it signals a withdrawal from competition for power, the current apoliticism of the Bali Aga is still a political strategy. At the very least, their participation within a Balinese political economy beyond the highlands may have provided an additional and powerful incentive for the Bali Aga to unite through joint participation within regional ritual domains.

The analytical focus in Part 2 on the wider context of a Balinese representational landscape develops my initial argument about the intersubjective nature of representation in general. I shall argue that the imperative for cooperation that is intrinsic to the construction of a shared knowledge, though it may be more obvious within the fluid status economies of Bali Aga society (especially at a regional level), is also noticeable and important where mutual symbolic representations are formed among larger groups of people and on a more uneven political and economic playing field. While the Bali Aga have competed for symbolic resources with a southern Balinese elite from a position of economic and political disadvantage, the evidence also suggests that there has been a considerable degree of representational cooperation among the two parties. To the degree that it has been based on a conceptual notion of interdependence and been socially coproduced in practice, the resulting knowledge system has simultaneously endorsed and constrained the power of Balinese kings and modern power holders in relation to the Bali Aga.

Part II

In the Shadow
of Paradise

The Bali Aga and the Problem
of Representation

Chapter 8

REPRESENTATION BEYOND THE HIGHLANDS
Preliminary Reflections

Processes of mutual representation within the regional status economy of Bali Aga society are based on voluntary association, and status differentiating relationships are perpetually negotiated in the terms of an inherently process-oriented idiom of fluid temporal distinctions in an order of precedence. Moving beyond the highlands, to the larger world in which the Bali Aga engage in a process of mutual representation with more powerful others, this chapter and the following ones explore their place within Balinese society and discourses, and in the Western anthropological literature about this island. This exploration leads back, inevitably, to problems of representation in anthropology and in the world at large.

The current crisis of representation relates to the institutional and historical context and the general mood in which contemporary ethnographic texts are composed. In attempting to capture this general mood my purpose is to describe, in a self-consciously rhetorical tenor, the intellectual and political climate in which this and other contemporary ethnographic texts have been written. I will illustrate in the process how the representational systems of Bali Aga society are relevant to our own representational practice, both as researchers and as people.

Cultural anthropologists have become insecure about their mission as intellectuals and as members of a changing academic discipline. Serious epistemological, ethical, and political objections have been raised that cast doubt on whether ethnographic texts can be trusted to provide accurate and unbiased representations of other cultural worlds. The fundamental challenge has been the "subjectivity" of specific representors and the associated bias of their representations.

Particular aspects of the epistemological challenge of subjectivity could be shrugged off to some degree. Innocent mistakes in the representation of foreign cultural worlds could be classed as simple errors, and error as a necessary part in the trial and error process of scientific discovery. The idea that all past, present, and future ethnographic representations may be doomed to suffer the distorting effects of their authors' subjectivity to the same degree, however, could not be reconciled with a positivist research paradigm. For many scholars over the last two decades, the idea of subjective bias as a universal aspect of the human condition has seemed to call instead for an attitude of epistemological humility, of lamenting rather than attempting to overcome the limitations of anthropology as a scientific mode of human understanding.

The epistemological problem of subjectivity aside, an ethical component has rocked the very foundations of cross-cultural research. A moral concern about the scientific representation of other cultures arose from the realization that representors are not just prone to occasional or even systematic errors of perception and interpretation but may be swayed by an underlying self-serving purpose. Representations created in the spirit of such a self-serving purpose could be expected to conflict with the interests of the represented and, at times, to have a negative sociopolitical effect on their lives. The problem is most acute where the self-serving purpose in representations of other cultures reflects not only the diverse personal interests of particular representors, but their shared interests as a group of agents similarly positioned within a wider political arena. This broader issue of a representational conspiracy has been raised especially in relation to the historical period in which many academic disciplines concerned with the study of non-Western cultures, languages, histories, and societies originated, the age of Western colonial expansion (e.g., Said 1978). Though it may have been dedicated to a humanist project of promoting mutual understanding across cultural divides, anthropology could not escape the suspicion of complicity with a more sinister project of Western imperialism.

The effect of this epistemological and moral challenge has been profound and prolonged, with no adequate solution in sight. Practicing anthropologists, however, have had to make practical and immediate choices about how to proceed under a condition of uncertainty.

Many anthropologists practicing ethnography abroad in the current climate tend to argue, in defense of their activities, that this crisis has provided a positive impetus for paradigm shifts and new discoveries, as scientific crises generally tend to do (Kuhn 1970). Perhaps a dwindling minority of Neo-Popperians have interpreted the positive potential in the crisis of representation from a positivist position. Most others have simply urged that uncertainty be met with an openness to new and multiple forms of knowledge, rather than with a desperate search for a new certainty.

An example of this approach in the United States is *Anthropology as Cultural Critique* by George Marcus and Michael Fischer (1986).[1] The title of this work, raising the question of anthropology's moral obligation, points to what was to become a moot point. If some finite form of knowledge about other cultures could be derived from a process of epistemological and methodological experimentation, and if such knowledge was no longer to serve as a symbolic support structure for coercive power, as it presumably had, then what precisely would be the moral foundation for such a critical anthropology?

One option was to envisage a morally acceptable role for Western intellectuals as culture critics or even as political activists. To fulfill this role, anthropologists would retain their authority and lend it to those victimized and disempowered by the knowledge structures arising from biased popular representations. Such a proposal, however, could be denounced as a disguised regression to an untenable position of paternalistic authoritarianism. Written from a position of power by privileged Western subjects, as some have objected, all scientific representations of non-Western cultures would be doomed to repeat history and destined to become instrumentalized in the service of new and ever more insidious patterns of cross-cultural domination. The only viable option seemed to be to deconstruct unfair popular representational knowledge structures without offering an alternative. Representational knowledge would thus be exposed as a tool and disguise of political interests but without attempting to redeem such knowledge for the service of humanity.

Unfortunately, writing without raising validity claims proved to be problematic in itself. In view of the near impossibility of saying anything at all about people of other cultures without constructing a further representation in the process, Western scholars—unwilling to stop writing altogether—were thus called on to undermine their own narrative authority as authors by paying careful attention to their style of writing. In keeping with a nonauthoritarian, self-reflexive, or postmodern style, the new-age ethnographer would simply channel or evoke the voices of cultural others rather than represent them from an external and politically suspicious position (Tyler 1986).

In its new conservatism, this approach did not resolve the central moral issue of representation. Authority overtly denied could after all resurface as an authority concealed, with the postmodern author like an invisible conductor hidden among an orchestra composed of the appropriated voices of others. In response to this intractable problem, those who did not entirely abandon the idea of studying other cultures abroad moved toward a more practical and less immediately dubious solution. Their solution was based on a clever choice of subject matter under the banner of a new "postcolonial anthropology."

If complicity in the cultural mechanics of Western imperialism had tainted Western scholarship in the past, the remedy was to direct the critical project of anthropology inward to become exclusively a self-critique of Western power. In this context, and this alone, representations could still be put forward with a morally legitimate flair of scientific authority. Even a constructive (rather than purely deconstructive) critique was made acceptable and the danger of an authoritarian regression banished by avoiding a boundary-crossing from a strong self to a supposedly weaker other. The academic Western self in its narratives was entitled to evaluate and criticize the power-sustaining narratives of an imperialist Western self, promising scholars a new image as heroes in a quest for the redemption of Western civilization.

My own response to the underlying epistemological challenge of subjectivity is captured in part by Renato Rosaldo: "All interpretations are provisional; they are made by positioned subjects who are prepared to know certain things and not others. Even when knowledgeable, sensitive, fluent in the language, and able to move easily in an alien cultural world, good ethnographers still have their limits, and their analyses always are incomplete" (1989:8). This ethnography, like any other text of its genre, provides no more than a limited and positioned account of another culture, an incomplete portrayal of a Bali Aga world as experienced from the unique position of a particular subject. But scaling down the scope of anthropology's validity pretensions is a response with limited utility unless the reasons for particular failures are addressed. As Rosaldo implies, the legitimacy of anthropology as a mode of scientific inquiry rests on the assumption that some representations of foreign cultures are indeed more complete and less biased than others.

A project of developing a better method of ethnography does not require an objectivist view of "legitimate knowledge," a knowledge that corresponds to some monolithic and unchanging truth. Rather, the crux of the epistemological challenge is to ground anthropological knowledge in a fuller understanding of the structure of subjectivity or, rather, "intersubjectivity," through critical reflection on human interests and the social aspect of human psychology. This approach assumes that the content of subjective knowledge cannot be divorced from the means of its production, that is, from the facticity of thinking, feeling, and embodied human subjects.

While current debates on the relationship between subjectivity and the anthropological project of cross-cultural representation seem to be departing from a specific set of assumptions about the human psyche as well, progress has been slow. Some of the covert assumptions about the "knowing subject" that have informed contemporary attitudes in anthropology can be summarized as follows: Representations of cultural others are knowledge structures designed to serve the strategic interests of those who construct them, and the specific strategic interests of individual or groups of representors are necessarily and intrinsically at odds with those of the people who are represented. In short, representors strive to enhance their own power, wealth, and status at the expense of those whom they represent. Human nature is intrinsically sinister, propelling us to dominate others as best we can, and knowledge is but a servant of power on the battleground of society. In popular Marxist terms, for example, representations feature as the building blocks of an ideological superstructure usually designed to conceal, legitimize, or support material conditions of economic and political inequity. Similarly, a cursory reading of Nietzsche would suggest that the driving force of human civilization is nothing but a burning will to power. And in the terminology of a popularized Freudian theory, individuals and interpersonal relations are to be judged with similar skepticism. Human nature entails the concealment of powerful, selfish drives and intentions from others and even from oneself.

This may seem like a somewhat superficial analysis in the light of what I have written about Bali Aga society, and it is. What I am criticizing is not a theory but a mood, a lingering distaste for representation and for difference itself, which stands out in stark contrast against a background of Bali Aga theories of society in which difference is celebrated.

Some of the prevailing negative assumptions about human nature are not entirely misconceived, as my own field research experience revealed and as my critical position on cultural knowledge reflects. But I did not leave the highlands of Bali with a grim impression of people as ruthless Machiavellian subjects. Indeed, most theories of radical skepticism already evoke the shadow of their own nemesis. If a concern with power and self-interest were paramount to human nature, why would there be such an intense need to employ knowledge to legitimize power and conceal strategic interests?

The Bali Aga have taught me that the relationship between knowledge and power is complex and that the one cannot be reduced to the other. The intrinsic complexity lies in the fact that people have a communicative as well as a strategic interest in representing themselves and others. Among members of a species whose success has rested on a capacity for symbolic communication and social cooperation, individual self-interest is routinely redefined in the context of belonging to a larger group, and the collective self-interests of groups are redefined in the context of their involvement in even wider spheres of social cooperation. This dynamic is not reducible to the effects of a more enlightened form of self-interest. Knowledge may serve to disempower others, but it first arises from a cooperative sphere of communication and is thus a prerequisite for competition. Representational knowledge is also more than just a roundabout way to compete. It creates the opportunity for a systematic cooperation with others, which is an important end in itself.

Highland Bali may be a very particular region of an already very particular island, but it is by no means an insular world. The specificity of Bali Aga experiences with representation as a practical problem has been an important influence in the course of this specific research. Patterns of distorted intercultural or interethnic representation, however, are an endemic and global problem. Representation has become a more important practical and politicized issue in an age of globalization than it has ever been before, even in the age of Western colonial expansion.

The world in which anthropologists now conduct their field research is characterized by increasing economic interaction, mobility, and cultural hybridization among societies. Societies unaware of each other's existence or bound together in an earlier colonial system of domination until recently are now encountering one another as participants in a dynamic world of global communication and economic interdependence. Culture can no longer be thought of as something occurring in single, bounded, and localized systems. Pertinent examples are the birth of immigrant diaspora cultures in Western metropolitan centers and the establishment of permanent miniature tourist worlds in the east. Many anthropologists recognize these dramatic changes and have responded by abandoning the notion that other people's worlds can be defined in terms of fixed cultural properties or spaces (Appadurai 1988; Clifford 1988; Malkki 1995).[2]

However, the idea of representing, localizing, and thus separating oneself from others on cultural grounds has by no means become a thing of the past at a popular and political level. To the contrary, the strategic stereotyping of other people on account of their culture, ethnicity, or religion is a characteristic feature of political struggles in this postmodern age of globalization (Sahlins 1999).[3] Ironically, the recent political history of a world characterized by growing interdependence across cultures shows no indication of a corresponding decline in the importance or prevalence of cross-cultural misrepresentation. The more tenuous economic, social, and conceptual boundaries between different cultures or ethnic groups have become, the more vehemently they seem to be defended as lines of political control, as is illustrated by a proliferation of interethnic violence in recent years.

Even "remote" and "marginalized" peoples like the Bali Aga have been drawn into the cultural politics of this emerging global sphere of interaction or have entered into it deliberately in the hope of turning the tide of new external influences to their own advantage. By challenging the way they are characterized by others, they and other marginalized groups are seeking to hold their position or reposition themselves among old and new foes or allies within changing power and communication structures. These changed practical conditions of research have affected contemporary ethnographers. No longer just a science of the local, anthropology has recognized a need to examine intersections between global, national, regional, and local spheres of interaction and meaning.

Bali Aga lives, for example, have become transparent to the administrative gaze of the Indonesian nation-state and exposed to the political ambitions of its Balinese representatives, and exposure to a global economy has drawn them into new alliances and conflicts across established cultural fences. A gradual softening of interactive boundaries has reduced some of the obstacles the Bali Aga have faced on account of their negative cultural image, but in other contexts they may also regard it as a threat to their "identity," conceived positively as a symbolic resource. In short, the world of the Bali Aga—both as an experienced reality and as an, in itself, already regional representational map—is shaped by practical encounters and representational struggles in larger and increasingly global contexts.

In the course of writing a representational account of highland Balinese society, the practical consequences of their marginalized status at first seemed to call for an act of deliberate intervention on their behalf. Given that their practical problem with representation is not so much unique as it is exemplary of similar problems in the world at large, it also seemed to suggest a more general need and moral imperative for an anthropology of engagement.

Adopting this approach led to some unexpected results. It seemed safe enough at first to assume that external representations of the Bali Aga, on account of their biases, needed to be critically analyzed, deconstructed, and then juxtaposed—if at all possible—with their own counterrepresentations of themselves and others. The first surprise in taking this road was that the marginality of the Bali Aga does not appear to be a product of colonialism in any simple way or simply a product of the power and discourse of a modern Indonesian nation-state. Their condition of political marginality far preceded the event of colonization and the advent of modernity and, even now, seems to be anchored squarely in a Balinese politics of identity. Power in Bali had been drawn from external sources from the fourteenth century at least, when Bali was first incorporated into the empire of Majapait—with the notable exception of the Bali Aga. A permutating external power, again and again, had been successfully appropriated by some Balinese to be wielded against others.

This realization forced me to depart from the established method of postcolonial studies, in which critical focus tends to rest on colonial systems of knowledge and domination and their enduring repercussions for postcolonial societies. Insofar as there was a need to be critical also of Balinese systems of knowledge and domination, the epistemological trap door of representation began to loom even larger than it already had, in the form of the generic revisionist paradox. Though a critique of Balinese knowledge systems could be morally justified on account of their negative outcomes for some sectors of Balinese society, even a purely deconstructivist project could be accused of evoking another truth—and of doing so in the absence of any sound epistemological foundation. The analysis of a Balinese politics of identity, however, was to reveal further unanticipated complexities that could no longer be reconciled with a naive moral concern for the oppressed. Instead, it offered a way of eliminating the trap door of epistemological uncertainty—by knocking out the entire floor of subjectivity.

Closer observation of pan-Balinese identity constructs revealed that the highland people are by no means passive victims of external representations. For many centuries, they have responded effectively to the force of external discourses by generating reciprocal representations of their other and alternative representations of themselves, in accordance with their own political interests. To characterize the Bali Aga simply as passive objects of external representations would have meant to ignore their remarkable success as agents of representation and to underestimate their contribution to Balinese society. It would be necessary instead to pay close attention to their celebration of "marginality" as a source of symbolic capital in its own right.

Thus, the current project of exploring broader issues of representation is intricately linked to the preceding ethnographic account of ritual domains and alliances among Bali Aga communities. It was essential to gain an understanding of these regional institutions insofar as they have provided the organizational platform for a remarkable Bali Aga success story. Previous ethnographic research has underestimated the organizational complexity and regional unity of Bali Aga society and hence has been hard-pressed to account for its cultural survival through centuries of opposition.

But mutual representations between Bali Aga and southern Balinese were not only a contested field of knowledge; they were also partially commensurable with their respective narratives about themselves. Both parties were involved in coproducing an image of Balinese society as a unified whole in which the other is a necessary part. Their narratives are differently positioned, but they also overlap in content and in their idiom. This element of coproduction was the second suggestion that a purely competitive model of human relations in the spirit of a liberal political and economic theory—the model of human nature whose special focus on individualism and subjectivity forms the very foundation of the representation debate —would not suffice to explain the phenomenon at hand.

One further observation and subsequent insight was to shape the entire ethnographic project and the theoretical approach of this text. As the preceding chapters have illustrated, Bali Aga society is anything other than a homogeneous whole, though first impression and external portrayals sometimes may have encouraged such a perception. The Bali Aga instead are engaged in a local politics of representation of their own. Though intermeshed with pan-Balinese, national, or global contexts, internal struggles among different Bali Aga communities in the context of regional ritual association involve processes of mutual identity construction and contestation on a miniature scale. The characteristics of these representational practices within Bali Aga society could not be reconciled with a totally cynical view of human nature or explained with a purely deception-oriented theory of knowledge.

I began this book by analyzing the regional system of representation embodied in the ritual domains (*banua*) of highland Bali. *Banua* have been contemplated as status economies wherein the social distribution of symbolic resources is negotiated by reference to a temporal logic of precedence. I also suggested that theories concerned with hierarchy, precedence, or other forms of status distribution among persons or groups ultimately address the same issues on a different scale as theories of interethnic or cross-cultural representation and that the former may shed new light on the unresolved epistemological issues raised by the latter.

The impression gained from an ethnographic investigation of the specific knowledge and status system of Bali Aga society is that the strategic pursuit of status or other forms of symbolic capital relies on communicative or intersubjective processes of representation and that the tension between strategic interests and a communicative imperative for cooperation defines a fundamental paradox of human interaction. As in every other culture, the people of the highlands have had to establish a set of communicative and interactive conventions as a prerequisite for social cooperation. Conversely, while communication is essentially cooperative, specific instances of communicative interaction necessarily involve unequal exchanges of information and thus provide a constant opportunity for asymmetric exchanges of approval. I have explored how this inherent paradox of status (and of representation in general)—the paradox of having to cooperate in order to compete for social approval—is manifested in Bali Aga society and how this society has attempted to manage the resulting tensions.

In Bali Aga society the predominant representational knowledge systems are designed specifically to accommodate the possibility of difference and thus to regulate the impact of the competitiveness that is automatically introduced into the dynamics of association by the strategic interests of different participants. The basic principle of their solution to this fundamental human conundrum is, first, to acknowledge that society and representational knowledge about society are the products of a historical and intersubjective process and, second, to create an interactive setting marked by voluntary cooperation and culturally managed (rather than unrestrained or liberal) competition among individuals or groups. In short, research on the *banua* suggests that—at least under certain favorable conditions—representation is a communicative or "intersubjective" game. I shall illustrate that the same applies even to cases where this game is played out on a field of social interaction marked by significant political and economic disparities. If it can be shown that representation is always not just a subjective but an intersubjective process, this may provide a solution for the problem of representation in social science.

An intersubjective theory of representation would hypothesize that the impact of subjectivity and positioning on representation (in the form of bias) is always limited by an imperative for communicative and social cooperation, but to significantly different degrees under different historical conditions. From this perspective, the legitimacy of knowledge is conditional on the process of its production within a particular field of cultural performance. Such an intersubjective theory of knowledge and representation does not deny the relevance of subjectivity and agency, nor does it have to resort to an objectivist or "correspondence" theory of truth.

Chapter 9

PEOPLE OF THE MOUNTAINS AND PEOPLE FROM THE SEA
A Balinese Model of Society

Moving beyond the ethnography of highland Bali, I now explore how Bali Aga people and their culture are situated in the representational landscape of Bali as a whole. Insofar as the Bali Aga have been portrayed with a negative bias by other, more powerful Balinese people, I assume that there is a moral responsibility to amplify their counterdiscourses. At the same time, Balinese identities are the product of a historical and intersubjective process in which the Bali Aga have participated with an ambivalent attitude of competition as well as cooperation. In adopting this perspective, I aim to prevent a fetishization of either power or resistance.

Balinese Models of Society:
From Identity to Representation

The Bali Aga are broadly conceived of (and see themselves) as the island's indigenous people, descendants of the first ancestors who cleared the island's forests and whose spirits still protect the land. As such they are vested with a sacred duty to appeal to Bali's founding ancestors on behalf of all its inhabitants so that the land may remain fertile and the vital rains will never fail. As one Bali Aga elder once put it: "We guard the mountain of life, the temples of Bali's origin; we are the old trunk that supports the fresh tip. If we neglect our [ritual] duty, the world shall rock and all its peoples shall tumble" (Jero Tongkog, Bali Aga elder, 1994).

Their conceptual counterparts are now the majority of the island's population. Most other Balinese regard themselves as the descendants of magically powerful Javanese ancestors from the kingdom of Majapait. These Javanese ancestors are believed to have invaded and conquered Bali in the fourteenth century. Foremost among them are the royal ancestors of Bali's still powerful aristocracy. As "stranger kings" from across the sea, they became the local representatives and embodiment of a world more powerful than Bali, a world that has always been at its doorstep. Once Bali's wider nonaristocratic population had embraced and appropriated the narratives of a new and powerful Bali Majapait as well and had claimed a Javanese ancestry as best they could, the Bali Aga remained as a necessary residual category, representatives of an "older," more "original," and, in some ways, more sacred Bali.

The conceptual, ritual, and political relationship between Bali Aga and Bali Majapait, between indigenous people of the mountains and people from across the sea, has evolved over a period of six centuries. The contemporary position of the Mountain Balinese in the fabric of Balinese identities can only be appreciated by tracing this precolonial history of struggle, negotiation, and compromise. Representations of the Bali Aga were also redefined—both in content and in their idiom—in the wake of a more recent colonial and postcolonial history. The following is thus a contemporary analysis of a postcolonial Bali Aga condition with a long precolonial history.

For the Balinese the landscape of their identities is a testimony to a history of encounters among people of different origins. In this sense, it is less a landscape of identities, or bounded cultural universes of sameness (from Latin *idem*, "the same"), than it is a landscape shaped by representation (from Latin, *prae-esse* "to be in front of or confronted by [someone else]"). That Balinese concepts of ethnicity so recognize "otherness" as a product of historical encounters or confrontations, as a product of contact rather than isolation, may relate to the specific conditions of their historical experience.

Since prehistoric times, Bali has been a site for encounters among different but often related peoples arriving from across the sea in countless waves of migration. Having begun their migrations in southern China and Taiwan some three or four thousand years ago, even the first Austronesian ancestors of the Balinese to land on the island's shores found the island inhabited already, by people whose name has been forgotten. Whenever they arrived and whoever they were, each group of immigrants had to establish a way of relating to groups who had settled before them and to others who were to arrive later. Some newcomers were perhaps content to be tolerated and left no major impression. Others, however, among them the people from Majapait, were to gain political ascendancy over those whom they encountered upon arrival. Whenever such a takeover occurred, the status of earlier settlers in the social landscape of Bali had to be redefined.

Such encounters with the foreign were not necessarily experienced in the guise of human migration. Often the scenario may have been that local groups became agents for the promotion of new and foreign items of knowledge within Balinese society, such as Indian notions of divine kingship. Some Balinese could claim for themselves the status of virtual newcomers simply on the grounds of their privileged communicative or economic access to the outside world.

In response to a long history of encounters with new peoples or knowledge, a specific cultural model of identity developed in Bali. In this model, notions of time, mobility, and change are central, as is the conceptualization of difference in the terms of a recursive dualism. Rather than being fixed for all time, the status of a group in such a precedence-based model of society is always relative to that of another (paired) group as well as being changeable, at least in practice if not always in theory. Newcomers can become the "original people" in this schema, particularly after an earlier people are forgotten, or have to relinquish their position to even more recent and powerful newcomers.

The Bali Aga were probably not the first people to have arrived on Bali, and some among them explicitly claim that they were not. They are simply the earlier people, in the sense that they were presumably the ones encountered by the conquerors and immigrants from Majapait. The position of the latter has since moved in a similar direction. As a consequence of having lost some of their power to later newcomers (notably the Dutch), the people of Majapait are by now approaching a moment of transformation. They may become the new original Balinese and are already adopting a corresponding role as protectors of tradition and carriers of ritual obligations. The public ritual role of the Bali Aga may become less prominent as a result, on the condition that they can be made to become an absorbed and forgotten people.

The strong focus on time, mobility, and change in a pan-Balinese model of society is highly significant not only for Balinese lives but as an inspiration for social science. Its inspirational value lies in the model's fundamental departure from such essentialist notions of cultural identity as have been prominent in Western maps of the world's ethnic landscapes. Cultural identity has often been assumed to be a sameness born of deliberate or accidental isolation or boundedness rather than a historical product of contact, confrontations, and mutual representations among different groups of people. This attitude has its own historical roots.

Western culture theory has often contemplated the effects of "culture contact" from the historical perspective of an expanding Western culture. Such contact was not believed to produce culture but to destroy it. As European civilization extended its horizon in an age of discovery, it presumably overpowered or contaminated all other cultures in its wake. From this perspective, the world of the Bali Aga would seem like a bounded universe of meaning and interaction, a small, unique, and fragile world on the brink of becoming open to and absorbed within an expanding or globalized Western world. Their shrinking stronghold of traditional culture would seem to owe its very existence to a fortunate state of isolation, confined, as it may appear to have been, to the refuge of a geographically remote corner in a former colonial empire, now a distant outpost in a postcolonial "global village" (MacLuhan 1969).

In rejecting this perspective, I am drawing inspiration from a seminal paper by Hau'ofa (1993). Hau'ofa argues that the boundedness, smallness, and gradual shrinkage of other cultures is a figment of the Western imagination. Referring to Pacific nations as his specific example, he suggests that exotic miniature worlds were invented to provide the logical counterpart to the image of an enormous and still growing Western universe of meaning, a cultural empire with a history of technology-driven expansion. Hau'ofa argues that the idea of small nations acquired a semblance of reality only after the once boundless Pacific had been carved up into tiny colonial territories.

This smallness of the other, according to Hau'ofa, was and still is a hoax. To its inhabitants the Pacific was not a cluster of small isolated islands but a nearly infinite world of sea and land. It was a place of many encounters to Polynesians (like the Balinese, speakers of Austronesian languages), who were able to traverse this world with remarkable skill and ease. The colonial encounter with the West did not compress this world. In fact, the incorporation of Pacific cultures within colonial empires can be interpreted as a new impetus for migration and expansion. An even larger contemporary Pacific world is manifested, for example, in the web of relations among people living in diaspora communities in Western nations along the Pacific rim and their relatives back home.

Hau'ofa's observations are relevant to the Mountain Balinese. There is no evidence to suggest that their world has ever been small and isolated, and no denying that it has witnessed a second expansion in its encounter with colonialism and modernity. Many Bali Aga have relocated to the urban centers of Bali and beyond in recent decades, in search of education, employment opportunities, or a more "modern" lifestyle. Others have accepted government offers of land and transmigrated as farmers to the more sparsely populated outer islands of Indonesia. A few have even lived and studied in Western countries. The majority of those who have left the highlands return regularly as a matter of filial and religious duty, and thus act as an extension to the world of those who stayed behind.

The impact of increased contact among societies in global and national contexts on their cultural uniqueness is a matter of fundamental concern for anthropology, as a science inspired by and dependent on cultural difference. Whatever prognosis may be proposed for the future of human cultural diversity, Hauʻofa's observations illustrate a need for caution with regard to another potential essentialism and reification process. A technology-driven process of globalization, whether it is regarded as a cultural world expansion or shrinkage, affects the world as a whole. Global interaction is not simply an encroachment of Western modernity on other societies that must precipitate a decline of their cultures. Cultural boundaries can be said to be softening only on the essentialist assumption that they have been "harder" at some time in the past. If anthropologists are prepared to contemplate the current process of globalization instead as yet another multidirectional process of encounters and negotiations, we stand to learn much from a dualistic and dynamic Balinese model of identity as representation.

Akin to Austronesian-speaking peoples in many other island societies of the Southeast Asia–Pacific region, the Balinese are no strangers to the experience of cross-cultural encounters. Over many centuries they have thus been compelled to develop practical and conceptual strategies for coping with the periodic arrival of sometimes powerful and dangerous, but often simply fascinating, newcomers seeking to trade at their shores or choosing to make Bali their new home. What seems to have emerged from their efforts to negotiate and control the cultural and social changes precipitated by such encounters is a notion of society that encompasses at least two categories of people with separate origins. These origin categories distinguish relatively indigenous people from others who are more obviously of foreign extraction or have arrived more recently. Such a temporal distinction, applied recursively, gives rise to a social order of precedence.

Balinese images of their own society envisage a social whole forged from dual origins or from repeated encounters among different historically adjacent dyads of earlier and later peoples. This image acknowledges difference but also speaks of a perpetual effort to regulate its negotiation, as powerful newcomers and powerful new ideas find a passage into the core of Balinese civilization. The Balinese view of historical change as a necessity of life has a twofold advantage. It allows for maintaining a sense of connection to a sacred past as a basis for cooperation among competing groups of earlier people and newcomers. It also values the positive potential and acknowledges the practical challenges of encounters with what is foreign and different, thus recognizing the twofold inevitability of cooperation and competition in society.

The importance of Bali's precolonial history for understanding a contemporary Balinese model of society and the inspirational value of this model need to be stressed. It would be contrary to the spirit of this same model, however, to suggest that traditional Balinese conceptions of their society have remained unaffected by the island's more recent history, that is, by a colonial and postcolonial experience, or that the effects were the same as those that precipitated from earlier cross-cultural encounters. The Dutch were not a related Austronesian people, had no intention of treating Bali as their new home, and certainly did not see a spiritual need for connecting with the Bali Aga as the island's original people and the custodians of its sacred mountains and most ancient temples. More important still, they brought with them a system of administration and a way of conceptualizing society that was almost completely alien.

While the foreigners from the West who colonized Bali arrived comparatively late and may not have stayed on the island for very long, their foreign ideas certainly did. Western forms of government and an associated idiom of modernity became an integral part of a local reality. Still, the Bali they encountered was not unfamiliar with or unprepared for living under the rule of powerful strangers. A culturally alien model of society was quickly appropriated by Balinese, at least in part, as they began to participate in the Dutch colonial administration. This process continued with the rise of a new and independent Indonesian Republic, created in the image of a Western nation-state.

The degree of local participation and empowerment in this process of "modernization" varies across different sectors of society. At one level, the aspiration of owning a television set and other modern commodities, for example, may be shared by a vast majority of all Indonesians. But the most active promulgators of modernist discourses and the most prominent social representatives of a recently acquired layer of modern identity are the new and rather small political and economic elite of Indonesia, of Bali, or of other provinces. They are not newcomers in an ethnic sense, and they need not be. It is sufficient that they are a cosmopolitan group who have domesticated the once foreign project of modernity and seek to install it at the center of their own society (Warren 1989).

In contrast, those who are regarded as yet to be "modernized" through government and private development initiatives tend to be people in such geographically remote localities as the Balinese mountains. Remote peoples are now increasingly depicted as comparatively "traditional" in the negative sense of being backward or underdeveloped (Lowenhaupt-Tsing 1993). At the same time, they also represent a pool of indigenous Indonesian cultural capital, a resource in a nationalist struggle against wholesale Westernization and, in some cases, a valuable commodity in the context of global tourism. A long-established notion of dual identity may thus have played a role in the construction of Indonesia's national culture.

How then does one appropriately acknowledge the fact that Bali is a former Dutch colony without reifying power or essentializing culture in the process? Looking from the perspective of a global distribution of power and knowledge, it may be tempting to describe the Bali Aga of central Bali (or others like them) as a politically marginal people on a marginal island in a marginal nation. But the very sense of contradiction in this act of sociospatial positioning, in allocating its cultural periphery to the island's geographical center, presents an admonition. The Western spatial metaphors "center" and "periphery" may or may not have equivalents in local discourses about power, and even where they do, it does not justify a moral endorsement.

As Craig Reynolds (1995) and Deborah Tooker (1996) have recently pointed out, Western perceptions of the centers and margins of traditional states in Southeast Asia have carried an element of complicity. Portraying smaller polities as the outer layer of a mandala, for example, as peripheral and lackluster replicas of a powerful and exemplary center, has meant that "marginal" groups "have been defined from the perspective of dominant political groups. . . . As a result, theorists have inadvertently reified this perspective in a set of analytical concepts that reaffirm existing power structures" (Tooker 1996:324).

Even though center-periphery metaphors do feature in some Balinese discourses, sometimes it is important not to endorse such local discourses blindly or to overestimate their efficacy in shaping local realities. The temptation to do so may arise because these metaphors are highly familiar and hence intelligible to Western observers. Indeed, to allocate the Bali Aga to the periphery of the world would be to reinforce a spatial idiom and a materialist perspective in a global discourse in which power and wealth form the center of all concerns, and fragile culture occupies a precarious position at the margins.

Apart from these questions of legitimacy and efficacy, a further problem is that inherent ambiguities in the discourses of local power holders are easily ignored. A classification of the Bali Aga as marginal, while it may echo the centralist discourses of the modern Indonesian state administration, would ignore the countervalue of "culture as a national asset" within that same discourse. What is, in effect, the status allocated to presumably marginal people in the dominant discourses of Indonesian and Balinese power holders? Even informants from among Bali's new political elite explained to me that human society is a fragile middle sphere, a dualistic world balanced between the powerful and the sacred, the newly acquired and the indigenous, the modern and the traditional. Contemporary Balinese continue to see life as a necessary struggle among "two that are different" (*rua bineda*), a struggle to be continued rather than won.

In response to the earlier question about how to approach the study of a previously colonized society, I would therefore argue that local models of society should be taken very seriously indeed, even in a postcolonial setting. Rather than being simply precolonial or postcolonial, these models have a continuous history that needs to be traced as far back as is possible. In the present case, the local model of Balinese society is not predominantly "centrist." Rather, it is a model of identity as encounter, informed by a recursive, dynamic, and time-focused notion of dualism.

Balinese Categories and Idioms of Social Difference

Leaving aside more recent changes for now, Balinese models of society display a characteristic focus on time, movement, and historical processes. In this encounter-oriented model, recursive dual classification is an important conceptual ingredient. Paired categories are employed as an idiom for describing and evaluating spatiotemporal processes and associated categories of people. "The original" and "the new" (people) are not absolute categories in opposition but represent relatively extreme points along a living continuum, and life is defined by complementarity and difference. Furthermore, this temporal continuum is not a sliding scale of measurement in relation to a single and paramount value. Each of its two polarities is charged with a value of its own, thus allowing for the construction of at least two basic forms of social authority—ritual and political.

The model, with its paired categories and values, inspires two very different local perspectives on the cultural heritage of the highland Balinese. Within this Balinese schema of graded difference, the Bali Aga may be devalued as a culturally immobilized indigenous people in a state of relative powerlessness. At the same time, they may be valued highly as a people who have remained at the place of sacred origin, and whose relative immobility, like that of the mythical turtle at the foundations of the Balinese cosmos, is the stable foundation and spiritual source of sustenance for its ever-changing civilization.

Although the label is disliked by the mountain people because of its potentially derisive connotations, and while they prefer to regard themselves simple as "*the* Balinese" (*wong bali*), many accept the designation "Bali Aga" with some reservations. They do so in the understanding shared by all Balinese that the mountains are the epitome of the sacred and the abode of the gods, while the sea is a place of dangerous and destructive forces. Exploiting this ambiguity, and as a counterdiscrimination, the Bali Aga sometimes sarcastically refer to the "newcomers" from Majapait as "*wong bali dataran*" or "*wong bali kelodan*," the people who dwell on the plains or nearer to the sea. This designation is based on the understanding that the sea is home to powerful demonic beings of uncivilized disposition and semi-human shape and, on a more practical level, is an important gateway to foreign powers.[1]

The paired spatial categories of mountain and sea or Bali and Java (Majapait) are particularly prominent in Balinese narratives of origin and relate to a wider Balinese schema of paired social categories. Both suggest a distinction between an inner and earlier core and a relatively external layer of the new. A similar contrast is contained in the paired terms *wedan-pendonan*, "people of the trunk (*tuwed*)–people of the leaf (*don*)." This botanical metaphor is employed to distinguish between first settlers and newcomers within the context of a village community. Such botanical metaphors index social difference not simply in terms of a polarized or layered whole. They are used to depict society as a single living entity evolving from a temporal process of growth and transformation. The position that was once the new leaf or "tip" (*muncuk*) moves relatively closer to the stump, trunk (*tuwed*, *bongkol*), or root (*akah*) of the plant in a historical process of growth, just as newcomers may acquire the status of locals subsequent to further waves of immigration.

Some Balinese creation myths conflate idioms of topography and botanical growth. They describe how the peak (*pucak* or *pucuk*) of Bali's primordial mountain grew from the sea, like a tree made of stone. The myths suggest that the island's coastal area emerged later than its peaks and highlands. The image is again one of relative and graded distinctions along a continuous scale, "from the sea" (*kelod*) and the level earth (*bumi*) "to the mountains" (*kaja*) and the sky (*langit*), rather than proposing an absolute and unmediated juxtaposition of categorical opposites. A very similar image of continuous gradation along a mountain-sea axis is conveyed by reference to the flow of water through Bali's rice irrigation system. Water travels along a path with a theoretically infinite number of way stations, marked by irrigation temples, from its origin and source in the mountains to its final destination in the sea.[2]

The common element among these paired categories is the conceptual importance they give to the passage of time, to movement, and to historical processes of social change. "Mountain" and "trunk" are metaphors of a sacred origin (*kemulan*). An origin in the distant past is linked through a sequence of events to the present, as mountain is to sea and trunk to tip. If there is a paramount value in this schema at all, it is the value of life. Life is conceived as a continuity or pathway through time and space, a process of mediations between the original and the new, the nourishing trunk and the powerful growing tip, female and male.[3]

In keeping with the prevalence of temporal concepts in Balinese models of society, history is an all-important and problematic issue in this society. Accounts of the past are typically contested knowledge in Bali, because such accounts are vital in determining the relative social status of people in the present. History is also vital to my own ethnographic model of Balinese "identities," a model that, inspired by the nonessentialist epistemology of a local model, seeks to understand identities as representations—as the products of a specific ethnohistory of encounters and negotiations.

The actual history of the encounter between the indigenous Bali Aga and a politically dominant Bali Majapait is difficult to reconstruct. Written sources or oral narratives about the island's past are not often historically reliable in the Western sense, because of the contested character of historical knowledge in Bali. Nor is it easy to infer a historical truth, located somewhere in between the different historical discourses of the two groups, given that the two groups' interpretations of Balinese history are voiced from positions of unequal power.

A fruitful alternative is first to consider a dualistic Balinese model of society and associated origin narratives from a perspective of comparative Austronesian ethnology. A cultural distinction among political and ritual forms of authority, allocated respectively to groups of people identified as relatively indigenous and foreign, is a theme that forms part of a shared cultural heritage among Austronesian-speaking peoples. Distinctions not unlike the one between Bali Aga and Bali Majapait have been reported in a growing literature on the narrative origin histories of societies from Madagascar to Polynesia. Before returning to the question of actual "history" in the next chapter, I shall first describe how this thematic encounter is treated in Balinese narratives of origin.

Dualism, Precedence, and the Contingency of Encounters in Balinese Narratives of Origin

It is somewhat surprising that a still increasing majority of contemporary Balinese, even though they are very proud of their separate Balinese identity within the Indonesian nation, consider themselves to be the descendants of non-Balinese ancestors or "foreigners." According to the dominant myth of Balinese origins, the ancestors of these newcomers originated from the legendary Hindu kingdom of Majapait on the neighboring island of Java and are said to have invaded Bali in A.D. 1343 under the leadership of a famous general by the name of Gajah Mada.[4] The invaders achieved victory by cunning, deception, and trickery as well as military prowess. Following the introduction of Islam and the collapse of this and other Hindu empires in Java (and elsewhere), the surviving Balinese contingent of Majapait came to celebrate themselves as the only remaining heirs to an epic legacy of Indic civilization in the Indonesian archipelago.

Majapait's violent military intervention is legitimized in southern Balinese literary sources and oral histories alike by portraying it as a liberation of the indigenous Balinese people from the unjust rule of their last king. This Balinese king, Raja Mayadanawa of Pejeng, is described as a demonic and semihuman tyrant and as an atheist. His defeat was supported and thus legitimized by the gods, whose proper worship had been neglected and prohibited under his rule.[5]

According to the Babad Dalem, a dynastic origin narrative of which there are several versions, the emperor of Majapait, acting on the request of Patih Ulung of Bali, eventually sent the Javanese prince Sri Kresna Kapakisan to rule and restore order in a still turbulent post-conquest Bali. The emperor equipped him with a royal dagger (kris) and other magically potent (*sakti*) regalia in order to help him accomplish his "mission of peace." The victorious and well-meaning newcomers thus began to establish a political order, a new dynasty of kings from which numerous branches of noble houses began to grow (Geertz 1980). A number of greater and lesser palaces (*puri, jero*) were constructed in the irrigated plains and southern foothills of Bali by the new aristocracy. Ironically, their occupants began to refer to themselves as "*anak jero*," literally "the children of insiders." The majority of Balinese-born commoners who lacked a Majapait pedigree were now the "outsiders" (*anak jaba*), that is, from the perspective of the new aristocracy and their palaces. Those indigenous *anak jaba* who were in the service or under the influence of the aristocracy eventually came to be distinguished from the more evidently indigenous Bali Aga. The mountain people were outsiders by preference rather than for a momentary lack of genealogical credentials. They were a Balinese people who had chosen to continue their own traditions in the highlands and maintain their identification with Balinese ancestors rather than embrace a presumably superior Majapait civilization and a fictitious Javanese ancestry.[6]

In order to create a new Balinese society and to confirm their status as its political insiders, the newcomers established not only a new political structure but a new and supportive ritual order and status economy. The ritual order of Majapait Bali was redefined by reference to the presumably innovative teachings of legendary priests of Javanese extraction. These newcomer priests are still recognized as the ancestors of contemporary Balinese Brahmana clans. Foremost among them and appropriately named was Mpu Sakti Wahu Rauh, "the powerful priest who only just arrived." The centers of the new ritual order were Pura Besakih (Stuart-Fox 1987) and a number of other, smaller state temples. Until today Brahmana priests (*pedanda*) cooperate with secular authorities in a relationship of mutual support. They officiate at most state temple ceremonies sponsored by traditional ruling houses or, nowadays, by modern political leaders.

A general development can be observed in the narrative structure of these southern Balinese origin histories. Initially, the newcomers are praised for their extraordinary and magical prowess as they dissemble an old and corrupted political system. Once victory has been achieved, however, the status of the stranger kings is gradually transformed. Increasing emphasis is placed on the establishment of ordered relations in society and on a general civilizing mission. In their quest to gain symbolic capital within Balinese society, the new leadership construct themselves as the potent carriers of a superior secular civilization and as the champions of a more appropriate form of Hindu ritual and worship. Majapait kings became builders or restorers of temples and generous benefactors and protectors of fellow immigrant Brahmana priests. In the context of this discourse, the Bali Aga officially became less and less relevant to the new political as well as ritual order of Balinese society.

This dominant account of the origins of Balinese civilization is only one, and by no means an uncontested, narrative perspective on a complex, local politics of ethnicity. Bali Aga renditions of the legendary conquest of Bali, in particular, do not portray the invasion of Bali as a justifiable act of liberation, but as a contingent and rather unfortunate event. This perspective is epitomized in their interpretation of the well-known tale of Raja Bedaulu. This alternative name for Bali's last indigenous ruler literally means "the king with a different head."[7]

Unlike his demonic double Mayadanawa, Raja Bedaulu was a saintly personage, capable of temporarily detaching his head from his torso and of elevating it to the heavens during his yogic practice. On one occasion the prolonged absence of the royal head led an overly anxious attendant to place a pig's head on the king's neck, acting on the unjustified fear that he would otherwise meet his death. Raja Bedaulu's original head thus was permanently prevented from rejoining its body.[8]

Bali Aga construct this myth as a metaphor for foreign rule. The ghastly animal head represents a Balinese king of Majapait extraction, a potent and yet unrefined and alien power that has come to head and rule the genuinely human body of the Balinese people. What is elsewhere constructed as a mission of civilization is portrayed here as an unsolicited and misguided act of replacement, substituting an already civilized rule with a barbaric power. Nevertheless, the installment of the foreign head at the apex of an organic whole is described as an accident that had been waiting to happen, given the inherently fragile link of magical power between the royal head and the body of the people in indigenous Balinese society. Overly immobilized and concerned with spiritual practice, Raja Bedaulu had ceased to be a repository of worldly power.

While they may officially discount the validity of these alternative Bali Aga discourses about Balinese history, the so-called *wong majapait*, aristocrats and commoners alike, are aware of their claims and silently acknowledge the existence and ritual authority of a more ancient Bali in the course of their religious practices. Thousands of people travel into the mountainous interior regions to participate in annual festivals held at the ancient regional temples that lie at the heart of highland ritual domains. These ceremonies include crucial and islandwide harvest and fertility rituals directed toward the guardian deities of land and water. Most of the temples concerned have remained entirely under the ritual authority of the indigenous Bali Aga and their non-Brahmana priests, though there have been repeated appropriation attempts.[9]

Some among the many southern Balinese people who attend Bali Aga temples conceal the embarrassing truth of their ritualized submission to non-Majapait (and hence low-caste) priests by construing their visits as "devotional acts" (*mabakti*) and by stressing that they do not "carry an ancestral responsibility" (*nyungsung*) for these temples. They are quite prepared, however, to acknowledge at least the spiritual authority of the deities enshrined at temples like Pura Pucak Penulisan or Pura Batur in matters of fertility and irrigation. It is interesting to recall in this context that the temple of Penulisan was a state temple of ancient Balinese kings, whose statues are still venerated in its inner sanctum and whose identities have merged into that of the deity Ratu Pucak, the king of the mountain peak. The severed royal head thus has survived in the heavens, and the sacred authority of ancient Balinese kings and ancestors continues to be acknowledged in the worship of their deified manifestations.

Even this brief discussion of a complex body of Balinese origin narratives and associated ritual practices reveals that power and its human representatives are attributed with a foreign origin in this society. The notion of power as a stranger strikes a resonance across the Southeast Asian and Pacific region. In societies as widely separated as Hawai'i and Sumatra, local origin histories feature the common cultural theme of a powerful outsider and newcomer, who arrives at the shore and gradually begins a symbolic journey to the interior. By means of powerful heirlooms, magical efficacy, prowess, and sheer cleverness, or by a strategic marriage, the outsider gains political control over an indigenous community. Newcomers may also challenge the locals' special ancestral relationship to the land and their role as ritual leaders in the worship of the deified ancestral protectors of the land. Such a transformation of "newcomers" into "original people" may also be triggered by the arrival of other newcomers in several successive waves.

In view of its underlying distinction between political and ritual forms of authority, this pattern has been referred to as "dual sovereignty" (Wouden 1968) or "diarchy" (Cunningham 1965; Needham 1980; Valeri 1982). Other authors have highlighted the dominant position of the newcomers within this dyad by focusing on the notion of a "stranger-king" (Sahlins 1985) and the "power of strangers"

(Barnes 1996) or have attempted to describe a variable process of "installing the outsider on the inside" (Fox 1994a). This variable terminology is not just a result of each author's semantic preference or subjective interpretation. Rather, the different labels reflect the very different outcomes of a historical struggle over the division of authority between these two thematic parties in various Austronesian societies.

It would be short-sighted to suggest that a cultural theme such as a distinction between ritual and political forms of authority is mechanically actualized in the course of social history. If this were the case, one could assume a conflict-free relationship whereby one of two groups would claim power and the other, ritual status as it own and inalienable right. The diversity of narrative histories and social arrangements among societies in the region, instead, is a testimony to the specificity of local political histories and the underlying indeterminacy of historical encounters. In presenting a case study of how one particular relationship between newcomers and indigenous people has been constructed and managed, in Bali, my aim is therefore not simply to provide a further example of a common cultural theme, but to illustrate how thematic cultural representations of authority have to be negotiated in the practical context of a specific historical process.

In the Balinese case the outsiders violently installed themselves at the inside of an earlier political order, that is, at the old political center in Pejeng. In order to erase the moral blemish of this military intervention, they gradually established alternative political and ritual centers and partially liberated themselves from the memory and authority of an indigenous Bali.[10] This dominant origin narrative contains no hint of "domesticating" the stranger and thus departs from Sahlins' description of how "stranger kings" are constructed in Polynesia: "Kingship makes its appearance from outside the society. Initially a stranger and something of a terror, the king is absorbed and domesticated by the indigenous people . . . the draconian feats by which they [kings] come to power are foreign to the conduct of 'real people' or 'true sons of the land,' as various Polynesians express it. . . . Power is a barbarian" (Sahlins 1985:73, 78–79). In Bali's dominant myth of origin, the strangers from Majapait are claimed to have been on a civilizing mission and to have transformed a barbaric indigenous society by bringing the monster Mayadanawa to his justified death.[11] It is only the Bali Aga counternarrative of Raja Bedaulu that shows elements of a theme in which power is a barbarian who becomes integrated into a preexisting and already civilized social order.

On another level of origin history, however, there are some remarkable similarities between Bali and Polynesia. When Sahlins reflects on Fijian origin narratives and describes how "the stranger wanders into the interior where he is taken in by a local chieftain, whose daughter he eventually marries" (1985:79), he may just as well be describing the origin narrative of Bali Aga villages like Sukawana (Part 1) and Trunyan (Danandjaja 1980:40). These myths narrate how the son or royal emissary of a foreign king is sent to Bali, where he encounters an already civilized people. He marries the daughter of a local ruler and becomes the founder of a new and prestigious ancestral origin group.

These origin narratives also illustrate that a number of Bali Aga clans or origin houses consider themselves to be newcomers in a local context. Their immigrant ancestors are said to have moved to the inside of an even earlier society, whom they may refer to as *bali mula*, the "original people," or as *wedan*, the "people of the trunk." In short, the Bali Aga are themselves a heterogeneous group and need not evoke Bali Majapait as the paradigmatic image of the powerful stranger when it comes to representing the polarities of their own local and regional identities. Nor does Bali Majapait regard the Bali Aga as the sole representatives of ritual authority, given that Brahmana priests can fulfill this same role in most other religious contexts.[12]

In order to comprehend the character of a sometimes contradictory but otherwise complementary relationship among the two groups and their discourses, it is necessary to contemplate the peculiarities of Balinese history. The picture that is drawn in Balinese sources may be sketchy and distorted, but it seems to indicate that the journey of the newcomer to the ritual center may not have been completed in this case.

There is evidence suggesting the Bali Aga actively resisted external political and economic control from the very beginning. Their unwillingness to lend their acceptance to the new Majapait rulers, even in the form of a nominal sovereignty, is said to have triggered several military expeditions in the time of Sri Kresna Kapakisan and numerous raids by later kings such as Panji Sakti of Buleleng (Worsley 1972).[13] In the Babad Pasek it is claimed: "After the noble warrior families from Java had settled in Bali, it became obvious that the leaders of the Bali Aga were not content to see them rule and hold power in Bali. They expressed their displeasure by rebelling against the new government and trying to destroy the state. The rebellion arose in the villages of Batur, Cempaga, Songan, Serai, Manikliyu, Bonyoh, Taro, Bayad, and Sukawana, the headquarters of the rebellion" (Babad Pasek, 63a).[14]

The Bali Aga villages reported to have resisted the political take-over of the island are among those that, until today, are tightly orga-nized in several and interconnected ritual domains, or *banua*. As I will discuss further in the following chapter, it may have been their alliances within such domains that allowed the Bali Aga to present a unified front to the newcomers. Even though they were repeatedly violated, the people of the highlands evidently resisted eradication or cultural absorption, although they accepted the political status quo in the end.

Again according to the Babad Pasek, it was only after the first Maja-pait king had sponsored a ritual in the Bali Aga temple Pura Penu-lisan that the conflict began to subside.[15] The terms of this truce clearly specify a distinction between secular and ritual authority, and a mutual recognition, if only in a context of limited and guarded interaction among the two parties. Such ceremonial interactions have taken place as long as anyone can remember and have followed the established division of authority.[16] Although the people of Bali Maja-pait have their state temples and Brahmana priests, they participate in the festivals of ancient mountain temples. Bali Aga, however, still refuse to accept Brahmana priests and recognize no formal obliga-tion toward the newer Majapait temples.[17] By the same token, the Bali Aga have never succeeded in establishing a secular kingdom of their own, though they may have tried to do so.[18]

While each group had its own social reality to live, each with its own inner distinctions between wielders of secular and ritual authority, there have always been limited but important interactions between these two worlds of Bali. The pattern of their encounters reveals a mutual recognition as necessary partners in a dualistic schema of society but also a historical encounter among competitors. Neverthe-less, a number of political factors may have encouraged the creation of an overall arrangement that is predominantly cooperative. Perhaps the instability created by competition among rival Majapait princes on the plains made it advantageous to maintain a politically neutral space in the island's interior, a place of exile following a military defeat.[19] Perhaps the legitimacy of some rulers was bolstered by main-taining an exclusive ritual relationship with Bali's "original people" (e.g., the king of Klungkung and Pura Batur). Cooperation may also have been necessary in facing the threat of renewed invasion from the outside, for example, from Islamic sultanates on neighboring islands, or to support the imperialist adventures of Balinese kings in Lombok and elsewhere.[20]

It is not possible to substantiate these speculations in the absence of more reliable historical sources, and among the majority of Balinese there has been no great desire to do so. A greater abundance of historical documents and a more explicit concern with "history-as-a-science" began to emerge, however, with the arrival of a new group of colonizers. Colonization by the Dutch precipitated major changes in Balinese culture and politics, and the process continued after Indonesian independence. In the wake of these changes, the positions of the Bali Aga and of Bali Majapait had to be renegotiated. These very categories were also redefined, at least to some degree, in a new idiom.

Modern Identities and the Narratives of the Nation-State

I shall argue in the following chapter that an earlier Balinese model of society, based on precolonial notions of a necessary encounter and a dynamic relationship between "indigenous" and "foreign" peoples or ideas, has had a profound effect in shaping colonial and postcolonial representations of Balinese society. At the same time, these Balinese models of society were also transformed by the experience of colonialism and modernity. In short, contemporary ideas about Balinese society both in Bali and abroad are coproductions; they are the products of yet another historical encounter and process of social negotiation, with its own peculiar blend of competitive and cooperative tendencies. My present aim in discussing this process of coproduction is to look at how it has shaped the image of the Bali Aga espoused by modern Balinese society and promoted in its dominant state discourses.

Even casual visitors are bound to notice that modernity and globalization have become a major part of material and social realities in contemporary Bali. The current situation has many of its historical roots in Bali's colonial encounter. But Western cultural influence also continues unabated as an endless stream of foreign tourists passes through Balinese temples and palaces armed with cameras and video recorders rather than cannons and rifles. The cultural innovators and political instigators bringing modernity to Bali once again originate from the outside; they are resourceful and powerful strangers.

How much relevance traditional models still have in shaping local representations of a contemporary Balinese society embedded in a modernizing and globalizing world is a difficult question. In seeking to answer this question there is a danger of becoming caught somewhere between the twin follies of romanticism and cynicism, of searching for pockets of cultural authenticity and of proclaiming the gloomy dawn of a global monoculture. In investigating the relevance of dual authority as a cultural theme in the modern Balinese setting and throughout a recent period of unusually rapid social change, I attempt to avoid these extremes by adopting an interactionist or intersubjective approach. A global discourse of modernity is contemplated as it has been experienced and interpreted by the Balinese themselves against the backdrop of an earlier society and a model of society with its own and distinct cultural history.

This approach has a major advantage. It may be useful to develop a general social theory of marginality for the analysis of the modern condition of the Bali Aga and other ethnic minorities, in Indonesia and other modernizing nation-states around the world. It is regrettable, however, that many marginality studies in contemporary anthropology attribute the politics of marginality with too great a significance and with universal properties. It is generally admitted that power is culturally constructed, but it is rarely explored whether the very notion of power itself may be culture-specific and, hence, variable (see also H. Geertz 1995).

One insight these studies offer is that the condition of political marginality is a coproduction insofar as underprivileged minority groups do tend to object to dominant discourses and resist outside interventions. Some of the best marginality studies have further avoided romanticizing local responses as political struggles against a nameless national or international political conspiracy and have paid detailed ethnographic attention to the actual process of negotiation between representors and representations positioned at the centers and margins, between the worlds of the powerful and those of the fringe dwellers of the modern world.

In many of these studies, however, the culturally specific elements in the discourses of the people concerned are no longer important. The focus instead is on presumably universal aspects in the purely political narratives of modern nation-states. These narratives are assumed to be so similar because the non-Western nation-states in which they are produced are themselves assumed to be the homogeneous products of a global process of cultural homogenization. Indonesia, for example, is often portrayed and judged by political commentators in the Western media not as a political system with a history and destiny of its own but as the still imperfect replica of a Western democracy. Anthropologists have not sufficiently criticized this global (or cultureless) approach to contemporary non-Western politics, even when they have been in a position to do so.

A prominent and recent example of a marginality study in the ethnographic genre is Anna Lowenhaupt-Tsing's (1993) study of an indigenous Dayak people in the Meratus Mountains of southern Kalimantan and their relationship to the coastal people of the provincial capital and former kingdom of Banjar. She notes in passing the Banjarese claim that their ancestors were immigrants from the empire of Majapait, hinting at the long precolonial history of their relationship without exploring its contemporary relevance. In its basic focus on marginality as an interactive process, this study has substantial merit, even though the author may sacrifice too much of the cultural specificity of local experience in her own representations of this process. The following analysis of Bali Aga marginality combines this interactionist approach with a strong focus on the cultural specificity of Balinese and Bali Aga models of society.

In modern Bali the meaning of the term "Bali Aga" conflates notions of physical, historical, and cultural remoteness. The Bali Aga are regarded as prehistoric survivors from a distant past and as "survivors" only on account of their isolation in the remote mountains. Their continuing adherence to different customs—falsely presumed to be primitive—is taken as evidence of their lack of exposure to a civilizing process that is thought to have produced a refined courtly culture in other parts of Bali under the banner of Majapait. This positioning in the past is constructed on an act of selective amnesia.

The historic significance of the mountain region in the development of Balinese civilization has been systematically ignored by most Balinese. This is remarkable, given that there are hundreds of *prasasti* that bear testament to the importance of Bali Aga communities during a period of approximately six hundred years before the presumed Majapait invasion, when Balinese dynasties had already established a complex Hindu civilization on the island. The category Bali Aga is only sustainable on the fallacious assumption that a vast cultural chasm divides the Bali before the mythical conquest from the Bali thereafter (Chapter 10). Although they are quietly acknowledged as first settlers and as custodians of the most ancient temples on Bali, the mountain people are not acknowledged as the true founders of its living civilization. They are living relics from a forgettable past.

Actual knowledge or curiosity about the details of current Bali Aga traditions is limited among fellow Balinese. Most often such knowledge is conveniently phrased as a negative description: "The Bali Aga do not cremate their dead, they do not acknowledge caste, they do not consult Brahmana priests, they do not use Sanskrit *mantra* (sacred words) in their prayers, and they do not elect village leaders on the basis of aptitude" (these statements are taken from recordings of conversations with urban Balinese). Impoverished, uncouth, and un-educated hill dwellers they are deemed, ignorant of the sophisticated process of Balinese wet rice agriculture, awkward in their use of re-fined Balinese language, and without literature or literacy. In short, any known difference between the traditional practices of the two groups is interpreted as a deficiency on the side of the mountain people, indicating an absence of important elements of a proper social order and ritual procedure. Wherever Bali Aga traditions are more elaborate than those in southern Bali, the relevant information fails to be registered.[21]

Contemporary narratives about the Bali Aga build on and extend this traditional schema of historical and cultural differences. The mountain people are also remote from the ideals of a contemporary Indonesian project of modernity. This construction of the Bali Aga as a people at the margins of the sphere of influence surrounding modern political, administrative, and economic centers becomes evi-dent in the context of state development initiatives.

The Bali Aga have been selected as the most appropriate targets in Bali for a range of development projects sponsored or initiated by the national government. Indonesian tertiary students, for example, are required to take part in compulsory community service intern-ships (B.I. Kuliah Kerja Nyata, or KKN).[25] These group internships are in part a means by which the government seeks to proliferate pro-gressive ideas at a local level wherever development is seen to be re-tarded. In Bali it is the village communities of the Bali Aga who enjoy the dubious status of being among the most-favored internship targets and are thereby identified as belonging to the most undereducated sector of society.

In recent years, Bali Aga villages have also been identified by local Balinese authorities as appropriate targets in relation to a nationwide government initiative for the advancement of Indonesia's economi-cally and socially most backward communities (B.I. *desa tertinggal,* lit. "villages left behind [by progress]"). In Bali Aga villages this has meant, for example, that some people have had to destroy their tra-ditional wooden houses with earthen floors and replace them with concrete structures. These new dwellings are said to be more hy-gienic or healthy (B.I. *rumah sehat*) than traditional homes, and rela-tively low-interest government loans were provided to fund their con-struction. The affected families were often left with no other choice than to sell land, trying to meet the repayments for a forced lifestyle change that they could not sustain. The only local beneficiaries of this scheme were members of village elites who could redirect such housing loans toward more profitable investments.

Bali Aga marginality is not merely a matter of forgetting ancient Balinese history and the dynasties of pre-Majapait kings. It is reproduced through an ongoing process of reinterpretation. Modern interpretations are framed in terms of a state discourse, with education (B.I. *pendidikan*), development (B.I. *pembangunan*), and progress (B.I. *kemajuan*) as its key metaphors. Although the Bali Aga are no longer explicitly juxtaposed with a glamorous Majapait civilization in such state discourses, there are a number of continuities. The empire of Majapait is evoked frequently as a historical precursor to the current Indonesian nation-state, for example, in order to justify the continuing political centrality of Java.

The distancing rhetoric, denial of history, negative description, negative targeting, and other marginalizing strategies of a modern Balinese administrative elite are directed toward Bali Aga culture as a legitimization for its systematic and deliberate eradication. The interventions experienced as the most imposing by the Bali Aga themselves relate to a politics of tradition (*adat*) and religion (*agama*). Government policies on these matters are implemented through the provincial and local branches of state-controlled institutions such as the Badan Pelaksana Pembina Lembaga Adat (Agency for the Implementation and Cultivation [i.e., Restructuring] of Traditional Institutions) and Parisada Hindu Dharma Indonesia.[23]

The concepts *adat* and *agama* are as pivotal to nationalist discourses concerning Indonesia's future as are notions of modernity and progress, and their inclusion produces a deep ambiguity. On the one hand, the outside forces of modernity are to be tempered and civilized by promoting an indigenous heritage of "Indonesian tradition." On the other hand, tradition and religion are perceived as potential obstacles to progress and national unity unless they are reconstituted according to the needs of a modern state. The state thus gains a mandate to intervene in the traditional and religious affairs of local groups, particularly those in marginal and "disorderly" (B.I. *belum diatur*) regions, and for eliminating the extremes of cultural and ethnic diversity they seem to represent.[24]

However, the power of the nation-state presents itself to the Bali Aga with a Balinese face, as it is wielded and manipulated by local politicians and administrators. The latter are generally members of a privileged urban Balinese elite. Many of them are also the children of a former traditional elite and may still have a considerable stake in the myth of Majapait.

While the Bali Aga thus regard many state interventions as originating from an old opponent under a new cloak, they now have an opportunity to compete with other Balinese in the borrowing of state power. For example, they have welcomed calls by Parisada Hindu Dharma Indonesia for a simplification of ritual procedure. Bali Aga people have long voiced opposition to what they describe as inessential pomp in southern Balinese ceremonial life. The casteless Bali Aga also claim (perhaps rightly so) to have more democratic traditional institutions, in the spirit of the Indonesian constitution (*panca sila*), than what is to them a neofeudal southern Bali. In general, however, the Bali Aga have not become organized as a modern political faction, and their efforts to borrow the power of the state by adopting some of its narratives are mostly related to specific issues arising in a local context.

State discourses and interventions are diverse and elicit an equally broad range of local responses, from accommodation, appeasement, and opportunism to noncooperation, subversion, and public protest. Some specific examples of Bali Aga experiences of and responses to state interventions illustrate how these negotiations may unfold.

Over the last two decades, the Badan Pelaksana Pembina Lembaga Adat has tried to impose changes on customary village (*desa adat*) organization throughout Bali. Mountain communities differ in their organization from those of the south. They are organized around a council of paired elders (*ulu apad*), who are ranked in order of precedence (Chapter 7). The standard critique is that traditional leadership selection is not based on aptitude and qualifications such as literacy. Little credit is given to the fact that a senior position in these councils is only obtained after a lifetime of experience and practical learning as a junior council member and that any individual lack of aptitude is absorbed through the collective nature of local leadership.

The government's real concern may be that a seniority system of succession to positions of community leadership is quite impervious to manipulation by institutions like the Badan Pelaksana Pembina Lembaga Adat, which elsewhere in Bali approves and educates elected *adat* leaders. Village communities in coastal Bali are headed by a single *klian adat* and one assistant, rather than by a large council of paired and ranked elders. These *klian adat* must be literate in Bahasa Indonesia and, until the recent fall of the Suharto regime, had to support the ruling Golkar party before being approved as candidates by the authorities. Once elected (or perhaps, rather, selected), they must regularly attend educational sessions chaired by the Badan Pelaksana Pembina Lembaga Adat branches in the nearest district or regency capital.

Suggestions of dismantling the councils of village elders have been rejected by most Bali Aga communities. Such intervention attempts are discussed among local leaders from different villages during regular gatherings at regional mountain temples. Individual villages often respond to pressure from government officials by evoking their regional religious obligations as a justification for maintaining village councils. The Badan Pelaksana Pembina Lembaga Adat, in turn, has recognized this unity as a problem by officially declaring its determination to force the Bali Aga into line. In a formal statement of its program for the future, the committee proclaims that it is its aim "to integrate the social structure, culture, and Hindu religion of old Balinese [Bali Aga] villages into that of the appanage villages [villages under the cultural influence of the Majapait courts] so that in the long run the cultural difference between them becomes less acute" (*Hasil-Hasil Pesamuhan Majelis Pembina Lembaga Adat, Daerah Bali*, 26 Feb. 1993, item 3, p. 35, my translation). Other passages of the text leave little doubt as to who is to be assimilated and who is to provide the blueprint for the committee's vision of a culturally homogenized Bali. Bali Aga culture, it seems, has been earmarked for systematic destruction.

Local responses have not always taken the form of unrelenting resistance. Many Bali Aga villages accommodate the wishes of the government by electing a *klian adat* as well as maintaining a full council or by allocating the office of *klian* to an elder of a particular rank. Other villages have indeed decided to disband or modify the council of elders itself. Such cases are rare and tend to indicate not only external pressure but serious internal conflicts among political factions in the villages concerned (Reuter, in press).

A different set of interventions has originated from the religious institution Parisada Hindu Dharma Indonesia, which had begun to rationalize and homogenize Hindu religion and ritual practice in preparation for a quest to gain recognition for Hinduism as a state-approved religion in Indonesia. This quest finally succeeded in 1958 (Bakker 1995). Their national agenda has inclined leaders of the organization to be critical of the idiosyncrasy of religious practices within different Balinese villages. Again, it is the Bali Aga whose local traditions show the greatest discrepancy from a new national religious norm.

One issue relates to Hindu temple architecture. Many Bali Aga communities do not have the "three essential village temples" (*kayangan tiga*, i.e., a *pura dalem*, a *pura bale agung*, and a *pura puseh*) that are officially required under Parisada Hindu Dharma Indonesia recommendations, though many have now renamed their existing idiosyncratic sanctuaries in order to create an appearance of conformity. In addition, their temples do not contain all of the shrines that are deemed to be essential in southern Bali. To name but one case, the leaders of the temple committee of Pura Penulisan have suffered repeated criticism because this important regional sanctuary does not feature a *meru*, a tall shrine with a multitiered roof, or a *padmasana*, a stone seat dedicated to Sang Hyang Widi, the paramount Hindu deity promoted by Parisada Hindu Dharma Indonesia in response to a monotheism requirement for state-accepted religions under the Indonesian constitution. The significance of the shrines that are typical of Bali Aga temples is not understood or appreciated by the authorities.

Perhaps the most contentious religious issue for the casteless Bali Aga, however, is the use of priests of Brahmana extraction (*pedanda*). In one incident, the temple of Penulisan was visited by a Parisada Hindu Dharma Indonesia–organized delegation of worshipers under the ritual leadership of a Brahmana priest from Bangli. The uninvited visitors had the support of the *bupati* of Bangli, who belonged to the same Brahmana family as the priest who led this party. Local leaders were outraged about the outsiders' attempt to appropriate their temple ritually, and responded by constructing the visit as a ritual defilement. In this they focused on the fact that the delegation had brought a sacrificial pig to the temple, an offering forbidden and despised by the local deity. The thirty thousand members of the temple's congregation first allowed and then responded to this violation of local tradition and authority by holding an elaborate three-week-long purification ceremony. The ceremony included a journey to a seaside temple maintained by Sukawana's ritual clients in Tejakula at the northern coast. There, the polluting influence was finally returned to the sea by ritually "bathing the deities" of Pura Penulisan. This ritual protest created such negative publicity and embarrassment for the unwelcome visitors that they have never since returned.[25]

In another incident, the dominant political faction in a Bali Aga village, under the leadership of the administrative village head, called in a *pedanda* to officiate at a village ritual. In this fashion they managed to enamor themselves to the political leader of the regency, the *bupati* of Bangli. The *pedanda* whom they invited was the same relative of the *bupati* who had led the fateful visit to Penulisan. As a reward, the faction's hold on the important office of *kepala desa* has since become virtually unassailable. This is because the *bupati* has had the power to reject candidates from rival factions.

Attempts to involve the Bali Aga passively in modern forms of state-sponsored ritual have also led to considerable local resentment. In one case I experienced personally, the *kepala desa* of a mountain village reported to the village elders during a new moon meeting how he had been summoned to Bangli in order to receive *tirta* from an annual blood sacrifice (*taur agung*). This ceremony is held under government sponsorship in Bangli and other regency capitals on the day before *nyepi*, the southern Balinese festival of the new year. "Where did you throw it?" they asked in puzzlement, given that "*nyepi pemerintah*" (the *nyepi* of the government calendar) is not observed in this and other Bali Aga villages and that, hence, the *tirta* had no specified use. "With respect," answered the *kepala desa*. "I just put the bottle on my kitchen shelf, opened it, and—let the water evaporate!" Government pressure does not evaporate quite as easily, and the excessive laughter in the assembly over this small victory only accentuated the gravity of the situation. The *kepala desa* later urged the village elders to instruct people to show consideration for the religious authorities by not working or commuting too much on the official holiday of *nyepi*, when everyone in Bali is supposed to stay at home.[26]

The future of Bali Aga society is shrouded in uncertainty, though perhaps not more so than that of all Balinese, as their lives are reshaped by an ever deepening engagement with national and global issues. Notions of the indigenous and the foreign acquire a new meaning as Bali is swept by other waves of newcomers, including an increasing number of economic immigrants and wealthy investors from Java, who seek their fortune in Bali's thriving tourist industry. In one sense, mainstream Bali's ongoing romance with Majapait is still a metaphoric border crossing, a renewed borrowing of power from an outside political center situated once again in Java and beyond.

Following the violent arrival of the Dutch, some of the surviving Balinese rulers and their descendants eventually became politically emasculated figureheads under colonial control (Vickers 1989; Wiener 1995). Faced with an initially unfamiliar political establishment, at first colonial and later national, members of this privileged class soon began to regain a measure of power by obtaining a Dutch education and securing positions in the colonial administration. In general terms, their traditional role as power holders has been eroded.

Some royal houses, however, have been rather successful in borrowing and subverting colonial and postcolonial state power to suit their own purposes. Some of those who failed to manage such a self-transformation into modern power holders began to retreat toward a more traditional and religious sphere of life. This secondary inward movement of the newcomers from Majapait has sometimes led to a renewed assault on the remaining ritual authority of the Bali Aga, an assault fought on both sides with weapons borrowed from the arsenal of the modern state.

The preceding discussion of the relationship between the people of Bali's mountains and the increasingly urbanized political and cultural elites of the Balinese plains, between presumably indigenous Bali Aga and the children of Majapait, and, nowadays, between those who face and those who wield the borrowed power of a Javanese-dominated nation-state has provided a preliminary glimpse of transformations and continuities in Balinese models of society. Traditional narratives of origin acknowledge that the distribution of ritual and political authority is always a complex and contested historical process, and this notion has been emphasized once again as earlier perceptions of society became fused with the new narratives of colonialism, nationalism, and global modernism. The continuities of a Balinese politics of ethnicity lie in a historical experience of perpetual exposure to outside forces and in a preoccupation with the cultural management of encounters between ever new categories of "foreigners" and "genuine Balinese people."

Balinese models of society are not entirely unique in this. They invite comparison with other Austronesian-speaking societies in which notions of dual ethnicity and authority are prevalent and have been documented. In a recent article, James Fox (1994a) provides a preliminary list of such thematic features, based on an analysis of origin narratives from Fiji, Timor, Roti, Palembang, Besemah, and Bali. He emphasizes that various social arrangements between groups of classificatory or actual newcomers and indigenous people can and do occur. His inventory of thematic options can be summarized as follows:

– a stranger from across the sea encounters indigenous inhabitants

– a king from abroad is requested by the autochthons to restore order

– the male outsider moves inward by marrying the daughter of insiders

– the stranger is installed as ruler, but indigenous people retain control over land and fertility; a permanent compact or diarchy is established

- the outsider creates a new organization for the domain; the insider disappears (or is explicitly said to have been chased out)
- the outsiders violently usurp the insiders' authority over the land and enter into a dichotomous relationship with a new wave of outsiders
- the new ruler eventually becomes immobilized at the center

The Balinese case, while it strikes many resonances, shows a number of idiosyncratic features. A distinction between secular and ritual authority is clearly significant. This dual distinction has been actualized, however, within a specific historical struggle over the control of symbolic resources, an open-ended process with unpredictable outcomes. As the original insiders, the Bali Aga have managed to retain their ritual authority and a measure of political autonomy by entering into an enduring, though context-limited, diarchic relationship with the newcomers or new political insiders of Bali Majapait.

With the entrance of Bali into an arena of national identity and international tourism, and with Indonesia's engagement in a transnational political scenario and a global economy, notions of the indigenous and the foreign are given new meanings. Nevertheless, old and new notions of the foreign and the local merge in the thinking of modern elites and the modern experiences of the Bali Aga alike. For the present time, at least, precolonial Balinese concepts of dual authority relating to a wider Austronesian cultural heritage still seem to inform contemporary Balinese strategies for negotiating encounters with the foreign and remain relevant as a foundation for local and ethnographic models of Balinese society. Even in the general discourse of the modern Indonesian nation-state, a system of complementary values seems to be operating. The present representational landscape of Bali thus continues to be a product of negotiation and cooperation, though it may also be the outcome of a competitive struggle over symbolic resources on a social playing field marked by significant and still increasing economic and political disparities.

Chapter 10

THE ANTHROPOLOGICAL COPRODUCTION OF THE BALI AGA
A Mirror of Changing Relations

The situation of the Bali Aga within changing Balinese representations of their society is part of a contested and emergent knowledge system, drawing on a range of culturally specific metaphors of time and movement and, more recently, on a more "global" and Western-influenced vocabulary of modernity. But how do these local representational models compare and relate to Western portrayals of the Bali Aga, as reflected in an abundant and changing anthropological literature on Balinese society?

While the way Balinese conceptualize their own society has been influenced significantly by Western ideas over the last century, the reverse may also be the case.[1] It is thus necessary to trace in some detail the twisting historical course of a Western project of representation that began with the reports by Nieuwenkamp, Haga, and others —the early colonial administrators in Bali who first felt a need to establish for themselves who and what the Bali Aga really were. Subject to forms of distortion other than those of Balinese representations, Western representations of the Bali Aga certainly reflect the specific colonial and postcolonial agendas of their proponents. However, their vision of the highlands has been obscured even more by what other Balinese have told them. Western observers have listened in on a dominant Majapait discourse more often than they have gone to the interior to hear what the Bali Aga people have had to say for themselves.

The following review of Western interpretations of the Bali Aga and their culture therefore aims to be more than a critique of the colonial or postcolonial anthropological literature. It is concerned with the distorting effects of cultural brokerage. Anthropologists do not perceive a people as an ethnic minority or a culturally marginal group simply on the grounds of their own position of power or even in acknowledgment of the facticity of local power structures. Their evaluations are shaped by local constructions of power, presented to them by local cultural elites. Some observers may reify and reinforce local narratives of power within their own narratives or even issue them with a stronger accent of reality than they previously possessed.

Cultural brokers can be defined as members of another culture whose discourses appear authoritative, articulate, and coherent to Western listeners, and who thus seem predestined to become key informants. Other local discourses and potential informants may be excluded from the ensuing ethnographic dialogue. In the present case, representations of the Bali Aga may have been coproduced by Western scholars and their Balinese hosts, that is, their primary informants in the palaces and Brahmana households of southern Bali.[2] In this process, the people of the mountains were gradually reduced to shadows—strangers in a paradise created without their participation.

The Bali Aga and Colonial Policy

The status and place foreign visitors and researchers have allocated to the mountain people within the fabric of Balinese society has varied over time in keeping with changing Western agendas. After a more favorable interpretation of a Bali Aga heritage in the early stages of the colonization process, when Balinese princes were still regarded as willful tyrants and ferocious enemies, the mountains receded into the ever deepening cultural shadow of a now celebrated southern Balinese civilization. Foreign commentators have thus contributed to local marginalizing discourses concerning the Bali Aga, unwittingly perpetuating the views of a Balinese cultural elite whose courtly refinement had imposed a lasting impression on their imagination.

Western commentators, as well as constructing their own knowledge systems, have been important contributors to a Balinese politics of representation, though they may have been unaware of this to some degree. The first step in this process was their acceptance of the preexisting Balinese designation "Bali Aga" for a presumably separate people and cultural tradition. F. A. Liefrinck, who was among the first Dutch colonial civil servants, compiled a survey of northern Balinese villages in the 1880s. In it he mentions the community of Sembiran as exemplary of a different, "Bali Aga" type of village organization

(1934:465–466). Around the same time, the medical doctor Julius
Jacobs went so far as to suggest that the entire Kintamani area was inhabited by an archaic "Bali Aga tribe" (1883:52).

Later visitors, among them military officer Le Roux and the cartog-
rapher Roon, observed an actual pattern of cultural differences between plains and mountain peoples, and the adopted local term
"Bali Aga" was confirmed on these grounds (Le Roux 1913:20; Roon
1916:254). A first survey of Bali Aga villages and their characteristics
was compiled by B. J. Haga, the Dutch administrator (*controleur*) of
the regency of Klungkung, who was responsible also for the regency
of Bangli, including the district of Kintamani (Haga 1924:453–469).[3]
Despite these attempts to collect empirical data on Bali Aga communities and, hence, to form an independent impression of their society,
the more powerful formative influence on Dutch perceptions of the
Bali Aga was to be their relationship with Bali's traditional elite.

Western images of Bali in general, and more specifically of its
secular rulers, have not always been a romantic glorification. During
the early stages of colonial rule, the predominant view was that Bali
had passed its earlier golden age under the leadership of the kings
of Gelgel. The island had apparently lost the peace and prosperity
induced by a once unified political system, under the later reign of
an exploitative and ferociously competitive host of minor despots.
Only colonial conquest would restore order and liberate the population from their slave-trading and opium-addicted petty kings (Geertz
1980:45; Vickers 1989). There is an uncanny similarity between this
Dutch discourse of "legitimate conquest" and the one created by invaders from Majapait long before the dawn of Bali's so-called colonial
period.

The solid and healthy foundation of Balinese society to the Dutch,
in this initial period of colonial contact, was not its courts and aristocracy but its villages and peasants. Particularly prominent as examples of original, pre-feudal Balinese "village republics" (Korn 1933)
were the few Bali Aga communities that had escaped the yoke of
"oriental despotism." In silent agreement with a well-known Marxist
argument, stating that the power of oriental aristocrats—in Bali and
elsewhere—had been based on the centralized organization of rice
irrigation and an associated taxation system (see Wittfogel 1957:53–
54), Dutch researchers argued that the Bali Aga, with their more localized dry rice and mixed gardening economy, had been able to remain
independent.

This independence was also defined in more general political and
historical terms. As Vickers puts it: "According to Liefrinck and his

successors, the original or Bali Aga villages in the mountains reflected the true, republican, if not democratic, nature of Balinese society, over which the fourteenth-century Javanese kingdom of Majapait had imposed a despotic aristocracy" (1989:90). Most of the Bali Aga villages presently known to scholars and tourists alike are those few that attracted the attention of colonial explorers in their initial search for pristine Balinese villages, among them Tenganan, Trunyan, and Sembiran.

The political motivation for seeking out presumably self-sufficient and autonomous Bali Aga village communities ceased quickly as the Dutch began to consider the advantages of governing the island through respected local agents. From a contemporary perspective, it may be difficult to appreciate why Balinese "self-government" (*zelf-bestuur*) became so attractive to the Dutch. Seeking to extract revenue from a complex and alien social and economic system and hampered by problems of communication, however, the members of a tiny contingent of Dutch administrators must have felt a desperate need for soliciting the help of cultural brokers. In 1938 it was thus decided to reinstate the very same degenerate despots whom they had initially denounced and defeated as the tamed and tethered heads of territorially defined regencies, each under the watchful eyes and heavy hand of a colonial officer (*controleur*).

The lively debate leading up to this change of attitude focused on the advantages of "self-rule" for a colonial economy. Van der Heyden (1925) and others began to argue that at least the larger of Bali's irrigation systems had to have been constructed with the help of once powerful kings, though many of them had since lost control over their management. By restoring their sovereignty and power to what it presumably had been in a classical Bali under the Gelgel dynasty, the Balinese economy could be expected to become productive once more and more easily taxable.[4]

Once the local aristocracy had been enlisted as administrative collaborators, acknowledged as the prime carriers of Balinese civilization, and nominated as cultural brokers, the initial interest in the peasant communities of the Bali Aga declined. A new and romantic enchantment with Bali's courtly culture became the paradigmatic feature of Western representations of Bali from the 1930s onward (Vickers 1989). Bali became the icon of a now peaceful tropical island paradise, a utopia in which a culturally sophisticated people lived in harmony with nature and the arts flourished under the graceful hands of talented natives and the sponsorship of traditional rulers. But most important, Bali was a land where ancient Hindu traditions from Majapait flourished still, or once again, under the benevolent rule of a new colonial government.

Once the proud Bali Aga peasants had been dismissed as relatively irrelevant to the flow of colonial power and profits, Western commentators instead began to endorse their social classification as a group of ancient survivors from a time before the dawn of Bali's Hindu civilization (e.g., Covarrubias 1937). Even so, a scholarly fascination with the Bali Aga phenomenon lingered on. This interest was essentially historical, fueled by the possibility of using their ancient tradition as a window to Bali's past. Blended in with these comparative historical and ethnological concerns was a degree of genuine admiration for the Bali Aga, who, for better or worse, had survived six centuries of Majapait rule.

On Isolation, Cultural Survival, and Complicity

Misrepresentations of the Bali Aga are not the most striking feature of Western discourses on Bali. More often, the mountain people have simply been ignored and forgotten. In the rich and voluminous ethnographic literature on Bali, rarely more than a glancing reference is paid to those presumed to be the island's aboriginal people. And that limited interest has declined in the historical course of Balinese studies. Much of what is now known about them is owed to the pioneering research efforts of Dutch colonial scholars.

Among the first of these scholars, Jacobs (1883) and Berg (1927) portrayed the Bali Aga as the last survivors from a distant past and as carriers of an ancient culture that predated the Indianization of the island. In a handful of remote and inward-looking communities, they were still guarding archaic traditions and an animist religion that had been discarded and superseded in the more accessible regions of Bali. This initial evaluation generated a basic research question that was to dominate Western approaches to an understanding of the Bali Aga phenomenon: How was it possible that a distinct and ancient Bali Aga culture had survived into the present?

The answers to this question about cultural survival have all revolved around a notion of isolation, though different researchers have periodically redefined its nature and cause. The fundamental flaw in this approach has been the imposition of an essentialist notion of culture on the lived traditions of the Bali Aga. With a concept of culture as a bounded system of similarities, cultural survival became a function of isolation. In order to persist, a culture had to have permanent and unassailable boundaries.

Drawing on insights gained in the course of more detailed ethnographic investigations and from a study of early Balinese inscriptions, Korn (1932f) and Goris (1932) later criticized the premature classification of the Bali Aga as a pre-Hindu people. V. E. Korn, perhaps Bali's most accomplished colonial ethnographer, pointed to the improbability of a group of people remaining untouched by the influx of Indic cultural elements on an island as small as Bali for more than a millennium (1932:77). Nevertheless, Korn retained the basic idea of physical remoteness and isolation as the most likely explanation for the evident cultural differences between Bali Aga and other Balinese villages. Instead of classing Bali Aga villages as pre-Hindu he designated them as old Balinese (*bali kuno*), as communities preserving an earlier "Hindu Balinese" tradition. He thus distinguished them from the appanage villages of a southern Balinese heartland that had been placed within the sphere of influence of the new courts of Bali.[5] The newcomers from Majapait had brought with them a new brand of "Javanese Hinduism," had promoted it from the fourteenth century onward, and had forgotten or ignored the highlands.

Korn managed to compile detailed and invaluable information on some of the local traditions of Bali Aga villages, particularly in his excellent ethnography of Tenganan in eastern Bali. In evaluating the general significance of the Bali Aga phenomenon, however, he is content to locate them beyond a Wallace line of cultural diffusion. Although his approach is broadly ethnohistorical and acknowledges a process of culture change, his view of culture is still essentialist. He assumes that the cultural difference between the two parties was already a given fact at the moment of their encounter and that it was more or less preserved by some kind of natural boundary. Assuming a limited sphere of courtly influence, Korn's basic explanation for a sustained Bali Aga culture difference is still physical remoteness.

Korn's explanation of Bali Aga survival in terms of cultural and political isolation from a newer, Hindu-Javanese Bali is difficult to sustain. The Javanization of Bali did not begin suddenly in A.D. 1343, though the popular Balinese mythology of Majapait origins may strive to convey this same claim. Old Javanese had become the court language of Hindu Balinese kings long before the time of the conquest. Contact among Balinese and East Javanese courts in particular had been very close and apparently quite cordial.[6] Pre-Majapait Bali therefore cannot be classified as untouched by cultural, political, and religious influences from Java, nor can it be assumed that the flow of inspiration was unidirectional. If changes to Balinese forms of religious practice and statecraft did occur after the Majapait conquest of the island, they probably cannot be explained in terms of a mechanical process of diffusion whereby "foreign" ideas were simply taken from Java to Bali as a ready-made cultural package.

It can be argued instead that cultural change in Bali unfolded in the specific context of a local political history. Ritual activities were part and parcel of statecraft in traditional Hindu kingdoms (*negara*) in Bali and beyond, as Clifford Geertz (1980) has shown. For the new political rulers from Majapait, controlling the island meant either becoming involved in an existing ritual order, creating a new one, or some mixture of both.

Creating an innovative version of Hindu religion and ritual or claiming to have brought such a new order with them would have had clear advantages. Rather than negotiate an involvement with a local ritual establishment, the new rulers may have preferred to build for themselves (and for their Brahmana priests) a new, controllable, and exclusive ritual world. Perhaps the claim that a cultural divide had already existed between the original inhabitants and the newcomers at the time of their initial encounter was politically more useful still than the alternative claim to have been strategic innovators after the fact. By arguing that a different and better knowledge of Hindu religion had been carried to Bali, the invaders provided themselves with a justification for the political takeover of the island in the form of a civilizing mission. The actual events are perhaps impossible to reconstruct with historical certainty. It is known, however, that the cultural traditions of Bali and Java were rather similar at the time of this "civilizing conquest" (Supomo 1995) and that these similarities have been vigorously denied thereafter.

Korn's history of cultural diffusion does not acknowledge the specific political interests of historical agents. By viewing culture as something people carry along unwittingly, like an infectious virus, rather than something they actively fashion, he underestimates the political motivations behind the culture changes initiated by Bali's new political elite. At the same time, he also belittles the historical agency of the mountain people in their response to this challenge. I would argue, to the contrary, that the cultural distinctiveness of the Bali Aga must be considered in the context of historically constructed and mutually negotiated Balinese categories of ethnicity.

It cannot be assumed that Bali Aga resilience against external domination arose independently of the specific features of their culture or, indeed, that their culture was left unaffected by their stance of resistance in relation to Bali Majapait. Furthermore, a mutual construction of cultural difference presumes some kind of shared communicative framework for negotiation. In this case, negotiation may have been facilitated by a shared (though provisional) cultural ideal that indigenous people should be granted some ritual authority as custodians of the land and that they in turn should eventually cede political power to illustrious stranger kings rather than oppose them. Assuming that the two parties shared a common dualist model of society, a cultural similarity that in itself facilitated a construction of difference, does not mean that culture is again essentialized as a fait accompli. I am suggesting instead that the actual division of political and symbolic capital between Bali Aga and Bali Majapait has been a matter decided by intense contestation and negotiation over the last six centuries of Balinese political history. A knowledge of the Bali Aga, as representatives of the past, may have been of genuine interest to Korn as well, as a scholar working within a diffusionist model of cultural history. But unfortunately, this knowledge carried an element of complicity in that it confirmed a Bali Majapait definition of the preconquest past.

The encounter with Majapait has not resulted in a total obliteration of Bali Aga traditions but in a degree of mutual recognition. Limited but important aspects of ritual authority remain vested in the mountain people. There is also evidence suggesting the mythical conquerors from Majapait did not manage to establish tight political or economic controls over the highlands following the fourteenth-century "invasion" or at any time thereafter.[7] Hence the question remains: How was this possible with the capitals of Gelgel and Klungkung no more than one or two days walking distance from the mountains?

While Korn's isolation hypothesis of cultural survival continues to be promoted by Western scholars as an answer to this question, there have been several attempts to dress this hypothesis in a different guise. One option was to argue that the "cultural survival" of the Bali Aga had nothing to do with either culture or agency. The notion of geographical isolation could be refined and reinvented as an isolation produced not by sheer distance but by the special characteristics of a specific environment. Rejecting earlier isolation hypotheses, some Western researchers began to suggest a relatively low population density and the limited productivity of a mountain economy had caused the Bali Aga to be ignored by the new secular rulers. In short, Bali Majapait had not been interested enough in the highlands and its sparse, poverty-stricken population to prompt any attempt to incorporate them more completely.

The earlier quoted excerpts from the Babad Pasek seem to suggest the contrary. If military expeditions were indeed organized in order to break Bali Aga political resistance, the suggested lack of political interest seems highly questionable. Similarly, there is no compelling reason to preclude that Bali's new rulers would have had an interest in controlling the material resources or the important trade routes leading through the mountains.

Clifford Geertz (1980) is among those who have continued to account for the cultural distinctiveness of Bali Aga society independently from a study of the dialectic processes of its cultural and political history. Unlike Korn and other Dutch predecessors, he suggests that the social organization and culture of Bali Aga villages is a random variant adapted to the specific demands of their isolated existence in a difficult natural environment. It is indeed beyond doubt that the ecological conditions of life in a tropical mountain environment, in the highlands of Bali and similarly in neighboring Java (Hefner 1985, 1990), have had an impact on people's economic and social practices. Nevertheless, I agree with Stephen Lansing's objections to this argument—"Contrary to Geertz, it may be observed that widely separated Bali Aga villages share a distinct cluster of characteristics which are not easily explainable by reference to the mountain environment in which they are found" (1983:114)—particularly since the very same traits can also be found in a number of coastal Bali Aga communities. Moreover, ecological and economical changes similar to those that have occurred in the Tengger Highlands of Java, as reported by Robert Hefner, have also taken place in the highlands of Bali. The mountain ecology of Bali thus cannot be regarded as a historical constant that would account in itself for a prolonged state of cultural stability. In addition, the mountains were always an integral part of the island's domestic economy as a whole, particularly given that Bali's point of access to a wider network of sea trade was its harbors along the northern (rather than southern) coast. Imported goods had to be transported through the highlands before reaching the southern courts, with export goods traveling in the opposite direction.

In one way or another, the Bali Aga have been portrayed as living fossils—preserved in a solid immutable layer of cultural or environmental bedrock or by the accidents of historical sedimentation. My alternative suggestion is that they survived as historical agents with specific interests and a specific arsenal of cultural and organizational resources, adapting their interests and culture to ever-changing conditions. If they were able to offer resistance to the political and cultural imperialism of Majapait, and the evidence seems to suggest that they were, then the question should be rephrased as follows: What specific cultural and social resources allowed the Bali Aga to be successful in their struggle for self-determination?

A more satisfactory explanation for the resilience and adaptability of Bali Aga traditions must be derived from a closer study of their content, and it is all the more unfortunate that few have cared to inquire further as to what these traditions entail.[8] The villages Tenganan, the topic of an entire monograph by Korn (1933), and Trunyan, famous for its presumably unique mortuary practices (Spies 1933), were indeed studied in considerable detail and later rediscovered by postcolonial researchers with different agendas (Ramseyer 1977; Danandjaja 1980). But while these initial and repeated village studies were ethnographically thorough, they only further entrenched the view of Bali Aga communities as isolated, quaint, archaic, and—from a pan-Balinese perspective—"marginal in the extreme" (Geertz 1959:1012).

The lack of interest in a discussion of the wider issues surrounding the Bali Aga phenomenon may be a reflection of their marginal status in the discourses of fellow Balinese who were acting as cultural brokers, but it is linked also to the inherent methodological limitations of a village studies paradigm that has been particularly prominent in the anthropology of Bali. Numerous monographs on individual Balinese villages, though they have provided detailed descriptions and invaluable insights into the cultural life of the Balinese, have revealed a bewildering array of forms. Observed variations among different types of local social organization and culture became a major theoretical challenge (Geertz 1959). The fact that the Bali Aga village type presented the greatest deviation from an already elusive norm may have prompted Geertz' frustrated remark on their marginality cited above.

General texts on Balinese culture have followed his lead by avoiding a serious examination of Bali Aga traditions, deeming them to be insignificant or exceedingly problematic in the context of their models. Even the few ethnographers who did conduct their village studies among Bali Aga people have been unable to deconstruct their well-established image as isolated and obscure remnants of a long declined and superseded civilization, though some of them may have striven to do so.

Dunker Schaareman's (1986) monograph on "Tatulingga," the pseudonym for a Bali Aga village in the regency of Karangasem, is an example that illustrates the basic problems of a village studies approach in relation to the Bali Aga. Schaareman's ethnography is of admirable quality and explicitly seeks to rekindle a discussion on Bali

Aga culture as a key to a better understanding of Balinese culture as a whole. By the same token, his study does not present evidence that would have demolished the isolated-community hypothesis of earlier researchers, or brought the attention such a reevaluation deserved. Its impact might have been more significant if the study had not been focused once again on an isolated village.[9] The author does not describe a striking pattern of regional ritual alliance in Karangasem, though he was most likely aware of its existence. Tenganan, in fact, maintains close and mutual ritual ties with several neighboring villages featuring a Bali Aga type of organization, among them "Tatulingga."[10]

For a general textbook account of Balinese culture as a whole, Stephen Lansing's *Three Worlds of Bali* (1983) is also unusual, in that it aspires toward a more general understanding of the Bali Aga. Lansing devotes an entire chapter of his book to a comparative description of the few Bali Aga villages that had been studied at the time. Drawing on these isolated village ethnographies, he concludes that "Bali Aga temples . . . do not link the members of their congregations to institutions that transcend the boundaries of the village. They are, instead, entirely inward looking" (1983:114). As is clear from Part 1 of this book, nothing could be further from the truth. Lansing's conclusion simply testifies to the utter lack of a regional (rather than village-based) study that would have granted the Bali Aga people an existence beyond their doubtful status as cultural oddities and isolates.

The entrenched perception of the Bali Aga as an isolated people continues to affect the few works that genuinely attempt to include them in a general account of Balinese culture. Howe (1989), for example, reiterates an insular community hypothesis, citing the above passage from Lansing. It is truly remarkable that even the most recent researchers report that in the mountain district of Kintamani, "intervillage alliances are largely absent. All the more remarkable is that the settlements, which are widely separated from one another, should show so many cultural similarities" (Leemann 1993:8, my translation).

The portrayal of the Bali Aga as isolates has ipso facto denied them recognition as an organized group of historical agents. As isolated communities, they could not have sustained a significant civilization of their own or have been key participants in the creation of an overall Balinese civilization that, in all its complexity, has long fascinated foreign observers. Seen through Western eyes, physical remoteness, cultural isolation, and economic insignificance were the only defenses available to protect small islands of Bali Aga tradition from more powerful, external cultural influences. Isolation came to be regarded as their raison d'être. Western researchers thus succumbed to a way of thinking that can be traced back to some of the oldest written accounts of other cultures: "Out of sight from subject shores, we have kept even our eyes free from the defilement of [foreign] tyranny. We, the last of the free, the most distant dwellers on earth, have been shielded till today by our very remoteness and by the obscurity in which it has shrouded our name" (Calgacus of Britain's speech before the final battle against the Romans, romantically reconstructed by the Roman historian Tacitus in his *Agricola*).[11]

The Bali Aga Phenomenon: Historical and Organizational Foundations

The isolation hypothesis of Bali Aga cultural survival is linked to a dominant Majapait-oriented reading of Balinese history. It is also founded on a paradigm of localized and localizing ethnographic study in Bali, in which regional forms of organization—beyond the *desa* and below the *negara*—have been largely ignored. The second factor has reinforced the first, insofar as village-focused studies among the Bali Aga have indirectly confirmed their state of isolation, both from the Majapait courts of Bali and from one another. The following is a re-examination of the history of Bali Aga culture and ethnicity—as they themselves tend to portray it.

Amplifying this alternative Bali Aga perspective may help to generate a more balanced perception of Balinese history in general. Bali Aga villages have cooperated and been united within regional institutions throughout that history, providing them with a specific organizational foundation in their struggle to maintain a separate set of traditions and a measure of self-determination—a situation that has been difficult to explain in terms of their isolation. Entering into a debate over their cultural survival, however, is not meant to deny that social change has been a constant companion to Bali Aga lives. My claim is merely that specific cultural, historical, and organizational factors have made it possible for the Bali Aga to exert some control over the direction these changes have taken.

The positioning of the contemporary Bali Aga as a distinctly indigenous and marginal minority people stands in stark contrast to the prominent position occupied by their communities in a pre-Majapait Balinese history. This early history has become either a matter of popular mythology or a research topic for prehistorians. But this past was a formative and integral period in the history of Balinese civilization. It was a time when the first Hindu-Buddhist states began to flourish on this island and across mainland and insular Southeast Asia. Ironically, Bali was integrated then within a larger world of Indic civilization rather than being isolated, as was the fate of classical Bali Majapait after the Islamization of the Indonesian archipelago.

The earliest written sources of Balinese history are royal edicts issued by early Balinese kings. Inscribed on durable bronze plates (*prasasti*), the overwhelming majority of these edicts are addressed to the Bali Aga communities in the central highlands and along the northern coast that have been the subject of this study (compare figures 2 and 4 above). They may appear as remote settlements of the interior nowadays, far from a tourist-invaded coast, but mountain villages were the site of a bustle of activity for several hundred years from the ninth century onward. The royal inscriptions contain valuable information about the privileges of mountain villages (not yet classed as belonging to a separate ethnic group), the building and economic support of monasteries, the existence of a stringent taxation and ritual obligation system, and the regulation of travel and trade from the northern coast into the highlands.[12]

The courts of early Indic states in Southeast Asia were not always established in the vicinity of coastal trading cities. In many cases (e.g., Angkor), inland capitals controlled overseas trade as well as domestic production from the relative safety of the interior (Heesterman 1989). In the Balinese case, however, the location of the political centers or courts of the earlier Indic kingdoms has remained difficult to ascertain. One hypothesis is that they too lay in the agricultural hinterland of the interior. The most likely location of Bali's political center, at least for the period immediately preceding the arrival of Majapait, is thought to have been somewhere in the Pejeng region, famous for its many archeological remains (Bernet-Kempers 1991).

The earliest *prasasti*, however, were issued to villages higher up in the mountains where archeological research has been sadly lacking. There are also some later literary sources, as already discussed, explicitly referring to a relatively late downhill shift of the royal court (*puri*) from Puri Balingkang in the Kintamani area to Puri Pejeng. A downward expansion, from its original center on the island's upper slopes toward the sea, has also been attributed to the institution of the *subak*, the system of rice irrigation management that is commonly regarded as one of the pillars of Balinese civilization (Korn 1932:102–103).[13] Another piece of evidence supporting the hypothesis of an early inland center higher up in the Balinese mountains is their physical proximity to early interisland trade ports. For Bali, the only shore open to interisland trade networks was in the north. The steep northern coast is the one section of Bali's shoreline with natural harbors facing the relatively calm Java Sea. The important trade routes from India and China to the spice islands of Eastern Indonesia passed Bali on its northern side, whereas its southern shores were largely inaccessible.[14] The highlands were therefore of great strategic importance as a gateway to the protected hinterland of Bali and an ideal site from which to control a bidirectional flow of trade goods.

There are some clues in the inscriptions that may explain why Bali's central highlands and northeastern coast were of special significance to the rulers of Bali during the many centuries of Indianized civilization before the Majapait conquest. This period, as far as is known, began with the establishment of the Warmadewa dynasty and lasted for some time after the reign of King Jayapangus. Royal edicts from this period are addressed to communities in the mountains and along the northeastern coast who are still united as participants in a network of ritual alliances or domains (*banua*). The domains of highland Bali are reminiscent of similar institutions on a number of eastern Indonesian islands beyond the range of Indic cultural influence. They may thus predate the formation of Indic states in the archipelago. Nevertheless, the first Hindu kings of Bali are likely to have built a political system or state (*negara*) by using these ritual forms of regional organization as its foundation. They may also have adapted and transformed *banua* to better suit their specific purposes.

Several of the temples at the centers of contemporary ritual domains are mentioned in the earliest royal edicts. They appear to have played a prominent role in statecraft, particularly in the collection of tax revenue. Most prominent among them is Pura Pucak Penulisan, located in the village of Sukawana, home to Bali's oldest bronze plate inscription (Sukawana A 1, A.D. 882). The first direct reference to the temple is found in Prasasti Dausa A 2 (A.D. 1061), in which the king grants the people of Parcanigayan their request to be released from duties as long-standing participants in the cult of Bhatara Mandul, whose statue is located and venerated in Pura Penulisan until this day. The text illustrates that Pura Penulisan and other temples have been in a position of regional importance for as long as a millennium.

Contemporary *banua* maintain traditional connections to the coast, in terms of both ritual and trade. These links point directly northward, to villages on the eastern coast of Buleleng, which can be reached on foot in a few hours. Excavations near the coastal villages of Pacung and Julah (Ardika and Bellwood 1991) have confirmed that Indian trade goods first reached Bali's northeastern shores some two thousand years ago. Possibly, there was also direct contact with Indian traders long before local Hindu kingdoms were established. Moreover, the villages between Pacung and Les are mentioned in royal edicts from as early as A.D. 922 (Sembiran A 1), indicating that they lay within the sphere of influence of the Warmadewa kings who issued these earliest inscriptions. In order to be able to participate in interisland sea trade, Balinese kings must have collected local goods for the purpose of exchange, as well as securing routes of transportation for local produce to be carried to the coast and imported valuables to be taken back inland.

Until recently traders from the coast came by foot with their pack-horses to visit the ancient market of Kintamani, still held on every third day. The market forms the economic center of the entire highlands and may well have been among Bali's oldest inland centers of trade. One inscription (Prasasti Kintamani E 3a, A.D. 1200) mentions trading privileges held by the mountain people of Kintamani. They were granted permission to trade with coastal villages—among them Les, Tejakula, Bondalem, Julah, and Tajun—a privilege explicitly denied to others.[15] Until it was shifted by the Dutch in the 1930s, Kintamani Market was located in Kuta Dalem, the oldest part of Sukawana, a stone's throw from the ritual center of Pura Penulisan. The proximity of the two centers, of trade and ritual, allows for speculation that a political center may also have been situated nearby. This is what local people believe to have been the case, given that "*kuta dalem*" means "the fortified town of the king" and that legends speak of a palace located there before a shift to nearby Puri Balingkang.

All of the mountain and coastal communities mentioned in the *prasasti* are nowadays led by the elders of a bipartite council (*keraman desa, keraman banua*), headed by one or several pairs of priest-leaders (*kubayan, bau*), as is characteristic for Bali Aga communities in general. The inscriptions frequently address pairs of village leaders with these very same titles and are issued to the *keraman desa* or *keraman banua* as the general organization of local communities.[16] In other words, the edicts suggest that a Bali Aga type of village organization was the Balinese norm rather than an exception in that period. Even in contemporary Bali, Bali Aga villages are much more common than is generally believed. The sheer number of Bali Aga communities (see Figure 1) suggests that this organizational variant is not as obscure as it has been deemed, but remains a viable and important form of organization for a significant portion of the island.[17]

The strategically located Bali Aga villages of the central highlands and the ancient harbors along the northern coast with whom they still maintain important ties seem to have been some of the first settlements to become involved in early state formation and Indian-ization in Bali. Insofar as can be deduced from the evidence that they were indeed prominent in Balinese society throughout a preconquest period, it may no longer seem surprising that they were also the last to fall under the cultural influence of the fourteenth-century arrivals from Majapait and loath to accept their claim of a civilizing mission. The new rulers may have found it difficult to challenge a well-instituted regional network of Bali Aga communities or to undermine their concerted ritual authority over Bali's sacred mountain temples.

Organizational flexibility, genuine social change, and constant innovation must have been central ingredients to the persistence of a living Bali Aga tradition. Perhaps no other part of Bali was as imme-diately exposed to Indian notions of kingship and early processes of state formation as were the highlands and the northern coast. More-over, the contemporary ritual domains of this region are not simply an organizational relic from long lost kingdoms but an ingenious adaptation to a more recent condition of foreign rule. For example, if relations among participants within a *banua* were once regulated by the higher authority of an indigenous Balinese king, then the main-tenance of an autonomous ritual domain without a king (or under a distant and dissociated Bali Majapait king) must have demanded a different set of controls in order to avoid a collapse of the association.

This brief portrayal of early Balinese history from a Bali Aga perspec-tive identifies the Bali Aga as possible heirs to Bali's first Hindu king-doms, a well-advanced civilization hidden away by deliberate omission, distortion, and selective historical amnesia within the textual tradition and identity of post-Majapait Bali. As C. Geertz has phrased it, "In Bali-nese eyes, the foundation of a Javanese court, first at Samprangan and then at Gelgel . . . created not just a center of power—that had existed before—but a standard of civilization. The Majapait conquest was (and is) considered the great watershed of Balinese history be-cause it cut off the ancient Bali of animal barbarism from the rena-scent Bali of aesthetic elegance and liturgical splendor" (1980:15).

The actual history of Bali may never be known in full, though there is evidence that the people of the highlands played a significant role in it. In presenting this alternative view of Balinese history, my main concern is to show that the well-maintained "memory" of their former Bali-wide centrality, whether it be historically founded or imagined, and their enduring status and unity as the custodians of major ritual centers have made it possible and worthwhile for the

people of the mountains to preserve a distinct culture and some independence from the new political centers of the south.[18]

Regional cooperation through participation in ritual domains has
been a major factor in making this achievement possible. At the same
time, *banua* have also been a podium for status competition among
the people of the highlands, a point of reference—other than the new
courts—to which the Bali Aga could orient their own social ambitions. An emphasis on regional organization thus provides a more
plausible explanation for the resilience of Bali Aga culture and society
to external control or absorption than the isolation hypothesis proposed on the basis of earlier village studies.

As Paul Feyerabend once suggested, "Successful research does not
obey general standards; it relies now on one trick, now on another,
and the moves that advance it are not always known to the movers
[in advance]" (1987:281). Indeed, the merits a regional study of Bali
Aga society would have over another village study were not known to
me in advance of my research. It was a stroke of fortune that regional intervillage alliances and similarities among Bali Aga communities came to my attention in the early stages of fieldwork. Ironically, my initial anxiety over choosing the ideal site for an intended
village study in the district of Kintamani propelled me to consider
more than one community. In the process of conducting preliminary inquiries at a number of possible fieldwork locations, it soon
became obvious that there were striking similarities and important
regional ties among the villages concerned and that a regional study
was called for.

My decision to conduct such a study was not taken lightly. The
project would involve much commuting among villages scattered
over a large area, traveling on steep trails or unsealed roads and often
hampered by the cold and wet climate of the highlands. The real
obstacle, however, was conceptual rather than logistical. Few models
were available in the ethnographic literature on Bali regarding how
a regional social phenomenon was to be investigated. One important conceptual inspiration, however, was Stephen Lansing's work on
regional irrigation-temple networks.[19]

Toward an Ethnography of Critical Engagement

Oh lord (*ratu*) who rests on my head, who is seated here. I am presenting these "offerings of reporting" (*bakti mapiuning*). Here is one
who has come from afar, who has lived here, and who now requests
your permission to leave (*nunas pamit*). He says he will write about this

land, your sacred domain, about the ancient knowledge that has passed
from mouth to mouth, from the root to the tips. What we could tell him
was only what little we know, and he has listened. But all knowledge
comes from you. Ratu, we ask your blessing so that the people of "Java"
(the outside world) will come to value our tradition and the people of
the plains will remember their origin. May he return safely. (Sukawana
priest informing the deity at Penulisan of my departure in 1994)

I now return to the ethical question about representation that I raised
earlier, to reflect on it from the perspective of the Bali Aga. Can prac-
titioners of social science indeed afford to abandon their task of
promoting cross-cultural understanding, and if not, how can this be
achieved?

The preceding analysis has been carried out on the assumption
that ethnographers, in particular, cannot at all afford to abandon the
moral project of challenging biased popular and politicized systems
of representational knowledge, no matter whether such a bias is encountered in a "participant" or an "observer" model of society. But
the task is not simply one of deconstruction. Representational models
of Balinese society carry a degree of legitimate validity insofar as
they have been coproduced, at least in part, in the context of historical encounters. They are the product of complex negotiations conducted in a spirit of competitive cooperation and always involve an
element of mutual historical transformation.[20] This element is anticipated in Balinese models of their society, with their prominent focus
on time, encounter, and change. In short, knowledge and culture
are founded on intersubjectivity rather than belonging within clearly
bounded islands of subjectivity. This model hints at a way of acquit-
ting anthropological knowledge as well from the charge of being intrinsically subjective.

The analysis has also shown, however, that people struggle to increase or protect their symbolic capital at the expense of others and
that different persons, groups, or societies may have unequal opportunities to participate in particular processes of negotiation as they
unfold within a specific historical context and under specific economic
and political conditions. Subjectivity may be carved out from a primary sphere of intersubjectivity, by means of essentializing notions
of self and other. Nevertheless, artificial cultural fences, once they
have been constructed, are real enough to have practical consequences
for those incarcerated within them.

Two general questions arise in the context of these observations.
What does an ethnography of moral engagement entail, and how is it to
be tailored to a variety of historical contexts and material conditions?

We live in a world where representations are often formed on the basis of first impressions and where knowledge may be wielded, to varying degrees, as an instrument of domination. Awareness of this situation may call for a general critique of cultural knowledge, but it does not clarify how to address specific situations, given that such knowledge can also be embedded, to varying degrees, in a context of genuine social cooperation. The preceding analysis of representational processes and relevant historical conditions across some very different contexts—in Bali Aga society, in Balinese society as a whole, and in the colonial and postcolonial Western literature on Balinese society—has shown just how much variation there can be across different symbolic economies, depending on the distribution of economic and political resources among the people involved. This comparison can serve as a model for understanding the conditions that give rise to genuine knowledge or knowledge abuse and for tailoring a methodology of moral engagement to these variable conditions.

My experiences as an ethnographer among the Mountain Balinese propel me to call for a fundamental and general critique of all cultural representation systems. Representing and being represented by others should be regarded as matters of universal strategic interest to all social agents. In this general sense, every person has the potential to be a biased representor or a victim of biased representation. The process of representation, however, also fulfills a second and equally general purpose, relating to the basic communicative interests of human beings. A first answer to the question of where to direct the moral project of cultural critique is, therefore, toward every form of representation—but without lapsing into an unwarranted wholesale cynicism with regard to human nature.

This generalized mode of critique is particularly relevant to situations where acts of mutual representation occur on a level playing field. In this hypothetical situation no participant is positioned in advance as a potential victim of misrepresentation by factors outside the process of representation itself, because power and wealth are distributed rather evenly among the mutually representing agents. Even then, strategic interests remain important, and corresponding representational biases must be anticipated. The representational knowledge system in this type of society is likely to permit relatively free argumentation concerning a wide array of conflicting validity claims. The nature of this competition is communicative. Contradictory claims must appeal to a shared conceptual framework in reference to which their validity pretension can be assessed. Apart from this basic need for communicative cooperation, participants would also be propelled to build mutually acceptable representations of one another in order to establish a foundation for practical social cooperation and joint action. The representational system would tend to fluctuate between moments of compromise and cooperation and times of conflict and renegotiation, with corresponding shifts in the overall flow of mutual approval and an associated distribution of symbolic capital.

The conditions I have just described were found to prevail, to a limited and varying degree, in the context of interactions among different Bali Aga groups. The predominant (but not the only) expression of a strategic interest in representation was a pursuit of symbolic capital in relation to ritual status. The critique of the negotiated knowledge structures of this society did not warrant a cynical judgment. Even though strategic interests were evident in people's interactions, systems of mutual representations in Bali Aga society were found to contain effective checks and balances. A moral imperative for a generalized critical stance was still operative in this case, but it related not so much to a preexisting pattern of flagrant domination as to a potential for creating such a pattern. There is always a danger that ethnographers may lend authority to the particular claims of a particular group and thereby upset an existing state of relative equity.[21]

The need to remain critical of individual knowledge claims also relates to the epistemology of ethnographic inquiry. Even in societies where representational knowledge structures are rather freely negotiated and not overly tarnished by inequitable economic and power relations, ethnographers are well served by a measured skepticism in relation to any particular validity claim, as raised by a particular person or faction. A proper account of a contested representational system, in its full historical actuality, must reflect the momentary balance among competing truths, that is, the limited practical consensus on which participants base their collective and cooperative performances. Through a comparison of competing narratives, an ethnographic account must also identify the common conceptual foundations on which they are variously constructed and the common idiom in which they express their different claims.

The suggestion that there is a general and moderate need for critique in relation to all representational knowledge structures must be qualified for situations where the game of representation is not played on a level playing field. Where there is an inequitable distribution of economic and political resources among the populations or persons concerned, the moral project of cultural critique may still be directed everywhere, but not with uniform intensity. How they are represented by others on account of their cultural identity is a universal practical concern to any group of people, in that status is vested in the opinions of others. But variations in the object and intensity of this concern can be momentous. Where economical and political relations are markedly skewed, the knowledge structures of a symbolic economy may reflect, reinforce, or help to escalate these material inequities. In such a situation cultural critique may need to become skewed in the opposite direction. Popular knowledge claims that are in part based on coercion rather than on free argumentation or other social validation procedures may need to be subverted.

The contemporary relationship between the Bali Aga and other Balinese represents such a case to some degree. The mutual representations constructed by the two groups do not issue from positions of equal power and wealth. While the Bali Aga have contested their misrepresentation in the narratives of changing Balinese elites, their negotiation efforts have departed from a position of political and economic disadvantage. Expressed in Gramscian terminology, one could argue that a hegemonic discourse of domination can be distinguished from a counterhegemonic discourse of resistance. The projects of hegemony and resistance are inconceivable, however, unless there is some cultural provision for mutual intelligibility among proponents of politically strong and weak validity claims. Both projects assume that a cultural self and other are bound together in a larger order of things. In other words, people are still communicating and expecting a limited degree of cooperation and acceptance from one another even in a setting where there may be considerable hostility. Nevertheless, an ethnographer should not endorse or even reinforce a representational model that exists in symbiosis with a pattern of political domination.

A critical response to a local representational knowledge structure that is in the service of power must be seen as an act of intervention and must be very carefully considered. A first precautionary step is to determine the actual degree of disparity in political power among the proponents of two competing discourses in a society. This assessment may begin with an analysis of the discourses of the more powerful group for their intended effect, but it also requires measuring the actual successes (or failure) of these discourses in achieving the intended social outcomes. Rather than overestimating the power of hegemonic discourses or fetishizing resistance, this assessment must be realistic.

It has been argued that the Bali Aga have been disempowered by a long process of marginalization, at least from the perspective of modern Balinese society. I have noted, however, that their village communities have retained a greater measure of local autonomy under a modern state administration than many southern Balinese communities, precisely by appealing to their local traditions as Bali Aga. In the larger context of Balinese Hindu religion, the Bali Aga may have been marginalized as a recalcitrant opposition to the authoritative ritual knowledge of southern Balinese Brahmana priests and, more recently, as a people with supposedly primitive or animist religious traditions. Nevertheless, they have retained almost complete local ceremonial autonomy as well as a measure of ritual authority in relation to Bali as a whole, again on account of their Bali Aga identity. This assessment does not lend itself to a portrayal of resistance as a simple product of necessity. Resistance for the Bali Aga is a particular stance that in part has been pushed upon them and in part has been embraced deliberately as a special source of symbolic capital.

A further need for caution relates to the question of what different local discourses set out to achieve in the first place. In this case, the fact that the discourse of Bali's traditional feudal elite was partially received by the Bali Aga and vice versa may indicate a hidden complicity among the two parties. With the Bali Aga claiming a measure of autonomy and ritual authority as representatives of an ancient indigenous Bali and southern dynasties of kings claiming political authority as descendants of powerful royal strangers, the most disadvantaged group may in fact have been the majority of Balinese commoners who had access to neither of the two forms of authority.

Another problem is that knowledge structures and patterns of domination are historical and changeable phenomena. With the advent of colonial rule and the subsequent establishment of a modern Indonesian state, political and economic capital was partially redistributed in Bali. This redistribution has not been to the advantage of the Bali Aga. The changing discourses of urban elites in southern Bali have tended to characterize them in an increasingly negative way, though for the time being, the highland people still remain useful as a contrast to their own modernity. On a more practical note, however, modernity has also become an ally to the highland people. For example, many Bali Aga farmers are now becoming rather wealthy as a result of their efforts to incorporate new technologies and improved agricultural production methods. As a result, it may not be long before it will become very difficult indeed to portray them as an economically backward people. A critique of a local politics of representation must therefore be sensitive to historical changes, some of which may have been triggered by Western intervention.

Morally engaged ethnographers (or ethnohistorians) may also

encounter far more extreme situations, where struggles on an uneven political and economic playing field are not tempered by an element of regulated cooperation. Representational knowledge structures may still be important in such cases, in that they may "justify" systematic dispossession or even genocide, and thus illustrate a general need for justification even in relation to blatant abuses of power. The knowledge that enables a project of forceful domination in the first place, however, tends to be more technical than it is cultural. The critique of domination patterns sustained by physical violence is no longer a task requiring a special anthropological understanding of the cultures involved. To justify morally a protest on behalf of victims of systematic violence or intimidation, it should be sufficient to know that they are human beings. Fortunately, contemporary relations between the Bali Aga and other sectors of Balinese society do not reach such extremes. In its colonial and postcolonial experience, however, Bali has indeed suffered periods of violent upheaval.

Images of bloodshed in paradise are most frequently associated with the colonial conquest of Bali and in particular with the massacre of many Balinese aristocrats as they ran, armed only with ceremonial daggers and spears, into the heavy gunfire of Dutch soldiers. These events must not be forgotten, particularly insofar as the long-term effects of colonial rule are still felt today. Violence has not been the prerogative of Western colonial powers, however, nor did it cease in Bali with Indonesian independence. There were perhaps more Balinese killed during the collapse of the Sukarno regime in 1965 and the subsequent anti-Communist purge than ever fell victim to Dutch colonial aggression. Under the so-called new order regime of his successor, former president Suharto, there have been other forms of violence. In recent years, for example, many southern Balinese people were forcefully dispossessed of their land and compensated inadequately or not at all. This dispossession occurred in the wake of tourism-related development projects in which family members and corporate allies of President Suharto were deeply implicated. Similar projects were envisaged for highland Bali. Particularly worrying for my hosts was the proposal to establish a large golf course at Lake Batur. What will happen to these plans following the demise of Suharto's regime is uncertain. If they are revived, one form of intervention from the position of a social scientist would be to bring the concerns of local people to world attention.

The proposal for an ethnography of moral engagement remains problematic even if these precautions are observed. The main problem is that the cultural critique implicit in this approach is no longer focused exclusively on the ethically safe target of the anthropologist's own culture. Critique across cultural boundaries may well be interpreted by some as an unwarranted meddling in the affairs of other people on questionable moral grounds. But there are at least four important arguments to the contrary.

Taking the position of an unconcerned bystander to a struggle between others, particularly on an uneven playing field, is an act of passive complicity. There is no neutral moral ground to walk on for people, for example, who turn their backs to a rape scene or an act of genocide. Even where violations occur on a comparatively moderate scale, as in the present case, the same basic principle applies.

A second issue arises for Western anthropologists whenever they encounter a scenario of cultural politics in which their historical predecessors have already intervened. In many cases Western scholarship has been the accomplice of colonial rule, and in Bali, at least, the colonizers also collaborated with local elites and thereby helped to legitimize and strengthen local structures of domination with their foreign knowledge and power. Presenting a people like the Bali Aga people in a more positive light may help to balance the score in an otherwise irrevocable history of Western colonial intervention.

A third consideration is that the analysis of strategic aspects in non-Western knowledge systems may help to define the problem of biased representation in more general terms than has been possible by a critique of Western knowledge alone. Failing to perform such an analysis is to lend support to the fallacious notion that power has been and remains the historical prerogative of Western nations.

Finally, and on a more positive note, the analysis of non-Western power-knowledge systems may actually reveal that some other cultures have found a rather effective way of balancing strategic and cooperative interests within their societies by adopting a specific mode of representation. In this case, to engage in the critical analysis of a particular non-Western knowledge structure does not imply that the result of the analysis will be nothing but criticism. On the contrary, the analysis of such a culture-specific knowledge system may reveal that it successfully accommodates an inevitable potential for difference without precipitating severe economic, political, or symbolic forms of oppression. I am suggesting that Bali Aga society is commendable in this sense and that ethnographers stand to learn much from an analysis of their representational procedures and the resulting knowledge systems. The same may also be true to some degree of Balinese knowledge systems in general.[22]

A different way of assessing the merit of a proposal for a generalized critique of cultural knowledge is to contrast it with more narrow alternatives. Examples will illustrate the point where the present study departs from more familiar approaches.

In self-critical recognition of a link between power and knowledge, and prompted by accusations of complicity from some of their non-Western colleagues, Western anthropologists have struggled to come to terms with their predecessors' involvement in a history of colonial domination. A postcolonial project of researching and deconstruct-ing colonial disguises of power has offered a welcome but temporary solution. By focusing on the past, anthropologists have been able to escape their deep sense of apprehension about becoming implicated in the creation or legitimization of neocolonial power structures in the present. There is a sad irony in the timing of this response. In a world marked by increasing cross-cultural contact, cooperation, and conflict, there is perhaps a greater demand for debunking popular myths and mutual prejudices between people of different cultures than there ever was before. A further irony is that postcolonial studies unwittingly celebrate the former power of Western colonial empires. By focusing their attention on it, they implicitly define the often brief historical period of their colonization as the key to understanding all there is to know about contemporary postcolonial societies.

These problems are reflected in the state of contemporary Bali-nese studies. Changing images of Bali promoted by foreign scholars, expatriates, colonial administrators, and a rapidly expanding tourism industry have been examined critically for their political implications. One example is an important study by Adrian Vickers (1989). This and similar research has exposed how specific images of Bali evolved in the course of the island's colonial and postcolonial history. Western representations are also shown to have been instrumental in the crea-tion and legitimization of a colonial structure of domination. Vickers argues that the legacy of a colonial project "to know Bali" is still felt in contemporary Western images, where the island features as a fetishized object of consumer fantasies and a commodity for interna-tional tourism.

This and similar analyses are enlightening and convincing, but they have a number of limitations. Vickers is to be commended for acknowledging the existence of a diversity of Balinese self-images and of another, local power structure (1989:6–7). But the local "image makers" whose views he finally turns to in search of a counterweight to the excesses of Western fantasy are not members of a dominated peasantry—they are Balinese emperors, kings, queens, and princes.

Peasant voices, it seems, do not carry sufficient weight as a counter-discourse to colonial narratives.

Dutch images of Bali and colonial accounts of the island's conquest have been juxtaposed more directly and systematically with Balinese self-representations in a recent study by Margaret Wiener (1995). In the course of her Foucaultian and postcolonial analysis, Wiener contrasts the narratives by which the foreign colonizers expressed their sense of legitimate power with a very different perception of the world. Her counterweight, however, is again the narratives that supported precolonial power structures and the views on the historical advent of colonial rule in Bali as entertained by the island's aristocratic elite. The study discovers in the narratives of the paramount dynasty of Balinese kings in Klungkung an idiom and conceptual model of power relations that remained more or less alien and invisible to the Dutch invaders. The focus on "local" narratives of power allows Wiener to move away from an exclusive preoccupation with the deconstruction of Western colonial or neocolonial narratives. Balinese narratives of power, however, are not subjected to the same process of deconstruction as are colonial narratives. This omission leaves two important issues unresolved.

For centuries before the arrival of the Dutch, the kings of Klungkung had maintained a Balinese structure of domination and had legitimized their power with mythical histories of another, much earlier invasion. They claimed, and still claim, that their royal Javanese ancestors legitimately conquered and colonized Bali in the fourteenth century. The memory of this event was carefully preserved (and constructed), as Wiener's study also illustrates, for example, in complex genealogical records of royal succession. These acts of legitimization suggest that a correlation between power and knowledge structures is not confined to the unique historical phenomenon of Western imperialist expansion. Intent on viewing the discourse of a precolonial Balinese elite as a discourse of resistance to colonial domination, however, Wiener does not expose Klungkung narratives of power as a discourse that has produced a class of dominated people and a world of subjugated knowledge all of its own. Those dominated are as invisible in the discourses of Bali's traditional elite as a world of magical power in Klungkung was invisible to the Dutch. The world according to a small group of aristocratic Balinese who have maintained some of their power to this day is still a world apart from a "native point of view" conceived in a democratic sense. Amplifying the voice of this local elite (now that the Dutch are no longer in power) may actually reinforce a knowledge structure that even now is striving to silence the vast majority of Balinese commoners, as well as the Bali Aga.

It is significant that the somewhat derisive term "Bali Aga," for example, cannot be traced to a Western imagination. A distinction of this kind is evidently absent in the oldest written sources on Balinese history and society. The designation first appears in Balinese palm-leaf manuscripts (*lontar*), some of which have been referred to in this book. These texts often defy accurate dating (Davies 1992), and hence it has not been possible to ascertain when exactly the label "Bali Aga" first became a designation for a separate ethnic group on this island. It is highly likely, however, that at least some of the texts predate the Dutch colonization of Indonesia and Bali.[23] There is also no hint in the earliest Dutch reports about the Mountain Balinese that the label was invented by the colonizers. On their sporadic excursions from the centers of a reconstructed Balinese political organization to the distant mountains, Western explorers and colonial administrators did not come empty-handed. They carried the baggage of expectations about the Bali Aga, heaped on them by a Balinese elite with whom they had come to cooperate as mutual accomplices in ruling the island. I hope that in declaring its complicity, I have eluded in the present attempt to pursue an ethnography of engagement some of the pitfalls of unconsidered complicity.

By demonstrating that local conflicts of representation have been a crucial dimension of Balinese lives and political history from the beginning, this study has departed from the subject matter of most other postcolonial studies. My aim in stressing the inequities of a local politics of representation has not been to shift attention away from the injustice of colonialism. My project has been to show that a need to share knowledge for the purpose of cooperation and a simultaneous struggle to control that knowledge for strategic purposes are both inevitable and that the tension between these conflicting needs defines an essential human conundrum. Assuming that all societies have had to find a way of living with this tension, anthropology has a contribution to make by assessing the relative merit of the solutions they have found and by comparing the different conditions under which they have negotiated the problem.

Human Encounters and
the Intersubjective Construction of Knowledge

The problem of representation cannot be resolved through deconstruction, as even a deconstruction is itself a form of representation.

The crux of the matter is the question of how one's subjectivity and self-interest affects the way one represents others. One way to approach this question is to invert it by examining the self-concept, the theory people have about themselves, on the assumption that the two are closely related.

As cognitive psychologists define it, the self-concept is "a theory that the individual has unwittingly constructed about himself as an experiencing, functioning individual" (Epstein 1973:407).[24] The possibility of drawing inspiration from such a contemporary psychology of the self is based on the assumption that a better understanding of the processes of representation that lead to the development of personal self-concepts will be useful also in trying to understand how collective self-representations or culture-concepts are formed. Both processes, even at an interpersonal level, are intrinsically intersubjective or social rather than resting solely on the mental performances of a solitary individual subject.

The paramount domain of reality in which knowledge claims about the self and the other are expressed, validated, and revised is a world of intersubjective encounters. It is in reference to this shared sphere of social interaction that representations of self or other can be said to have meaning and can be evaluated as true or false. The knowing human subject is a social subject, and theories of knowledge therefore must contemplate self-representations and representations of others as products of intersubjective rather than narrowly conceived psychological or subjective processes. Representational knowledge is founded on competitive subjective interpretations of cooperative intersubjective exchanges of approval. The intersubjective nature of this process acts as an intrinsic constraint on subjective bias and, hence, offers a way of meeting the challenge of subjectivity in relation to ethnographic knowledge.

Although it can be argued that representational knowledge never directly corresponds to some kind of numinous self or other, this does not mean that such representations are intrinsically false. From the perspective of an intersubjective or performance (rather than correspondence) theory of truth, the social constructedness of knowledge does not herald the end of epistemology (see Habermas 1984: 94). One comfort for the epistemology of the social sciences lies in the fact that subjective biases arising within the *process* of representation are phenomena accessible through empirical research and can be subjected to critical analysis. The more fundamental comfort, at a level of *content*, is that all representational knowledge (including ethnographic knowledge) is contested and can be appropriately validated within the intersubjective field to which it belongs as long as the conditions of the field concerned allow for voluntary association and free negotiation.

For ethnography, an intersubjective theory of truth implies that reliable knowledge of other people and cultures is obtainable through a continuing process of mutual engagement in a world in which free intersubjective knowledge production is possible. Like the ritual domains of highland Bali, though perhaps no more so, the intersubjective field circumscribed by anthropology in its current historical and institutional context meets these requirements. Anthropologists are able to negotiate, contest, or validate each other's representations, and they generally can do so without having to fear violence or economic penalties. While these principles may be compromised in some cases, the more serious problem may not lie in the character but in the scope of anthropology as a field of intersubjectivity.

Until recently there were no non-Western anthropologists, which meant that none of the people represented in classical ethnographic texts were able to participate in this field, except perhaps at its fringe —as informants, less often as readers, and, occasionally, as nonprofessional commentators. This situation is changing quickly in the wake of a globalization the effects of which have been acutely felt in the academic world. There are exciting opportunities on the horizon, given that anthropology is now taught in universities around the world, and ethnography is conducted both at home and abroad, by both Western and non-Western scholars. In the interim, however, one would have to say that the validity pretensions of anthropological knowledge must confine themselves to the scope of the limited intersubjective field on which this knowledge is currently produced.

The contemporary world, outside of such special social contexts as the ritual-focused associations among highland Balinese villages or the knowledge-focused associations among academics (akin in their unusually strong emphasis on symbolic economy), is not usually like this. It is a world in which fields of intersubjective knowledge are typically skewed by disparities of power and wealth within the social performance contexts from which they arise. Social scientists are presented with a moral challenge and a formidable task as they themselves are becoming more and more politically marginalized in a globally dominant discourse of power and economic rationalism. Like the Bali Aga, we may still enjoy a certain status as the apolitical custodians of a "sacred" domain of relatively disinterested knowledge, but the shrinking relevance of this domain can only be halted in the course of a conscious historical struggle.[25]

Anthropologists cannot pretend that the political problem of knowledge production in the typically less-than-level playing fields of the real world can be resolved by social science simply through an evocation of the ghostly voices of others at the level of the ethnographic text. What we can do, until anthropology has become a truly global and politically equitable project of mutual understanding, is to remain critically aware of the cognitive biases that affect all knowing subjects and of the embeddedness of all knowledge claims in intersubjective validation processes unfolding under sometimes adverse historical conditions. By exploring regularities in patterns of subjective bias and systems of economic or political domination, as well as recognizing the emancipatory potential of intersubjective knowledge, social scientists from across the world are still able to contribute much to a better mutual understanding among the peoples of the world.

Anthropology in particular must therefore remain committed to creating a foundation in knowledge for a more practical global "we" relationship beyond the multitude of our separate positions, without dismissing genuine cultural differences or obliterating the reflexive capital that lies dormant in them. We have something important to learn from the highland Balinese people.

Chapter 11

REPRESENTATION AND SOCIETY
A Bali Aga Perspective

This final chapter asks what people generally and social scientists in particular can learn from the highland Balinese and from their approach to representation. We all have a practical interest in representational models insofar as they have a tangible effect on all of our lives, for better or worse, as models for living. Social scientists also have a theoretical interest in representational models, as they struggle to gain a general understanding of particular societies and of society in general. The Bali Aga, likewise, approach representation from these two inseparable perspectives as they negotiate practical conflicts among self-interested subjects and simultaneously satisfy their shared theoretical interest in understanding and responding to the intersubjective condition of their humanity. The ethnography of highland Bali illustrates how the practical problem of subjective bias can be contained in a society by adopting at a popular level an intersubjective social theory that sees society as a historical sequence of culturally mediated encounters.

In making this argument, I am not attempting to glorify Bali Aga society. Rather, I am responding to one of the demands of an intersubjective theory of representational knowledge. If representations of other societies are inherently intersubjective coproductions, and especially if we wish to define and encourage them to be such, then our theories about our own societies must also be coproductions. In short, the way to determine whether our new ideas about others are just new self-projections or the products of mutually transformative encounters is to ask whether our previous ideas about ourselves have had to change as well.

The ethnographic part of this book has explored processes of mutual representation in a particular society in the hope of finding a solution to the general theoretical dilemma of representation as it relates to ethnography. Taking its departure from within Bali Aga society, this exploration has shown that representation is indeed a mutual or integrated process of theorizing self and other. The theories ethnographers have of ourselves and others and of our own society and those of others are the products of encounters within specific fields of intersubjectivity shaped by variable historical, political, and economic conditions. Given that these conditions are favorable within Bali Aga society, especially as far as the free associations of villages in regional ritual domains (*banua*) is concerned, the study of a highland Balinese status economy may provide an example of a best-case scenario. Nevertheless, as people carve out their theoretical notions of self and other from a primary sphere of intersubjective experience and communication, they are also prone to a variety of subjective biases, even under a material condition of relative parity. Status systems may strongly reflect these representational biases by becoming oppressive at a symbolic level. Since there is a dialectical relationship between the control of symbolic and material resources, this in turn can contribute to a historical change of material conditions in the direction of greater disparity. Such intense symbolic oppression has not been observed within the regional status systems of Bali Aga society nor have any concerted attempts to translate status into permanent political or economic advantage.

The tension created by having to cooperate in an intersubjective process of representation so as to be able to compete for symbolic resources and by having to reconcile theoretical and practical interests defines the fundamental paradox of status systems and of representational knowledge systems in general. As the ethnographic focus shifted in the second part of this book from highland ritual domains to an analysis of interethnic and cross-cultural (Western) representations of the Bali Aga, this tension was still noticeable at a level of both discourse and practice—in the form of a more limited degree of representational and social cooperation and a less restrained mode of competition. The analysis of a representational process under less equitable conditions has thereby demonstrated the impossibility of denying intersubjectivity and communication altogether, even though they may be partially eclipsed by self-interest and the use of symbolic violence. Nevertheless, the Bali Aga are remarkable in that they seem to have recognized and accommodated the problem of self-interest in the form of difference within their theory of society and have thereby gained a means for regulating this problem successfully at the level of social practice.

In simultaneously drawing on and moving beyond the situational specificity of this ethnographic inquiry, my aim is to contribute to the wider anthropological project of critical cultural comparison for which ethnography is a necessary foundation. Encounters with other cultures ultimately challenge social scientists to examine the taken-for-granted representational theories that inform our own way of life. This self-critical dimension in the project of cultural comparison cannot be accomplished by completely diverting critical attention away from other cultures to the dark legacy of our own colonial history. To approach other people and their cultures uncritically or not to examine them at all, in keeping with an ill-conceived notion of cross-cultural charity or a sense of postcolonial anxiety, is to deny them their humanity and a full status as contemporaries and equals. Perhaps the only way to show appreciation for the cultural knowledge of others as a serious alternative to our own is to treat it as a set of criticizable validity claims in relation to fundamental existential conundrums that concern everyone.

A critical cultural comparison between Bali Aga and contemporary Western society involves a translation from the particular to the general. It therefore needs to be considered in advance whether such generalization is feasible and how it should be carried out.

A major concern in generalizing about cultural knoweledge is its inherent practical specificity. Local theories of society cannot be fully appreciated or critically evaluated simply through an examination of their objective knowledge content or their underlying epistemological approach. A people's knowledge also relates to their practice and affects their lives for better or for worse. Systems of cultural knowledge thus need to be considered in their practical relation to the intersubjective social fields to which they belong.

Agents operating within a particular field of intersubjectivity have a practical as well as a theoretical interest in the pursuit of knowledge. In contemporary Western societies, the propensity and opportunity to construct "disinterested" knowledge—including abstract theoretical models of our own and other societies—is available only to a limited degree and within the distinct subuniverse of scholastic or similarly constituted social fields in which at least some practical concerns can be excluded. As Pierre Bourdieu (1998) has argued, this scholastic social field provides the necessary material and sociopolitical conditions for a privileged minority of scholars to pursue knowledge at relative "leisure" (Greek *skhole*) and is designed to cultivate within them a genuine interest in disinterested or leisurely understanding.

Popular knowledge systems rarely operate under such leisurely conditions. Nonetheless, people in other cultures too have contemplated the possibility of disinterested understanding within specific subdomains of knowledge embedded in specific subfields of inter-subjectivity. The Bali Aga, for example, are well familiar with an ideal of disinterested understanding in relation to a special social field of ritual action that is set apart—at least in theory—from practical con-cerns (and set apart in actual practice perhaps no less so than the Western project of scientific understanding). As ritual relates in prac-tice to a distribution of status, the academic subfield of intersubjec-tivity in Western societies is one of the few remaining refuges in which a pursuit of status is permitted, while notions of a formal and intrinsic difference are otherwise suppressed in Western societies by an egali-tarian ideology and model of society.

Bali Aga knowledge systems, their general epistemological princi-ples, and their specific content thus belong to a people with "disinter-ested" as well as "interested" interests. The latter include a practical interest in constructing theoretical knowledge, that is, knowledge with a flair of universality and a corresponding power of legitimiza-tion. When Bali Aga construct theoretical models of their society, they tend to depict it in an idealized fashion, as a ritually articulated order whose participants wish to partake in a state of disinterested or sacred unity. Ironically, the people with the greatest proclivity to construct such totalizing theoretical models are likely to be those who have the greatest practical interest in maintaining an associated ritual distri-bution of symbolic capital. Nevertheless, I would not venture to deny that Bali Aga persons or groups have a genuine desire for transcend-ing the fragile truths of their self-concepts and the finite worlds of their competitive self-interest by embracing a broader intersubjective truth and participating in a larger universe of social cooperation and meaning.

The feasibility of cultural comparison thus rests in part on the assumption that people generally strive for some form of disinterested knowledge and do so by accentuating the intersubjective aspect of their human condition. In another part, it rests on the assumption that there is also a common ground for the instrumentalization of knowledge because human beings share similar practical interests. Nevertheless, the cultural specificity of a particular form of knowledge and intersubjective field is important, first, with regard to their mutual relatedness and, second, insofar as a particular form of knowledge is the product of a particular history. From a comparative perspective the historical specificity of knowledge is what accounts for its unique-ness, and hence it is a bonus as well as a potential impediment.

While it has long been argued in anthropology that the embed-dedness of cultural knowledge in specific worlds of practice is important, this insight sometimes has been used as an excuse for discounting other people's ability to produce knowledge sufficiently disinterested or self-conscious to compete on equal terms with Western social theory (see Crapanzano 1986:52). As a consequence, there has been a tendency to view other people's knowledge not as their models of society or social life, but only as their models for living.

A critical comparative appreciation of Bali Aga knowledge, nevertheless, is impossible without a critical analysis of its practical relationship to a specific field of intersubjectivity. To widen artificially the gap between knowledge and practice in search for objective "truth" is deeply precarious, as our Western history has taught us. After all, to attempt this has been a defining feature not only of science (in the tradition of both rationalism and logical empiricism) but also of totalitarian political ideologies (Horkheimer and Adorno 1979).

Within Bali Aga models of society, the gap between knowledge and practice—and an associated gap between winners and losers in a social game of symbolic and material exchanges—is sufficiently wide to warrant a moderately critical response. At the same time, it is not wide enough to warrant a portrayal of their society as one in which blatant domination is disguised by a veil of ideological enchantment. Comparatively mild forms of symbolic domination in Bali Aga society are reflected, for example, in the relative faintness of younger men's voices in public contexts and in the temporary exclusion of powerless newcomers from many village councils. But the ambitions reflected in Bali Aga theories of society are not necessarily realized. The symbolic domination of younger men and other disadvantaged groups appears more blatantly in local discourse than it actually is in practice. Surprisingly perhaps, to those who would fetishize cultural critique in the place of fetishizing knowledge, this example suggests that the critical exploration of a gap between representations and social practice in a particular society can also reveal power structures more equitable than associated structures of knowledge may insinuate.

Within Bali Aga society, for example, the prevalent form of silence is not a silence of the oppressed but a silence akin to the one observable among participants in a game of cards. This is not a coincidence but a remarkable cultural achievement, based on a complex system of regulated practice and knowledge that recognizes and celebrates the contingencies of history and the sediments of human agency.

The practical interests of particular representors bring an element of subjective bias and distortion to personal, local, regional, interethnic, and cross-cultural processes of mutual representation even under the best possible conditions, and ethnographic representations are no exception. A critical ethnography may help to explore such biases and may attempt to avoid them in providing an alternative representation. In the final analysis, however, an ethnographic representation of another cultural world is itself a set of validity claims, to be validated or rejected by others within another, scholastic field of intersubjectivity. Ethnographers must dare to posit such preliminary validity claims and dare to acknowledge them as such, if their studies are to serve a more general anthropological project of critical cultural comparison. Another advantage to this approach is that it may help to stimulate and facilitate new research and alternative interpretations of the society concerned.[1] This dual purpose of comparison and contestation cannot be accomplished through a discourse of denial.

A critical cultural comparison and scholarly debate can be initiated by presenting a self-consciously and temporarily totalizing theory of Bali Aga society, a theory that remains critical but faithful to already somewhat totalizing local discourses about society, without wishing thereby to absolve the anthropologist from responsibility. Insofar as the following validity claims appropriately reflect some of the validity claims made by the Bali Aga themselves, it is also their knowledge that is hereby posited as their contribution to a wider comparative project to understand our social condition as human beings.

Bringing the Past into the Present: Origin, Precedence, and Dualism in Bali Aga Society

The people of highland Bali frequently allude to the provisional character of individual human knowledge. Few claim to understand fully the society and culture in which they are embedded: why it is the way it is, how it was, and how it should be. This does not prevent local participants from viewing themselves as parts of a society conceived as a whole. They are active agents in a living society and cosmos that in its totality is sacred and in its facticity cannot be ignored. The participants' quest for knowledge arises from the existential imperative to take appropriate action.

The order of the cosmos, according to Bali Aga theory, is as dynamic as life itself. It is a fundamentally social universe composed of relationships among paired categorical complements. The cosmological dualism of the highland Balinese does not seek to partition the world into static binary oppositions among mutually independent categories, as has been attempted in some Western philosophical and theological traditions. Cartesian dualism may have speculated on a mind existing independently from matter, and Christian prophesies may anticipate a final split of the quotidian world into domains of pure good and pure evil, heaven and hell.[2] Bali Aga cosmology, however, depicts a world of eternal mediations among complements that owe their very existence to one another and to their separateness. Their philosophy of life is to seek a graceful balance in a world of dynamic dualisms. There is no ambition to deny the necessity of difference or to resolve the tension among complements by permanently uniting or separating them. "Two that are different" (*rua bineda*) are the fundamental prerequisite for the perpetuation of a living social tradition (*adat*), as they are for the continuity of life itself.

In a world made up of dynamic relationships among the paired elements of conceptual and social complements, there is no room for stagnation. The eternal duality of life is irrevocably inscribed, as a gender or right-left distinction, onto natural as well as social bodies. This eternity of difference does not effect eternal separation. The perpetual tension among complements is punctuated by the recursive occurrence of creative and highly salient moments of unity. Life is predicated on a recurrent, temporary union (e.g., husband-wife) and on a subsequent re-creation of the initial difference in the products of this union (e.g., brother-sister). The notion of a perpetual dualism does not create a static world. It creates the necessary conditions for a history of mediations—for an order of recursive dualism in a temporal world of replicating differences.

The temporal dimension of dualism in the Bali Aga cosmos is prominently reflected in the idiom of their social philosophy. Society is recognized in a physiological or botanical idiom as the living product of a continuous growth process. From a retrospective point of view, it may appear to be a received order of things laid down in the past, the comparatively solid bones of the sacrificial body or the hard trunk of origin. At the same time, however, society produces or reproduces itself in the softness of the flesh and at the plant's tender tip, that is, in the here and now. The contingency of today is the inherited facticity of tomorrow's past, just as today's trunk was yesterday's tip. A tree without new growth is a dying tree, and a social body that does not evolve and reproduce itself, to the Bali Aga, is a society whose past does not lead to a future. The "social theory" of the highland Balinese, for all the complexities of their society, is founded on this one remarkable insight: Human society and life itself is a dynamic process in time, and human self-understanding is a product of deliberate retrospection.

Time is not defined as a separate dimension independent from the logic of action. It is human actions that fill the emptiness of time with meaning by creating sequences of memorable events. The regularity of human actions allows the events they produce (births, marriages, house/temple/village foundations) to be classified as recursive elements in sequences of categorical relationships (parent-child, elder-younger sibling, earlier-later foundations of houses or temples, and so forth). Embodied human existence, in contrast, is an ontological state defined in terms of the temporal divisions, conceptual and social, that are the hallmark of the quotidian world (*sekala*, "countable [or historical] time"). In short, in highland Bali it is human beings who make time, and it is time that defines them as humans, in both a physiological and social sense.

Human actions occur not only in temporal sequence. They are carried out by particular persons and at particular locations in space.[3] The Bali Aga attribute some significance to the ancestry of action, that is, to the identity of the human agents whose actions precipitated specific events that are retrospectively held to have been important. But they more often contemplate their world as a topography of action. Historical events are not only sequenced in time, they are movements between distinct localities. The spatialization of time is a method of reducing its continuous invisible flow to a visibly punctuated sequence and the continuity of human experience to a fixed number of localized events. Historical topographies thus help to index temporally distant events by reference to cultural artifacts, as well as their being memorized more directly in narrative accounts of the past. Important social events leave a trail of physical evidence to support people in the frailty of their memory, most pertinently a network of related human or divine dwellings. Ancestral houses or temples are therefore primary markers in the historical topography of Bali Aga spaces.[4]

Social categories based on a notion of common residence or place have the advantage of greater social inclusiveness as compared to categories based on ideas of ancestry or name. The coexistence of the two modes of conceptualizing social relationships suggests that a balance is sought in Bali Aga society between a cooperative principle of social inclusion and a more competitive principle of exclusion from access to group membership and associated resources. The predominance of more inclusive spatial categories (even the ancestor who founded a *sanggah kemulan* temple is rarely remembered by name) suggests that the current scarcity of and competition for material resources such as arable land may be the result of relatively recent demographic developments. For the larger part of Bali Aga social history, it is likely that localized conditions of resource scarcity could be alleviated by clearing additional land for cultivation at a nearby location. In this sense, the dynamic temporal structure of Bali Aga social topographies probably reflects a genuine history of human expansion.

Bali Aga concepts of topography and ancestry are linked by a common logic of temporal ontology, reflected in the way they define relationships between the parts of a whole. The people in an expanding domain (*banua*) could not have migrated from place B to place C without a prior migration from A to B. Likewise, the member B of a village assembly (*ulu apad*) could not claim to be the predecessor of member C without simultaneously declaring himself the successor of a member A. And in a house of origin group (*sanggah kemulan*), person B could not become the parent of his descendant C without first having been the child of the parent A. The resulting pattern of recursive dual distinctions among members of temporally adjacent social categories has been referred to as a social order of precedence. In view of the ontological dependence of the later on the earlier element, the relationship among temporal categories and their social representatives is usually asymmetric. The earlier or preceding element is often classed as superior. The central value of a society organized within social orders of precedence is thus the notion of a common origin, a sacred moment of social unity in the past.

Precedence acts as a principle of classification at all levels of social organization among Bali Aga, and the specific features of these organizational structures certainly are unique. Nevertheless, a similar logic of precedence has been observed in Austronesian-speaking societies throughout the Southeast Asia–Pacific region (Fox 1980, 1988, 1990c, 1994b; Lewis 1988; McWilliam 1989; Reuter 1992; Vischer 1992; Bellwood, Fox, and Tryon 1995; Fox and Sathers 1996). An important aim of this book, therefore, has been to situate the ethnography of Bali Aga society within an ongoing comparative ethnological project.

Bali Aga society, however, raises some problematic issues for the development of a more general theory of precedence in Austronesian studies. Origin as a definitive cultural value and precedence as a classificatory index of social relations both are important elements of a common cultural heritage among societies in the region. A general anthropological theory of origin and precedence as ideas-in-action must be constructed with caution, however, if it is to avoid a mimetic reproduction or further amplification of an idealizing character even within local models of society. A general theory of precedence in Austronesian societies needs to be grounded in an understanding of particular social orders of precedence as shifting and contested sites of practical interaction.

The need for a critical analysis is particularly strong in relation to the value of origin. Origin is the moral principle that transforms a merely classificatory order of precedence into a system of social evaluation and permits it to inform an asymmetric distribution of symbolic (and sometimes material) resources. In the process of constructing an anthropological theory of Bali Aga society, it is precarious but ultimately necessary to follow this lead by shifting the focus of critical analysis from categories to values.

The temptation in studying cultural values is that they seem at once to capture the essence of a social system and to issue an invitation for constructing sweeping generalizations. The dilemma with such value-based generalizations is that actual societies are not entirely cohesive wholes, nor is people's behavior a mechanical execution of their society's focal value principles. Nevertheless, it is by the power of values that a mere distinction (A precedes B) is transformed into a moral validity claim (A ranks above B). Insofar as the validity claims they raise have in fact gained general acceptance, by means of consensus or coercion, values do have the power to elevate a set of social categories to a practical system of symbolic resource distribution. This practical social impact of value systems necessitates their phenomenological study and simultaneously generates a need for cultural critique. In this case one might ask, what is the practical significance of placing a superior value on origin for different participants in Bali Aga society?

Posing this question initiates an anthropological evaluation of a Bali Aga system of evaluation. This external evaluation can be made legitimate only in the context of a simultaneous project of cross-cultural critique. Cross-cultural critique departs from the assumption that the focal values of specific societies are moral validity claims raised in response to some of the most fundamental conundrums of human existence and thus of concern to us all.

Losing the Present to the Past or the Future

"The task to be accomplished is not the conservation of the past, but the redemption of the hopes of the past" (Horkheimer and Adorno 1979:xv). The source of inspiration for a human inclination to posit universal or sacred values as the moral foundation of society, following the most profound insight of Durkheim's sociology of religion, is none other than society itself. This sacred character of society, in turn, reflects a primal human experience of social participation. Individuals experience society as an intersubjective, self-transcending, and, thus, potentially numinous reality. Similarly, individual self-concepts are framed within the representational economy of a larger social world. Theories of society, as a transindividual or transcendental reality, are thus likely to evoke a universal value or truth, a set of universal validity claims that aims to transcend subjective individual judgments to become a general standard of propriety.

The transcendental aspect of social experience, however, has its limitations. It is also part of the human condition to suffer experiences of society as a somewhat unholy battleground of strategic action where self-interested individuals or groups compete for limited resources. Any totalizing value system that appeals to society as the ontological and communicative foundation of its universality, no matter whether it posits a sacred or a more explicitly social value, is vulnerable to evident divisions of interest in society, divisions that are often further accentuated or defined by such a value in the first place. A singular vision of a sacred society thus helps to create its own nemesis.

The divisive and unifying aspects of social life are both so fundamental to human experience and knowledge that it may be better to speak of societies having a weak or strong proclivity for hierarchization rather than of their being either egalitarian or hierarchical. A strong proclivity for hierarchization can be defined as a propensity to employ a particular interpretation of the sacred (*hieros*)—of society as a presumably unified whole—in order to determine the appropriate form of government (*arkhia*) for that society. This logic of hierarchization is in some ways a tautology. Hierarchization often merely defines the current social order (society as it is) as an ideal order of things (society as it ought to be). Theories of society are hierarchical, one could argue, insofar as they discount the need or potential for positive change in the historical present.

It is necessary to establish a universal value or truth against the underlying paradox of human social experience in society, because societies, like individuals, are bound by an imperative of action. There are differences among the cultural values and social theories promoted within various societies, however, and these have important practical consequences. These differences relate to the particular logic of universalization in various local theories of society.

In Western Europe, the notion of the sacred (society) in local theories of society since the Enlightenment has been the concept of reason. Enlightenment theories imagined an ideal (sacred) society as one with a secular system of government so thoroughly rational that all persons (insofar as they are rational) would be spontaneously propelled to cooperate for the common good, even at the cost of restricting their own liberties. Society was to be founded on a secular morality rather than the Christian morality that had dominated societies in the postclassical "dark age" of Europe, but on a morality nonetheless. One advantage of this theory was that a social expression of collective rationality in the form of a contemporary democratic government was not final, because knowledge was seen as the historical product of a cumulative process of reasoning. Any particular government could be put into question by legitimate acts of reasonable opposition (e.g., voting or publicly protesting against the government) and within institutionalized processes of rational debate (e.g., parliament). A further advantage was that, while the intersubjectivity-based concept of democracy acknowledged a need for cooperation, the idea of competition was also embraced, by developing a bipartite system of government and opposition. In short, reason was an interpretation of the sacred explicitly recognized as society, as an intersubjective or democratic process driven by a dialectic of unity and division. The ultimate aim of this process was to bring a utopian or futuristic vision of a perfectly rational society closer to the present.

A fundamental tendency toward hierarchization could not be banished once and for all by displacing the danger inherent in the notion of a final truth from the present into a utopian future. All governments, given that they wish to remain in office, have a tendency to deny the recursive process of reasoning and the necessary dualism of the democratic political system (the need for a strong opposition) by positing themselves as the perfect and final product and manifestation of Reason (with a capital "R"). The peril for a democratic government is thus that it may lose the present to the future by portraying itself as the embodiment of a utopian future in the present and by declaring all expressions of opposition irrational. Over the last century, the long descent of many European countries into totalitarianism has shown that this danger is not just hypothetical. Reason in the form of an absolute truth becomes a dictator.

More recently, and in part owing to these failed experiments with bringing utopian ideals into reality, there has been widespread skepticism toward the very idea of a utopia. This skepticism could prove to be even more dangerous, though in a less spectacular way. In contemporary democratic societies, strong sentiments of disillusionment with politics, low rates of voter participation, declining democratic institutions, and fewer expressions of public protest all seem to indicate a surrender to the idea that the present is as good as it gets, even though it may not be very good at all. Abandoning the idea of a utopia of reason can thus lead to the abandonment of the notion of reasoning as a process on the grounds of futility. The present is lost to a future that is the same as the past, to the iron cage of a natural, eternal, and final here and now.

Akin to the social philosophy of a modern democratic system, Bali Aga theories of society have the advantage that, in principle, they idealize a continuous sociohistorical process rather than an immutable social order or product. Furthermore, the two theories are similar in that they do not celebrate the social order of the present for being necessarily perfect, though society should always strive for perfection. Insofar as they may consider this project to be already accomplished, the Bali Aga too encounter the threat of hierarchization, but in a rather different way.

The fundamental difference from the social philosophy of the Enlightenment is that the Bali Aga find their model of an ideal society not in the future but in the past. Society had its moment of perfect unity and sacredness at the time when it originated, just as a plant's multitude of leaves is united in the singularity of its trunk. The opportunity for hierarchization therefore presents itself in a very different and, perhaps, less acute way. It is not that the status quo of the present would be portrayed as the full realization of a utopian ideal. Rather, a Bali Aga denial of society as a continuous process of mediation, between unity and division or cooperation and competition, would theoretically take the form of a present envisaged as the self-evident product or perfect embodiment of a sacred past.

The difference between the two theories is significant. A critical examination of how the specific danger of losing the present to the past and the more general danger of hierarchization is averted in Bali Aga society illustrates that the specific danger of their social theory may be inherently less acute in comparison to the danger we in the West face of losing the present to the future (or to a loss of hope in the future).

I have argued that an inclination toward hierarchization or denial of process in theories of society arises from their ambition for establishing an absolute, noncontingent value or truth as the foundation for a stable government. At the same time, theories of society are hard-pressed to posit a permanent truth, given that the very object of their representation is evidently and inherently unstable. The ensuing conflict precipitates an ambivalent attitude toward social change, and this ambivalence toward change is ultimately directed at the transformational potential of human agency. For better or for worse, human agency (or choice) can modify society by producing difference and emphasizes society's character as a productive process of action that cannot be completely objectified in advance. However, human action is the means by which people and societies may indeed objectify themselves in retrospect (see Ricoeur 1981), and insofar as this action is regulated and recursive, societies may also reproduce themselves to some degree. Hierarchization comes into play when a theory of society expects mere cultural reproduction (the limited continuity of a social process) to become the cultural preservation of a perfect and final social product. Action, in this case, is no longer just regulated but dictated.

Bali Aga theories of society, at a conceptual level, are not designed to preclude the possibility of social change or to deny the emancipatory potential of human agency. To the highland Balinese, the historical journey of social life is a sequence of classifiable but nevertheless unique events originating in the distant past and coming to a preliminary end in the present. In its specificity, a sequence of human migrations, for example, could not have taken place or be perpetuated into the future if human agents were unable to select among alternative courses of action. However, this does not mean that the Bali Aga celebrate the present—the moment when human agency comes into play—as a space of unrestrained possibilities and freedom. The present is a site of creative potential as well as genuine peril. The power of agency as a motor of social change is therefore celebrated only in retrospect, after it has taken an irrevocable effect, rather than while it is in process and its outcomes remain uncertain.

The Bali Aga employ botanical idioms to convey their specific form of ambivalence toward social change. The metaphor of organic growth implies a process of social change as well as continuity. A historical process of becoming is indeed the very essence of the *sekala*, the human world of time and action, of which society is a part. But no matter how much human beings in their embodied state and human societies in their historical facticity are creatures of time, they are also meant to partake in the time-defying continuity of the *niskala*. Ironically, individual human beings are transformed into immortal ancestors by virtue of their very mortality. As people grow old and die, time for them travels backward to a sacred state of original unity, and the future becomes a return to the past. Absurd as it may sound from a linear perspective on time (as an absolute quantity), this image of life as a process of temporal inversion is logically consistent with what one could call a social theory of relativity. As we travel forward into the future, we are destined to move back farther and farther into the past; the past, that is, from the perspective of our successors in a future here and now.[5] A process of status changes is thus expected and accepted in relation to persons as they move ahead on their journey of transformation into "people of the sacred past" (ancestors). The Bali Aga quest for universal values and for the associated stability of a sacred society does not come at the cost of creating immutable person categories. In contrast to modern Western societies, where individual worth is supposed to be the rational measure of and reward for extraordinary individual achievements or personal qualities, one could argue that the highland Balinese consider gradual status increases as one of their basic human rights.[6]

Time unfolds as an inverted progression of transformations leading back to a final state of original timelessness for the individual. The place of time and change in Bali Aga theories of society, however, is not as easily negotiated. In their ambition for society to partake in a similar state of disembodied timelessness, the main obstacle is that, unlike individuals, societies do not normally have access to the transfiguring and immortalizing experience of death.[7] Compared to individuals, society is virtually immortal already or is at least a faint reflection of the *niskala* in the *sekala*. Society's greater continuity provides the path along which the more transient individual may safely navigate his or her passage of life back to a sacred time of origin. From another angle, however, this greater continuity introduces a vulnerability to society precisely where the individual's greater vulnerability to time introduces a strength. What if society experienced something resembling death? What if it lost its sacred unity and disintegrated into smaller fragments? When this occurs, as it frequently does, the continuity of the individual's path to immortality (which society normally provides) is put into question. The social time machine that transports a person into the sacred past works on an assumption of a continuous social velocity. If there are none in the future for whom today is the past, then the individual of today has no future as an immortalized ancestor.

Society is more permanent than the individual but cannot escape the contingency of the present in a final moment of disembodiment. This conundrum is elegantly expressed by the Bali Aga in their logic of sacrifice. The body of the sacrificial victim represents society. Society is brought to death, its body is dismembered, it comes "alive" again (*wangun urip*) for a moment in the *niskala* sense of a perfect or timeless existence, only to be consumed once more by society in its embodied state. The timelessness of society is thus recognized as the fragile and transient product of the work of immortalization that society carries out on itself. This logic does not amount to a general denial of process and cannot be described as an attempt for permanent hierarchization.

The Bali Aga nevertheless believe that a relatively durable society can be produced through a more regulated process of production, that is, by the collective symbolic labor of a people who perpetuate their ancestral traditions (*adat*) deliberately and with diligence. The notion of *adat* suggests not a fixed product but a set of procedures or regulated modes of appropriate action. This acknowledgment of process in itself indicates a weak tendency toward hierarchization. Nevertheless, even a deliberate quest to enhance the continuity of process (rather than to preserve a finished product) must meet with a twin challenge. Like every other society, the Bali Aga work to reproduce their social order in the face of practical opposition from external and internal sources. Their response to specific practical contingencies may help to establish how the value of origin and the concept of precedence are put into action and whether this entails a hierarchization in practice.

The ethnohistory of the Bali Aga suggests that they have met the perpetual challenge of external contingencies, such as the arrival of powerful newcomers from abroad, with a practical strategy of accommodation. Society in its historical facticity had to tolerate the periodic creation of new social entities by addition (or, in other contexts, by division). The theoretical classification and value system modeled on participants' lived experience of this society may have followed suit by embracing a concept of dual (or multiple) origins. A notion of dual origin is employed to characterize the relationship between Bali Aga and Bali Majapait, between founders and newcomers in some regional domains, between original people and immigrants in many local villages, and between the *sanggah* of kin and affines.

The impetus for a value fragmentation was pressing in cases where the newcomers were powerful enough to affect the government of social relations. As newcomers from Majapait gained political control in Bali, as newcomers from Desa Dausa appropriated the domain of Pura Indrakila, and as the descendants of the three immigrant brothers came to dominate the village of Sukawana, the interests of the two parties (local and foreign) were served by establishing separate orders of precedence for two distinct social contexts or value spheres. The distinction between them was conceptualized in terms of internal and external points of origin. In theory, the value of origin could have escaped fragmentation in other cases where the new-comers were simply absorbed within an existing origin structure, as dependent clients whose separate origin had no bearing as a positive point of reference (e.g., the newcomer client villages in Gebog Satak Selulung). Society, however, even in the absence of external interference, is more than a sacred and timeless domain of origin and ritual status. It is also a domain of social competition in which the main reference point is the ability to accomplish and sustain a change in the social order that is to one's own advantage.

The evident duality or multiplicity in a Bali Aga value concept of origin cannot be described as a practical response to a particular type of external challenges alone, though it may indeed reflect a long history of successive immigrations. A distinction between dual identity layers in society has become an a priori assumption of local social theory. For example, village assemblies (*ulu apad*) feature a division into ceremonial moieties and an associated twofold division of labor and value.[8] The maintenance of functionally distinct but purely ceremonial moieties (where membership is neither fixed nor related to birth) in villages where there has been no discernible historical immigration or any other practical incentive to develop a notion of dual origin is a clear illustration that a twofold social division (or one based on recursive dualism) is conceived as a necessary precondition for the very existence of a society.

The possibility for drawing a distinction between two different value spheres and social identities is already implicit in the concept of origin itself. Origin is only relevant in relation to a living totality, and life itself is thought to evolve from an original creative moment of unification between the complements male and female. Duality is thus a logical prerequisite for origin, and, in its most basic form, this duality is one of gender. Similarly, the most fundamental division of labor and value in society is a gender-based division. The social tensions among persons with gender-specific roles is also exemplary of a more general tension between society as a sphere of cooperative unity (among the members of complementary social categories) and as the site for a competitive struggle between people of different status. All this suggests an awareness of the dynamics of society as a process and a low propensity for hierarchization. The multiplicity of Bali Aga values or value spheres negates the notion of a single and universal value, which is a necessary prerequisite for widespread hierarchization.

In their quest for a relatively continuous tradition, Bali Aga responses to internal challenges—such as a sudden or gradual refusal to recognize a common origin, identity, or shared ritual obligation—require more detailed discussion. Where the source of contingency and the impetus for social change is no longer a stranger but a local participant, theories of society must finally face or conceal their ambivalence toward the contribution of human agency to processes of cultural production.

Bali Aga social theories tend to celebrate the imperfections or creative impulses introduced by human agency to a process of cultural reproduction. Social history is often depicted as a fragmentation process and time as the very principle of conceptual and social divisions. The ultimate challenge for society is not to prevent fragmentation but to define particular fragments as new and integral parts of an ever-expanding whole. Ritual domains, villages, and ancestral houses are alike in that they anticipate and tolerate a process of branching. That society may thus grow without disintegrating is an achievement based on human memory. The fragmentation process of history does not destroy a social unity so long as it is counteracted by the time-inverting power of memory, expressed in the social recognition of a common origin. This paradox of unity in division again implies a necessary distinction, in these cases, between politicoeconomic and status-oriented value spheres or what can be referred to as secular and sacred contexts. Branch villages or houses will indeed participate in the ritual labor of commemoration and accept the ritual precedence of their origin village or house—so long as they are granted a great measure of economic and political autonomy.

The commemorational unity of a domain, village, or house group remains problematic even though it concedes to the partial symbolic and more complete material autonomy of its constituents (villages or households). The concept of an original unity still generates a possibility for asymmetric distinctions in the present and simultaneously provokes a social response from those who are thereby placed at a symbolic disadvantage. Strategic interests come into play insofar as people's varying categorical proximity to the sacred (origin) establishes an inequitable distribution of symbolic capital among them. Relative status distinctions in terms of precedence avoid symbolic hierarchization—on a conceptual level, by retaining the idea of a process and, on a practical level, by allowing for an incremental process of status gain. Nevertheless, time-based distinctions may still have negative social consequences for people who are associated with the recent rather than the original and who are unable to define their "newness" as an alternative point of origin. One reason why disadvantaged members of Bali Aga social institutions may accept their condition is that their disadvantages are more modest than they may appear to be. The formal and official asymmetry of rank among predecessors and their successors often conceals an underlying practical interdependence.

Even though the status differences within an order of precedence are mutable in principle and of relatively modest significance in their practical implications, they can and do precipitate some discontent among those who are "temporarily" disadvantaged.[9] Bali Aga social philosophy therefore does not operate on the assumption that a balanced state of sacred unity in diversity can be taken for granted. As a countermeasure to the disenchantment that comes from human agents' experience of society as a field of competition, the Bali Aga have created a social technology for amplifying natural transcendental experiences of society as a unified whole. This technology is ritual or, more precisely, a ritualization of human interaction.

Bali Aga people do not draw an absolute distinction between secular and ritual action (both are referred to as "work," *gae* or *karya*). Even the most contingent and obviously self-interested human actions of the present may gradually acquire the sanctified status of pertinent events in a sacred past. An action that leads to a split in a *banua*, for example, may be seen as an active violation of tradition at the time when it occurs. If the split does not precipitate misfortune and is not revoked, however, this action will eventually come to be regarded as a sacred moment of origin and the beginning of a new unity.

Ritualized human actions in the here and now can acquire this same sanctity in a more immediate sense, because they are explicitly devoted to the enactment of the sacred past. The ritual process is a symbolic manipulation of time, an alternating movement between a state of temporal and social divisions in daily practice and a sacred and timeless (*niskala*) state of quasi-original unity in ritual practice. To pay respect to the ancestors means to commemorate and retrace the itinerary of their journey in a ritual act of returning to the source of life, topographically represented by their sacred dwellings or temples. A heightened sense of unity in diversity is achieved by bringing the past into the experience of the present, that is, by supporting oral origin histories with regular ritual performances.

Ritual experiences act surreptitiously as an antidote to social discontent by providing relief for some of the more general discontents of human social existence. Participants tend to describe their experience of ritual as a complex blend of emotions. For all its apparent repetitiveness, ritual can be a welcome reprise from daily routines in a society with few other provisions for entertainment.[10] It is a spectacle to be observed and a drama to participate in, as everyone dresses in his or her finest garments to receive the ancestors. Temple festivals with their dance performances, colorful offerings and extraordinary culinary delights, and blood sacrifices in their boisterousness and raw aggression are festivals of sensory stimulation. Nevertheless, rituals can provide moments of tranquillity and a powerful sense of security as well. As people display their pious devotion to the ancestors, they also affirm their devotion to one another as members of a sacred community. Working and feasting together, with an intimacy normally reserved for a domestic setting, they are able to forget for a moment the sense of loneliness instilled by the pursuit of self-interest. Sheltered in a haven of togetherness, they may also face a potentially callous and more powerful outside world with greater serenity. Ritual further provides an escape from the finitude of embodied existence. It is a religious drama whose participants do not ever leave the stage of life, even in death, but who only change their positions. And, finally, ritualized action provides a social technology for contemplating and coordinating the cyclical dance of more mundane (e.g., agricultural) activities dedicated to material survival. As a celebration of life, ritual is a celebration of unity. It exemplifies the kind of social cooperation—human and divine—without which the practical task of survival would be infinitely more difficult than it is already.

A number of Bali Aga rituals can also provide moments of symbolic compensation by openly acknowledging that the theoretical rank asymmetry among representatives of different social categories may have practical limitations. These rituals tend to invert or emphasize the circularity of a temporally indexed linear rank order of precedence. The funeral tower of a deceased is symbolically pulled by a male child from the youngest generation of his or her successors, the aged priest-leaders of a village work hand in hand with prepubescent child priests or village youth associations, and the head elder's food portion, normally a symbolic index of his rank, is stolen by young men in some rituals of fertility. Such inversions of precedence suggest that the already composite value of origin is further compromised by a silent counter value of becoming. In a botanical idiom of growth, the old trunk cannot live without the power of a fresh tip, just as social predecessors cannot be acknowledged or remembered if they fail to produce successors and to secure their cooperation.

The benefits of participation in a *banua, ulu apad,* or *sanggah* generally carry sufficient importance to outweigh the relatively modest strategic losses of disadvantaged members. Participation in cooperative socioritual organizations, despite their less endearing aspect as

sites for strategic games of status competition, may also be a superlative strategic end in itself. A Bali Aga status economy based on
notions of origin and precedence acknowledges that a struggle for
control over a shared present becomes possible only by accepting
the general assumption of sharing a common past and, possibly, a
common future.

The preceding analysis illustrates that Bali Aga theories of society,
though they contain the element of universalization that is characteristic of all social theories, do not encourage a denial of society as a
process. This is because their central classificatory concept is temporal sequence or precedence and because their origin-focused value
systems in their multilayered dualism recognize the fundamental tensions of social experience. In this general sense, they are not inclined
toward hierarchization. It may also be said that the danger inherent
to this specific theory of society—the danger of losing the present to
the past—appears to have been averted in practice.

I argued earlier that a Western democratic theory of society faces
the same general danger of hierarchization, in the specific and opposite guise of losing the present to the future, to a final utopia or dis-
topia. This danger has not always been successfully averted in practice. The reasons can be traced to the basic principles of our own
local social theories.

One problem is the inherent future-orientation of popular Western
theories of society. Ricoeur (1981), Schutz (1976), and others have
argued that our concept of self is derived from apperception, that is,
from reflecting on our actions in the past. Reflection on past actions
and on our general historical condition is a more reliable source of
knowledge and more profitable in enhancing our self-understanding than to reflect on a hypothetical future (perhaps the imagined
future is in fact no more than a knowledge of the mistakes of the
past).

Another problem in Western theories of society has been their
reliance on egalitarian individualism. This focus on the subject and
on agency may counteract hierarchization in theory and may have
done so successfully in some limited contexts of practice. But the
assumption of a nominal equality also can and has been abused as a
legitimization of vast differences arising in the course of practice. By
denying the kind of formal but nominal difference that Bali Aga
theory posits as intrinsic to all life and all ways of living, and by declaring it as irrational, popular Western theories of society lose the
opportunity to acknowledge and regulate actual differences. Furthermore, in positing a highly competitive model of human relations, with

society as its unholy battleground, the need to create heightened experiences of sacred society as a field of cooperative intersubjectivity tends to be neglected. Some examples may illustrate how the two basic problems of popular Western theories of society come into effect in practice.

The intense desire of the highland Balinese to bring the past to bear on the present, through the commemoration of shared historical origins and the ritual reenactment of ancestral journeys, may not hold much immediate appeal for a contemporary Western audience. However, it highlights the first problem of Western self-representations, their exaggerated future orientation. From the time of the Enlightenment, Western social theories began to portray the objective social conditions, religious institutions, and traditions that had been inherited from historical predecessors as an encumbrance to the creation of a more rational social order in the present. Following the recognition of a dialectic link between external social conditions and the social conditioning of individuals, the past has also been cast as an impediment to personal freedom, as unwanted baggage to be disposed of rather than a treasure chest of valuable heirlooms.

This denial of the relevance of the past, however, has not prevented the past from entering into the present in a more clandestine manner. Like it or not, we are still embedded in a historical process that comes to a preliminary end in the here and now. Worse still, we also engage in practices designed actively to reproduce the past, and we mystify this engagement insofar as we deny it. So-called modern societies or nation-states also preserve their "new" social orders, institutions, and ritual traditions, and perhaps no less diligently so than the Bali Aga. Nor can it be concealed that there are privileged groups within modern societies with vested interests in maintaining the current social conditions and the universalizing knowledge system that sustains them. By fetishizing rational progress and underemphasizing the inherent potential and human craving for cultural continuity, modern societies have not been able either to realize the positive reflexive potential of the past or to exorcise the malignant ghosts of the past. Rather, processes of cultural production and reproduction in Western societies have become ever more opaque to their participants.

It could be argued that the political dimension in processes of cultural reproduction is covered by fewer veils of enchantment in Bali Aga theories of society than it is in the mythologies of modernity. The people of the highlands openly disclose their concern for reproducing the past in the present, though individual stakeholders may attempt to conceal their particular interests. By deliberately celebrating their origins and inherited traditions, they successfully redeem hidden mechanisms of cultural reproduction for a more self-reflexive project of ritual production. In the course of reenacting past actions, ritual practices do not simply institutionalize the past as the ideal model for the present. Ritual institutionalizes a process of examining the past and its power to shape the here and now, for better or for worse. As a project of retrospective progress, ritual commemoration encourages historical reflection and inadvertently opens avenues for a redefinition of the present in the image of a newly reinterpreted or reimagined historical self.

A similar argument could be applied in a comparison between Western egalitarianism and Bali Aga notions of precedence. This comparison reveals the second problem of popular Western theories of society, the formal denial of (nominal) difference. The most dominant and influential of these theories has been liberal individualism. This theory rest on the idea that all human individuals are equal and have equal rights. The formal ideal of egalitarianism does not anticipate a need for status differentiation but tolerates enormous differences in power and wealth in the very name of equality. For example, exploitation is fair and the successful accumulation of wealth is to be admired because economic competitors in a free market are assumed to have had equal opportunities initially insofar as they are equal by nature. It is not considered that equality must be created by regulating the competitive pursuit of material as well as symbolic capital. Moreover, with formal status difference by and large no longer an option, self-serving ambitions are strongly directed away from the acquisition of status (and to some degree of political power) to the accumulation of wealth and economic power. Much of this dominant economic sphere now operates as a global oligarchy that democratically elected national governments can no longer control and, worse still, that they must serve to their utmost ability in order to avoid a catastrophic withdrawal of global capital investment from their national economies.

Bali Aga cultural theory differs in that it does not deny difference. By anticipating formal differences at a level of theory, an opportunity is gained to regulate difference and the associated flow of symbolic capital in practice. The acceptance of social differentiation as a necessary condition for the survival of society means that competitive human ambitions can be satisfied and contained within a rank-distinguishing social organization and thus diverted from an indulgence in material greed. In short, the Bali Aga have developed a social technology to avoid the gross and permanent material inequities shared by truly hierarchical or nominally egalitarian systems.

No matter how different Bali Aga society may be from our own, the preceding comparison has shown that the challenges to which different cultural systems of theory and practice respond, with different degrees of success, are ultimately rather similar. Historical challenges and cultural responses may vary widely, but there is only one earth and one human species. In a globalizing world, and a world that has been slowly globalizing for centuries, our future will be inextricably linked with the future of the Bali Aga and other geographically distant peoples, just as our pasts are irreversibly joined. What kind of future will it be?

The futures of the Mountain Balinese and of people in societies similarly positioned at the fringe of emerging global fields of power and knowledge depend in part on how their cultures are represented in the minds and words of others. If this book were to dispel some of the prejudices that, until now, have relegated the highland people to the shadowy recesses of Balinese civilization and to the footnotes of anthropological literature on the island, its most urgent purpose would have been accomplished.

The present modus vivendi of the Bali Aga people will inevitably need to be adjusted in response to changing social and economic conditions in Bali and increasing involvement in a national and global scenario. Their ethnohistory provides reasonable grounds to conjecture that this adjustment may not necessarily herald a complete loss of their unique way of life. Bali Aga tradition has never been stagnant or monolithic but has reserved a special place in its midst for the incorporation of respectable newcomers and new knowledge from the outside world.

As they were entering the twenty-first century, most of my informants still argued that the received wisdom of the ancestors is a gift rather than a chain around their hands and minds. Some suggested explicitly that if their society were to disregard or deny the past, it would become ignorant of itself. In Weberian terms, they would enter into the iron cage of a disciplinary society that is no longer understandable or contestable but has become an entirely self-evident reality.

The dominant ideology of present-day globalism is economic rationalism, the pseudopostmodern tip on the old tree trunk of liberal individualism, and it has certainly grown dominant enough to have reached Bali. With its focal metaphor of an ever-changing market and its obsession for "up-to-date information," this ideology depicts such an enchanted present without a past. Having failed the original aims of the Enlightenment project of modernity, the once sacred ideal of reason has become instrumentalized rationality, a mere tool for the maximization of profit. This celebration of the competitive pursuit of economic interests has led to a condition of alienation in a society without community, a condition that is now becoming increasingly familiar to urban Balinese (including a sizable contingent of Bali Aga expatriates). Similarly, the Hegelian call for the cultivation of a critical historical consciousness has been eclipsed by a less inspired concern for minimizing production time. With their awareness depleted by the twin demands of rapid production and breathless consumption, time for the global citizen has shrunk to a narrow present without much space for reflection, let alone retrospection.

With Weber, Horkheimer, and Adorno, I would argue that new forms of domination and irrationality were inadvertently created in the pursuit of the Enlightenment's hopes for a more rational modern world. If the experiment of modernity—with its sinister dialectic of knowledge and domination—is to become a lesson of the past, genuinely postmodern societies of the future must either examine this past or face the tyranny of a timeless pseudopostmodern present. Perhaps the Enlightenment's hopes for a more rational future may yet be salvaged through an escape from the philosophy of (subjective) consciousness into a utopia of emancipatory reason—based on processes of free, intersubjective argumentation—as outlined by Jürgen Habermas (1984) in his theory of communicative action. Or perhaps, as suggested by Michel Foucault, the Western vision of a better society may pitch its hopes not on a single and universal utopia but on a heterotopia (1970:xviii).[11] May it be a future in which there is room for difference and retrospection, and room for a people like the highland Balinese to pursue their own aspirations as a critical alternative to our own.

Notes

INTRODUCTION

1. During my major fieldwork stay in Bali, I resided in two communities in the district of Kintamani. Both villages participate in the largest among a number of ritual alliance networks in the highlands, the domain of the Penulisan temple. My first two visits to Bali in 1981 and 1984 were as a culturally interested traveler.

2. Indonesian words, written in italics in this text, are Balinese unless stated otherwise. B.I. stands for Bahasa Indonesia, the national language of Indonesia.

3. Briefly in advance: I do not deny that status claims tend to be raised and contested in a spirit of competition. As long as participants in the social field concerned cooperate voluntarily rather than simply being coerced into cooperation, however, such claims and counterclaims are likely to rely for their validation on the general acceptance of a shared cultural logic of argumentation and on compliance with regulated social procedures of contestation. Bali Aga alliance networks are of great interest precisely because they are heavily reliant on voluntary association.

4. I define discourse as the cultural practice of communication, through language or other forms of symbolic expression, in speech or in writing. Discourse is more than the sum of the individual speech acts of a set of speakers. It is shaped in both form and content by culture, ethnicity, or other forms of affiliation set in a specific historical context. When I speak of Balinese or Bali Aga discourses, I am thus referring not simply to the common content of the utterances I have listened to but to the cooperative elements I have observed in the way individuals express and support the validity of their views. Unlike a grammar in the more conventional sense, a discourse expects of utterances that they not only are intelligible but contain claims that seem at least reasonable (if not necessarily valid) to other speakers by virtue of their conformity to a cultural standard of argumentation. The specific claims contained in the utterances of participants in a discourse may be shared as well, but this is not necessarily the case. Discourse may serve cooperation by setting a standard of argumentation, but it also allows different individuals or groups to pursue their own and often conflicting strategic interests by raising specific arguments and by contesting those raised by others. However, the strategic intentions of individual speakers and the ideological twist in their utterances alone are not sufficient to lend to a discourse the character of an ideology. Although the distinction may only be one of degree, I prefer to reserve the term "ideology" to designate a body of unverified discursive claims, with a false flair of universal validity underwritten almost exclusively by systematic coercion and institutionalized inequalities. This would be too harsh a term in relation to southern Balinese discourses about the highland people.

5. Intense wet rice cultivation is also impossible in most of the Bali Aga villages situated on the northeastern coast, though the reason for this is lack of water rather than climate.

6. The cultivation of coffee for export was initially encouraged by Chinese traders and then expanded significantly and forcibly under Dutch colonial administration. Large clove plantations were later added, with encouragement from the Indonesian government, to supply a growing clove cigarette (B.I. *kretek*) industry. Many of these plantations have since disappeared, their trees felled in anger by local farmers as clove prices began to plunge. Farmers blame this disaster on a government-supported cartel in the *kretek* industry that was able to dictate the market price. Reliance on cash crops has generally created a vulnerability to price fluctuations in global markets but also a certain resilience to major downturns in national economic cycles. Highland farmers, for example, were not affected negatively by Indonesia's recent economic crisis as a steep rise in international coffee prices (especially in rupiah terms) offset cost increases due to local inflation.

7. The national government has made a strong effort to provide basic health care and education to people in the highlands of Bali and elsewhere. Local population growth reflects a declining infant mortality rate and an increasing life expectancy due to better health care, hygiene, and a more steady food supply, where epidemics and famine were once common. Nevertheless, living conditions are still harsh in many mountain villages. Local participation in national family-planning schemes (B.I. *keluarga berencana*), which promote the idea that "two children are enough," may eventually lead to a decline in population growth.

8. In Trunyan and some other highland villages, the body of a deceased person is exposed to the elements rather than buried, which is the more common form of corpse disposal in the highlands. Unlike a Tibetan sky-burial, the corpse is protected from scavenging animals by a loosely plaited bamboo structure. While an exception is made in the case of Trunyan, for the benefit of tourism, this practice has to be concealed elsewhere to avoid criticism from state authorities, who regard it as a threat to public health.

9. This is possible only on the assumption that difference and distance, though they sometimes coincide, are not the same. At a basic interpersonal level, human subjectivity is shaped by a psychology of distance as a result of our condition of embodiment. Cultural subjectivity, as I have attempted to illustrate, is often similarly embedded in a psychology of distance. Knowledge as such, however, is about particular (in this case cultural) differences rather than about distance, no matter how much distance may serve to insinuate difference in general.

CHAPTER 1: THE *BANUA* AS A CATEGORY AND A SOCIAL PROCESS

1. I am grateful to Dunker Schaareman for providing me with copies of Grader's unpublished field notes on his research in Kintamani. The notes suggest that Grader's evident research interest in Kintamani never came to fruition. Dr. Schaareman also passed on to me some unpublished notes from his own preliminary research in Kintamani in the 1970s. Both sources contain information on local patterns of village organization gathered by the authors in the course of several short visits. The data were valuable in allowing me to add some temporal depth to my perception of Bali Aga village organization. Systems of intervillage alliance, however, were not explored.

2. I am referring here to a mutual autonomy among highland villages only, rather than a condition of absolute political and economic autonomy. The people of a village (*desa*) and their local institutions (*desa adat, banjar*) are no

longer autonomous even in regulating their own internal affairs, given that they are incorporated into the political system of the Indonesian state as its smallest units of administration (*desa dinas, banjar dinas*). Such political incorporation can be traced back to colonial and precolonial times. As participants in an increasingly global system of production and trade, especially with a gradual shift from subsistence to cash crops, local farmers also no longer can be described as locally autonomous in economic terms, if, indeed, they ever were.

3. Using gift exchange as an example, if a patron were to bestow identical gifts on all his clients as an expression of approval, these gifts would be of no value for distinguishing between them in terms of their relative status in relation to the patron. Nevertheless, the gifts would still be useful as a general expression of stronger approval toward clients relative to nonclients.

4. The use of words such as "territory" and similar Western terms is inherently problematic because of the implications they carry in relation to their origin in Western political history. Such problems cannot be avoided except by describing in detail in what limited and specific sense *banua* can be conceived as territories. For now, I simply wish to stress that *banua* provide a place-focused more than a kinship-focused rationale for social participation.

5. For a more detailed discussion of reflexes of **banua* that may connote a house or inhabited territory, see Fox 1993:12. On the meaning of the term "*wanua*" in Old Javanese, refer to Supomo 1995:295. Reflexes of the constructions **tanah* and **daRat* often carry similar meanings in these languages, as in Balinese *tanah desa* (village land). Note that comparative linguists use an asterisk to indicate a reconstructed term in the hypothetical protolanguage from which a family of contemporary languages in which reflexes of this term occur is said to have evolved.

6. The terrain of the central temple of a *banua* and all land directly attached to it (*tanah laba pura*) are "owned by the deity" (*duwen bhatara*) of that temple in a more immediate sense than the land of the domain as a whole. In theory all proceeds from the use of *tanah laba pura* should be consumed in the temple's festivals. However, in practice it may happen that the leadership of the village in which the temple is located diverts these funds to other purposes. This allegedly occurred and caused many disputes at Pura Balingkang (Chapter 5).

7. One of the most elaborate blood sacrifices includes a red dog with a black snout.

8. Clifford Geertz, drawing on the Babad Tanah Jawi and his ethnographic research, reports about similar cultural schema of human-spirit relations in Java (1960:23). This island too is believed to have been in the possession of spirits (*bangsa alus*) before the arrival of the first human colonizers. It is the original covenant between people and land, and continuing good relations among contemporary occupants and those who first used the land that established and maintain human prosperity and the fertility of the fields.

9. In this book I follow the modern spelling conventions of the Balinese dictionary officially sanctioned by the provincial government with few exceptions. For example, in modern Balinese the silent "h" in *daha* (maiden) is no longer written (*daa*). When referring to Balinese gods I make an exception: I use the more old-fashioned and polite spelling "*bhatara.*" It is polite in that it conforms to the spelling of the word in the more refined language of Kawi (Old Javanese).

10. The supreme human ancestor of an extended and dispersed clan group (*warga*), for example, is referred to as Bhatara Kawitan, "the god of origin." It is

remarkable that even the sun god, Bhatara Surya, can be constructed as an ancestor of human beings. In an origin myth from Trunyan, the sun is said to have impregnated the mother of the original human twins and ancestors of this village (Danandjaja 1980:40).

11. I shall later explore how and why this transformation process has occurred and how, in the course of this process, certain historical factors have led to the rise of a regional field of interaction in which the major concern is status rather than political power.

12. The aversion to the falling apart of a natural whole is exemplified in folk beliefs. Locals claim horrifying creatures may sometimes be encountered in graveyards at night taking the shape of severed body parts (e.g., hands: *tangan-tangan*).

13. *Pangamong* is derived from *among*, "to take care of, stand guard," or *ameng*, "to hold or wield a weapon"; while *pangempon* is derived from *empon*, "to take care of a task" or "to organize an event," or perhaps from *empu*, "to nurse or look after [a child]." Both of these local terms are more suggestive of extraordinary duties than of superior rights. This qualification needs to be added in speaking of their status as one of ritual authority or leadership.

14. The term "*pura banua*" is also occasionally used to designate a temple marking the boundary between the territories of the two villages who jointly support it.

15. The *gebog banua* is the group of villages whose people are the foremost supporters of the domain's principal temple, whereas the wider membership of a domain may include other supporters.

16. Prestations offered by a village (*atos desa*) are seen as an acknowledgment of a link beyond concepts of kinship and an obligation beyond the general observances of religious piety. They differ significantly in content and size from prestations offered by a family group or individual (*aturan pribadi*).

17. However, even in societies oriented toward the accumulation of material possessions as the most salient status markers, some material objects have personal as well as monetary significance and are not readily alienable or exchangeable.

18. There are exceptions where only one faction within a branch village may *mabanua* at a regional temple. This tends to be an indication of a power struggle in the village. In one case, a group of "village founders" continued to *mabanua* at the source temple when their village as a whole had stopped attending. In this manner, they reminded everyone that their claim to a position of prominence as branch village founders was still accepted within the domain, even though it was beginning to be denied by other factions in their own village.

19. Note that the term "*k(e)rama desa*" refers to the village council as a whole, while the term "*keraman desa*" refers to the group of its actual members at any given time.

20. Some versions of this narrative attempt to establish in what order these villages were founded. None of these has gained general acceptance.

21. It is common practice for narrators to ask the gods for forgiveness of any mistakes or omissions in advance or after they have finished reciting an origin narrative.

22. Sometimes all the villages within a *banua* are included within a *gebog banua* and are required to pay *peturunan*. But, more commonly, some participants in the rituals of a domain are excluded from the *gebog banua* and therefore only contribute *atos desa*. Both types of supporters may also provide a third kind of contribution called "*cucukan*," which consists of specific indispensable and essen-

tial ingredients for producing the key offerings used in a ceremony at the *pura banua.*

23. As among the Bali Aga, the ceremonial division of sacrificial animals is an important aspect of Kédang ritual, and the name of the body part received by a group of persons may be used as the designation for the social category to which they belong (Barnes 1974:236).

24. Several subcategories of reconstructions of the Proto-Austronesian word for "leaf" (**da'un*, where "au" is blended into "o" in Balinese *don*) feature an initial "n" or "en." An example is the Proto-Oceanic **ndaun* (Wurm and Wilson 1975:118). This may explain the derivation of the Balinese verb "*endon*" (to come, arrive), which is more commonly regarded as the free morpheme in *pendonan* than the noun "*don.*"

25. Often their decision to conform to a local and distinctly Bali Aga tradition meant a major change for newcomers to the domain of Selulung. Many came from southern Bali and were unfamiliar with local customs. Those among them who had a high-caste title had to renounce it formally. Their villages are among the many that are difficult to classify as either *bali aga* or *bali dataran.* They themselves argue that their *adat* and current status is *bali aga,* but not their ancestry.

26. Bali's major temples are of relevance to rituals of ancestor worship even where they become the abode of more abstract local or Hindu deities. An example is the ritual practice called "*mendak hyang*" (to receive the purified spirit of an ancestor). It is believed that as an ancestor is gradually purified by the postmortuary ritual performances of his or her descendants, that ancestor will merge with the ultimate source of creation. Since this source is identified with the paramount temple of the domain, the fully purified ancestor must be recalled to the family temple by visiting the relevant regional temple. Once the ancestor has been brought back, he or she will dwell in the temple of the kin group (*sanggah*). Penulisan is traditionally seen by many as the appropriate place for recalling ancestors and is still frequently visited for this purpose. Recently it has been eclipsed in this respect by the more heavily promoted Pura Besakih.

27. Pura Besakih would come close to representing Bali as a whole in its ritual, at least if one were to believe the claims raised in the official discourses of the religious state organization Parisada Hindu Dharma Indonesia. Similarly, the degree of political control that the national government wields over the island is unprecedented. And yet, while religious and political state discourses may be dominant, they are not entirely successful at a level of ritual practice or in silencing counterdiscourses. Pura Penulisan may have been a temple that occupied a similar position in the past, before Pura Besakih's more recent ascendancy. Note that Pura Besakih is not mentioned in any of the Balinese *prasasti* (royal inscriptions).

28. The forty-five villages in Batur's core support network are said to correspond symbolically to the forty-five core elders in the village council of Desa Batur. The number of actual supporters of Pura Batur is much greater and is steadily increasing, as is the wider membership of Desa Batur's village assembly. The sacred slit-drum (*kulkul*) of Batur is also struck forty-five times each morning as a reminder of these two core groups: the forty-five *pasihan* and the forty-five members of the council of elders and priest-leaders.

29. This has been illustrated by Graeme Macrae (1995) in his research on ritual connections between the temples of communities in the upper Wos valley

and Pura Gunung Lebah in Ubud, and also by J. S. Lansing (1987) in his work on ritual networks relating to irrigation in Bali.

30. It is futile to attempt a premature resolution of a global political problem at the level of style in ethnographic writing. It may be more profitable to promote the direct participation of local participants in the construction of a global anthropological knowledge. I am partly responsible for the fact that anthropology is now taught for the first time in a secondary school in Kintamani as it has been for decades at a tertiary level at Udayana University in Denpasar and at many other Indonesian universities. This is only a small step, but it is part of a general trend. Anthropology can no longer be described as an exclusively Western project. Direct global participation in the construction of knowledge (symbolic resources) may still not suffice to correct existing imbalances in global patterns of political participation, however, insofar as power is also derived from the use of force and wealth (material resources).

Chapter 2: Pura Pucak Penulisan

1. There are numerous other stone artifacts preserved in this and other mountain temples. Conspicuous is the large number of *lingga* among them. *Lingga* are upright, phallus-shaped objects commonly associated with the worship of the great god Siwa in India and in early Balinese Hinduism. Some of the oldest stone statues in mountain temples were apparently made before a period of Indianization and share many features with Polynesian statues of chiefs. These statues still await a proper classification by archeologists.

2. I have recorded an almost identical creation myth in Desa Gobleg that describes the origin of lakes Buyan and Tamblingan. Again, the water first erupted from the top of a mountain peak associated with a male deity, before it settled into lakes associated with a female deity. The male god is the creator of life, and the female deity represents the repository of fertility. In a similar metaphor of cosmic ejaculation, descendants in Balinese may be referred to as "*damuh,*" the dewdrop that forms at the tip of a blade of grass or a leaf. It is worth noting that there was no tale of Mt. Batur itself erupting anything other than fire and ash. This it did once again during my stay in 1994.

3. *Tasik* also means "salt" in contemporary Balinese. Salt is an important item of trade and is harvested from the sea in Bali, particularly on the northeastern coast between Tianyar and Tembok.

4. The creation of a relatively flat coastal area is attributed to the efforts of two mythical birds, the white-feathered and crested duck and chicken (*bebek/ siap putih jambul*). The chicken (male) scratched away at the primordial mountain with his strong feet to loosen up some dirt, and the duck (female) compacted the earth with her large feet until it became flat.

5. The term "Ratu Pucak" (deity/king of the summit, from Old Javanese *ratu/ datu,* "grandfather, ancestor, ruler of a domain") is a gloss commonly used to refer to the principal deity of this temple. The identity of this deity is not clearly defined. If locals are questioned, some may identify the deity as Bhatara Siwa, Guru, or even Wisnu, and yet others as Sang Hyang Widhi. However, most prefer to designate deities by reference to their temples (deity of temple X) rather than risk divine retribution for having used an inappropriate form of address.

6. In 1961 the temple committee was approached by representatives of Pari-

sada Hindu Dharma Indonesia (National Indonesian Office of Hindu Religion) and asked to construct a permanent *sanggaran surya*. They refused, arguing in this case that all of Bali would suffer a drought if the sun god was permanently tied to the temple.

7. Hands are raised in formal greeting with the fingertips touching and the wrists slightly apart, thus forming a "peak." It was explained that the converging of the hands "at the tip" symbolizes a coming together of potential adversaries, who in their greeting express their readiness to put all differences aside in good faith. The final gesture of priestly prayer is similar but (in this area of Bali) traditionally begins with both hands open and stretched upward before they are folded together as described above (see cover photo).

8. For a review of published textual evidence in support of the historicity of these events, see Buchari 1968.

9. In one form of adoption, the child is symbolically left at a bathing place near a river or spring before it is picked up by the adoptive parents. The latter pretend that they are unaware of who the birth parents were, and the former revoke all rights as parents. Poverty is the most common motivation for this kind of abandonment of a child.

10. Farmers say that garlic is difficult to cultivate and requires constant fertilization and care, whereas onion will grow all the better for being neglected. Hence the idea of spoiled *kesuna* and neglected *bawang*.

11. In the local mythology of Gobleg, the goddess of the lake, Dewi Tirtha Mangening, also remains forever unmarried but symbolically paired with the male deity Bhatara Lang-Lang Buana, who dwells atop Gunung Raung and has likewise ejaculated the waters stored in her lake.

12. This passage is an extract from the origin narrative of Sembiran. The myth shows a number of similarities to those of the Wintang Danu, including the arrival of four emissaries of Dalem Solo later on in the narrative. In Bayung Gede's origin myth a (white) monkey is also mentioned. He brings the water of life (*tirta kamandalu*) used in the creation of the first human beings. Informants in Sukawana itself knew only fragments of this myth but accepted the fuller Sembiran version as accurate.

13. In another version, from Desa Mengani, Ni Daa Tua is a resourceful spinster of unknown origin. She was unjustly ordered to prepare all the sweet sticky rice (*kukus ketan*) for the meetings of the village council (*ulu apad*), normally a task that is shared by all households in the village. No matter how late they informed her, she was able to produce a huge amount of sweet rice in no time at all. Thus the villagers began to hate her and sought a pretext for executing her. They requested her to prepare *kukus* for the next day, for the full moon meeting, when in fact the next day was the meeting of Anggara Kasih and no *kukus* was required. Thus they created an occasion for accusing her of a mistake and threw her own hot rice upon her until she was buried beneath it and died. Before that she cursed the village to be reduced from two hundred to seven households. Later the curse was neutralized. A temple was built and dedicated to Ratu Daa so that the village population could safely increase once again. Desa Kintamani and Satra also maintain a temple for Ratu Daa Tua.

14. In a rather bawdy narrative about Ni Daa Tua recorded in Ulian, a number of humorous inversions bring out some of the sexual connotations of this theme. The tale points out that the division of labor between men and women may be arbitrary but is necessary for good relations, even though the only natural

division of labor lies in sexual reproduction: "Ni Daa Tua was clever and hard-working and able to do *everything* by herself. One day she was hoeing the fields (a task for men) on the downstream side of Ulian when Kaki Raksasa (grandfather ogre) approached her. 'Hey, Daa Tua, what are you doing?' 'I am hoeing.' 'What are you planting?' 'I am planting rice.' 'After it is ripe, then what?' 'I'll cut it.' 'After it is cut, what next?' 'I'll thresh it.' 'After it is threshed, what else?' 'I'll cook it.' 'And when it's cooked?' 'I'll eat it.' 'And when you have eaten?' 'I go to bed.' 'And when you are in bed?' 'I'll have sex!' When Kaki Raksasa heard this, he laughed so hard that he fell over and his tusks became stuck in a tree. Ni Daa Tua saw her chance and killed him, smashing his skull with her hoe."

15. It should be noted that according to the rules of a local numerology, $3 + 3 + 6 + 6 = 18 = 9 = 2 + 2 + 5 = 225$. In this esoteric sense 225 is equivalent to the sum of 33 and 66 coins.

16. These interpretations are not just the product of my own analysis. This paragraph contains in summarized form an explanation of these offerings that I received in a long conversation with an elder of Sukawana. This man was not the most senior elder but was recognized widely as a specialist in offerings, a local intellectual, and one of the few willing to verbalize their understanding of ritual symbology.

17. The root morpheme in *penulisan* is most likely *tulis*, "to write," but there are other, linguistically unfounded local interpretations. Some informants, for example, saw a metaphoric link between the topography of the Penulisan hill-top and the word "*tulih*" (to view).

18. Goris' (1954) system of numbering *prasasti* is adhered to in this text, except as specified.

19. Mpu Sakti Wahu Rahu is known also under a number of other names in southern Bali, including Dang Hyang Niartha and Sri Dwijendra, and as Sang Pasupati in Lombok.

20. In southern Bali, the Kubayan Kiwa is replaced by a *pedanda buda* and the Kubayan Tengen by a *pedanda siwa* in the context of "three-priests rituals" (with a *sengguhu*).

21. The following anecdote on the politics of holy water describes an event at this festival in 1994. It demonstrates some of the difficulties experienced by the people of Sukawana in dealing with distant visitors who do not share their Bali Aga traditions: The *pemangku* of Pura Puseh Malinggih lodged a complaint about the *tirta* produced by Sukawana elders, pointing out that no proper Sanskrit *mantra* (incantations) had been used, as specified in Parisada Hindu Dharma Indonesia ritual guidelines. Spokesmen for Sukawana countered that Sanskrit was only another language and that it is the gods who make *tirta*, not the human officiant. They became quite infuriated when the *mangku* pulled out a little bottle of *tirta* that he had prepared at home, with Sanskrit *mantra*, and asked permission to mix it in with the other *tirta* as a supplement. They angrily questioned why he had come at all if he could make his own *tirta*. In the end permission was granted on the basis that more *tirta*, after all, could do no harm. The *mangku* emptied his bottle into the larger vessel, but, alas, his *tirta* floated to the top! After an instant of silence, the bystanders broke into a roaring laugh, and even the elders were grinning. The *mangku* had consecrated the wrong bottle back at home, and spoken his *mantra* over a batch of coconut oil! All the *tirta* had to be discarded, and the rite was repeated for a new batch—with prayers spoken only in Balinese!

22. The Pura Bale Agung is perhaps the most important local temple in all

Balinese villages, and in the mountains it is the most common location for village assembly meetings on the new and full moon. The literal meaning is "the temple of the great pavilion [of assembly]." A *pura penataran agung* is a "temple yard" for a remote summit temple and is situated at a less elevated and more convenient location.

23. This larger festival was celebrated last in 1992 and will be held again in 2002 if there are no prohibiting circumstances.

24. People from Sulahan reported how a violent quarrel had erupted during a festival at the Pura Puseh of their village. When all had calmed down, it appeared that no one remembered who had caused it. Talk began of a "divine warning," and shortly thereafter several people saw a pale and ghostlike female figure appear in their midst, riding on a huge black bull (*sampi wadak*) of the kind only found in the Kintamani district. She said that they would all perish in a *perang saudara* (civil war) unless they accompanied her to visit her father at Pura Pucak Penulisan. They instantly obeyed, and the apparition walked with them until the very boundary of Desa Sukawana, where it finally vanished.

25. Some of my eldest informants reported a radical increase in the number of formal *barong* visits during their lifetime. They suggested that *barong* journeys used to be mainly an entertainment in the past. The masked carriers would go from house to house and ask for small amounts of cash or rice in exchange for a dance performance. In a similar but more recent move toward ritual formalization, the utterly secular and bawdy *joget* dance is beginning to be sponsored as a part of temple festivals. It is conceivable that such performances could become more obligatory.

26. This ritual is formally referred to as "*mapurowita*," from *purohita* (Sanskrit), "the priest of a royal household," or "high priest in a kingdom." Local mythology has it that when the king of Bali resided in nearby Puri Dalem Balingkang, his *purohita* resided at Penulisan. A Jero Kubayan or Jero Bau of Sukawana who has undergone this ritual is indeed claimed to be "of equal rank with the paramount ruler of Bali and the Jero Gede of Pura Batur" in the Catur Dharma Kelawasan. This is a palm-leaf manuscript from the Klungkung era of which I found two exemplars with only slight differences in content. A more colloquial term for the same ritual is "*mapodgala*." Note that a Jero Bau ranks below a *kubayan*, the most senior elder, but is already a priest-leader and may represent him in most of his ritual duties whenever necessary.

27. One exception are the people of Desa Blantih, who always bring a special offering for the deity of Pura Gaduh when they attend the annual festival at Pura Penulisan.

28. It is worth noting that Pura Penulisan has been classified as a tourist object and a historical site by Bali's provincial government (Pemda, *pemerintah daerah*). The temple is guarded constantly by Pemda staff to prevent the theft or damage of artifacts. The guards charge a small entry fee to tourists for insurance purposes and to cover their own wages. Groups of tourists arrive in buses almost on a daily basis. There is no tourist accommodation locally available that would allow them to stay overnight.

CHAPTER 3: *GEBOG DOMAS*

1. The above data were taken from the financial report of the temple committee (Panitia Pura Pucak Penulisan) about the annual temple festival and

repairs carried out at Pura Pucak Penulisan in 1992. The money is normally collected in each village and passed on to the chairman (*ketua*) of this committee. This contribution is not a donation (*dana punia*). It may be voluntary in principle, but in practice it is an obligation that few would dare to neglect. The amount was Rp 4,000 per household in 1992.

2. These figures are based on the "Laporan Kependudukan Kecamatan Kintamani," a government demographic study completed in October 1994.

3. In other parts of Bali, the *banjar* is an association of neighbors and is concerned with the more mundane aspects of cooperation within the community but also with mutual help in the context of mortuary and other rituals. One *desa adat* usually comprises several such neighborhoods. However, the norm in the Kintamani district is one *desa adat*–one *banjar*, whereby the *desa adat* has more stringent membership criteria than the *banjar*. The term "neighborhood" is thus somewhat misleading as a translation. These *banjar* are often referred to as "*banjar dalem*," indicating that members are responsible for the rituals celebrated at the Pura Dalem, rituals that are related to mortuary and postmortuary rites as well. These issues are discussed further in Chapter 6. Note that the word "*dalem*" is also used to refer to a king.

4. From his analysis of Javanese inscriptions, S. Supomo has reconstructed that the smallest unit of Javanese political organization before Indianization was probably the *wanua* (village, settlement), which came under the authority of a group of elders (*rama*, "father") (1995:295–296). *Wanua* were in turn organized into larger clusters called "*watak*" or "*watek*," under the authority of a *rakai* (grandfather/elder). Several *watak* in turn were encompassed by a *kedatwan* (from *datu/ratu*, "king/apical ancestor"). It is not impossible that the word "*satak*" may be related to Javanese "*watak*," perhaps as a contraction of "*sa-watak*" (one *watak*).

5. Note the thematic similarities with the narratives concerning Ratu Daa Tua that have been discussed earlier.

6. A temple dedicated to this saint has been built (or rebuilt) recently on the southern slope of Mt. Raung in the village of Wono Asih (Glenmore district).

7. The narrative of Maharishi Markandeya is particularly significant as a charter of origin for villages around Ubud and Payangan, where it is told differently and in much more detail (Graeme Macrae, personal communication).

8. Note that all these distances are based on straight lines. The travel distances by road or walking track can be twice as long.

9. Relevant examples are the villages Belok, Sidan, and Tambakan, which are located outside the boundaries of Kabupaten Bangli. The lack of contact between administrative village heads (*kepala desa dinas*) at *kecamatan*-level meetings was cited as a cause of this estrangement. The *banua* temple of these villages (Pura Pucak Antap Sai) was linked to Penulisan in the past (see Chapter 6).

10. Banjar Haa (from *lahah*, "dirty, ugly") is a small *desa adat* northwest of Sukawana and was settled by outcast *adat* offenders from Sukawana (as was Desa Adat Kubusalia) and Bangli. The derogative name was recently changed to Desa Angansari. Banjar Haa is no longer allowed to attend festivals at Pura Pucak Penulisan. Their offerings began to be considered polluted and unacceptable only after the village became a place of exile for offenders from Bangli.

11. Even priest-leaders are often unwilling to comment on the precise genealogical relationships among the many deities of the center, subcenters, and member villages of the domain. The present narrative is not widely known outside Sukawana. Although informants in other communities were aware of part

of the story, their knowledge was usually confined to elements that directly concerned their own village.

12. In the Subaya version of this narrative, the one who desires human flesh is a male deity who came from Lake Bratan. In this narrative there is also mention of a child of Ratu Pucak who came to Subaya, but she is female and is known as Ratu Ayu Subandar.

13. Bantang's position of precedence over Selulung and Kintamani in this sequence is reflected, for example, in intervillage marriages. People from Sukawana will rarely allow their daughters to marry outsiders, but when they do, the men are most often from Bantang.

14. Versions of the Usana Bali kept at Pusat Documentasi Bali also speak of such a relocation of the royal palace. Unfortunately, I have not yet had the opportunity to publish on the *lontar* texts that I have managed to collect in the highlands.

15. A statue of Bhatari Mandul ("the childless goddess or queen") is still found in Pura Pucak Penulisan. It was dated A.D. 1077 by Stutterheim (1929).

16. I would like to emphasize that the political aspect of a ritual domain is not the primary dimension of its meaning, as a superficial interpretation of the evident competition for status may lead one to conclude. Though religious and political discourses or activities cannot be clearly separated in the case of the Bali Aga, the moderate competitive concerns of participants are for status rather than power. The authority and status gained by prominent members remain confined to a ritual context in this politically rather egalitarian society.

17. Until today it is the villagers of Pengejaran who provide the rattan rope (*penyalin*) for the ritual swing that is erected in the Pura Bale Agung of Sukawana whenever there is an *usaba ngawiji* (this is a special festival held on the rare occasions when the village has a full set of six consecrated priest-leaders at the time of the *usaba*). A ritual swing of this type is also used in the Bali Aga village Subaya (*usaba ngapitu*), and ritual "Ferris wheels" (*jantra*), in Trunyan (Pura Pancering Jagat), Les (Pura Puseh Panjingan), and Tenganan.

18. When a subsidiary center can manage to attract clients from outside the larger and encompassing domain, it is often a significant step toward gaining ritual independence. For example, one factor that helped Pura Balingkang to a degree of independence from Pura Penulisan is that some of its clients have no direct link to Penulisan at all (see Chapter 5).

19. Given that some of Selulung's traditions are rather different from those of other villages in the *gebog domas,* it is also understandable that the second myth speculates about Selulung's official status as first settlers in this western *gebog satak* of Penulisan. They may indeed be later arrivals who had belonged among the people of the Batur area, with whom they share many specific traditions and close ritual ties.

20. In some cases the mere rumor of physical evidence, such as a hint that a particular person possesses a written (*lontar*) version of the origin narrative, can suffice to silence possible critics.

21. See Connor 1982 for a detailed description of the practices of *balian* and their clientele.

22. It is very common in Bali that conflicts are expressed by mutual avoidance or by "not acknowledging one another's presence" (*puik*).

23. The alternating location of festivals between the two temples is related to the polluting effect of postmortuary rituals. These are held during the second

month (*sasih karo*) and are polluting to the spring from which water is drawn for the purpose of the rituals. The polluted spring cannot be used in the same year as a source of *tirta* for the regional temple. Pausan thus holds its postmortuary rituals only in even years, when the festival is held at Langahan, and vice versa. Note that the springs in the two villages are the sources of two branches of the river Tukat Tampus. The *subak* thus ask for *tirta* at the one of the two river sources that is unpolluted by postmortuary ritual in any given year. Tukad Tampus irrigates much of the eastern Payangan area, together with the larger Tukad (Anak) Ayung to the west, which originates at Penulisan and unites with Tukad Tampus just south of Desa Buahan (Payangan).

24. The wood for a *barong* mask is often obtained from a tree or location that is considered sacred or magically potent (*tenget*). If the subsequent ritual practices in which this *barong* plays a part were justified by reference to its mere physical origin, then it would at first seem that the human agency and sociality of the visit had become utterly objectified. However, the original selection of a location for obtaining wood represents a rather arbitrary human choice, with no socially binding effect beyond the life span of the particular *barong* mask. By contrast, the genealogical relations between *barong*-riding deities represent in principle an immutable condition, depicted as ontologically prior to any human choices. It is therefore inaccurate to suggest that literal objectification (in a physical rather than metaphysical sense) is the most extreme means of denying human agency.

25. One reason why I would describe these temples as relay stations is that most of Pausan's *subak* clients are also *subak* clients of Pura Pucak Penulisan.

26. Some of Penulisan's distant allies will be mentioned throughout Chapter 6, including the villages Bayung Gede, Tejakula, Les, Margatengah, Belok, and Sidan.

27. Desa Tejakula once (genuinely) forgot that a buffalo was due, probably because this additional sacrifice occurs only once in ten years. A buffalo was purchased and sacrificed nonetheless, to the utter embarrassment of Tejakula. They later refunded the amount expended for the purchase to the *gebog domas*.

28. Note that the *bali rama* (*krama desa*) of Batur until today consists of forty-five members. Forty-five is an ideal number and is related to the concept of *nawa-sanga*, the nine directions of the cosmos and their corresponding deities. The link is that forty-five in numerological terms equals four plus five, or nine (*sanga*).

29. Desa Les is also indirectly connected to Sukawana through its membership in the *kanca satak* of Pura Balingkang (Chapter 5). The following list of offerings brought by Les for the festival at Penulisan is an example of the composition of *atos desa*, though it also includes some items that are part of the unique contribution of this village (*cucukan*): one *salaran* (an offering including a duck and a chicken), two times ten coconuts (yellow and green variety), ten *catur* (2.5 kg) each of white and black rice, six types of saltwater fish (*ikan umbul-umbul, udang pantung, suda mala, mas, bera, rerontek*), ten *bila* fruits, traditional Chinese coins, and a number of accompanying flower offerings. *Atos desa* often also includes a pig and is usually accompanied by substantial cash donations.

30. *Benang tukelan* are worn as belts by high priests at Penulisan and are also used for a special rope by which the sacrificial buffalo is led in procession.

31. The napped cotton fabric for the jacket worn by the *kubayan* of Sukawana (*baju jujut*), however, is obtained in Manikliyu (or alternatively in Payangan). Manikliyu's *prasasti* describes the village as a "community of weavers." This may explain why they are still held responsible for providing this jacket even though there have been no weavers in Manikliyu in living memory.

32. Prasasti Kintamani E (A.D. 1200) states the specific privileges held by the traders of Kintamani (over those of the lake villages, or Wintang Danu) with regard to the cotton trade *from* the mountains *to* villages on the coast, including Julah. Prasasti Sukawana D (A.D. 1300) grants similar privileges to the people of Sukawana and also states that there were extensive cotton plantations between Sukawana and Balingkang. Note that the symbolically female activities of weaving and planting rice are prohibited in Sukawana.

33. In 1937 Grader published the results of a study he had conducted in Madenan. He reported that this and many other villages in Eastern Buleleng regularly attended at Pura Penulisan on the fourth full moon (p. 97).

34. Pecatu's troubles have been amplified recently by an enormous government-sponsored tourism development plan for the Bukit peninsula. Locals explained to me how in the political and legal intrigues that led to the appropriation of their village land by outsiders, their claim to a *patih* relationship with the royal house of Pamecutan was rejected by the latter in return for a payoff from the developers.

35. A written version of this narrative is contained in a *lontar* in the possession of Warga Tambiak, Desa Pecatu. The narrative shares several themes with the tale that explains the *baris goak* dance of Selulung (Riana 1992), wherein the Raja of Badung is attacked by enchanted black birds (*goak*) and aided by a Bali Aga culture hero.

36. There is a legend that suggests why the sacrificial buffalo has to be purchased in Kabupaten Badung: "Once there was a large festival at Pura Besakih for which several buffaloes were offered. In the end there were two animals that had not been sacrificed, and they were sold off, one to Buleleng and one to Negara. Ever since, the buffalo to be offered at Pura Penulisan was purchased in Badung, because an animal obtained from these two other areas could be a descendant of the Besakih buffaloes, which were the leftovers of Bhatara Besakih and therefore unfit as sacrifices to Ratu Pucak Penulisan." The myth suggests that Pura Penulisan's status is higher than that of Pura Besakih, according to some.

37. The most explicit links relate to Songan's involvement with Sukawana-dominated Pura Balingkang, to the Pasek Kayuselem origin narrative (chapters 5 and 6), and to the belief in an underground water channel that originates at Gedong Puser Tasik and feeds into Lake Batur at Songan.

38. The ethnic Chinese population of Kintamani deserves further study. For a brief comment on the Chinese in Bali in general, see Eiseman 1990:114–128.

CHAPTER 4: THE RITUAL PROCESS OF A DOMAIN

1. References to a recent death in the village can sometimes be used as a polite excuse to stay away when other motivations are in play.

2. For a succinct exposition on the complex Balinese calendar systems, see Goris 1960.

3. A film based on video recordings of this festival is available from the author.

4. Highland Balinese is sometimes described as a form of "low" Balinese, as opposed to the high Balinese used in southern Bali when people of lower status address individuals belonging to a higher caste. I find this labeling unfair. While there are also degrees of politeness in the local Balinese, a distinction between high and low Balinese is not a relevant one in relation to the language practice of the casteless highland people.

5. The upper platform of the square *sanggaran tawang* (Old Javanese "shrine of the sky") is dedicated to Bhatara Surya (the sun god). Its lower structure contains a miniature hearth with an iron cooking vessel for deep frying. There are numerous allusions to ritual as a cooking process in other contexts.

6. Visitors will prepare such personal offerings at home as are required for the act of individual worship and prayer.

7. There are also some written manuals on offering composition (*bebanten*) and ritual procedure (*anteb-anteban*). These are not consulted by women, nor do the texts attempt to describe in detail the structure of individual offerings and their often already complex smaller components. Such *lontar* usually provide a list of finished offerings, and the knowledge of how to construct them is taken for granted.

8. The term is derived from *bangkit*, "delightful, delicious," or *bangket*, "rice field." A *bebangkit* offering depicts the world and its content, including a human effigy (*adegan*) made of cooked rice. It is used to propitiate demonic beings (*buta kala*), especially their corpse-devouring queen, the Hindu deity Bhatari Durga. Men take the leading role in the blood sacrifices and preparation of offerings for such chthonic beings. Note that the *bebangkit* offering also contains an array of animal species, including the fish brought by Les and (if available) a scaly anteater (*kelesi*), porcupine (*landak*), and various bird species.

9. From *sayut* (Kawi, Balinese *andeg*), "to stop, retain," as in "to stop menstruating owing to a pregnancy," or possibly from *sayub*, "calm." The offering is aimed to seek a divine blessing so as to ward off disaster, misfortune, and the loss of crops. The singing of a male elder is likened to a husband giving support and strength to his pregnant wife (*aji*, "father"; *kembang*, "to grow, blossom").

10. Some uranian deities are female in gender, and some chthonic deities are male. Gender is also context-dependent. Durga (female), for example, is the male deity Siwa in his overtly female aspect, while Kala (male) is a demonic manifestation of Siwa and thus female in symbolic function. I am here only referring to the general gender attributes of the two classes of supernatural beings associated with the upper and nether worlds of the Balinese cosmos.

11. I will here merely list the most important collective offering arrangements for this festival, for comparative purposes. It would introduce another major and complex topic if I were to describe and analyze their composition and meaning in detail. These main offerings include *pula kerti, pula kerta, pula kedaton, bakti kampuh jero gede, suci sorohan, jerimpen, sayut agung, bebangkit, tutuan, siwabau, sapa degdeg, rantasan, sayut alit, pregembal, banten dulangan*, and *sekar taman*.

12. The *nyuh titikan* can also be obtained at Pura Puseh Panjingan in Les and at a village temple in Madenan. In each case, they originate from a coconut palm growing inside a village sanctuary.

13. The *saya bunga* and their families are also responsible for the numerous other utensils and ingredients required for the divination ritual. All of these have to be purified at home by the *balian desa* of Sukawana before they can be taken to Pura Penulisan.

14. The timing of the festival sometimes diverges from the standard Balinese calendar during leap years with an additional, thirteenth lunar month (*nampih karo*). In such years, the fourth full moon is identified by reference to the position of the constellation Pleiades (*bintang kartika*), which is named "*kartika*" after

the fourth month in the Indian lunar calendar. When this constellation is positioned in the zenith at sunset, it is assumed to be *sasih kapat* (the fourth Balinese month). Hence the festival in the leap year 1993 was held on what was the third full moon according to the official pan-Balinese calendar.

15. The tempo and composition of gamelan music varies according to the ritual context. The music accompanying processions is particularly fast and vigorous.

16. The elders of Sukawana had begun a tour of village temples before dawn in order to invite the deities of all nearby temples to gather at Penulisan. Groups from other villages had engaged in similar gathering rituals at home and had visited way-station temples on the road to Penulisan.

17. The rite is associated with Pura Daa primarily. However, its courtyard is far too small to allow for a collective prayer by a crowd of this magnitude.

18. This twenty-one-day festival is not yet the most elaborate held at Pura Penulisan. The *lontar* Catur Dharma Kalawasan mentions several larger sacrifices, the highest level involving the centennial sacrifice of twelve buffaloes. None alive can remember the celebration of this ritual, which is said to "revive the entire island" and is the responsibility of the paramount ruler of Bali. Locals say that many of Bali's current social problems are due to the neglect of the temple by the secular authorities. Yet they also fear such involvement, for it could end in a challenge to their own ritual authority.

19. In the wet season this same rock is heated in order to gain a respite from rain during ritual events.

20. A precedence ordering of female before male is most clearly symbolized in the *salaran*, an important offering carried at the head of any ritual procession. This offering consists of two sticks tied together, one of *kayu sakti/dapdap* (*Erythrina lithosperma Miq.*, female) and one of *kayu tebu* (sugar cane, male). The arrangement is carried with the base (*bongkol*, female) of the branches pointing ahead and the tip (*muncuk*, male) at the back. At the front is a basket with a duck (female), at the back another with a chicken (male). It is also common practice that women walk ahead of men except when going steeply uphill. Women are said to walk with small steps like a duck (because of their tight sarongs), while men take large strides "like a fighting cock."

21. If one of the coconuts in the first set is imperfect, the reserves are used, and failing that, the coconuts brought by the relatives of the *saya bunga*, or as a last resort, any coconuts that can be found in the village. Old people tell of an occasion when it came to this extreme and "the temple was flooded with coconut juice." In the end, the very last coconuts in the village, which belonged to a "*daa tua*" (old spinster), were found to be perfect. Though the harvest was said to have been minimal in that year, at least there was no starvation.

22. The rope (*penandan*) used for leading the buffalo in procession had been blessed earlier by presenting it to the deity at Pujut Ayah, a shrine at the spring beneath Pura Penulisan from which the River Ayung originates.

23. For some unknown reason the procession proceeded in clockwise direction during the 1993 festival.

24. The order of procession is rather more complex than has been described. Suffice to say that each group is headed by *sekaa daa* and *teruna* (organizations of unmarried village girls and boys) who carry the seats of the gods and their "beauty utensils" (combs, mirrors, perfume, and even soap).

25. Signe Howell mentions a similar distinction between the symbolic and

actual slaying of the victim in her study of sacrifice among the Northern Lio of Flores (1996:94). She interprets the initial drawing of blood from a live animal as a means of separating the life-giving significance of blood from the event of the victim's death.

26. The interpretation that ritual sacrifice is an act of reciprocal exchange, punctuating momentary reversals in a cosmic flow of life, has been put forward in many studies of Indonesian societies. For example, Elizabeth Traube notes that in the cosmology of the Mambai of East Timor, "a principle of reciprocity integrates the two poles of existence. Life and death are defined in this scheme as reciprocal prestations, complementary gifts which call forth each other in the dialectic unfolding of an exchange relationship" (1986:11).

27. It is exceptional that the buffalo bones are later buried at the conclusion of this festival. In village-level festivals, however, each elder receives the bone of a sacrificial pig that is specific to his rank and the attached meat as part of his ritual food portion. This is true not only of Sukawana. The rank-specific division of a *wangun urip* is a common element of ritual in all Bali Aga villages.

28. The word "*baris*" (to line up) is a descriptive label, given that *baris* dancers always line up in a linear formation.

29. Why some *subak* attend in the fourth and some in the fifth month remains unclear, but it may relate to variations in the commencement of rice planting in different areas.

30. These offerings included the *pula kerta, pula kerti, pula kedaton,* and *sapa jambeng*. Note that the terms "*pula*" (to plant), "*kerta*" (law), and "*kerti*" (discipline) suggest that these offerings relate to a (regional) ordering or synchronization of the planting of crops.

31. An additional rite was conducted at this point during the 1993 festival. The *sekaa teruna,* who accompany the *ngluaran* procession with their spears, divided into two groups that formed two concentric circles with the elders of Sukawana in the center. The two groups of boys then started running around the elders in opposite directions. This rite was explained as an expression of the immanent separation between a *niskala* and a *sekala* world, with the elders symbolizing the power of establishing a ritual link between them.

32. Even from the ethnographer's perspective the festival became an exciting experience, prompting a cheerful reunion with countless friends and acquaintances from all the different villages of the domain. As it may be for participants, it was an opportunity to celebrate the social network and the understanding of a ritual world I had gained during my stay.

33. I am not arguing that material capital cannot be converted into symbolic capital. Wealth can be and is frequently converted into status in Bali by means of ritual extravaganzas, though perhaps less so in the mountains than elsewhere. The point is that such a conversion, if it were made too obvious, would contradict the notion that ritual authority is legitimate only insofar as it reflects a group's symbolic proximity to a sacred origin (see also Bourdieu 1986).

34. One might suspect that the continuity of Sukawana's prominent position is due to a lack of challenges from others. This is not the case. For example, some years ago a group of ritual and informal leaders from Kintamani attempted to wrest control over the temple committee of Penulisan from Sukawana. Some even questioned Sukawana's ritual precedence, pointing to the fact that the *prasasti* Sukawana A 1 is issued to "the people of Cintamani" rather than mention-

ing Sukawana. A later discussion of Sukawana's lost or diminished prominence in relation to Puri Dalem Balingkang will further illustrate that it has not remained stable for lack of interest from other parties (Chapter 5).

CHAPTER 5: BENEATH AND BEYOND PENULISAN

1. Several local versions of these texts were collected by the author, and copies are available on request.

2. The term "*kanca satak*" is sometimes used exclusively to refer to these five coastal villages. This is because a force of "two hundred" men are said to have been sent by Dalem Balingkang to the coast, ready to guard against any invasion from the sea (hence the name Sembirenteng, from *sami ranta,* "all in readiness"). Alternatively, there are said to have been two hundred refugees who immigrated to the coast after the collapse of his kingdom. Sembirenteng and Gretek form a single *desa dinas,* just as Les and Penuktukan form a single *desa adat.* Van der Tuuk and Brandes' comments about two mountain and four (instead of five) coastal "villages" as supporters of the temple may thus be explained.

3. There are shrines at Pura Balingkang that testify to these connections, including a shrine for Bhatara Pucak Indrakila (Dausa) and one for Bhatara Pucak Penulisan (Sukawana).

4. The Kubayan Kiwa Sukawana also "kills" the buffalo at the rite of consecrating a Jero Bau (*mapurowita*) in Desa Blantih/Selulung and at temple consecration ceremonies (*nenteg linggih*) in Subaya and Batih.

5. Pura Pagonyongan is in fact a kind of *pura penataran* for the small seaside temple Pura Kanginan. After the opening ceremony of its festival has been held at this sea temple, all further ritual is conducted uphill in the larger Pura Pagonyongan. The temple is maintained jointly by Gretek and Sembirenteng.

6. As is the case with many of the origin narratives presented in this book, some elements of the stories can be found, perhaps in a different order and context, in other parts of Bali. An example is the story that explains the origin of the *garuda* figure in Balinese shrines (version 3).

7. Masula and Masuli are enshrined in the eastern part of Pura Balingkang's inner court (*jeroan kangin*), and a grave mound outside the temple is believed to be the cremation site (*tunon*) of Sri Mahadewi.

8. During the postmortuary ceremony called "*nangun*" (to wake up [the deceased]), a bamboo cannon is fired. This device is known as "*keplogplogan.*" Water and carbide (or alternatively, kerosene) are heated in a bamboo tube, and the gas produced is lit to cause an explosion, as in the birth described above. However, the name Dalem Keplogan may also be a play on the similar sounding word "*belog*" (stupid).

9. The narrative continues:

Once, after the festival at this temple had been concluded, a cockfight was held there, attended also by the crew of a foreign vessel. The foreigners brought a formidable white cock with a red marking (*siap siginongseng*), which, as everyone knows, can only be defeated by a white cock with a black marking (*siap siginangsi*). So the people of Panjingan decided to trick the foreigners by attaching a black feather to an ordinary white cock. The visitors immediately wanted to acquire the animal and were invited to swap it for their own. This offer was gladly accepted, and high stakes were put on the fight. But, to the locals' surprise, the false cock won, and the village lost a fortune to the outsiders they had tried to cheat. In the end they simply robbed and killed the visitors: all but one, who ran to his ship, spilling sesame seeds along the way. Some years later the foreigners returned with many ships to ransack the village in revenge. Following the sesame trees that had sprung from the seeds, they found Panjingan and killed most of its inhabitants. The survivors established a new settlement, well hidden by the side of a river. They called it Ngenes (to move [one's residence]), which eventually became shortened to Les.

For a similar version of this tale, but concerning the origin of Desa Tulamben, see Babad Pasek Gelgel, 95a–97b (Gedong Kirtya, 963/6).

10. The purification rituals following the birth of opposite sex twins are often explained by reference to Masula Masuli. Human twins are a threat to the boundary between a human world of practical conflict and an ideal world of divine balance reserved for the gods.

11. The theft of the *rejang* dancer by a cannibalistic ogre is a common theme that appears in many myths about a cave-dwelling Kaki Raksasa (Grandfather Ogre). I have recorded different versions of this myth in Sukawana, Manikliyu, Kutuh, Singaperang, Ulian, and Gunung Bau.

12. In a myth from Blantih, a *porosan* is also used to kill an evil teacher, Raden Jaya Sakti, who impregnates his own student and thereby violates a generational boundary (i.e., he contracts an unlawful "marriage"). A *porosan* is also used, in a story from Songan, to kill an otherwise invincible half human, half buffalo figure named Kebo Iwa.

13. The reason Sembirenteng became responsible for the opening ceremony is that Pura Makulem, where the *prasasti* were once kept, is also known as Pura Ampel Gading. Ampel Gading is said to have been a saint from India, who landed in Sembirenteng before coming to Balingkang.

14. Sukawana still maintains its connection to Pura Pagonyongan and last visited the temple for a purification ritual (*makiis*) in 1989.

15. The deciding factor in this discussion was that some of the younger leaders of Desa Pinggan were unwilling to support the *cokorda*'s request. My own opinion about historical ties between Sukawana and Balingkang was also sought in the course of the debate.

16. There is no direct connection to nearby Pura Pucak Indrapura (Tajun), except for an agricultural ritual, held in Cenigayan, which is directed toward its deity. In this fertility ritual, a model of a bull (*sampi sambuk*) is made from a wooden frame (of *kayu kem*) and covered with the fiber of coconut husks. The effigy, which also contains seeds, is then carried in procession around the *sanggar tawang* shrine in the Pura Bale Agung of Cenigayan. A similar ritual, but with a live bull, is performed in Desa Bantang.

17. There are also claims about direct links to Pura Penulisan. For example, the duck submerged in the well in Gedong Puser Tasik (Penulisan) for the *pekelem* rite is said to have once traveled along subterranean channels and emerged in a spring inside Pura Kelaga in Desa Satra (the water from this spring is used for irrigation here and in Desa Tamblang).

18. It is possible that the content of the text was known all along but never heeded or made public.

19. Some informants claim that the *bupati* of Bangli at that time became involved on the side of Dausa and that he actively supported the split with Penulisan.

20. Batur also is engaged in territorial conflicts with Songan over an area called Batu Magantung and likewise with Kedisan over an area called Nungut Danu.

21. In recent years a number of villages in the Kintamani district have established *pura subak abian* (dry *subak* temples) on request of government institutions and in order to gain the associated government subsidies. These *subak abian* have the character of agricultural cooperatives, and their temples are often idiosyncratic, traditional village temples that have been renamed to please the authorities.

22. According to the annual financial report delivered by the *kepala desa* (administrative village head) of Batur during the *maperani* rite in 1994, the temple's total revenue was Rp 55,000,000, while expenses were only Rp 14,000,000. The huge surplus was allocated to building projects and various village-level non-profit foundations (*yayasan*) in Batur. One of them is dedicated to maintaining local participation in the development of tourism in Toyabungka (Batur).

23. Van der Tuuk and Brandes published an article with a transcription of a Prasasti Pakwan (1885), and the myth is of relevance in confirming the location of the village to which this inscription was issued.

24. Selulung is the only village in the *gebog domas* of Pura Penulisan where the office of Jero Gede is known and has a similar meaning to that in Batur and other Wintang Danu villages.

25. The link between ritual activities and trade is emphasized by the fact that the people of Batur are forbidden to engage in trade for the duration of the *usaba purnamaning kedasa*, in other words, from the tenth full moon until the following new moon. The end of this trading prohibition is marked by a reopening ritual (*upacara petangi*).

26. The exclusion of Desa Bondalem is perhaps linked to its connection with Desa Buahan, which also does not participate in the ritual network of Wintang Danu, of which Batur is (or was) a part.

27. Informants in Tejakula claim that they suddenly received a letter from Batur in 1971 asking for this buffalo. At first they ignored the request, but in 1975 they were told that the buffalo would be asked for again and again until they paid. Afraid of insulting and being cursed by the deity and of being refused *tirta* at Batur, they finally conceded, but they felt that they were forced into it. By contrast, they are well aware of their duty to provide a buffalo for Penulisan every ten years, although they are never reminded or asked to pay. They also know the water sale myth but claim that it refers to the deity of Pucak Penulisan and that Batur has simply appropriated the narrative. Note that the myth does not depict them as willing trading partners—they fail to greet the (trading) goddess. Rather, the trade is forced upon them. Despite all this, Tejakula's ritual responsibilities to both centers are clearly described in a *lontar sima desa* (charter of village regulations) dated 1932 (Gedong Kirtya, 2a:3611). It may be that the informants simply took sides in the conflict between Batur and Penulisan.

28. The local produce currently traded between coastal and mountain villages includes salt, palm sugar, fish, coconuts, and coconut oil (uphill), as well as bananas, maize, root vegetables, spices, coffee, and meat (downhill). Traders traditionally traveled by foot from Pasar Kintamani (on Hari Pasah) to Pasar Penuktukan the next day (on Hari Beteng) and back to Kintamani two days later, allowing additional time for the more difficult uphill journey.

29. This theme of buffaloes magically hidden in a small vessel also occurs in a relationship narrative from Desa Trunyan (Danandjaja 1980:43).

30. Unlike in Tejakula, the obligation to bring a buffalo to Pura Batur is fully accepted by these villages.

31. The desire to construct a more permanent relationship is likewise a contributing motivation for modern department stores, who offer their customers special arrangements according to the system of "buy now–pay later" with interest-free terms.

32. Chinese coins were used as a currency in Bali in the past, but nowadays they are used as ritual money. These coins form an important part of most temple offerings, and often their number is specific to a type of offering. One *kepeng* was worth about twenty-five Indonesian rupiah at the time of research.

33. The lost copper bowl is said to be symbolically related to Dewi Danu's sanction on prayer bells. In order to convert a metal bowl into a bell, one only needs to add a clapper. These two components of a bell are female and male in their symbolism, and their combination is a metaphor for the marriage that the goddess refused. Despite the terse ritual relations, Bangli still requires irrigation water and thus Batur's blessing for the fertility of its fields. Bhatara Kehen's sanction on the right of passage may relate to Batur's need to gain access to markets in the south, which was equally essential.

34. It is worth noting that the cultivation of rice is forbidden in both Penulisan and Batur, a prohibition that is often justified by reference to Ratu Daa Tua or Dewi Danu. She is said to be afraid of the leeches (*lintah*) that are prolific in rice fields. If it is correct to assume that ritual is a means of deemphasizing the relationship between a status order and the processes and relationships of material production, it is only logical that the paired temples, centers of ritual practices elaborating on the mundane practices of rice agriculture, should be spatially distanced from the mundane aspect of their raison d'être.

35. I am aware of only one case where a village (Desa Catur) is a full member of two separate *banua*, rather than belonging to two *banua* one of which encompasses the other entirely. The explanation may be that Desa Catur is located at a boundary between domains and that the two domains concerned are not entirely unrelated (Chapter 6).

36. That Maharishi Markandeya finally settled in Penulisan was also claimed by informants in Payangan. In Batur, Bhagawan Siwagandu is believed to have been the spiritual adviser and high priest of Dalem Balingkang, the king of Bali before the shift to Pejeng and the defeat by Majapait. In the times of Sri Jayapangus, the *kraton* is said to have been shifted from its original location in Kuta Dalem to Puri Balingkang near Desa Pinggan. When Dalem Balingkang decided to take as a second wife a Chinese girl who was an opium trader, he was cursed by Bhagawan Siwagandu so that his own descendants would fail to remember him as their ancestor, and he was transformed into a *barong landung*.

37. The *lontar* Bhagawata Purana and some versions of the Usana Bali mention a marriage between Bhagawan Kasyapa and Dewi Danu.

CHAPTER 6: A RITUAL MAP OF THE HIGHLANDS

1. See Warren 1991 on the difference and interactions between *desa adat* and *desa dinas*.

2. The inscriptions are regarded as sacred objects, and hence it is dangerous

to examine or handle them. The archaic script and language in itself has often prevented locals from deciphering and analyzing the texts.

3. On alternate years a smaller "*usaba pekiling*" (meeting [at different temples] in rotation) is celebrated and attended by villages of the domain. This gathering involves visits to all major village temples individually rather than a gathering of all village deities in the Pura Bale Agung. This biannual alternation is common in Bali Aga villages. In Bantang, for example, the *usaba gede* during odd *saka* (Hindu calendar) years alternates with an *usaba ideran* (*ider,* "to circle around") during even years, as in Bayung Gede. Note that most festivals at *pura banua* take place on *purnama kapat* or *purnama kedasa* (the fourth or tenth full moon).

4. The *barong* of the Pura Puseh in Sekardadi also visits Bayung Gede, and so do many others. See Belo 1949 for an introduction to the history and origins of the Balinese *barong* mask.

5. Note that attributions of agency to a collectivity are made as frequently in the Western media (e.g., "the United States is threatening to engage in a trade war with Japan") as they are in Bali.

6. There are some exceptions. One *barong* is located in Desa Pausan itself, but it does not reciprocate the visits it receives. Like the *barong* of Desa Lembean and Mangguh, it only visits upstream destinations within the *banua* of Pura Pucak Penulisan, namely, to its origin point (*kawitan*) in Sukawana.

7. Some say that this son-in-law is the deity of Pura Puseh Katung, the husband of the deity at Pura Gunung Sari. In the mountains a son-in-law has numerous obligations to his wife's father, marking this relationship as asymmetric. Some informants stressed this asymmetry by saying that being a *mantu* means being a *pembantu* (B.I. a helper or servant, from B.I. *bantu,* "to help"). This is a play on words rather than indicative of the etymology of the Balinese word "*mantu*" (B.I. *menantu*).

8. The motif of a sacred tree whose fragrance attracts the attention of outsiders is common in Mountain Balinese mythology. For example, the divine founders of Trunyan are said to have followed the perfume of a sacred benzoin tree (*taru menyan,* hence "Trunyan"), whose perfume also prevents unpleasant odors that would otherwise result from the practice of sky-burial (Danandjaja 1980). In Bayung, a sacred tree of the same genus prevents a possible bad odor from the human placenta (*ari-ari*) that is put into coconut shells and hung in its branches following a birth (also in Desa Bonyoh).

9. The people of Bayung Gede provide a particular type of banana leaf (*don biyu gerutuk*) as a *cucukan* offering on the occasion of an *usaba* temple festival at Trunyan and prepare the main pillar for their *pamaruman* shrine.

10. The entire village of Bayung Gede visited for four days at the festival of Sukawana's Pura Bale Agung in November 1996, bringing *atos desa* and even contributing a work party of forty-five men to help with the preparations.

11. Batur, Bayung Gede, and others symbolically associated with the lake, with its female goddess, and with being Bali's most "original people" (*wong bali mula*) are sometimes contrasted to the "people of the mountain" (*wong bali aga*) with their male deity on Mt. Penulisan. Some locals speculate that the earliest Hindu Balinese kings displaced an even earlier civilization and its leadership when they first took residence in the mountains. Other locals see this distinction as unfounded and use the terms "*bali mula*" and "*bali aga*" as synonyms, similar to southern Balinese usage.

12. Presenting a coherent account of the "traditional" relationships of the

Wintang Danu or of the ethnohistorical genesis of this network would contradict a reality of political polarization. From a local perspective, such an account would not merely represent a scholarly endeavor aimed at achieving consistency but would be an attempt to resolve the present political tensions. Such an endeavor would be difficult and inappropriate, even though many ordinary participants are hoping for a more cohesive narrative charter, an end of the disputes, and more harmonious and ordered relations in the future.

13. There is currently still a small fish market near this temple. The market is said to have been a major center of trade in a broader variety of goods for the Wintang Danu villages in the past.

14. The sister occupies an ambiguous position in both versions. Her mission is in some ways beyond that of her brothers, particularly in the second version, where she is also their senior. The sister's status as the virgin goddess of the lake (or her follower) transcends the human domain of patrimonial status and ownership of land, just as a real sister will usually leave behind the concerns and property of her *sanggah* of origin at the time of marriage. From a structural and descent ideology point of view, sisters instead represent an opportunity to engage in relations with other *sanggah* by contracting an outward marriage. This option is not explored in the narrative, however, since the sister of the newcomers remains unmarried. One explanation may be that the possibility of an exchange of sisters, in this case with I Bang, is ignored as a practice that is generally frowned upon. Similar to relationships in barter, such immediate reciprocation is unproductive insofar as the life tension of relationships rests on a state of indebtedness. Immediate reciprocation amounts to mere swapping. Another reason may be that the ideologically favored type of marriage among high-status groups is within their own extended *sanggah*. This strategy avoids the pitfalls and added cost of forming an association with outsiders. Female celibacy fulfills a similar function when a suitable partner is unavailable in the woman's own *sanggah*. Most commonly, however, from the point of view of the *sanggah*, the sister is replaced by an inmarrying wife. In this case, the wife is Ni Kuning, the younger sister of I Bang. She is also an ambiguous figure since it is she, rather than her newcomer husband, who brings a patrimony of land into this uxorilocal marriage. Both narratives share the theme of a twofold line of ancestry traced to a female local ancestor associated with the land and a male ancestor who is a royal outsider (but not necessarily from Majapait).

15. Peter Bellwood argues that a distinctive feature of Austronesian societies is "a culturally sanctioned desire to found new settlements in order to become a revered or even deified founder ancestor in the genealogies of future generations" (1995:103), a desire leading to the continuous lateral fission of origin groups and encouraging territorial expansion in search of fresh resources.

16. The design of the *kampuh pujawali* features a white background with seven brown stripes and yellow borders at the ends. The *kain wulan matanai* depicts the cyclical movements of the moon (*wulan*, white diamond shape) and sun (*matanai*, yellow diamond shapes) across the sky. The *kain leluhu* is checkered with white, yellow, and brown. Finally, the *kain lelancang* is plain and dark colored, and the *kain putih polos* is plain white. Photos are available from the author on request. Note that the warp of these cloths must be left uncut if they are to serve as the gods' attire.

17. It is a common requirement to undergo a rite of purification before commencing a study of *lontar* texts. This measure reflects feelings of respect for the

sacredness of these manuscripts as well as a need for protection from the possible dangers of handling the knowledge contained in them. The perception of *lontar* as sacred objects rather than objects containing sacred knowledge is a rather recent phenomenon in this area. This objectifying attitude has arisen in response to a situation where such texts have been used increasingly as weapons in struggles for political or ritual supremacy. After I examined several hundred *lontar* manuscripts in the Kintamani area, it became apparent that until quite recently local origin narratives were not formalized into texts. Most older manuscripts are instead devoted to problems of magic, medicine, divination, and ritual procedure. While such knowledge presented a possibility for increasing the student's personal efficacy (*kesaktian*), it was a private and personal endeavor rather than one concerning the community as a whole.

18. This summary is derived from Budiastra's (1989) transcription. It differs significantly in content from the alternative version known in Batur. Budiastra himself was active in establishing a new Pura Kawitan Pasek Kayuselem at Pura Jati (by the lake) in 1986. This new temple was supposedly meant to provide easier access for worshipers, given the remote location of the original temple in Songan, but the project also reflected internal disagreements.

19. It will be recalled that there is still a Pura Song Pasek on Bukit Penarajon in Sukawana. Note the implicit reference to a possible shift from Bukit Penarajon (Penulisan) to Balingkang, which has been mentioned above.

20. Most Pasek Kayuselem members live in the districts of Kintamani (Bangli), Kubu (Karangasem), and Tejakula (Buleleng), but their dispersion has increased in modern times. Many now reside in Bali's urban centers.

21. The excerpt also shows that the pattern of the ancestors' migration from Songan to various other places is carefully recorded in the text. Memorizing places still serves at least as a mnemonic device in support of genealogical knowledge. None of my informants were able to name their ancestors all the way back to the founders named in the text. In other words, the partial idiomatic transition from places to names did not lead to a truly systematic recording of family trees among the Bali Aga.

22. Note that there is an important branch temple of Pura Kawitan Pasek Gelgel (in Klungkung) located in Songan. Festivals here are attended by small Pasek Gelgel groups from about eighty different villages.

23. For example, the Pasek Gelgel members in Songan cremate their dead in contempt of local traditions that prohibit and condemn this practice. Pasek Gelgel and Pasek Bendesa members in Sukawana more or less follow local traditions concerning mortuary practices, with only some minor elaboration to funeral towers.

24. Part of the reason why Abang Suter sought independence from Abang Batudinding in 1972 was to gain access to a government subsidy. From 1969, villages in Kintamani received *bantuan desa* (village assistance), an annual benefit paid to administrative villages by the central government for the realization of village development projects. The projects are chosen by village leaders but must conform to government-specified criteria. This pro rata funding provided an incentive to village fission as a means of doubling the amount of funds received by a community. In most cases, this economic justification for administrative fission concealed existing factional ambitions.

25. Note that there is a *barong* in Pengotan's Pura Kanginan that is regularly taken to Pura Pucak Penulisan in Sukawana in order to "renew its life force." The origin of this connection could not be established.

26. Some of the sharecroppers were refugees from Desa Pemuteran (Kec Rendang, Karangasem). Legend has it that they fled when they heard the war gongs of the approaching army of Panji Sakti. After a brief stay in Bangli, they were forced to leave. They established a Banjar Pemuteran on Abang territory (*alas lateng*) and later settled the village of Pengotan. Desa Pengotan still visits during the *usaba* at the Pura Bale Agung of the distant Desa Pemuteran (Karangasem). The *prasasti* held by Pengotan are issued to the *keraman muteran* (villagers of Pemuteran), which confirms their origin narrative.

27. Some informants conceded that the appearance of a Pura Tolukbiyu in Batur was the last straw that led the desire for unity to outweigh the preoccupation with internal strife. This temple posed the threat to the scattered people of Abang II of losing control of their symbolic resources, particularly since the founders of this new sanctuary are the descendants of the original founders of Er Awang (Abang I) and are in possession of its *prasasti*.

28. C. J. Grader conducted research in Pacung, Bangkah, and Sembiran. However, the results were never published. A copy of his notes can be made available on request.

29. In Desa Subaya, once the eastern boundary of Banua Indrapura, some origin narratives are still told that link Subaya to Lake Bratan and nearby Desa Candikuning, not far from Gobleg. The male deity of Pura Puseh Subaya is said to have married a female deity from Candikuning, and mutual visits between the two villages at the festivals of their respective Pura Puseh continue until today.

30. Refer to Simpen 1986 for an account of the traditions of Bali Aga villages involved in this network.

31. The Prasasti Pura Kehen A (2a) is addressed to the "*wanua di* [of] *Simpat Bunut.*"

32. There are also regular visitors who bring *atos desa* but do not pay *peturunan*. Desa Trunyan is one of these visitors, and it is believed that one of the village deities of Trunyan is the child of Bhatara Pura Kehen (according to Bangli informants).

33. Puri Semarabawa was even stripped of some of its prime real estate in Bangli, which the new *bupati* managed to claim as government property (*milik pemerintah*).

34. The most significant change in the nature of worldly leadership is that the powers of the modern state exceed by far the powers of even the greatest royal dynasties in Balinese history. The same applies to religious institutions. Recent changes in ritual practice are not merely based on Brahmanization but also reflect the new orthodoxy of a reformist and politicized Hinduism promoted by more influential state religious institutions.

35. According to the origin narrative of Buungan, its founding ancestors fled from Asti, a village on the eastern slope of Mt. Agung (Karangasem), after a devastating attack by I Panji Mikuh (*mikuh*, "[having a] tail [like a monkey]") and his army. Only seven of the two hundred (*satak*) heads of households survived. After a brief interlude in Desa Selat (Karangasem), they eventually found a new home in present-day Buungan, at a location that reminded them of their home village. The uninhabited place was known as Alas Pengharuman (the scented forest). The migrants brought with them a sacred *kulkul*, two baskets of salt, and a pillar of the old *bale agung* (assembly pavilion), which was rebuilt in Buungan to the exact likeness of the original in Asti. Every *purnama kedasa*, Buungan will visit the festival of the Pura Puseh Asti in Karangasem. This path of origin, re-

traced by the *desa adat* in its annual journey to Asti, is a supporting mechanism for maintaining internal unity, since it requires the group to act as a whole in relation to another community.

36. An example of a similar spatial arrangement is the blood sacrifice (*caru*) referred to as "*manca sata*" (five chickens [of different color]), in which four sacrificial poles surround a central pole that represents unity.

37. The modernist term commonly used to designate private (and voluntary) offerings is "*aturan pribadi.*" The composition of these offerings differs significantly in quantity and content from the offerings made on behalf of an entire village (*atos desa*).

38. The relevant part of the narrative is the one that describes the creation of human beings from clay (and more or less stands in contradiction to another part that describes their creation from a wooden figure): A brother-sister pair of divine twins arrived in Taro, where the younger sister created three human siblings from clay. A second set of siblings was created by the older brother in Songan, the next stop on their journey. Some of the descendants of the first humans continued on a journey with the divine twins. One settled in Bayung Gede, one in Margatengah, and others returned to Taro.

39. Pura Agung Gunung Raung, also the origin temple (*pura kawitan*) of Pasek Taro, is located in the village of Taro. A group of Pasek Taro from Blantih attend the festivals at this temple regularly, for they believe that their ancestors migrated from Taro via Sukawana to Blantih. It is worth noting that in both villages certain cows are considered sacred, namely, the black *sampi wadak* of Blantih (also Selulung and Tambakan) and the albino cows (*lembu putih*) of Taro, although for different reasons. Cows are not normally regarded as sacred animals in Balinese Hinduism as they are in India.

40. Desa Adat Pujung Taleput is located just west of Taro and at a similar elevation. The ritual leader is a *kubayan*, but this office is hereditary. Nine villages attend the festival of a local temple named Pura Bale Bang, including Taro Kelod. The village is said to have been founded by Bali Aga ancestors from Darmaji, a village in Karangasem on the eastern slope of Mt. Agung (see also Howe 1980).

41. One indication supporting this claim to recent settlement is the absence of *prasasti* in any of these communities, unlike in most other Bali Aga villages.

42. It was common that ritual visitors were presented with a gift by the people of Sukawana, "as a king would present a gift to a visiting vassal (*patih*)." These gifts were usually ritual utensils made by silversmiths in Tejakula. Several such gifts from Sukawana are still kept at Pura Pucak Bon.

43. I also recorded a version of this legend at the hot springs near Wongaya Gede, on the slope of Mt. Batukaru. This version is said to be based on a *lontar* text titled Buana Tattwa (unconfirmed). The baths are said to have been built by Dalem Penulisan, who was cured by the sacred water of a skin disease.

44. According to the origin myth of Pengejaran (above), one of their male village deities is the son of a deity from Mt. Batukaru and the local goddess Ratu Manik Penyalin. It is impossible to offer a reliable interpretation of this and other references to links between the Kintamani and Batukaru regions without further research. It may be that both once lay within the sphere of influence of old Balinese kingdoms centered on Penulisan.

45. Local informants claim that they joined the *banua* of Pura Pucak Bon when Desa Catur became a part of the kingdom of Mengwi (from A.D. 1801 to

1891). Formerly the village had been claimed by or had given allegiance to the king of Bangli. The kingdom of Mengwi exerted some control over the domain around Pura Antap Sai and Pura Manggu until they were defeated by enemies from Tabanan and Badung. This part of Mengwi was appropriated by the kings of Badung.

46. The sea temple in Desa Seseh is still visited for the *melasti* ceremonies of the deity at Pura Pucak Manggu.

47. The so-called dry field but actually rain-fed rice (*padi gaga*) that was traditionally grown in this area had a rather lengthy growing season of five to six months. Following the introduction of fast-growing irrigated rice varieties in other parts of Bali over the last decades, spontaneous cross-pollination and hybridization has occurred with the indigenous varieties. Consequently, even some of the *padi gaga* that is currently grown in mountain areas may reach maturity in as little as four months.

48. It will be recalled from Chapter 4 that similar procedures are also carried out at Pura Pucak Penulisan on *purnama kapat*. The sacred objects of Penulisan's male deity are taken out (*ngodal*) and washed in order to produce *tirta wangsu-pada*. An additional symbolic representation of maleness becoming submerged in the female sphere of the earth is that the male sacrificial buffalo and small parcels filled with seeds are buried at the end of the festival at Pura Penulisan.

49. In the Kintamani area rice is often stored in the attic (*tukub*) of residential houses rather than in separate rice barns (*lumbung*), perhaps because rice is no longer grown in large quantities, if at all. Rice has been replaced by cash crops or maize over the last century. Another reason may be that the attic is kept dry by the warmth of the hearth fire, a distinct advantage over separate rice barns under the damp conditions of the highlands.

50. The link between women or female deities and harvest ritual is not confined to rice agriculture. In Sukawana, for example, the ritual of the maize harvest involves the construction of an effigy of the female maize deity (*nini jagung*). It is prepared and performed entirely by the woman who "owns" (cultivates) the maize field. Men do not attend.

51. The ceremonies that mark the peak of the dry season are the postmortuary rituals of patrifocal origin houses. They are traditionally held during *sasih kasa* and *sasih karo* (July–August). In the annual cycle these "rituals of the dead" are diametrically opposed to blood sacrifices as rites of fertility (January–February).

CHAPTER 7: THE STATUS ECONOMY OF HIGHLAND BALI

1. The term "*pura bale agung*" (temple of the great pavilion) is the common designation for a type of temple found in most Balinese villages. In the highlands the same temple is also referred to as "*pura desa*" and sometimes forms a single complex together with the Pura Puseh. "*Pura bale agung*" is somewhat of a misnomer in relation to the design of mountain village temples. Additional "great" (*agung*) or "long" (*lantang/dawa*) pavilions (*bale*) can also be found in the Pura Puseh, Pura Dalem, or other village temples, where they similarly serve as meeting houses.

2. In most villages (but not in Sukawana) the lowest rank is marked with a specific title (*pamuit* or *pider*) and ritual task (e.g., serving palm wine to the elders).

3. In former times a large banana leaf was used by the elder of this rank to record attendance and rice deliveries by members at meetings. As each man

arrived, he would tear one strip of leaf along the small lateral ribs, on the appropriate side (left or right moiety) of the thick central stalk of the banana leaf (hence *keset don*, "to tear the leaf").

4. Note that in both ritual and everyday speech contexts, it is always "left and right" rather than "right and left"; likewise, it is always "*luh muani*" (female and male) and "*daa teruna*" (young girls and boys).

5. A male-female sibling pair in mythology usually incorporates an older brother and a younger sister, thus equating "younger sibling" with "female." When a couple are not yet married, the man will address his bride or girlfriend with the term "*adi*" (younger sibling), and she will address him as "*kaka*" or "*bli*" (elder sibling), even if the woman is actually older than the man (which is uncommon). Also, young men are often accused of going to the temple only "to worship Dewa Nyoman and Dewa Ketut [younger sibling, third and fourth born]," which means that they only attend to look at the young girls in their tight sarongs. Younger brothers are equated with females not only in a symbolic but also in a practical sense. Like sisters, they tend to receive less of the paternal inheritance in Sukawana than their older brothers and remain somewhat subservient to them until they are married.

6. No longer married (*balu*) can mean that the person's spouse has died or that a person is divorced. Members of the assembly must also retire (*baki*) when all of their children have married, that is, when theirs is no longer a productive household in terms of fertility.

7. Marriage ritual is explicitly tied to the concerns of the *desa adat* (rather than being just a *sanggah* affair) by a practice common to all Bali Aga communities whereby the groom must pay a kind of brideprice (*bakatan* and/or *kelaci*) to the village, to be divided among all assembly members. The payment varies but most commonly includes two live pigs as well as an array of other offerings.

8. The matter is rather more complex. Nonmembers may also approach the assembly with a suggestion or complaint under exceptional circumstances. Low-ranking members, in turn, may attend regularly and yet contribute rarely to council discussions. In general, rank is not as certain an indicator of informal influence as it is of formal authority.

9. An example is provided in an article by Cecilia Ng (1993) on Minangkabau houses. The household compartments in Minangkabau longhouses are ordered in a row. Again, the most senior couple dwell in the compartment closest to the point of origin, represented by the *pangkilan* pillar, literally the "trunk" or "origin."

10. *Sanggah*-endogamous marriages (especially among second or more distant patrilateral cousins) are also highly valued. Internal alliances can help to prevent a lapse of unity in the fourth generation or thereafter. Such marriages are most common in *sanggah* with high prestige, where the incentive for maintaining symbolic unity is stronger than the inclination to legitimize material autonomy through fission.

11. Jürgen Habermas (1984) has argued that communicative interests are prior to strategic ones, no matter how routinely strategic concerns may follow in the wake of communication. Before people are able to manipulate one another systematically, they must first be able to communicate, that is, they have to subscribe not only to the conventions of a language but to a shared set of beliefs and practical relations to the world. When people evoke the notion of "tradition" for strategic purposes, they have assumed that their communication partners will accept certain arguments and behaviors, because, as subscribers to

that tradition, they hold certain tenets to be true and consider certain actions appropriate in a given situation. But the manipulators must also hold the tenets of tradition to be true, because their communication partners will expect them to abide by those tenets also. A person or group could subscribe to a tradition only nominally, for the sake of short-term gains. But such a deception would become apparent as soon as their behavior contradicted the tenets they professed to adhere to. While Habermas' argument on the priority of communication may be too ambiguous, it seems unlikely, at least, that strategic interests could exist independent of communicative interests.

12. A village elder from Desa Bantang during preparations for the big festival of Pura Pucak Penulisan once commented as follows on the voluntary and compulsory aspects of *banua* participation:

> When we [people from participating villages] gather at Pura Pucak Penulisan, we know what our different positions are. But when all is prepared, we do not think of that any more. We feel ashamed to approach the gods incomplete and divided. There is no reward for participation, no fine for staying away. So why do we all come here? Hm, perhaps you know what happened to people in Dausa [who recently detached themselves from this domain]? Evil spirits (*roh jahat*) have entered their village. So they quarrel with their neighbors, they fight among one another, and they cannot even cooperate to repair their own village temples. No wonder so many of them are sick and their crops failing. That is what happens when we start dividing and are arrogant or forgetful of our responsibilities. We all come so that we can be here together. After all, it's the greatest [ritual] event of the year!

13. The local term used for describing what may be called "oral tradition" is *gugu tuun/tuonin*, "a belief that has passed down [from the past or from ancestors]/has been confirmed." Often it is only in response to government initiatives that orally transmitted rules of propriety are put into written form. Many locals consider it interference to have their *adat* put under such formal scrutiny. Neither written nor orally transmitted rules can be assumed to capture how people actually behave; the way individual agents conduct themselves cannot be reduced to a mere execution of rules. Nevertheless, the formulation of rules does have some impact on individual actions or, at least, on their moral interpretation.

14. I have heard reports of contemporary cases where a culprit was subjected to public flogging and humiliation. In a few extreme cases, where an individual's actions had threatened to destroy the village, there have even been executions.

15. I was told of an incident where a stall holder refused to oblige a traditional messenger (*jero saya*) who had been asked by the elders of Sukawana to request some hot water (free of charge). The trader told him to make his own hot water. When the head elder of the right (Kubayan Mucuk) was informed of this insolence, he said no more than "Fine. Rp 100,000." The trader paid, certain that a refusal would lead to his death by both magical and divine means. Indeed, after the payment, his fortunes improved dramatically (as he told me himself)!

16. Only in rare and specific cases have cremations been tolerated (rather than "approved") by a village council in defiance of regional traditions and despite feelings of resentment among other local factions. I witnessed a case in Sukawana where the body of a teenage boy was cremated. His parents were filled

with such grief and rage over his sudden and tragic death that they decided to violate tradition. The father told me in highly emotional terms that he relished the opportunity to offend the gods who had allowed his son to die. Others excused this act as one inspired by temporary madness.

17. There are also sufficient economic resources in highland Bali to provide for most of the population. While many young people move to the cities in search of education and employment, my observations show that the majority eventually return to their native villages. Economic opportunities are as good (or as bad) there as in the city, though many may believe at first in the myth that riches await all who are educated enough to join the "modern" sector of Balinese society. Often the income of an average farmer is several times higher than that of an average public servant or private sector employee. In the wake of the currency crisis that began to devastate Indonesia's economy in 1997, the advantages of engaging in primary production or local trade have become more pronounced than ever before. During a visit in early 1998, I had several conversations with local farmers in which they showed themselves to be unperturbed by the crisis and, on the contrary, reported significant increases in the market value of their products, especially coffee.

18. Temples are essentially the sacred dwellings of invisible beings. *Pura banua, pura desa* and *sanggah* are all objectified spatial representations of a point of origin. As the abodes of invisible persons, divine creators or deified founding ancestors, they are all dedicated to predecessors from the past who define social relations among their successors in the present. Places of origin and past acts of creation and foundation are situated within a continuing process of life unfolding. *Umah* may only be the humble dwelling places of visible human beings today, but each house and household is focused on a productive and fertile married couple whose socially legitimized reproductive capacity holds a necessary origin potential for the future. Visible and invisible persons are differently positioned travelers on the same road, and their mundane houses and sacred temples are signposts on the same path of life.

19. Contrary to Lévi-Strauss' definition, not all of these Austronesian societies are stratified in a way comparable to the earlier European societies ruled by noble houses, the specific case from which his general model was derived.

20. A fission of the *desa adat* has occurred in Songan, Kintamani, and Batur, to name but a few examples. Factional disputes may also manifest as a split into two separate *desa dinas*, as in Blantih/Selulung.

21. The common practices of adoption and uxorilocal marriage suggest that agnatic kinship ties are not even an entirely necessary condition for *sanggah* membership.

22. *Rama ngarep* are distinguished from affines, who are often referred to collectively as "*rama dia*" (*dia*, "to precede" or "the last," as in "last year").

23. From my limited research in Tenaon, the reasons why this step has not been taken cannot be established.

24. Spatial metaphors, though they are important as an index, are not the primary organizing principle in Bali Aga discourses about society insofar as spaces are ranked by reference to time. It is also significant that spatial metaphors, in this sense of being linked by time, are oriented inward and serve to define zones of similarity and inclusion, rather than being oriented outward and creating a distance between spaces. This may explain why the Bali Aga are not much concerned with defining villages and domains in terms of their boundaries.

25. Some of the evidence provided above points to the possibility of a historical shift in control over land from the *banua* to the *desa*, a shift that is consolidated in the context of modern Indonesian landownership laws for which the *banua*, much more than the *desa adat*, is not a relevant institution. The balance of economic power between *desa* and *sanggah* has been shifting as well and in the same downward direction. More and more village land, though still legally and ritually defined as such, is becoming inheritable (and the distinction between usufruct and ownership is becoming more and more intangible).

26. If it was decided, for example, that the highest-ranking village elder should receive two plots of village land instead of only one, then this would be of no specific advantage to him, because it would also apply to all others who would come to occupy his position after his retirement and in the future.

27. The different forms of capital in the three economies I have referred to are to some extent interconvertible, but this does not mean that a materialist reductionism is warranted. Such attempts to purchase status (the approval of others), for example, are always precarious to the degree that they are transparent to others. One man complained to me that for all the times he had fed half the village in the context of his own household's (private) ceremonies, his level of recognition in the village had improved very little. His fellow villagers, in turn, told me that his ambitions were all too obvious to them and not founded on any valid claim. Nevertheless, the elaborate ceremonies did help the man to retain support from other members of his own *sanggah*, not just because he had entertained them but because they interpreted his actions as appropriate and genuine in the spirit of cooperation among kin.

28. This idea will be explored further in the final chapter of this book, by means of a comparison with Western democracies under which severe and growing economic disparities are justified by an ideology of (nominal) equality and free competition. Such a discourse, unlike a discourse of precedence, ultimately fails to address the problem of difference.

CHAPTER 8: REPRESENTATION BEYOND THE HIGHLANDS

1. Marcus and Fischer's approach is somewhat similar to the interim solution I proposed in the Introduction, which was to proceed on the somewhat uncertain foundation of a critical humanism. However, my aim in the later part of this book is to develop a more solid epistemological and ethical foundation for ethnography.

2. Social science is also struggling to retain control of the very notion of "culture," however it may be defined. Multinational corporations have been situated at the forefront of globalization processes and economists at the cutting edge of their interpretation. In their narratives, cultural and political boundaries have been reduced to an obstacle or nuisance in the search for more lucrative business deals with Asia or other emerging markets. Culture has been redefined in a materialist idiom of global market exchanges as an obstacle to progress, a necessary consideration for local management and marketing strategies, or a commodity in its own right.

3. This culturalization of politics may have been a response to the threat of national politics becoming a mere adjunct to the imperatives and narratives of the global economic system or, perhaps, to the end of the great wars of political ideology (after the fall of the Berlin wall).

CHAPTER 9: PEOPLE OF THE MOUNTAINS AND PEOPLE FROM THE SEA

1. In a recent paper, Hildred Geertz (1995) discusses in particular how the exercise of power (*kesaktian*) tends to coincide with a demonic appearance in Balinese cosmology and society.

2. The ultimate source of (rain) water is, of course, the sky, the celestial realm of Balinese deities and purified ancestors. In this sense, the sacredness of the mountains may relate to their proximity to the heavens.

3. The words for "trunk" (*bongkol*) and "tip" (*muncuk*) also refer to female and male genitals. Female and male are perhaps the most fundamental categorical pair in Balinese thought, since the eternal difference and periodic unification of female and male is recognized as a necessary prerequisite for life itself.

4. There are many versions of this origin narrative, written and oral. The statement presented here is merely the minimum of what ordinary Balinese would know about these mythohistorical events. For an inventory of different published oral versions, see Geertz 1980:144, nn. 14–17. An example of a locally written version of this narrative is provided by Creese (1995).

5. It is remarkable that a similar accusation of atheism supported the legitimization for the government's violent purge of so-called communists in 1965.

6. The ships that carried Javanese ancestors from Majapait to Bali cannot have carried many. "Bali Majapait" must have initially comprised a very small minority. It is only through the "Majapaitization" of the *anak jaba*, the Balinese (commoners), that Bali Majapait now accounts for most of the population. Others argue that Sri Kresna Kapakisan himself was in fact of Balinese origins. Apart from the Bali Aga, there are a number of other important groups who retained a claim to Balinese ancestry and an associated ritual status, most notably the *pande* (smith) clans.

7. For a Bali Majapait–favoring interpretation of the tale of Raja Bedaulu, see Covarrubias 1937:37–38 or Wiener 1995:103.

8. I am presenting here a brief summary of a popular origin myth as most Mountain Balinese understand it and as they have narrated it to me on numerous occasions during my research. Minor variations have been ignored and optional elaborations omitted. For other Balinese the tale is merely a possible explanation of how King Mayadanawa came to his demonic shape and disposition in the first place.

9. Pura Batur is perhaps the only Bali Aga–dominated temple to have received attention in the literature on Balinese ritual systems. In a recent book Stephen Lansing (1991) confirms that ultimate ritual authority over the temple is still firmly in the hands of local priests and village leaders.

10. Puri Gelgel and Puri Klungkung are among the most significant of the "new" political centers. The situation is less transparent with regard to the new ritual centers of Bali Majapait. It is uncertain, for example, whether Pura Besakih was established or merely appropriated and transformed to become a state temple of the Gelgel and Klungkung dynasties. It is also important to note that Balinese terms for political centers are not easily translated. "*Jero*" implies the interior, as in the term "*jeroan*" (entrails, interior of the body or of a temple). Other common metaphors of centrality, such as the word "*puser*" (navel), also suggest a physiological rather than a spatial idiom.

11. The portrayal of the Majapait conquest as a civilizing mission is remarkably similar to the self-justifications of "benevolent colonialism," concerned with eradicating the "barbaric" aspects of native society, in other words, its political

powers. It is well established that a bodily form with both human and animal elements is commonly attributed to demonic beings in Balinese narratives and art. These demonic beings can be described as manifestations of raw, untempered power or efficacy (*kesaktian*).

12. J.-F. Guermonprez (1989) indeed argues that the relationship between Brahmana priests and kings is in itself a manifestation of dual sovereignty in Balinese society. He does not consider that this Indic conceptual dyad of Raja and Brahmana may have had local antecedents.

13. It is uncertain whether Panji Sakti and his successors conducted these raids on behalf of the paramount ruler in Klungkung or for reasons of their own. A history of warfare between the principalities of Buleleng and Bangli may explain some of these raids. References to the attacks staged by Panji Sakti in Bali Aga oral histories may also refer to raids conducted by other military leaders (*panji*, "soldier"). Some local histories concede that these attacks led to the destruction of entire villages, but others report cases of successful resistance and emphasize the cleverness and valor of the defenders. In later times, the rulers of Buleleng sought alliances and received military aid from "Bali Aga" villages (Sastrodiwiryo 1994:75). Informants in Bayung Gede and Seraya spoke of similar ties between their villages and the rulers of Bangli and Karangasem, respectively.

14. A translation of the Babad Pasek into Indonesian was published by I Gusti Bagus Sugriwa (1957), and this translation, as far as the above passage is concerned, corresponds with Balinese versions of the Babad Pasek kept at Gedong Kirtya in Singaraja and Pusat Documentasi Bali in Denpasar (serial number Va 963/6). The Babad Pasek is a text that must be considered with caution, for it may have been recently written in the political context of the Pasek movement. An earlier source, which contains the same passage, is the Pamancangah Bali (see Berg 1927).

15. Again, I emphasize that Balinese *lontar* are not very dependable as historical sources. But while they cannot provide a reliable account of how Kresna Kapakisan interacted with the Bali Aga, they indicate, at the very least, how he should have behaved according to the author of this text.

16. Older informants in Sukawana recall, for example, that Bali's traditional rulers still gathered each year at the conclusion of the festival at Penulisan in order to compete in a great cockfighting extravaganza (*tabu 'rah*, lit. "to spill blood"), which lasted for several days and was located on the lowest terrace of the temple complex.

17. Some Bali Aga are beginning to participate in ceremonies held at Pura Besakih, particularly in the context of their growing involvement in the Pasek movement. A rebel minority sometimes call on Brahmana priests for certain ritual services.

18. According to origin narratives I have recorded in Batur and Selulung, a small Bali Aga kingdom was once established around Lake Batur but was soon destroyed by "Panji Sakti." After his victory Panji Sakti gave public reassurance of his continuing respect for the sacred authority of the lake goddess at Batur and for her local Bali Aga priests.

19. I have encountered several families in Bali Aga villages who claim that their ancestors were political refugees of noble descent. These immigrants were granted asylum in the mountains on the condition of renouncing all claims to superior status.

20. Informants in the Bali Aga village Seraya, for example, claimed to have

provided warriors to accompany the king of Karangasem on his military expeditions to Lombok.

21. These stereotypes do not reflect the opinion of all Balinese. Those who come into regular contact with Bali Aga people tend to maintain much more balanced views. Some urban Balinese regard the Bali Aga with romantic admiration as an emblem of cultural "authenticity" (*bali tulen*).

22. Ironically, the acronym "KKN" nowadays stands more often for the English loan words *korupsi, kolusi, nepotisme*, with specific reference to the state of widespread corruption, collusion, and nepotism under the late Suharto administration.

23. A predominance of Brahmana is still evident among the ranks of the Parisada Hindu Dharma Indonesia, but this may change in the near future (see Pitana 1995).

24. Note that, under the dictatorial rule of former president Suharto, *adat* and *agama* also provided a last bastion for local political resistance (in an idiom of apoliticism), while other attempts to publicly express dissent were met with violent oppression.

25. Not everywhere has there been such well-organized and potent resistance. For example, some Bali Aga villages in western Buleleng have changed their religious practices almost to the point of abandoning their Bali Aga identity, at least publicly. My original plan to conduct field research in these villages was therefore abandoned in favor of the central highlands.

26. A local version of *nyepi* (*nyepi desa*) is celebrated in these villages at different intersections of the Balinese lunar-solar calendar, sometimes up to three times in a year. To be fair, it should be added that the specific traditions of some non–Bali Aga villages are just as unique and suffer equally from the cultural homogenization mission of the state.

CHAPTER 10: THE ANTHROPOLOGICAL COPRODUCTION OF THE BALI AGA

1. Riches (1990) has argued a similar case in relation to the impact Eskimo discourses about their tradition and history have had on the discourses of Eskimologists and vice versa.

2. One of the first foreigners to mix in courtly circles as a means of discovering Bali was the medical doctor Julius Jacobs, as is reflected in his travel reports (Jacobs 1883). His mentor H. N. van der Tuuk, in turn, had mostly consulted Brahmana priests as his key informants (see Vickers 1989:89).

3. I would like to thank Dr. Samuel Wälty for informing me about this early source.

4. Lansing provides a detailed critique of the theory of centralized irrigation control in Bali. He argues convincingly that the Dutch bestowed a form of sovereignty and power on Balinese regents that they had never before enjoyed and that it is more appropriate to speak of a reconstructed rather than simply reinstated aristocracy under the colonial political system (1991:32–36).

5. The distinction between "old Balinese" and "appanage" villages as is illustrated in the earlier quote from a Badan Pelaksana Pembina Lembaga Adat document, was later adopted by southern Balinese.

6. The first Balinese inscription in the Old Javanese language was issued in A.D. 994 by the Balinese king Dharmodayana Warmadeva (Udayana) and his Javanese queen Gunapriyadharmapatni (Mahendradatta). Their son Erlangga

left Bali to become the king of Kediri in East Java some thirty years later, while his younger brother (Anak Wungsu) ruled in Bali.

7. My own research has shown, for example, that while the former principality of Bangli (or Taman Bali) nominally included many Bali Aga villages, their rulers (*cokorda*) owned very little land in the mountain district of Kintamani. The situation changed with Bangli's rather late submission under direct colonial administration. The Dutch reinstated the precolonial ruler of Bangli as *zelfbestuurder* (regent) and thus gave him some control over vacant village land, reclassified as state forest (*tanah hutan*) or crown land (*tanah pemerintah*). Such land could be cleared and distributed to dependent clients. However, the Dutch administrative presence was not felt in Kintamani until the early 1930s and thus presented too brief an opportunity for the *zelfbestuur* of Bangli to capitalize on it.

8. The same can be said of the traditions that may have inclined the invaders from Majapait to accept the Bali Aga as a necessary and, in some ways, privileged class of indigenous custodians. It is only useful to speak of Bali Aga resilience insofar as other Balinese actually attempted to strip them of their symbolic and material resources.

9. Schaareman does pay due attention to the positioning of this village in a modern system of state administration. The isolation I am here referring to is an isolation from other villages of its own kind.

10. Regional ties between Tenganan and surrounding villages are mentioned in passing by Korn (1932:28–29; 1933), and they have been a subject of recent investigations by A. Francais-Simbuerger at City University, New York (personal communication).

11. As the Romans saw the last free tribes of Britain, so have the Balinese and Western scholars alike seen the relative independence of the Bali Aga as a product of their own obscurity and isolation. The curious combination of romantic admiration and condescending pity in Tacitus' representations of his cultural others reminds me of how the Bali Aga tend to be conceived.

12. For a discussion of the inscriptions' value and limitations as historical sources on Balinese society before the fourteenth century, see Goris 1941.

13. The reason for the importance attributed to rice rests on the argument that a differentiated society with a centralized authority structure, such as a kingdom, presupposes a surplus in agricultural production. Much depends on how much centralized authority one would wish to attribute to the Balinese "kings" of this early period. It may be worth noting that even so-called primitive economies may produce enough surplus to support a system of sociopolitical differentiation (Sahlins 1972).

14. Clifford Geertz notes that the island of Bali "faced south toward the Indian ocean, where given poor harbors and rough seas, there was hardly any traffic, rather than north toward the Java Sea, the Asian Mediterranean" (1980:87–88). This was the case at least until the middle of the nineteenth century, when Kuta was established as a first major southern port. Geertz does not consider the strategic advantage this situation gave to the mountain region as a trade thoroughfare for the entire island.

15. "*Ateher karaman i cintamani sapanjing thani tkeng ana kning karaman wnang adagang kapas mareng les, paminggir, hiliran [Tejakula], buhun dalem [Bondalem], julah, purwasidhi, indrapura [Tajun/Dapaha] bulihan dan manasa*" (Prasasti Kintamani E 3a:3–4). This reference focuses on trade in cotton, essential for local textile production (Prasasti Manikliyu), but other products are also mentioned.

Interestingly, the inscription also states that traders from villages of the Batur area (the Wintang Danu, or "Stars of the Lake") are forbidden to trade north—presumably their trade links were orientated southward. Between them these two clusters of mountain villages must have maintained a firm grip on inland trade, and, together with the important sea-trading villages in the north, they may have created a major source of tax revenue for the royal coffers.

16. The terms "*kabayan*" and "(*ke*)*raman*" first occur in Prasasti Dausa B 1 (A.D. 942); the term "*banua/banwa*," in Prasasti Bebetin A 1 (A.D. 896).

17. Elements of Bali Aga traditions can be found throughout Bali. For example, the most famous temple in Tabanan, Pura Batukaru, is still ritually led by the *kubayan* of Desa Wongaya Gede (Arsana 1991). I have also visited several villages that have only abandoned Bali Aga traditions, such as the ranking order in the *desa adat*, in the last few years. There are also contingents of people from Bali Aga villages in many lowland villages, towns, and cities. In this sense, to draw an overly formulaic distinction between the two types of villages, based on some list of necessary and optional cultural traits, would be unwarranted.

18. The study of ritual domains in Bali's highlands also provides the key to a better understanding of temple networks elsewhere in Bali. Ritual ties among village communities (*desa*) in Bali (rather than among other social units) have not received the attention they deserve until now. The availability of regional centers as a focus for people's social ambitions beyond the village is also important insofar as it may explain why the Bali Aga have not followed a tendency, evident among commoners elsewhere in Bali, to imitate the ritual practices of the aristocracy. A pertinent example is the popularization of elaborate cremation ceremonies, which at one time brought many Balinese commoner families to the brink of financial ruin (Connor 1996:186). Cremations never became popular among the Bali Aga.

19. Edmund Leach's classic monograph, titled *Political Systems of Highland Burma* (1954), has been another source of inspiration in the development of a method of regional research and comparison in the course of this study.

20. Though I have not carried out the necessary research to substantiate this, I am inclined to hypothesize that Dutch society, for example, was deeply affected by the general experience of colonialism and perhaps not much less so than the societies they colonized. Though it was a relationship of unequal power, the cultural specificity of Dutch society may well have been an important factor in shaping their peculiar version of colonialism, as compared to French, Spanish, or British colonialism. The many cultures they encountered, from Bali to Suriname, also may have affected the experience and self-image of the Dutch, each in rather different ways. As Richard Price (1990) has suggested for Suriname, a purely power-oriented analysis of colonial encounters in Bali (or elsewhere) may fail to register the aspect of mutual cultural transformation therein.

21. A critique of local theoretical knowledge is also important in that it draws attention to other, more practical forms of knowledge among local participants.

22. If one were to compare Balinese treatment of the Bali Aga with the record many Western nations (such as America and Australia) have in dealing with indigenous peoples, it might turn out that the Balinese have much less to be ashamed of than the latter.

23. The difficulty of dating Balinese palm-leaf manuscripts relates to the infrequency of references to the year in which they were composed. Another problem is the limited durability of the material itself, which calls for frequent

copying of the text. In the process the original text and its language may be altered. A philological method of dating is difficult to apply to such modified texts.

24. Much of the research mentioned above belongs to a new school of cognitive psychology that has overcome an earlier disdain for the study of mental processes and contents. A dogmatic rejection of speculative "mentalism," in part a reaction against Freudian theory, was prevalent during the heyday of behaviorist psychology. At that time, psychological studies of the Self or the self-concept were regarded as heretical. This may explain in part why many anthropologists still draw on Freudian theories of the self.

25. There are a number of parallels between this intersubjective theory of knowledge and Durkheim's sociology of religion. Intersubjective knowledge can be interpreted as something that has a transcendental or sacred character, that is, if it is interpreted from a religious perspective. I agree with Durkheim's basic insight that religious ideas of a self-transcending truth may arise, at least in part, from the social experience the Self has of itself as a participant in an intersubjective world.

CHAPTER 11: REPRESENTATION AND SOCIETY

1. This call for further research is directed not only toward anthropologists, local and foreign, but equally to political scientists, historians, archeologists, philologists, and others with an interest in Balinese studies or in the comparative ethnology of the Southeast Asia–Pacific region.

2. The dualism of heaven and hell has not always been as pronounced in Christian theology as it is now. It may be due to the later influence of Persian cosmological models, which envisaged the world as a battleground for the hosts of good (led by Ahura Mazda) and evil (led by Ahriman).

3. Bali Aga conceive of space as three-dimensional: mountain-sea, east-west, and above-below. The first two dimensions, however, do not depict a flat plane as in Western mathematics. *Kaja-kelod* and *kangin-kauh* combined describe a tilted plane, given that the *kaja-kelod* axis (unlike a north-south axis) is not independent of the concept of elevation. Note that the dimensions of space are joined with a fourth, temporal dimension in composite notions of movement. *Kangin-kauh*, for example, refers to the movement or path of the sun.

4. Another related class of event markers in the topography of the highlands are unusual rocks or stone artifacts. Some of these are found within nearly every temple, large or small, while others are scattered across the landscape. Offerings are placed on these stones regularly, even though people may not always know their stories. Informants explained that this apparent stone worship does not rest on a doctrine of animism at all. Rather, sacred stones are thought of as foundations beneath the pillars of ancient wooden dwellings or temples that have long since decayed but still persist in the invisible realm (*niskala*).

5. Einstein's relativity theory leads to a prediction that is remarkably similar to that of the social relativity theory of the Bali Aga: A forward journey through space (at great velocity) may be accompanied by a simultaneous movement backward in time (from the perspective of others).

6. The fetishism of youthful beauty in the modern mass media correlates with a general future or progress fetish and a corresponding lack of respect and appreciation for aged persons in contemporary Western civilization. The human

tragedy of this value orientation becomes obvious in comparing the social experience of a venerated Bali Aga elder, for example, with that of an aged person institutionalized in a modern old-age home.

7. The invisible *wong alus,* or "spirit people," may qualify as an exception in that theirs is regarded as a society that has become disembodied as a whole and immortalized in the process.

8. The social theories of Max Weber and Karl Marx concord in relation to this issue. Two important pillars of a Weberian theory of modernity are the increasing division of labor throughout history and an associated process of value fragmentation in relation to ever more specific value spheres (or spheres of action). In Marxist theory, labor and value are similarly linked. Value therein is not portrayed as inherent but as value added to objects or products by the expenditure of human labor (material or symbolic).

9. The meaning of "temporary disadvantage" varies among different Bali Aga organizations more or less in negative proportion to the practical degree of experienced disadvantages. Most people are compensated for the "disadvantage" of being someone's child or younger sibling by having children or younger siblings of their own. Young men have at least a decent chance of being compensated for having been subject to the authority of village elders as they become elders themselves. By contrast, it is much less likely that the most recent branch village in a domain is compensated by developing its own branches within the span of an individual lifetime.

10. Some younger informants admitted to an occasional and mild sense of boredom with ritual as a source of entertainment. But the same could probably be said of Western (or urban Balinese) people's experience and evaluation of such repetitive "entertainment rituals" as attending a discotheque.

11. Foucault's "heterotopia" is a fascinating concept, but one that he did not define and develop adequately. His basic insight is that power structures are embedded in particular spaces from which difference is excluded (e.g., self-referential nationalism) or in spatially defined relations where difference is accentuated in a negative sense (e.g., through a demonization of the spaces occupied by others). Little is said, however, about how the rather embarrassing differences revealed by anthropological or geographical knowledge can be accommodated within his evidently cosmopolitan project. This is in essence still a Kantian project, and the same problem I am noticing in Foucault's theory is already anticipated in Kant's cavalier treatment of anthropology and geography.

References

ABBREVIATIONS

BKI	*Bijdragen tot de Koninklijk Instituut voor Taal-, Land- en Volkenkunde*
KITLV	Koninklijk Instituut voor Taal-, Land- en Volkenkunde
MKLT	*Mededeelingen van de Kirtya Liefrick van der Tuuk*
TITLV	*Tijdschrift voor Indische taal-, land- en volkenkunde*
RIMA	*Review of Indonesian and Malaysian Affairs*

Appadurai, A.
    1988   "Putting Hierarchy in Its Place." *Cultural Anthropology* 3:36–49.
Ardika, W., and P. Bellwood
    1991   "Sembiran: The Beginnings of Indian Contact with Bali." *Antiquity* 65 (247): 221–232.
Arsana, G.K.G.
    1991   "Kedudukan dan Peranan Pemimpin Upacara di Pura Batukaru." In the team report *Temple Festival in Bali.* Osaka: Research and Exchange Program of Osaka University with the South Pacific Region.
Bakker, F. L.
    1995   "Bali in the Indonesian State in the 1990s: The Religious Aspect." Paper prepared for the Third International Bali Studies Conference, University of Sydney, 3–7 July 1995.
Barnes, R. H.
    1974   *Kédang: A Study of the Collective Thought of an Eastern Indonesian People.* Oxford: Clarendon Press.
    1996   "The Power of Strangers in Flores and Timor." Paper presented at the international conference Hierarchization: Processes of Social Differentiation in the Austronesian World, International Institute for Asian Studies, Leiden, 17–19 April 1996.
Bateson, G.
    1970   "An Old Temple and a New Myth." In J. Belo, ed., *Traditional Balinese Culture.* New York: Columbia University Press.
Bateson, G., and M. Mead
    1942   *Balinese Character: A Photographic Analysis.* New York: New York Academy of Sciences.
Bawa, I Wayan
    1990   *Frasa Dialek Bali Aga: Laporan Penelitian.* Denpasar: Jurusan Sastra Indonesia, Fakultas Sastra, Universitas Udayana.
Bellwood, P.
    1995   "Austronesian Prehistory in Southeast Asia: Homeland, Expansion and Transformation." In P. Bellwood, J. J. Fox, and D. Tryon, eds., *The Austronesians: Historical and Comparative Perspectives.* Comparative Austronesia Project. Canberra: Australian National University.

Bellwood, P., J. J. Fox, and D. Tryon, eds.
 1995   *The Austronesians: Historical and Comparative Perspectives*. Comparative
         Austronesia Project. Canberra: Australian National University.
Belo, J.
 1949   *Bali: Rangda and Barong*. Monographs of the American Ethnological
         Society 16. New York: J. J. Augustin.
Berg, C. C.
 1927   "De Middeljavaansche historische traditie." Ph.D. thesis, Leiden.
Bernet-Kempers, A. J.
 1991   *Monumental Bali: Introduction to Balinese Archaeology*. Berkeley: Periplus
         Editions.
Berreman, G.
 1971   "The Brahmanical View of Caste." *Contributions to Indian Sociology* 5:
         16–23.
Boekian, D. P.
 1936   "Kajoebii: En Oud-Balische bergdesa." Translated by C. J. Grader.
         TITLV 76:127–176.
Boon, J. A.
 1990   "Balinese Twins Times Two: Gender, Birth Order, and 'Household'
         in Indonesia/Indo-Europe." In J. M. Atkinson and S. Errington, eds.,
         Power and Difference: Gender in Island Southeast Asia. Stanford, Calif.:
         Stanford University Press.
Bourdieu, P.
 1977   *Outline of a Theory of Practice*. New York: Cambridge University Press.
 1986   "The Forms of Capital." In J. G. Richardson, ed., *Handbook of Theory
         and Research of the Sociology of Education*. New York: Greenwood Press.
 1998   *Practical Reason: On the Theory of Practice*. Cambridge: Polity Press.
Buchari
 1968   "Sri Maharaja Mapanji Garasakan." *Majalah Ilmu-Ilmu Sastra Indonesia*
         4:1–26.
Budiastra, P.
 1989   *Babad Pasek Kayuselem*. Denpasar: Warga Pasek Kayuselem.
 1993a   *Pangeling-eling Desa Les Penuktukan*. Denpasar: Museum Bali.
 1993b   *Prasasti Campetan/Bantang, Kecamatan Kintamani*. Denpasar: Museum
         Bali.
Clifford, J.
 1988   *The Predicament of Culture: Twentieth-Century Ethnography, Literature, and
         Art*. Cambridge, Mass.: Harvard University Press.
Connor, L. H.
 1982   "In Darkness and Light: A Study of Peasant Intellectuals in Bali."
         Ph.D. thesis, University of Sydney.
 1996   "Contesting and Transforming the Work for the Dead in Bali: The
         Case of Ngaben Ngirit." In Adrian Vickers, ed., *Being Modern in Bali*.
         Asian Studies, Monograph Series, No. 43. New Haven: Yale University
         Press.
Covarrubias, M.
 1937   *Island of Bali*. New York: Knopf.
Crapanzano, V.
 1986   "Hermes' Dilemma: The Masking of Subversion in Ethnographic
         description." In J. Clifford and G. E. Marcus, eds., *Writing Culture: The*

Poetics and Politics of Ethnography. Los Angeles: University of California Press.

Creese, H.
   1995   "In Search of Majapahit: Defining Balinese Identities." Paper presented at the Third International Bali Studies Workshop, Sydney, 3–7 July 1995.

Cunningham, C. E.
   1965   "Order and Change in an Atoni Diarchy." *Southwestern Journal of Anthropology* 21:359–382.

Danandjaja, J.
   1980   *Kebudayaan Petani Desa Trunyan di Bali.* Jakarta: Universitas Indonesia Press.

Darling, D.
   1990   "Kintamani." In E. Oey, ed., *Bali: The Emerald Isle.* Lincolnwood, Ill.: Passport Books.

Davies, P.
   1992   "The Historian in Bali." Paper presented at the annual conference of the Society for Balinese Studies, Denpasar.

Dirks, N. B.
   1987   *The Hollow Crown: Ethnohistory of an Indian Kingdom.* Cambridge: Cambridge University Press.

Dumont, L.
   1980   *Homo Hierarchicus: The Caste System and its Implications.* Revised English edition. Chicago: University of Chicago Press. First published in 1966 by Editions Gallimard, Paris.

Eiseman, F. B., Jr.
   1990   *Bali: Sekala and Niskala,* vol. 2: *Essays on Society, Tradition and Craft.* Hong Kong: Periplus Editions.

Epstein, S.
   1973   "The Self-Concept Revisited: Or a Theory of a Theory." *American Psychologist* 28:405–416.

Fabian, J.
   1983   *Time and the Other: How Anthropology Makes Its Object.* New York: Columbia University Press.

Feyerabend, P.
   1987   *Farewell to Reason.* London: Verso.

Forge, A.
   1980   "Balinese Religion and Balinese Identity." In J. J. Fox, R. Garnaut, P. McEarley, and J. Mackie, eds., *Indonesia: Australian Perspectives.* Canberra: Australian National University Press.

Foucault, M.
   1970   *The Order of Things: An Archaeology of the Human Sciences.* London and New York: Random House. First published in 1966.

Fox, J. J.
   1980   "Introduction." In J. J. Fox, ed., *The Flow of Life: Essays on Eastern Indonesia.* Cambridge, Mass.: Harvard University Press.
   1988   "Origin, Descent and Precedence in the Study of Austronesian Societies." Public lecture in connection with Wisselleerstoel Indonesische Studien, Leiden, 3 March 1988.
   1989   "Category and Complement: Binary Ideologies and the Organisation of Dualism in Eastern Indonesia." In D. Maybury-Lewis and U. Almagor,

eds., *The Attraction of Opposites: Thought and Society in a Dualist Mode.* Ann Arbor: University of Michigan Press.

1990a "Arguments in a Theory of Precedence: Sisters since the Trunk of Heaven, Brothers since the Rim of Earth." Paper prepared for the conference Hierarchy, Ancestry and Alliance, Comparative Austronesia Project, Australian National University, Canberra.

1990b "Austronesian Societies and Their Transformations." Paper prepared for the conference Austronesians in History: Common Origins and Diverse Transformations, Australian National University, Canberra, 12–14 November 1990.

1990c *Hierarchy and Precedence.* Working Paper No. 3, Comparative Austronesia Project. Canberra: Australian National University.

1993 "Comparative Perspectives on Austronesian Houses: An Introductory Essay." In J. J. Fox, ed., *Inside Austronesian Houses: Perspectives on Domestic Designs for Living.* Comparative Austronesia Project. Canberra: Australian National University.

1994a "Installing the 'Outsider' Inside: An Exploration of an Austronesian Cultural Theme and Its Social Significance." Paper prepared for the First International Symposium on Austronesian Cultural Studies, Universitas Udayana, Bali, 14–16 August 1994.

1994b "Reflections on 'Hierarchy' and 'Precedence.' " *History and Anthropology* 7(1–4): 87–108.

Fox, J. J., and C. Sathers, eds.
1996 *Origins, Ancestry and Alliance: Explorations in Austronesian Ethnography.* Comparative Austronesia Project. Canberra: Australian National University.

Geertz, C.
1959 "Form and Variation in Balinese Village Structure." *American Anthropologist* 61 (6): 991–1012.
1960 *The Religion of Java.* Chicago: University of Chicago Press.
1980 *Negara: The Theatre State in Nineteenth-Century Bali.* Princeton, N.J.: Princeton University Press.

Geertz, H.
1995 "Sorcery and Social Change in Bali: The Sakti Conjecture." Paper prepared for the Third International Bali Studies Conference, University of Sydney, 3–7 July 1995.

Giddens, A.
1979 *Central Problems in Social Theory: Action, Structure and Contradiction in Social Analysis.* London: Macmillan.

Ginarsa, K.
1979 *Pura Bukit Tunggal dalam Prasasti.* Singaraja: Balai Penelitian Bahasa.

Goris, R.
1932 "De positie der Pande Wesi." *MKLT* 1:41–52.
1941 "Enkele historische en sociologische gegevens uit de Balische oorkonden." *TITLV* 81:279–294.
1954 *Prasasti Bali.* Bandung: N. V. Masa Baru.
1960 "Holidays and Holy Days." In W. F. Wertheim, ed., *Bali: Studies in Life, Thought, and Ritual.* The Hague: W. van Hoeve.

Grader, C. J.
1937 " 'Tweedeeling in het Oud-Balische dorp' and 'Madenan.' " *MKLT* 5:45–121.
1960 "The State Temples of Mengwi." In W. F. Wertheim, ed., *Bali: Studies in Life, Thought, and Ritual.* The Hague: W. van Hoeve.
1969 "Pura Meduwe Karang at Kubutambahan." In J. van Baal et al., eds., *Bali: Further Studies in Life, Thought and Ritual.* The Hague: W. van Hoeve. First published in Dutch in 1940.

Guermonprez, J.-F.
1989 "Dual Sovereignty in Nineteenth-Century Bali." *History and Anthropology* 4:189–207.

Habermas, J.
1984 *The Theory of Communicative Action.* Vol. 1. London: Heineman.

Haga, B. J.
1924 "Aantekeningen van den controleur B. J. Haga." *Adatrechtbundels* 1924: 453–469.

Hau'ofa, E.
1993 "Our Sea of Islands." In E. Waddell, V. Naidu, and E. Hau'ofa, eds., *Rediscovering Our Sea of Islands.* Suva: University of the South Pacific, School of Social and Economic Development.

Heesterman, J. C.
1989 "The Hindu Frontier." In J. C. Heesterman, ed., *India and Indonesia: General Perspectives.* Leiden: E. J. Brill.

Hefner, R. W.
1985 *Hindu Javanese: Tengger Tradition and Islam.* Princeton, N.J.: Princeton University Press.
1990 *The Political Economy of Mountain Java: An Interpretive History.* Berkeley: University of California Press.

Heyden, A. J. van der
1925 "Het waterschapswezen in de voormalige Zuid-Balische rijkjes Bangli and Kloengkoeng." *Koloniale Studien* 1925 (2).

Hobart, M.
1991 "The Art of Measuring Mirages, or Is There Kinship in Bali?" In F. Hüsken and J. Kemp, eds., *Cognation and Social Organisation in Southeast Asia.* Verhandelingen 145. Leiden: KITLV Press.

Hooykaas, C.
1964 "The Balinese Sengguhu Priest: A Shaman, but Not a Sufi, a Saiva and a Vaisnava." In J. Bastin and R. Roolvink, eds., *Malaysian and Indonesian Studies: Essays Presented to Sir Richard Winstedt.* Oxford: Oxford University Press.

Horkheimer, T., and M. Adorno
1979 *Dialectic of Enlightenment.* London: Verso. First published in 1944.

Howe, L.E.A.
1980 "Pujung: An Investigation into the Foundations of Balinese Culture." Ph.D. thesis, University of Edinburgh.
1983 "An Introduction to the Cultural Study of Traditional Balinese Architecture." *Archipel* 25:137–158.
1984 "Gods, People, Spirits and Witches: The Balinese Sytem of Person Definition." *BKI* 140 (2–3): 1193–1222.

1989   "Hierarchy and Equality: Variations in Balinese Social Organisation."
        BKI 145 (1): 47–71.

Howell, S.
1996   "A Life for 'Life': Blood and Other Life-Promoting Substances in
        Northern Lio Moral Discourse." In S. Howell, ed., *For the Sake of Our
        Future: Sacrificing in Eastern Indonesia.* Leiden: Research School, Center
        for Non-Western Studies.

Jacobs, J.
1883   *Eenigen tijd onder de Baliers: Eene reisbeschrijving.* Batavia: Kolff.

Korn, V. E.
1932   *Het adatrecht van Bali.* The Hague: Naeff.
1933   *De dorpsrepubliek Tenganan Pagringsingan.* Santport: Mees.

Kuhn, T. S.
1970   *The Structure of Scientific Revolutions.* Chicago: University of Chicago
        Press. First published in 1962.

Lansing, J. S.
1983   *The Three Worlds of Bali.* New York: Praeger.
1987   "Balinese Water Temples and the Management of Irrigation." *American
        Anthropologist* 89 (1): 326–341.
1991   *Priests and Programmers: Technologies of Power in the Engineered Landscape
        of Bali.* Princeton, N.J.: Princeton University Press.

Leach, E. R.
1954   *Political Systems of Highland Burma: A Study of Kachin Social Structure.*
        London: G. Bell and Son.

Leemann, A.
1993   "Organisationsformen der balinesischen Gesellschaft." *Geographica
        Helvetica* 1993 (1): 6–18.

Le Roux, C.C.F.M.
1913   "Het bergland van Midden-Bali en et hoogland van Tjatoer." *Jaares-
        verlag van den topographischen dienst in Nederlandsch Indië over 1912*
        8:158–164.

Lévi-Strauss, C.
1983   *The Way of the Masks.* Second edition. London: Jonathan Cape.
1987   *Anthropology and Myth: Lectures 1951–1982.* Oxford: Basil Blackwell.
        First published in 1984 as *Paroles données* (Paris: Librairie Plon).

Lewis, E. D.
1988   *People of the Source.* KITLV, Verhandelingen 135. Dordrecht: Foris.

Liefrinck, F. A.
1934   "Desa-monographieën." *Adatrechtbundels* 37:453–469.

Lowenhaupt-Tsing, A.
1993   *In the Realm of the Diamond Queen: Marginality in an Out-of-the-Way Place.*
        Princeton, N.J.: Princeton University Press.

Macdonald, C.
1987   "Sociétés 'à maison' et types d'organization sociale aux Philip-
        pines." In C. Macdonald and members of l'ECASE, eds., *De la hutte
        au palais: Sociétés "à maison" en Asie du Sud-Est insulaire.* Paris: CNRS
        Press.

MacLuhan, M.
1969   *The Gutenberg Galaxy.* New York: Signet Books. First published in 1962.

Macrae, G.
  1995   "Ubud: Cultural Networks and History." Paper presented at the Third
          International Bali Studies Conference, University of Sydney, 3–7 July
          1995.
Malkki, L.
  1995   "Refugees and Exile: From 'Refugee Studies' to the National Order
          of Things." *Annual Review of Anthropology* 24:495–523.
Marcus, G. E., and M. J. Fischer
  1986   *Anthropology as Cultural Critique: An Experimental Moment in the Human
          Sciences.* Chicago: University of Chicago Press.
McWilliam, A. R.
  1989   "Narrating the Gate and the Path: Place and Precedence in
          South West Timor." Ph.D. thesis, Australian National University,
          Canberra.
Milner, M.
  1994   *Status and Sacredness: A General Theory of Status Relations and an Analysis
          of Indian Culture.* Oxford: Oxford University Press.
Needham, R.
  1980   *Reconnaissances.* Toronto: University of Toronto Press.
Ng, C.
  1993   "Raising the House Post and Feeding the Husband-Givers: The Spatial
          Categories of Social Reproduction among the Minangkabau." In
          J. J. Fox, ed., *Inside Austronesian Houses: Perspectives on Domestic Designs
          for Living.* Comparative Austronesia Project. Canberra: Australian Na-
          tional University.
Nieuwenkamp, W. O. J.
  1920   "De Batoer op Bali." *Nederlandsch-Indië oud en nieuw* 5:99–128.
Ossenbruggen, F.D.E. van
  1977   "Java's Monca-Pat: Origins of a Primitive Classification System." In
          P. E. de Josselin de Jong, ed., *Structural Anthropology in the Netherlands:
          A Reader.* The Hague: Martinus Nijhoff. First published in Dutch in
          1916.
Picard, M.
  1990   "Cultural Tourism in Bali: Cultural Performances as Tourist Attrac-
          tions." *Indonesia* 49:37–74.
Pitana, G.
  1993   *Subak: Sistem Irigasi Tradisional di Bali: Sebuah Canangsari.* Denpasar:
          Upada Sastra.
  1995   "Priesthood and Warga Movement: Observing Socio-Cultural Changes
          in Bali." Paper prepared for the Third International Bali Studies Con-
          ference, University of Sydney, 3–7 July 1995.
Platenkamp, J.D.M.
  1990   "Some Notes on Hierarchy in Eastern Indonesia: A Comment on J. J.
          Fox's 'Hierarchy and precedence.' " Paper presented at the Confer-
          ence on Hierarchy, Ancestry and Alliance, Research School of Asian
          and Pacific Studies, Australian National University, Canberra, 25–30
          January 1990.
Ramseyer, U.
  1977   *Kultur und Volkskunst auf Bali.* Zürich: Atlantis.

Reuter, T. A.
  1992   "Precedence in Sumatra: An Analysis of the Construction of Status in Affinal Relations and Origin Groups." *BKI* 148 (3–4): 489–520.
  in press *The House of Our Ancestors: Precedence and Dualism in Highland Balinese Society.* Leiden: KITLV Press.
Reynolds, C.
  1995   "A New Look at Old Southeast Asia." *Journal of Asian Studies* 54 (2): 419–446.
Riana, K.
  1992   "Baris Gowak dan Baris Omang di Selulung." *Antara Kita* 32:3–8.
Riches, D.
  1990   "The Force of Tradition in Eskimology." In R. Fardon, ed., *Localising Strategies: Regional Traditions in Ethnographic Writing.* Edinburgh: Scottish Academic Press.
Ricoeur, P.
  1981   "The Model of the Text: Meaningful Action Considered as a Text." In J. B. Thompson, ed. and trans., *Paul Ricoeur: Hermeneutics and the Human Sciences.* Cambridge: Cambridge University Press.
Roon, J.
  1916   "Enkele aanteekeningen omtrent Bali." *Jaaresverlag van den topographischen dienst in Nederlandsch Indië over 1915* 11:213–287.
Rosaldo, R.
  1989   *Culture and Truth: The Remaking of Social Analysis.* Boston: Beacon Press.
Rubinstein, R.
  1991   "The Brahmana According to Their Babad." In H. Geertz, ed., *State and Society in Bali: Historical, Textual and Anthropological Approaches.* Leiden: KITLV Press.
Sahlins, M.
  1972   *Stone Age Economics.* Chicago: Aldine-Atherton.
  1985   *Islands of History.* Chicago: University of Chicago Press.
  1999   "Two or Three Things I Know about Culture." *Journal of the Royal Anthropological Institute* (n.s.) 5:399–421.
Said, E. W.
  1978   *Orientalism: Western Concepts of the Orient.* Harmondsworth: Penguin Books.
Sastrodiwiryo, S.
  1994   *I Gusti Anglurah Panji Sakti, Raja Buleleng 1599–1680.* Denpasar: C. V. Kayu Mas.
Schaareman, D.
  1986   *Tatulingga: Tradition and Continuity: An Investigation of Ritual and Social Organisation in Bali.* Basel: Wepf.
Schulte-Nordholt, H.
  1988   "The Quest for Life." Paper prepared for the Annual Conference of the Society of Balinese Studies, Denpasar, 29–31 July 1988.
  1991   *State, Village and Ritual in Bali: A Historical Perspective.* Amsterdam: Amsterdam University Press.
  1996   *The Spell of Power: A History of Balinese Politics, 1650–1940.* Leiden: KITLV Press.
Schutz, A.
  1976   "On Multiple Realities." In A. Broderson, ed. *Alfred Schutz, Collected Papers,* vol. 2: *Studies in Social Theory.* The Hague: Martinus Nijhoff.

Simpen, W. AB.
   1986   *Adat Kuna Catur Desa (Tigawasa, Sidatapa, Pedawa, Cempaga)*. Denpasar:
          Fakultas Sastra, Universitas Udayana.
Spies, W.
   1933   "Das grosse Fest im Dorfe Trunyan." *TITLV* 78:220–258.
Stuart-Fox, D. J.
   1987   "Pura Besakih: A Study of Balinese Religion and Society." Ph.D. thesis,
          Australian National University, Canberra.
Stutterheim, W. F.
   1929   *Oudheden van Bali*, vol. 1. Singaraja: Publicaties der Kirtya Liefrinck–
          van der Tuuk.
Sugriwa, I Gusti Bagus
   1957   *Kitab Babad Pasek*. Denpasar: Pustaka Balimas.
   1968   *Babad Pasek Kayuselem*. Denpasar: Pustaka Balimas.
Supomo, S.
   1995   "Indic Transformation: The Sanskritization of *Jawa* and the Javaniza-
          tion of the *Bharata*." In P. Bellwood, J. J. Fox, and D. Tryon, eds., *The
          Austronesians: Historical and Comparative Perspectives*. Comparative Aus-
          tronesia Project. Canberra: Australian National University.
Tooker, D.
   1996   "Putting the Mandala in Its Place: A Practise-Based Approach to the
          Spatialization of Power on the Southeast Asian 'Peripery'—the Case
          of the Akha." *Journal of Asian Studies* 55 (2): 323–358.
Traube, E. G.
   1986   *Cosmology and Social Life: Ritual Exchange among the Mambai of East
          Timor*. Chicago: University of Chicago Press.
Tuuk, H. N. van der, and J. Brandes
   1885   "Transcriptie van vier Oud-Javaansche oorkonden op koper gevonden
          op het eiland Bali." *TITLV* 30:603–624.
Tyler, S. A.
   1986   "Post-Modern Ethnography: From Document of the Occult to Occult
          Document." In J. Clifford and G. E. Marcus, eds., *Writing Culture: The
          Poetics and Politics of Ethnography*. Los Angeles: University of California
          Press.
Valeri, V.
   1982   "The Transformation of a Transformation: A Structural Essay on an
          Aspect of Hawaiian History (1809–1819)." *Social Analysis* 10:3–41.
Vickers, A.
   1989   *Bali: A Paradise Created*. Harmondsworth: Penguin Books.
Vischer, M. P.
   1992   "Children of the Black Patola Stone: Origin Structures in a Domain
          on Palué Island, Eastern Indonesia." Ph.D. thesis, Australian National
          University, Canberra.
Warren, C.
   1989   "Balinese Political Culture and the Rhetoric of National Development."
          In R. Higgot and R. Robison, eds., *Southeast Asia: Essays in the Political
          Economy of Structural Change*. London: Routledge and Kegan Paul.
   1991   "Adat and Dinas: Village and State in Contemporary Bali." In H. Geertz,
          ed., *State and Society in Bali: Historical, Textual and Anthropological Ap-
          proaches*. Leiden: KITLV Press.

Wiener, M. J.
1995   *Visible and Invisible Realms: Power, Magic and Colonial Conquest in Bali.* Chicago and London: University of Chicago Press.

Winterton, B.
1989   *The Insider's Guide to Bali.* Hong Kong: CFW Publications.

Wittfogel, K. A.
1957   *Oriental Despotism: A Comparative Study of Total Power.* New Haven: Yale University Press.

Worsley, P.
1972   *Babad Buleleng: A Balinese Dynastic Genealogy.* KITLV, Bibliotheca Indonesia 8. The Hague: Martinus Nijhoff.

Wouden, F. A. E. van
1968   *Types of Social Structure in Eastern Indonesia.* The Hague: Martinus Nijhoff. First published in 1935.

Wurm, S. A., and B. Wilson
1973   *English Finderlist of Reconstructions in Austronesian Languages (Post Brandstetter).* Pacific Linguistics, Series C, No. 33. Canberra: Department of Linguistics, Research School of Pacific Studies, Australian National University.

Index

Page numbers in *italics* refer to illustrations, tables, and maps.

About the Author

THOMAS REUTER obtained a Ph.D. in anthropology in 1995 from the Research School of Pacific and Asian Studies, Australian National University. He subsequently taught for two years at the University of Heidelberg, then completed a three-year post-doctoral fellowship from the Australian Research Council at the University of Melbourne. He is presently Queen Elizabeth II Research Fellow of the Australian Research Council in the School of Anthropology, Geography and Environmental Studies at the University of Melbourne.

Dr. Reuter has been conducting ethnographic research in Bali and other parts of Indonesia for more than a decade. His current research is focused on new social movements in Java.